P
THE BERLITZ '

"Aimed at educated, experienced travellers, the [Berlitz Travellers] Guides capture the flavor of foreign lands."
—*Entrepreneur*

"Filling a needed niche in guidebooks . . . designed to eliminate the cumbersome lists of virtually every hotel and restaurant . . . . Special out-of-the-way places are detailed. . . . The books capture the personality and excitement of each destination."
—*Los Angeles Times*

"There's a different tone to these books, and certainly a different approach . . . information is aimed at independent and clearly sophisticated travellers. . . . Strong opinions give these books a different personality from most guides, and make them fun to read."
—*Travel & Leisure*

"Aimed at experienced, independent travellers who want information beyond the nuts-and-bolts material available in many familiar sources. Although each volume gives necessary basics, the series sends travellers not just to 'sights,' but to places and events that convey the personality of each locale."
—*The Denver Post*

"Just the right amount of information about where to stay and play."
—*Detroit Free Press*

"The strength of the [Berlitz Travellers Guides] lies in remarks and recommendations by writers with a depth of knowledge about their subject."
— *Washington Times*

"The most readable of the current paperback lot."
— *New York Post*

"Highly recommended."
— *Library Journal*

"Very strong on atmosphere and insights into local culture for curious travellers."
— *Boston Herald*

"The [Berlitz Travellers Guides] eliminate cumbersome lists and provide reliable information about what is truly exciting and significant about a destination. . . . [They] also emphasize the spirit and underlying 'vibrations' of a region—historical, cultural, and social—that enhance a trip."
— *Retirement Life*

"Information without boredom. . . . Good clear maps and index."
— *The Sunday Sun* (Toronto)

CONTRIBUTORS

MIKE BINGHAM, a longtime resident of Tasmania, is the travel editor of *The Mercury,* Tasmania's largest newspaper, and its sister publication, *The Sunday Tasmanian.*

CHRIS BROCKIE, a stockman, rodeo contestant, and freelance journalist, has covered the Outback since moving from New Zealand in 1972. A former bureau chief for two major Australian newspaper groups, he now lives in South Australia and is a freelance writer.

SHIRLEY MAAS FOCKLER, a member of the Society of American Travel Writers and the Travel Journalists Guild, has reported on travel in Pacific Rim countries since 1957 and writes for publications in North America, Oceania, and Europe.

HELEN GORDON was born in Sydney and has been in journalism all her life, working as a feature writer for magazines and newspapers. For the last 15 years she has been involved in travel writing, and was associate travel editor of *The Australian,* Australia's national newspaper, until 1990.

JANIS HADLEY has been a resident of Perth, Western Australia, for more than ten years. She writes on travel for a variety of publications within Australia and overseas.

KERRY KENIHAN, an author, radio travel broadcaster, and longtime journalist, lives in Adelaide, South Australia, and is a member of the Australian Society of Travel Writers.

IAN MARSHMAN, a lifelong resident of Melbourne, writes for many travel publications. He is a senior writer for Australia's *Traveltrade* magazine and hosts a travel-oriented radio talk show.

KIRSTY McKENZIE, a freelance food and travel writer based in Sydney, contributes to a variety of publications in Australia and overseas.

LEN RUTLEDGE, whose *Travelround* column was the longest-running travel column in Australia, is a contributor to newspapers and magazines in Australia, the Pacific, Asia, and Europe. He lives in Queensland.

CHARLES SRIBER came to Sydney in 1950 and worked as a journalist in radio and on newspapers. Former travel editor of the *Sydney Morning Herald* and *The Australian,* he received a Pacific Asia Travel Association Golden Award for a newspaper travel story in 1992.

THE BERLITZ
TRAVELLERS GUIDES

THE AMERICAN SOUTHWEST

AUSTRALIA

BERLIN

CANADA

THE CARIBBEAN

COSTA RICA

ENGLAND & WALES

FRANCE

GERMANY

GREECE

HAWAII

IRELAND

LONDON

MEXICO

NEW ENGLAND

NEW YORK CITY

NORTHERN ITALY AND ROME

PORTUGAL

SAN FRANCISCO &
NORTHERN CALIFORNIA

SOUTHERN ITALY AND ROME

SPAIN

TURKEY

THE BERLITZ TRAVELLERS GUIDE TO AUSTRALIA

Sixth Edition

ALAN TUCKER
General Editor

BERLITZ PUBLISHING COMPANY, INC.
New York, New York

BERLITZ PUBLISHING COMPANY LTD.
Oxford, England

THE BERLITZ TRAVELLERS GUIDE
TO AUSTRALIA
Sixth Edition

Berlitz Trademark Reg U.S. Patent and Trademark Office
and other countries—Marca Registrada

Published by Berlitz Publishing Company, Inc.
257 Park Avenue South, New York, New York 10010, U.S.A.

Distributed in the United States by
the Macmillan Publishing Group

Distributed elsewhere by Berlitz Publishing Company Ltd.
Berlitz House, Peterley Road,
Horspath, Oxford OX4 2TX, England

ISBN 2-8315-1706-0
ISSN 1057-4689

Designed by Beth Tondreau Design
Cover design by Dan Miller Design
Cover photograph by PaulSteel/The Stock Market
Maps by General Cartography, Inc.
Illustrations by Bill Russell
Fact-checked in Australia by Leanne Olsen
Edited by Kathryn Clark

Printed in the United States of America
1 3 5 7 9 10 8 6 4 2

THIS GUIDEBOOK

The Berlitz Travellers Guides are designed for experienced travellers in search of exceptional information that will enhance the enjoyment of the trips they take.

Where, for example, are the interesting, out-of-the-way, fun, charming, or romantic places to stay? The hotels described by our expert writers are some of the special places, in all price ranges except for the very lowest—not just the run-of-the-mill, heavily marketed places in advertised airline and travel-wholesaler packages.

We are *highly* selective in our choices of accommodations, concentrating on what our insider contributors think are the most interesting or rewarding places, and why. Readers who want to review exhaustive lists of hotel and resort choices as well, and who feel they need detailed descriptions of each property, can supplement the *Berlitz Travellers Guide* with tourism industry publications or one of the many directory-type guidebooks on the market.

We indicate the approximate price level of each accommodation in our description of it (no indication means it is moderate in local, relative terms), and at the end of every chapter we supply more detailed hotel rates as well as contact information so that you can get precise, up-to-the-minute rates and make reservations.

The Berlitz Travellers Guide to Australia highlights the more rewarding parts of Australia so that you can quickly and efficiently home in on a good itinerary.

Of course, this guidebook does far more than just help you choose a hotel and plan your trip. *The Berlitz Travellers Guide to Australia* is designed for use *in* Australia. Our writers, each of whom is an experienced travel journalist who either lives in or regularly tours the city or region of Australia he or she covers, tell you what you really need to know, what you can't find out so easily on your own. They identify and describe the truly out-of-the-ordinary resorts, restaurants, shops, activities, and sights, and tell you the best way to "do" your destination.

Our writers are highly selective. They bring out the significance of the places they *do* cover, capturing the personality and the underlying cultural and historical resonances of a city or region—making clear its special appeal.

The Berlitz Travellers Guide to Australia is full of reliable information. We would like to know if you think we've left out some very special place. Although we make every effort to provide the most current information available about every destination described in this book, it is possible too that changes have occurred before you arrive. If you do have an experience that is contrary to what you were led to expect by our description, we would like to hear from you about it.

A guidebook is no substitute for common sense when you are travelling. Always pack the clothing, footwear, and other items appropriate for the destination, and make the necessary accommodation for such variables as altitude, weather, and local rules and customs. Of course, once on the scene you should avoid situations that are in your own judgment potentially hazardous, even if they have to do with something mentioned in a guidebook. Half the fun of travelling is exploring, but explore with care.

ALAN TUCKER
General Editor
Berlitz Travellers Guides

Root Publishing Company
350 West Hubbard Street
Suite 440
Chicago, Illinois 60610

CONTENTS

This Guidebook	vii
Overview	5
Useful Facts	12
Bibliography	23
Sydney	33
Getting Around	61
Accommodations	65
Dining	72
Nightlife and Entertainment	78
Shops and Shopping	82
Side Trips from Sydney	87
The Blue Mountains	90
Broken Hill	93
The Hunter Valley	96
Canberra	99
Queensland	107
Brisbane, the Gold Coast, and the Sunshine Coast	110
The Great Barrier Reef Area	132
Cape York	175
Northern Territory	188
The Red Centre	190
The Top End	205
Tasmania	228
Melbourne and Victoria	255
Adelaide and South Australia	301
Perth and Western Australia	340
Historical Chronology	384
Index	389

MAPS

Australia   2
Sydney Center   34
Sydney Environs   59
Sydney Day Trips Area   88
Canberra   100
Southeast Queensland   108
Brisbane   112
Gold Coast   120
Sunshine Coast   126
Southern Reef Area   138
Townsville and Townsville Area   145
Central Reef Area   150
Cairns   162
Northern Reef Area   167
Cape York   176
Red Centre   192
Top End   208
Tasmania   230
Hobart   236
Melbourne   258
Melbourne Environs   276
Great Ocean Road   284
Adelaide   304
Barossa Valley   321
South Australia Coast   328
Perth   343
Perth Environs   354
Southwest Coast   362
The Pilbara and Central Western Australia   369
The Kimberley   373

THE
BERLITZ
TRAVELLERS
GUIDE
TO
AUSTRALIA

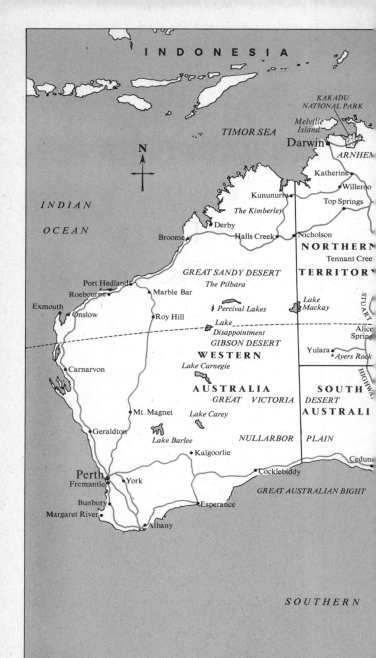

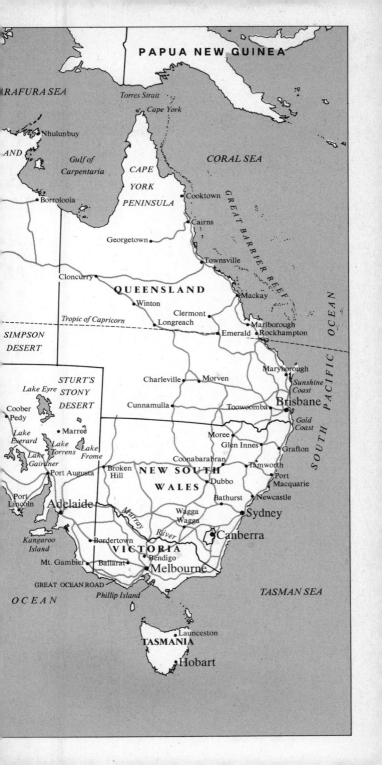

OVERVIEW

By Shirley Maas Fockler

Shirley Maas Fockler has reported on travel in Pacific Rim countries since 1957 and writes for publications in North America, Oceania, and Europe.

An ancient aboriginal myth—no one knows how many thousands of years old—attempts to explain how the first man and woman on earth managed to get together. The woman was travelling north, the man south, when they met on a plain in what we now call Australia.

The man asked, "Where are you from?"

The woman replied, "From the south. Where are you from?"

"From the north," he said. "Are you alone?"

"Yes."

"Then you will be my wife."

"Yes, I will be your woman."

It was all so simple then, but truth can be found in that myth even in modern-day Australia. It illustrates the lack of formality and the straight-from-the-hip directness that contribute to the charm of the Aussies. For those of us caught up in a more stress-filled world, the myth also helps explain why, of all the mysteries and peculiarities on this most unusual of continents, it is the Aussies themselves who are the greatest attraction Down Under.

In this regard Australia is very different from other places in the world. Many traditional vacation spots almost demand that we visit them not for liaisons with the citizens but for their cultural or historical worth. People packing for Paris no doubt have set their minds on seeing the Eiffel Tower and the Louvre. They are probably not anticipating long conversations in a pub with a neighborhood bloke. But in Australia there are no ancient ruins, no medieval cathedrals. No great battles were fought on its shores, and it is not a seat of world power. It is left to the Aussies to be Australia's greatest lure. Unpretentious, entertaining, and accommodating, Australians, far from having an inferiority complex about their distance from the rest of the world, almost pity the poor folks who don't live in their lucky country.

And why not? It's a laid-back life Down Under—life where a winter's day might call for a light jacket for a walk on the beach; where a ceiling fan stirs an ocean breeze that cools better than any air conditioner; where sun, sand, and sea all meld together; where the food is excellent and the beer is cold. No one seems to be dashing madly about, drivers don't honk their horns at each other or at pedestrians, and when five o'clock comes work is over. Ambition may not be the Aussies' strong suit; living the good life, on the other hand, is on everyone's mind.

Don't be lulled, however, into thinking Australia is a utopia. The biggest obstacle for visitors is that it is a long way from just about everywhere else. The trip from New York usually takes 24 hours when changing planes on the West Coast is factored in. Even from Los Angeles, a non-stop flight to Sydney is a bottom-numbing 15 hours. If you're flying from Europe, expect no mercy. It's a day's journey from most places on the Continent to Australia. Only those flying from New Zealand to Australia face more bearable flying times—about four hours to Sydney.

Once in Oz (another self-imposed Australian nickname), there are no better places to meet and chat up an Aussie than at a neighborhood pub or on the beach. A substantial portion of the population is bound to be at one or the other at any given time.

Then there's the Australian parlance known as "strine," a form of English spoken only in Australia. The actor Paul Hogan, Crocodile Dundee himself, introduced many outsiders to their first words of "strine." In the United States and Canada, "G'day" became a familiar greeting. Hogan also let us know that a barbecue grill is simply called a "barbie" where he comes from. But Croc left out a few other words and expressions in his 30-second spots for the Australian Tourist Commission that are equally handy to know Down Under. "Fair dinkum" is one—it means "the real thing." "He's a fair dinkum Aussie" tells us he's a homegrown boy. It's a popular expression on tee-shirts sold around the country.

At the pub, several words and expressions will come in handy. First, know how to order a beer: A "schooner" is a large glass of beer, a "midi" a small one. If the bartender only has a "tinnie" it means beer is served by the can. Second, know how to order a round for your drinking buddies: "My shout, mate," is the proper phrase here. On the beach it's important to know that the swimsuit you're wearing is a "cozzie."

Other key words that may require translation are "petrol"—gasoline; "boot" and "bonnet"—trunk and hood of a car; "brekkie"—breakfast; "tucker"—food; "pom"—an Englishman (from penal colony days, "Prisoner of Mother England,"); "rock melon"—cantaloupe; "prawn"—shrimp; "crayfish"—lobster; "good on ya' "—good for you; "brolly"—umbrella; "lolly"—candy; "sheila"—girl; "bloke"—guy. The list goes on and on, but these few words will get you started.

And now to tackle "Waltzing Matilda." Who, outside Australia, has ever understood those lyrics? Understanding the song helps you understand the country better. It is as essential to Australiana as "Home on the Range" is to Americana.

> Once a jolly swagman camped by a billabong
> Under the shade of a coolabah tree
> Down came a jumbuck to drink at the billabong
> Up jumped the swagman and grabbed him with
>   glee
> And he sang as he shoved that jumbuck in his
>   tucker bag
> You'll come a waltzing matilda with me

In the great Australian bush, or the Outback, as it is better known to non-Australians, a "swagman" is a hobo, a drifter who finds an honest day's work to his everlasting distaste, the type of guy who would much rather steal dinner than pay for it. A "billabong" is a pond, all the water left in an otherwise dried-up lake or river. In the vast Outback, a billabong is usually the only water to be found for miles around.

A "coolabah" tree is a gum tree, also known as a eucalyptus, where koalas live. In the bush, coolabahs provide what shade is to be had from the unrelenting sun.

A "jumbuck" is a sheep. In the song, the "swagman" apparently intended to have lamb chops for dinner, for he grabbed the "jumbuck" and shoved him in his "tucker" (food) bag. And he sang, "You'll come a waltzing matilda with me."

There have never been many women in the Australian Outback, leaving the men to resort to their own devices when it comes to female companionship. The "swagman" was no doubt a lonely bloke. He'd sit around the campfire under an endless, starry Outback sky and drink whiskey until he was plastered. Then he'd grab "matilda" and waltz with her by the light of the moon, blissfully ignorant, for the night at least, that matilda was only the backpack that held all his worldly belongings.

Australia's History

Australia's past has been checkered and its present is shaky, but Aussies are optimists. Few predict anything other than a bright future for a country that in 1988 celebrated a bicentennial marking the occasion when the first English convicts landed at present-day Sydney Harbour in January 1788. For the 50,000 or so years before that, Australia had been populated solely by native people or aboriginals, as they became known to the outside world.

When the British lost the American colonies as a potential spot for exiling convicts, it became imperative that a new location for prisoners be found. Naturally, one as far away as possible sufficed nicely for the Crown, and so Australia became England's newest and most dreaded penal colony. More than 700 prisoners were brought in that first boatload, and thousands more followed until 1868, when transportation of prisoners was halted forever.

Those prisoners and their jailers became the forefathers of white Australia. Many aboriginals were killed or died of imported European diseases—they were totally wiped out in Tasmania—but enough remained to give rise to later generations who are just now beginning to demand a place in Australian society.

In the 19th century Australia was closely tied to England's coattails. England was called "home" by just about every white person in the country, even though by midcentury most had been born in Australia. Few, in fact, ever set foot on English soil. Australia is still part of the Commonwealth, but many Aussies today resent the British presence and howl in derision when "God Save the Queen" is played.

Also in the last century, Australia had its own gold rush, which followed closely on the heels of the California Gold Rush of 1849. Indeed, many of the prospectors who had panned unsuccessfully in California made their way to the wilderness of Victoria hoping for better luck.

Today the gold is mostly gone, and the Australian economy is a bit of a mess; however, inflation has finally eased to almost zero, the lowest rate in a number of years. Unemployment is about 11 percent in a population of 17.9 million. The Aussie dollar, irreverently pegged the "Pacific peso," is a boon, however, for travellers exchanging U.S., Canadian, or New Zealand dollars or British pounds. At press time, it was worth about 75 cents U.S., making it possible for some travellers to stay at better hotels or eat at top-notch restaurants and still remain within their budgets.

The Visitor's Australia

There would still be plenty of reasons to travel to Australia were the place uninhabited—reasons like kangaroos, koalas, emus, wombats, Tasmanian devils, and platypuses. You may have seen most of those in the zoo back home—and that's probably where you'll have to go to see them in Australia if you don't venture out of the cities and into the bush. 'Roos, as they say in "strine," don't hop down Macquarie Street in Sydney or Collins Street in Melbourne.

Fortunately, there are some 500 splendid national parks and wildlife reserves scattered around the nation, and at some the animals are tame enough to eat out of your hand. Travelling beyond the cities and parks, you'll know you're in wild country when yellow and black warning signs alert you to the possibility of kangaroos or wombats (stocky, heavy badgerlike critters) crossing the road; in some places, the kangaroo and wombat signs are joined by one for camels. In forests you might be warned of koalas crossing. Australia's prolific birdlife is a continually surprising delight; in Canberra scarlet and royal-blue parrots and sulphur-crested cockatoos swoop down on suburban birdfeeders; in the bush the big kingfisher called a kookaburra serenades with a harsh song that's earned it the nickname "laughing jackass"; and at desolate Outback waterholes fragile zebra finches swarm at sunset for a drink.

Bushwalking is the best way to get close-up views of the rare flora and fauna that abound in Australia. There are more than 8,000 wildflower species and 700 varieties of eucalyptus trees alone. Apart from the cities and the desert, almost anywhere in the nation is a perfect place for a hike. Most national parks have well-marked trails for treks of 20 minutes' to two days' duration.

Another perfect reason to visit Australia is the tropics,

epitomized by the **Great Barrier Reef**, which stretches 1,200 miles along the **Queensland** coast. "Going troppo" is how the Aussies describe a trip to the tropics. To go troppo means to leave the real world behind. What becomes important is not a commute to the office but a swim in the translucent waters of the South Pacific; not a meal on the run but a leisurely banquet of lobster or shrimp or oysters; not a sleepless night but a good snooze, with drowsiness brought on by the pounding of the surf or the rustling of the palms.

In Queensland you can go troppo in the company of a crowd on the **Gold Coast** (Down Under's version of Waikiki), alone or with someone special in the **Whitsunday Islands**, or in a beach cottage on the **Sunshine Coast**. And going troppo almost demands that you go snorkeling or diving on the Great Barrier Reef for a Technicolor trip beneath the waves, or sailing in the shimmering waters of the Coral Sea. Surrounded by tropical waters—the South Pacific and Indian oceans, the Arafura, Timor, and Coral seas, and the Gulf of Carpentaria—Australia has no end of places to go troppo.

Still another good reason to take the plunge Down Under is the country's surprisingly sophisticated city life. **Sydney**, on the east coast in the state of **New South Wales**, is the nation's most exciting city and Melbourne its grandest, but the other large metropolitan areas—Brisbane, Perth, and Adelaide—are not without their own charms for visitors. Few sights in Australia are more exhilarating than the Sydney Opera House. Like the Statue of Liberty in New York, the Opera House is a symbol not only of the city but of the nation as well. Its white "sails," blinding against the harbor backdrop, represent the very hope of Australia that the future will be brighter than the past.

Grand old **Melbourne**, on the southeast coast in the state of **Victoria**, feels more European than other Australian cities. Forever locked in battle with Sydney over which is the nation's premier city, Melbourne claims supremacy as the financial center of the nation—a claim Sydney bankers hotly dispute—and as the epicurean capital of the continent, a notion scoffed at by Sydney chefs. However, no one denies that Melbourne's Victorian Arts Centre and National Gallery is Australia's richest repository of works by the great masters as well as Australian artists, or that its theater, music, and cabaret scenes are the most vibrant and trendsetting in the nation.

The spectacular **Great Ocean Road** ambles westward from Melbourne along Victoria's southern coast past surf-battered cliffs, lonely beaches, and forests that stop only where the ocean begins. It easily rivals such scenic drives as California's Pacific Coast Highway and Italy's Amalfi Drive. **Phillip Island,** south of Melbourne, is one of the country's must-see spots, a wildlife refuge that claims koalas, fairy penguins, fur seals, wombats, and untold numbers of seabirds among its citizens.

Yet another valid reason for visiting Australia must be mentioned: the forbidding **Outback.** A trip to the **Northern Territory,** in the heart of the Outback, may not be for everyone, but it is the quintessential Australian experience. (Queensland and other states have plenty of Outback, too.) The Outback is a tough place (except, of course, at the luxury resorts that have popped up in recent years), most of it a desert no-man's-land that promises a slow death to anyone who strays beyond what passes for civilization.

The aboriginals survived here for eons before the white man arrived. Aboriginal rock paintings scattered around the Northern Territory date back 20,000 years. One of the aboriginals' most holy places, **Ayers Rock** (Uluru in the aboriginal language), is also one of Australia's top tourist attractions. The single rock, eight miles in diameter at its base, soars more than 1,100 feet above the desert floor; nobody knows for sure how deep it plummets underground. Its penchant for changing colors at sunset, from deep red to burnt orange, is legendary.

Alice Springs, immortalized by Neville Shute in *A Town Like Alice,* is the closest outcropping of civilization to Uluru. There's not a lot to do in this dusty hotbox of a town, but just having reached Alice is a monumental accomplishment for self-respecting world travellers. Alice would seem to some visitors the last place on earth, but it is a jumping-off point for once-in-a-lifetime adventures that can be experienced only in the **Red Centre** of Australia. "Up the track" (up the road) a few hundred miles to the north lies **Darwin** and the magnificent wildlife reserve known as **Kakadu.** Rich in wildlife, the region is a new favorite among Aussies and their guests for bushwalking, camping, and going on safari in a four-wheel-drive vehicle.

Tasmania, or, "tiny Tassie," as Australia's smallest state is known, is likewise a wealth of the unknown. Some areas of the island are among the most treacherous places on earth and have never been fully explored, while others are as gentle as the English countryside. With beaches for swimming and mountains for skiing, Tasmania, off the south coast of Victoria, is another good reason to visit the land Down Under.

Though less often visited by travellers from North America, **South Australia** and far-flung **Western Australia** are filled with delights. **Adelaide**, capital of South Australia, is a genteel city, brightly colored with flowers and sunshine. Just outside the city, in the Adelaide Hills, small wineries produce boutique wines that are gaining popularity worldwide, and in the **Barossa Valley**, northeast of the city, sprawling vineyards yield some of what are already the world's most respected wines.

Perth is best remembered as the setting for the only America's Cup Race ever sailed outside the United States. (It actually was raced off nearby Fremantle, Western Australia's major port city.) This Indian Ocean city is closer to Southeast Asia than it is to Sydney and is, indeed, about as far away as you can travel from anywhere else on this planet and hope to find civilization. In the far north of the vast state of Western Australia, **The Kimberley**, a remote, sparsely populated, still largely unexplored region, is fast becoming one of Australia's most intriguing offbeat vacation destinations. The mountains and rivers in The Kimberley, geologists say, are among the oldest formations on earth.

On this smallest of continents there is a world of things to do, see, experience, taste, smell, and remember for a lifetime. We try in this book to tell you about some of the best; undoubtedly you'll find others on your own.

No manageable guidebook could completely catalogue the many sights and attractions in this country, but you won't have to go far for additional advice about what to do and see. Aussies are friendly enough to be concerned that you have a good time on their turf and that you see and do the things they think are Australia's best. Chat them up. They may be right.

USEFUL FACTS

Entry Requirements

A valid passport and Australian visa are required to enter Australia. Visitor visas for stays of up to three months are free; a one-time visa good for a stay of three to six months or a multiple-entry visa valid for four years cost U.S.$25. Visas are issued by Australian government offices worldwide and can be applied for in person or through the mail. In addition, the Australian Department of Immigration and Qantas have instituted a new service allowing Australia-bound travellers to obtain visas when they purchase tickets at Qantas offices in Los Angeles and San Francisco. Citizens of New Zealand do not need visas. No vaccinations are required before entering the country, unless the traveller is arriving from an "infected" nation as determined by the World Health Organization (the United States, Canada, Great Britain, and New Zealand are not infected nations).

How to Get There

Sydney was once the only arrival and departure city for flights between North America and Australia. In recent years, Melbourne, Brisbane, and Cairns have become important entry and exit points as well. Other international gateways are Adelaide, Hobart (for service from New Zealand), Darwin, and Perth.

There are daily flights between North America and Australia on a variety of airlines: Qantas (Australia's national airline), Air New Zealand, Continental, Northwest, and United. Canadian Airlines International serves Australia on a "share" arrangement, taking passengers from Vancouver to Honolulu, where they board a Qantas or Air New Zealand jet. If you go island-hopping in Fiji and Polynesia on the way to Australia from North America, the last leg of your journey to Sydney may be on a regional South Pacific carrier such as Air Pacific or Polynesian Airlines. Qantas and Air New Zealand fly between Australia and New Zealand. Both British Airways and Qantas make the long haul eastbound from London to Australia. If you include Australia in a circle-Pacific journey, you may find yourself heading south from Asia on Cathay Pacific Airways, Garuda Indonesia, Korean Airlines, Japan Airlines, Philippines Airlines, Singapore Airlines, or Thai Airways International. Sydney, Melbourne, Brisbane, and Perth are favored destinations for Asian airlines; some also serve Adelaide, Cairns, or Darwin.

Customs

Visitors may bring their personal effects into Australia, and those over age 18 may bring in 250 cigarettes or 250 grams of tobacco and one liter of spirits. Dutiable goods up to the value of A$400 are exempt from duty.

Agriculture is big business here, so the locals are nervous about pests and animal and plant diseases from overseas. Thus, you cannot bring fresh or packaged food, fruit, vegetables, seeds, cultures, animals, plants, or animal or plant products into the country.

Furs, jewelry, and artifacts made from endangered species are prohibited, as are drugs, weapons, and firearms.

Departure Tax
The departure tax is A$20 and must be paid in Australian currency.

Health, Disabled Travellers
Drinking tap water without fear of coming down with the classic traveller's stomach upset is one of the simple joys of travel in Australia. Standards of hygiene in such things as water supply and food handling are high. Medical care and hospitals are comparable to those in North America. In remote areas, the Royal Flying Doctor Service offers the comforting backup of emergency evacuation in the event of serious illness or injury.

The desert and seaside air is clear and the sun is harsh here, so pack a hat and SPF 15+ sunscreen as part of your Outback and Great Barrier Reef wardrobe. Sneakers are needed as protection against coral cuts when walking on exposed reefs.

Disabled travellers planning an Australia visit can obtain information about special facilities from the Australian Council for Rehabilitation of the Disabled, 33 Thesiger Court, Deakin, Australian Capital Territory 2605; Tel: (06) 282-4333.

When to Go
Seasons in the Southern Hemisphere are the reverse of those in the Northern Hemisphere; thus, summer in Australia is December, January, and February, while winter is June, July, and August. Many northerners find it difficult to conceive of Christmas as the major summer holiday. Another result of these opposite seasons is that there is a major school holiday in September, the middle of spring for Australians. The big school holiday occurs from mid-December through January. Keep this in mind if you plan to visit around these times, for accommodations are bound to be tight.

In a country about the same size as the continental United States, you will of course find variable weather. Cold weather is rare, though; in winter the southern cities—Sydney, Melbourne, and Hobart—are apt to be merely chilly, with lows in the 40 degrees Fahrenheit range. Morning frost is not unknown in Canberra, which is inland and more than 1,800 feet above sea level. Highs run in the 50s and 60s. Rain in the southern tier of Australia is also more common in winter than in summer, although torrential summer downpours do occur. The high mountain range shared by New South Wales and Victoria tops out with 7,316-foot Mount Kosciusko. The winter snowfields in this range support ski resorts. The high peaks of Tasmania also get a dusting of snow. Summer in Australia is hot everywhere. The best time to go trekking in the Outback is in the fall, winter, or spring, when temperatures are cooler and the flies of summer have ceased (or not yet begun) their rampaging. The best time to visit the Great Barrier Reef is any time—although the wettest time is January through March, and poisonous box jellyfish are found off the beaches then. The soggiest months for Darwin and other areas of the Top End are December through March; this is the season for nasty jellyfish there as well.

What to Wear

Aussies are hardly fashion mavens. They dress sensibly, as dictated by the weather. For much of the year this means lightweight, cool clothes, with shorts, tank tops, and flip-flops being favored by legions of the population. Few occasions call for dressing up, but no one cares if someone wants to put on a jacket and tie or party dress for a night at the opera or on the town. A lightweight jacket or sweater is usually plenty for a winter night in the south. An umbrella and raincoat might come in handy along the coast but would be distinctly out of place in the nation's midsection. A hat for protection against the sun will come in handy everywhere, and those who plan to walk along the Great Barrier Reef will need sturdy shoes to protect their feet against the cutting edge of the coral.

Currency

The Australian dollar is the unit of currency in Australia; it is divided into 100 cents. Bank notes come in A$5, A$10, A$20, A$50, and A$100 denominations, and each is a different color; notes increase slightly in size as the denomination increases. If you receive an A$5 note made of a plastic material, it's not a counterfeit, but a bicentennial commemorative issue. Coins have replaced one- and two-dollar bank notes; the dollar coin is the larger of the two. Other coins are 5, 10, 20, and 50 cent denominations.

Credit Cards. All major credit cards are accepted in Australia at hotels, restaurants, and shops and for air transportation and car rental. American Express, Bank-card, Diners Club, MasterCard, and Visa are the most widely recognized. Travellers' checks are also readily accepted; it is usually best to exchange them for Australian dollars at banks, where rates are more favorable. However, flat rate bank charges for travellers' check transactions can vary from as much as A$2 to A$10.

Tipping. Aussies are not big tippers, but the practice is catching on at finer restaurants around the country. When they tip, 10 to 15 percent is about the maximum. Cab-drivers and bartenders don't expect tips, nor do airport porters. No service charges are added to Australian hotel and restaurant bills.

Time Zones

There are three time zones in Australia: eastern, central, and western. Eastern time is two hours ahead of western and one-half hour ahead of central. Brisbane, Cairns, Canberra, Hobart, Melbourne, and Sydney are in the eastern time zone; Adelaide, Alice Springs, and Darwin are in the central time zone; Perth is in the western time zone. Except for the Northern Territory, Western Australia, and Queensland, clocks are advanced one hour during daylight saving time, October to March.

England, the United States, and Canada are all *behind* Australian time—London is behind Sydney by 9 hours, New York and Toronto by 14 hours, California and British Columbia by 17 hours, and Hawaii by 19 hours.

Telephoning

The international country code for Australia is 61. When dialing from outside Australia, do not include the initial zero in city codes.

To place overseas credit card or collect calls from Australia, dial 0014-881011 for the United States, 0014-881440 for the United Kingdom, or 0014-881150 for Canada. These numbers connect you with operators in the United States, United Kingdom, or Canada, eliminating the need to go through an Australian international operator.

Electrical Current

The electrical current in Australia is 240/250 volts, AC 50 Hz. Power outlets are three-pronged. An adapter socket and voltage converter will be needed by Americans and Canadians who want to run hair dryers, travel irons, shavers, and other small electrical appliances brought from home. Hotel bathrooms usually have 240V or 110V universal outlets for shavers.

Business Hours

Most banks are open 9:30 A.M.–4:00 P.M. Mondays through Thursdays and until 5:00 P.M. on Fridays. Post office hours are 9:00 A.M.–5:00 P.M. weekdays. Most stores and shops are open for business 10:00 A.M.–5:00 P.M. weekdays. In Sydney, Melbourne, and Southeast Queensland Saturday hours are about 9:00 A.M.–5:00 P.M.; elsewhere a noon or 1:00 P.M. Saturday closing is common. In bigger cities, some stores stay open late one night of the week. Seven-day-a-week shopping has made its appearance at a few big, touristy shopping malls and in city centers of Sydney and Melbourne.

Public Holidays

In addition to the national holidays listed below, individual states celebrate local holidays that generally cause a shutdown. National holidays are New Year's Day; Australia Day, January 26; Good Friday; Easter; Easter Monday; Anzac Day, April 25; Queen's Birthday, second Monday in June; Christmas; Boxing Day, December 26.

Where to Stay

Australia offers rooms for every taste and budget. There are deluxe city hotels and posh resorts (some on private islands), modest properties catering to the family trade, self-contained apartments for long-stay visitors, and thousands of motels serving the road traveller. Caravan (trailer) parks not only have space for recreational vehicles, they rent tidy tourist cabins or caravans to motorists who decide to bypass local motels. Bed-and-breakfast lodgings and farm stays satisfy other tastes. Details on all forms of accommodation, including bed and breakfast and farm or station stays, can be found in *Destination Australia* (see Further Information, below).

Because of frequent rate changes, the room rates given for hotels should be used as guidelines only. Rates fluctuate with market demand. Travel wholesalers dealing in volume negotiate room rates considerably lower than published "rack rates." It is therefore wise to make use of a travel agent for hotel reservations. Rates may also vary according to the season. The low season is generally from May to November; in the desert and tropics, however, winter is generally the most pleasant time of year and hence is the high season.

Hotel and motel rooms are universally supplied with electric kettle, tea bags, powdered coffee, sugar, and packets of long-life milk—or even a pint of fresh milk in the refrigerator. Toasters aren't uncommon; when you order room-service breakfast, sliced bread is delivered untoasted.

At most motels you can place an order at the front desk for room-service breakfast. On the other hand, some of the poshest hotels seem to discourage room service by exacting surcharges, particularly on weekends.

Dining in top-class hotels is expensive. For example, you'll pay A$12–A$15 for selections from a Continental breakfast buffet; a cooked breakfast will run A$15–A$19.

Getting Around by Air

Australia entered the unstable world of airline deregulation in late 1990 but thus far no new airline has survived to challenge Ansett Australia and Qantas, the only carriers with nationwide networks. Eastwest Airlines is a major carrier concentrating on the leisure market, with services mainly in the east. Numerous regional airlines in each state pick up where the majors leave off and fly to smaller cities and towns, sometimes in pretty small aircraft. The major domestic airlines can be very strict about baggage size—if your carry-on bag is larger than allowed you run the risk of having to leave it behind. Check with the airlines for their specific size restrictions.

Getting Around by Rail

Rail Australia is the national rail line that links most major cities. On long runs trains are equipped with sleeping cars, showers, cocktail bars, and dining cars. The longest run is the transcontinental Indian Pacific between Sydney and Perth, which takes 65 hours (three nights). *The Ghan,* the most luxurious of the long-haul trains, makes it between Adelaide and Alice Springs in 22 hours. The 1,045-mile, 32-hour coastal route of *The Queenslander* (between Brisbane and Cairns) is considered the most scenic.

Getting Around by Bus

Australia is crisscrossed with interstate and intrastate bus routes operated by Australian Coachlines and its subsidiaries, Pioneer, Greyhound, and Bus Australia. A bus trip from Sydney to Melbourne, for example, takes about 15 hours. Any travel agent can book domestic passage in

Australia. Australian Coachlines sells an Aussie Pass allowing for unlimited travel in periods of seven to 90 days.

Inclusive coach tours are popular here. Overseas visitors booking such tours enjoy the double advantage of economy and meeting local people. Some coach tours use conventional motels and hotels along their routes. For certain Outback tours coaches haul utility trailers that hold kitchen equipment, tents, and sleeping bags. Campgrounds at such places as Ayers Rock Resort have areas designed for coach groups. You can book a coach tour before your departure through your travel agent or directly through the offices of motorcoach operators listed in *Destination Australia*.

Getting Around by Car

You can make rental-car reservations for Australia before leaving home through such international franchise groups as Avis, Budget, Dollar, Hertz, National, and Thrifty. You can also arrange for a rental car on the spot at city, airport, and resort offices of these companies as well as local rental firms. Rates include unlimited mileage and some insurance, but drivers pay for gas and additional coverage. Rental rates vary, depending on company, season, locale, and length of rental. In general, small-car rentals start at about A\$65 per day, medium cars at A\$75, and large at A\$85. Day rates decrease for three-day, weekly, and monthly rentals. One-way rentals without a drop fee are available between some points; however, if you plan to make a long one-way trip, check out the drop fees and other restrictions carefully. Some companies don't want their cars dropped on the other side of the continent or even taken out of state. Gasoline (petrol) is sold by the liter and costs roughly A\$0.75 per liter (about US\$3 per gallon).

Rugged four-wheel-drive Land Rover–type vehicles, complete with kangaroo bumper bars and protectors to deflect rocks from windshields, can be rented for Outback travel on dirt and gravel tracks; Royal Flying Doctor Service Outback radios are offered by some companies to complete the four-wheel-drive safari equipment kit. A full array of recreational vehicles equipped with beds, kitchens, and toilets is available for exploration along paved roads.

A valid driver's license and a major credit card are required to rent a car in Australia, and most agencies will not rent to people under age 21. The law requires that all passengers must wear seat belts, and penalties for driving while intoxicated are severe—with no allowances made for foreigners. Police in Australia can stop motorists at any time to administer an on-the-spot breath test, and those who fail or refuse the test are hauled off to jail. Take note: Aussies drive on the left-hand side of the road.

Driving Tours. If you're planning a driving tour, visit an automobile association office as soon as you land. The New South Wales organization is called the National Roads & Motorists' Association (151 Clarence Street, Sydney); the others are the Royal Automobile Club of Victoria (422 Little Collins Street, Melbourne); Royal Automobile Club of Tasmania (corner of Murray and Patrick Streets, Hobart); Royal Automobile Association of South Australia, Inc. (41 Hindmarsh Square, Adelaide); Royal Automobile Club of Queensland (300 St. Pauls Terrace, Fortitude Valley, Brisbane); Royal Automobile Club of Western Australia (228 Adelaide Terrace, Perth); Automobile Association of the Northern Territory (MLC Building, 79-81 Smith Street, Darwin); and the National Roads & Motorists Association of the ACT (92 Northborne Avenue, Canberra). These offices should have touring directories, route maps, and other helpful information.

Most state tourism offices publish excellent motoring guides with route maps, color illustrations, and descriptions of points of interest; the Northern Territory Tourism Commission has a guide for four-wheel-drive exploration, and the Western Australian Tourism Commission has a guide to the best wildflower-viewing routes. Where motoring guides are not stocked, state offices have other material with information and suggestions for driving vacations.

Travel Bargains

Transportation companies, tour operators, and hotels offer discount schemes that can reduce travel costs in Australia. Many are detailed in *Destination Australia* (see Further Information, below). The Austrailpass, for example, allows unlimited first-class and economy travel on trains in Australia for periods of 14 to 90 days. The price of the pass does not include sleeping berths or meals.

Greyhound sells a road and rail pass that offers unlimited rail and coach travel on its routes for 14, 21, or 28 days. Express-bus companies commonly offer 7- to 120-day discount passes as well as savings on city sightseeing tours.

Domestic air travel is expensive, but air passes offered to foreign travellers by Qantas and Ansett Australia can reduce ticket costs from 30 to 60 percent, depending on the amount of mileage purchased and the current promotion. Advance payment for a rental car can reduce costs when you are dealing with international companies. Fly-drive and car-motel packages also reduce costs; fly-drive schemes include both regular cars and recreational vehicles. Advance-purchase hotel vouchers can sometimes reduce room costs by 20 to 25 percent. Companies offering voucher schemes include Southern Pacific Hotels (Parkroyal and TraveLodge properties), Flag Inns (500 properties), and Best Western (400 properties). Most discounts involve purchase outside Australia and have conditions and restrictions, so it's wise to work with a travel agent for bookings.

Special Interest Travel

Australia is a good destination for special interest travel, particularly for such active sports as scuba diving, golf, and tennis. Some tour operators outside Australia offer escorted group tours that focus on these sports Down Under; otherwise you can arrange all the action you want on your own before or after arrival. Wildflower viewing is a popular seasonal activity (see the Western Australia chapter), and birdwatching can be enjoyed almost everywhere. It is possible to join an Australian birding group or to stay in lodges where the proprietors specialize in birding excursions.

Another option is to span the continent, from the Hunter Valley in New South Wales to the Margaret River in Western Australia, satisfying particular interests in fine wine and food.

"Green Theme" eco-tours concentrate on flora, fauna, and wild country, including national parks and the country's nine World Heritage areas. Some Green Theme tours are for hikers, but many are designed as four-wheel drive adventure safaris. Or visitors can satisfy an interest in Aboriginal cultures by booking special tours of Aboriginal reserves (see the Northern Territory chapter).

Some special interest travel has a limited time frame: Through 1995, Australians are commemorating the 50th anniversary of World War II by inviting American and other Allied veterans of South Pacific campaigns to visit Australia for commemorations.

Further Information

U.S. residents can phone (800) 333-0199 and Canadians can phone (800) 231-6600 for a free copy of *Destination Australia,* published annually by the Australian Tourist

Commission, the national tourist office. The book contains information about tours, sights and attractions, accommodations, transportation, and discount schemes as well as handy travel tips.

For further information contact the Australian Tourist Commission. In the United States, 2121 Avenue of the Stars, Suite 1200, Los Angeles, CA 90067, Tel: (310) 552-1988; 150 North Michigan Avenue, Suite 2130, Chicago, IL 60601, Tel: (312) 781-5150; 489 Fifth Avenue, 31st Floor, New York, NY 10017, Tel: (212) 687-6300. In Canada, 2 Bloor Street West, Suite 1730, Toronto, Ontario M4W 3E2; Tel: (416) 925-9575. In the United Kingdom, Gemini House, 10–18 Putney Hill, London SW15 6AA, England; Tel: (081) 780-2227.

Most of Australia's states also maintain overseas tourism information offices, which you should contact for details on specific regional attractions.

Tasmania and Victoria. In the United States and Canada, contact Australia Naturally (Tourism Tasmania and Victorian Tourism Commission), 2121 Avenue of the Stars, Suite 1270, Los Angeles, CA 90067; Tel: (310) 553-6352. In the United Kingdom, contact Australia's Southern Tourism Promotion, Gemini House, 10–18 Putney Hill, London SW15 6AA, England; Tel: (081) 788-7088.

New South Wales. In the United States and Canada, contact New South Wales Tourism Commission, 2121 Avenue of the Stars, Suite 1230, Los Angeles, CA 90067; Tel: (310) 552-9566. In the United Kingdom, contact the New South Wales Tourism Commission, 7th Level, 75 King William Street, London EC4N 7HA, England; Tel: (071) 522-0306.

Queensland. In the United States, contact the Queensland Tourist and Travel Corporation, 1800 Century Park East, Suite 330, Los Angeles, CA 90067, Tel: (310) 788-0997; or 489 Fifth Avenue, 31st floor, New York, NY 10017, (212) 308-5520; in U.S. and Canada, Tel: (800) 333-6050. In the United Kingdom, contact the Queensland Tourist and Travel Corporation, Queensland House, 392/3 The Strand, London WC2, England; Tel: (071) 836-7242.

South Australia. In the United States and Canada, contact Tourism South Australia, 2121 Avenue of the Stars, Suite 1210, Los Angeles, CA 90067; Tel: (310) 552-2821. In the United Kingdom, contact Tourism South Australia at South Australia House, 50 The Strand, London WC2, England; Tel: (071) 930-7471.

Western Australia. In the United States and Canada, contact the Western Australian Tourism Commission, 2121

Avenue of the Stars, Suite 1210, Los Angeles, CA 90067; Tel: (310) 557-1987. In the United Kingdom, contact the Western Australian Tourism Commission, Western Australia House, 115 The Strand, London WC2R OAJ, England; Tel: (071) 240-2881.

Northern Territory. In the United States and Canada, contact the Northern Territory Tourist Commission, 2121 Avenue of the Stars, Suite 1280, Los Angeles, CA 90067; Tel: (310) 277-7877.

BIBLIOGRAPHY

If your local library and bookstores are not well supplied with Australian titles, ask for a catalogue from the Australian Book Source, 1309 Redwood Lane, Davis, CA 95616; Tel: (916) 753-1519. In addition to selling catalogue selections, the Book Source will make special orders; the service does not, however, search for out-of-print volumes.

Aboriginals

GEOFFREY BARDON, *Papunya Tula: Art of the Western Desert* (1992). Dramatic aboriginal paintings from the Western Desert have become hot items on the Australian art scene in recent years. This volume tells how Bardon, a Sydney art teacher, inspired and helped older aboriginal men in desert settlements to transfer archetypal ritual designs, previously produced only in sand paintings, onto board and canvas.

GEOFFREY BLAINEY, *Triumph of the Nomads: A History of Ancient Australia* (1975). Carbon dating has identified aboriginal sites nearly 40,000 years old. Blainey describes the ancient settlement of the continent by people who created a lifestyle around a harsh, ever-changing environment. Their skills in finding water and as herbalists, trappers, and hunters are part of a description that also shows how rising seas led to the isolation of the first Australians.

STANLEY BREEDEN AND BELINDA WRIGHT, *Kakadu, Looking After the Country—The Gagudju Way* (1989). An exploration of Kakadu National Park through the eyes of its traditional owners. Superb color illustrations.

BRUCE CHATWIN, *The Songlines* (1987). A travelogue/memoir/history focusing on the mythical "Dreamtime" of the aboriginals, when their ancestors walked across Australia singing the world into existence.

JENNIFER ISAACS, *Australian Dreaming: 40,000 Years of Aboriginal History* (1980). A standard text for aboriginal studies, this book recounts the history of the Australian continent and its first people through their myths and legends.

BILL NEIDJIE, STEPHEN DAVIS, AND ALLAN FOX, *Kakadu Man: Bill Neidjie* (1985). This little book contains the poetic, poignant response of Big Bill Neidjie, one of the last of the Bunitj people, to conflicting 1970s demands that tribal lands of Kakadu be made a national park or mined for uranium. (Park advocates won.)

Arts

ALBERT MORAN AND TOM O'REGAN, *The Australian Screen* (1989). A history of Australian filmmaking and television.

LEONARD RADIC, *State of Play: The Revolution in the Australian Theater Since the 1960s* (1991). Contemporary theater is examined by the drama critic of the Melbourne *Age*.

GEOFFREY SERLE, *The Creative Spirit in Australia* (1987). This volume provides newcomers to the Australian cultural scene with a Who's Who (and Why) in literary, visual, and performing arts.

MICHAEL STURMA, *Australian Rock 'n' Roll: The First Wave* (1991). The arrival of rock 'n' roll in Australia in the 1950s is likened to a bomb dropped "on a society steeped in the values of stability, conformity and sexual conservatism." The author examines those wild years.

Flora, Fauna, and Natural History

AUSTRALIAN GOVERNMENT PUBLISHING SERVICE, *Bush Dwellers of Australia* (1990). Revised edition of one of the most popular books ever published on Australian fauna. The book contains 132 color photographs of marsupials and other mammals, reptiles, birds, insects, and sea life.

BAY BOOKS, *Australia's Amazing Wildlife* (1988). Coverage of the entire range of unique Down Under wildlife, from the familiar kangaroo and koala to tortoises, turtles, and frogs. Full-color illustrations.

LEONARD CRONIN, *Key Guide to Australian Wildflowers* (1990). Six hundred of the most commonly encountered wildflowers are illustrated and described with a minimal use of botanical terminology.

GWEN ELLIOT, *Australian Plants Identified* (1990). Descriptions of more than 1,000 plants, with color photographs and line drawings.

ROBIN HILL, *Birds of Australia* (1967). A fine, illustrated introduction to the 700-plus species found Down Under. If this book (or birds on the wing) inspires you to birding, various compact field guides are available.

WILLIAM J. LINES, *Taming the Great South Land: A History of the Conquest of Nature in Australia* (1992). The author, a Western Australian, presents a 1990s politically correct view of the environmental devastation wrought on the continent during two centuries of settlement and development.

REG AND MAGGIE MORRISON, *Australia: The Four Billion Year Journey of a Continent* (1990). The story of Australia's evolution as a continent and its natural history. Illustrated with 500 color photographs.

ANN MOYAL, *A Bright and Savage Land: Scientists in Colonial Australia* (1975). Australia, continent of "all things queer and opposite," was a paradise for the 18th- and 19th-century scientists whose work is described here. The account begins with naturalists and navigators and ends with experimenters and inventors. Sketches, paintings, and plates of the time provide illustration.

GRAHAM PIZZEY, *A Field Guide to Australian Birds* (1980). More than 700 species are illustrated in this portable guide.

Reader's Digest Visitors Guide to the Great Barrier Reef (1988). Three hundred fifty color photographs illustrate this guide, which traces the evolution of the reef and its discovery and looks at the future of the coral barrier.

ERIC C. ROSS ROLLS, *They All Ran Wild* (1969). A tale of the ecological disasters wrought by foreign animals and plants Down Under. Rolls first looks at the ravages of the gray English rabbit, then examines the havoc caused by the hare, fox, trout, carp, sparrow, starling, feral pig, donkey, horse, camel, and goat. Not to mention the blackberry.

Food and Wine

STEPHANIE ALEXANDER, *Stephanie's Australia, Travelling and Tasting (1992)*. Alexander—a chef, award-winning restaurateur, and food writer—presents a gastronomic tour of her country, with a look at everything that's happening on the Australian food scene. She emphasizes the variety and quality of food grown in Australia and tells stories of people involved in the trade. Photographs by John Hay.

LEN EVANS, *Complete Book of Australian Wine* (1984). It takes 785 oversized pages to tell the history of Australia's wines and describe the wineries and regions, grape varieties, and white and red wines. Beautiful illustrations.

JAMES HALLIDAY, *Wine Atlas of Australia and New Zealand* (1991). The author, a wine-show judge and columnist for the *Australian,* introduces readers to the Down Under wine industry with detailed maps of production areas plus data on everything from soils to prices.

GRAEME NEWMAN, *Down Under Cookbook* (1987). A guide to Aussie cooking and eating traditions; includes recipes.

MARK SHIELD AND PHILLIP MEYER, *The Penguin Good Australian Wine Guide* (1991). This guide has a 1991 vintage guide and reviews of some 1,000 wines.

MICHAEL SYMONS, *One Continuous Picnic: A History of Eating in Australia* (1982). Looks at food and eating habits as part of Australia's history and national character; traces the evolution of cookery from colonial damper bread to fluffy pavlova and beyond.

History and Social Comment

H. M. BARKER, *Camels and the Outback* (1964). Camel drayman Barker provides a definitive account of the camel's role in exploration and frontier settlement.

D. L. BERNSTEIN, *First Tuesday in November* (1969). The complete story of the Melbourne Cup, the horse race that annually brings the nation to a standstill.

GAVIN CASEY AND TED MAYMAN, *The Mile That Midas Touched* (1964). Water was once almost as precious as gold in Kalgoorlie, Australia's last great gold-rush town. This history traces the settlement from Patrick Hannan's 1893 find through development of both the deep mines of the Golden Mile and the water pipeline from mountains far to the west.

C. M. H. CLARK, *A History of Australia* (five volumes, 1981). This work is said to have "made Australians interested in reading about their history for the first time."

ERWIN H. J. FEEKEN, GERDA E. E. FEEKEN, AND O. H. K. SPATE, *The Discovery and Exploration of Australia* (1970). The exploits of all of Australia's explorers, from the 17th-century Dutch to Frederick S. Drake-Brockman of 1901, are in this volume. It also contains a historical gazetteer of Australian place names.

DONALD HORNE, *The Lucky Country: Revisited* (1987). Hindsight of 1987 tempers the author's sometimes harsh look at the social and cultural climate of the 1960s. His topics range from the "first suburban nation" to "Australian ugliness."

ROBERT HUGHES, *The Fatal Shore: The Epic of Australia's Founding* (1987). The best-selling analysis of The System, the scheme that transported 158,829 men and 24,568 women from England's prisons to penal settlements in Australia between 1788 and 1868. Grimly fascinating reading.

THOMAS KENEALLY, PATSY ADAM-SMITH, AND ROBYN DAVIDSON, *Australia: Beyond the Dreamtime* (1989). A look at two centuries of Australian history from three viewpoints. Award-winning novelist Keneally (*The Chant of Jimmy Blacksmith*) examines the roots of the nation from the First Fleet to the Eureka Stockade battle; popular historian Adam-Smith focuses on class struggles, unions, and the maturing of the nation; and Davidson, famous for her solo camel trek across Australia, speaks from the perspective of the Vietnam War generation.

BRIAN KENNEDY, *Silver, Sin, and Sixpenny Ale* (1978). This history of the silver-mining town of Broken Hill—called "the Mecca of unionism" and "industrial magnet of Australia"—starts with the claim-pegging days of 1883 and ends with the great labor strike of 1919–1920.

W. F. MANDLE, *Going It Alone* (1978). Varied incidents, from strikes to the death of the racehorse Phar Lap, are used by Mandle to illustrate the development of national character in the isolated land Down Under.

ALAN MOOREHEAD, *Cooper's Creek* (1963). The story of the ill-fated Burke-Wills 1860 expedition, which attempted to cross the continent from south to north and return.

PETER J. PHILLIPS, *Redgum and Paddlewheelers* (1980). Paddlewheelers on the Murray, Darling, and Murrumbidgee rivers aided in the settlement and development of vast areas of inland southeastern Australia. This book tells the story of boats, captains, adventures, and disasters along the rivers.

JOHN PILGER, *A Secret Country: The Hidden Australia* (1991). Pilger, an Australian-born journalist and documentary filmmaker, takes a jaundiced and controversial look at the popular image of his homeland as an egalitarian nation and a workers' paradise. Genocide of the aboriginals and colonial manipulation (most recently by the CIA) are other themes.

ELIZABETH WEBBY, ED., *Colonial Voices* (1989). Letters, diaries, and journalistic efforts of 65 settlers and visitors in Australia from 1788 to the early 1900s provide a lively, impressionistic history of the new land. The reports range from "first impressions" to "floods, flies, and fauna."

JOHN YEOMANS, *The Other Taj Mahal* (1968). A look at the first ten years of squabbling, mistakes, and technical challenges in construction of the Sydney Opera House.

R. M. YOUNGER, *Australia! Australia!* (1987). Three detailed, pictorial volumes—*The Pioneer Years, March to Nationhood, Challenge and Achievement*—contain an overview of Australian history and cultural, social, and political development.

Language and Literature

DEBRA ADELAIDE, *Australian Women Writers: A Bibliographic Guide* (1988). Details on 450 writers, from settlement to the present.

JIM ANDERSON, *Billarooby* (1988). A hardscrabble Outback village, fear and hate of the inmates of a nearby Japanese prisoner-of-war camp, a guilt-ridden English immigrant family, and the untrammeled imagination of a boy are the cornerstones of this unusual, sometimes grim novel.

PETER CAREY, *The Tax Inspector* (1991). This novel by Booker Award winner Carey examines a bizarre, not-too-moral, not-too-honest family of car dealers in contemporary Sydney. The climax of the yarn has been termed Grand Guignol. His previous novel, *Oscar and Lucinda* (1988), was a study of 19th-century Australian religiosity.

MARCUS CLARKE, *For the Term of His Natural Life* (1874). Published more than a century ago, this grim and powerful novel of life in an Australian penal colony is considered an Australian classic.

JACK DAVIS, STEPHEN MUECKE, MURDOOROO WAROGIN, AND ADAM SHOEMAKER, EDS. *Paperback: A Collection of Black Australian Writing* (1990). The work of more than 40 aboriginal writers in this anthology ranges from literature based on tribal oral traditions to Western genres.

MILES FRANKLIN, *My Brilliant Career* (1901) and *All That Swagger* (1936). *Career* was the first novel by the then 21-year-old Franklin; *Swagger* is considered her best. Both ring with her affection for Australian country life and her feminist views.

PAM GILBERT, *Coming Out from Under: Contemporary Australian Women Writers* (1988). A study of top writers, with separate chapters on a dozen of the most important.

KEN GOODWIN AND ALAN LAWSON, EDS., *The Macmillan Anthology of Australian Literature* (1990). This volume contains an eclectic collection of more than 200 poems, fictional sketches, narratives of exploration, newspaper stories, speeches, and historical and biographical material. It also includes bibliographical guides to all authors and a chronological table of events in the literary history of Australia.

LENIE (MIDGE) JOHANSEN, *The Dinkum Dictionary: A Ripper Guide to Aussie English* (1988). Reviewers claimed that the 17,000 entries in this dictionary prove that "the speech of Australia is one of the richest and most creative parts of the English language."

LEONIE KRAMER AND ADRIAN MITCHELL, EDS., *The Oxford Anthology of Australian Literature* (1984). A selection of both the best and the most representative in Australian letters.

DAVID MALOUF, *The Great World* (1991). Malouf, whom Australians regard as a major contemporary talent, traces the lives of two Australians—Digger Kean and Vic Curran—who meet in a Japanese prisoner-of-war camp after the fall of Singapore. Reviewers have said that the story is epic in scope.

EDWARD E. MORRIS, *A Dictionary of Austral English* (1898). Reprinted in the 1970s, this volume is considered unsurpassed as a historical record of entirely new words and altered English words in the Australian and New Zealand languages.

LES MURRAY, *The Boys Who Stole the Funeral: A Novel Sequence* (1991). Australian poet Murray begins his verse

novel with two young men stealing the body of a friend—
an old soldier—from a mortuary and taking him to his
former home in the country for burial.

A. B. "BANJO" PATERSON, *A.B. "Banjo" Paterson's Collected
Verse* (1989). "The Man from Snowy River," "Waltzing
Matilda," and other famous and favorite poems are included in this reissue volume with original illustrations
by Norman Lindsay, Hal Gye, and Lionel Lindsay.

PETER PIERCE, ED., *The Oxford Literary Guide to Australia*.
A comprehensive and evocative account of the places
lived in and celebrated by Australia's writers, listing more
than 930 localities.

DORIS PILKINGTON, *Caprice: A Stockman's Daughter*
(1990). This story of an aboriginal woman's search for her
true identity won the 1990 David Unaipon Award (National Aboriginal Literary Award).

RHYS POLLARD, *The Cream Machine* (1972). A novel of
Australian involvement in the Vietnam War, considered by
many the best of its genre.

JOHN TRANTER AND PHILIP MEAD, EDS., *The Penguin Book of
Modern Australian Poetry* (1991). According to the edi-
tors, this representative collection of poetry, ranging from
Kenneth Slessor (1901–1971) to the present, was selected
for reading enjoyment.

PATRICK WHITE, *The Tree of Man* (1957). This novel by
Australia's first Nobel Prize winner (1973) was also the
first of White's work to draw universal acclaim overseas;
Australian critics, however, raged at his concept of the
national character.

Memoirs, Autobiography, and Biography

JOHN BERTRAND (as told to Patrick Robinson), *Born to
Win* (1985). Autobiography of the skipper who sailed
Australia II to victory in the America's Cup races of
September 1983. Says Bertrand, "I was pursuing ... the
sense of excellence, conquest, perfection—particularly
perfection—that is contained in the true Olympic spirit."
Bertrand's quest was inherited: His great-grandfather pre-
pared 19th-century Cup challenge yachts for Sir Thomas
Lipton.

PETER CONRAD, *Behind the Mountain: Return to Tasmania*
(1989). The evocative essays in this memoir of a child-
hood in Tasmania and of visits home after many years

abroad touch on historical, geographical, cultural, and other influences that make the residents of Australia's smallest state just a little different from the people who live on the mainland.

JILL KER CONWAY, *The Road from Coorain* (1989). At Coorain, the Outback station where Jill Ker spent the first 11 years of her life, "the silence was so profound it pressed upon the eardrums." Ker, who was seven before she met another little girl, followed a road from Coorain to alien Sydney and then to graduate school in America. She was the president of Smith College for a decade.

A. B. FACEY, *A Fortunate Life* (1981). A Western Australian everyman tells the story of his life: orphan boy on hard-scrabble frontier farms, jackeroo on remote cattle stations, Anzac soldier in World War I, and family man in postwar Perth.

MRS. AENEAS GUNN, *We of the Never-Never* (1908). The isolated life of a Northern Territory cattle station as described by Mrs. Gunn, who arrived at The Elsey in 1902 as a bride and departed a year later a widow.

DAVID MARR, *Patrick White: A Life* (1992). Australian biographer Marr explores all facets of Nobel Prize–winner White's writing and life—his sense of alienation, his homosexuality, and his love-hate relationship with both his family and his country.

—*Shirley Maas Fockler*

SYDNEY

By Helen Gordon, Charles Sriber, and Kirsty McKenzie

Sydney-born Helen Gordon has been in journalism all her adult life, working as a feature writer for magazines and newspapers. For the last 15 years she has been involved in travel writing, and she was associate travel editor of The Australian, *Australia's national newspaper, until 1990. Charles Sriber came to Sydney in 1950 and worked as a radio and newspaper journalist. Former travel editor of the* Sydney Morning Herald *and* The Australian, *he received a Pacific Asia Travel Association Golden Award for a newspaper travel story in 1992. Kirsty McKenzie, a freelance food and travel writer based in Sydney, contributes to a variety of publications in Australia and overseas.*

Sydney is a most distracting place. Imagine a city that combines the best of San Francisco and St. Tropez. Imagine a place where people take pride in their comfort and pleasure and hold them most dear. Imagine an urban sprawl of some 700 square miles trapped between sea and mountains, colored by eucalyptus trees, jacaranda, frangipani, hibiscus, and neon. Think Sydney.

It would be easy to call Sydney's four million people hedonistic. Tanned, slim, and often topless, Sydneysiders by the thousands grease themselves up and broil in the sun that bakes this city most of the year. They congregate in pubs and never say no to another beer, especially if someone else is buying. They feast on the freshest seafood, dance at the trendiest clubs, and soak up opera, dance, and musical music as if they were Viennese.

But it is not a hedonistic city. There's nothing even vaguely sinister about the way Sydneysiders grapple with

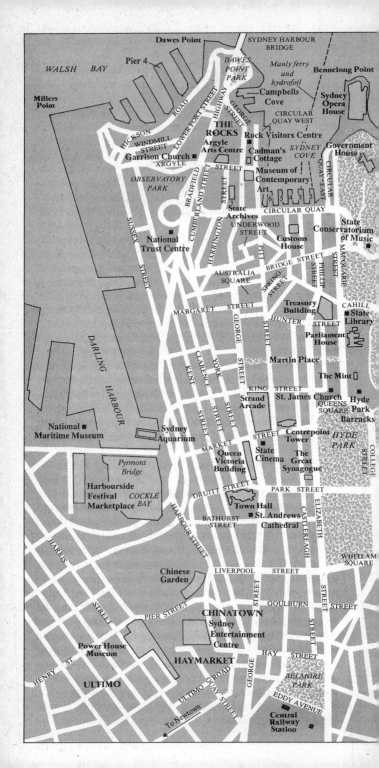

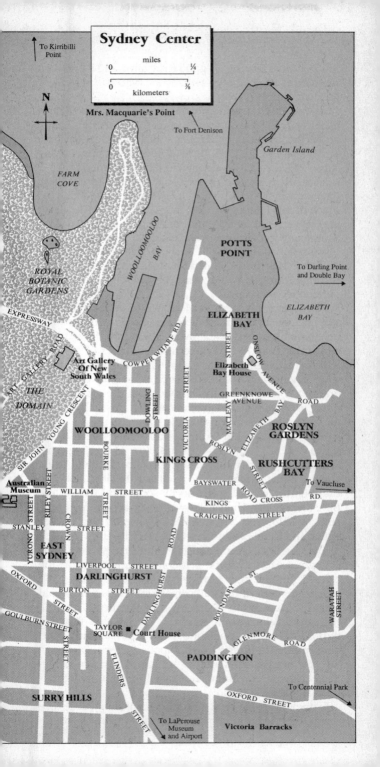

life. For most, it's fun, it's good to be alive, and it's great—the natives are happy to tell anyone who will listen—to live in a perfect place.

As the first outpost of white settlement in Australia, Sydney began its history in leg irons. Captain Arthur Phillip arrived at Botany Bay, 12 miles south of present-day Sydney, on January 26, 1788. He led a fleet of 11 ships carrying some 700 convicts—overflow from English jails. He chose Botany Bay as his landing spot on the recommendation of Captain James Cook, who had discovered and charted much of Australia's east coast in 1770. Although Cook had liked Botany Bay, Phillip was not impressed. He found the anchorage poor, the terrain exposed, and the natives unfriendly—they shouted "Warra, Wirra!" clearly meaning "Go away." He did, but only a few miles up the coast, after a reconnoitering party suggested Port Jackson might prove a satisfactory alternative.

Fleet surgeon-general Dr. John White wrote, "Port Jackson I believe to be without exception, the finest and most extensive harbour in the universe, being safe from all the winds that blow. It is divided into a number of coves to which His Excellency has given different names. That on which the town is to be built is called Sydney Cove. It is one of the smallest in the harbour, but the most convenient, as ships with the greatest burden can with ease go into it and heave out close to the shore."

Early days in the colony—christened New South Wales—were hard, with supplies slow in arriving from England and agriculture chancy, but free settlers using convict labor spread out to cultivate the land and run cattle on the coastal strips north, south, and west to the Blue Mountains. When a way was found across the mountains in 1813, New South Wales became an even greater wheat and cattle producer, with Sydney its hub.

The merino sheep-herding industry subsequently brought wealth to some settlers and reputation to the colony, but the real bonanza didn't come until 1850, when a veteran of the Californian goldfields found gold near the New South Wales town of Bathurst. The gold rush eventually moved south to Victoria, but that first flurry boosted the population, whose burgeoning wealth underpinned a flourish of pompous Victorian architecture. Sydney has continued to grow, its original predominantly Anglo-Celtic population swelling with immigrants from all over the world.

Sydney is truly multicultural. Thanks to successive waves of migration, almost every nationality is represented here; there are, for example, more Thai restaurants in Sydney than any city other than Bangkok. The sign on a doctor's surgery in the inner western suburb of Marrickville announces that Russian, Yugoslav, Greek, Italian, and Mandarin are spoken inside. Farther west, the district of Cabramatta is Sydney's Little Vietnam, where the supermarkets sell sticky rice, lemon grass, kaffir lime, and the foul-smelling delicacy fruit durian, and the banks, solicitors, and even the Medicare office are bilingual.

The Sydney outlook is outdoorsy, casual, and pleasure-loving, largely because of a weather pattern that seldom lets the city get really cold and that delivers oppressive heat only for brief periods. Seven racetracks, 30 or so public golf courses, and football and cricket fields are available in the city, and every weekend that "finest and most extensive harbour" complements the famous white sails of the Opera House with legions of billowing jibs and mainsails, as the serious yacht-racing fraternity sweats over the winches. The noncompetitive boaties drop anchor and raise their glasses in dozens of sandy bays around Sydney.

Sydney also has a thriving and frequently innovative cultural life, ranging the spectrum from chamber-music and symphony concerts to ballets (modern and classical), theater (mainstream and experimental), and, naturally—given the magnificence of the venue—opera.

MAJOR INTEREST

Sydney Harbour
The Rocks, Australia's first colonial settlement
Sydney Opera House
Beaches
Eating, drinking, and entertainment
Sports
Museums and galleries

SYDNEY HARBOUR

Still officially and correctly called Port Jackson, Sydney Harbour encompasses 22 square miles of sheltered waters. On weekends, particularly in summer, the harbor can be crowded with 10,000 or more sailboats, motor cruisers, runabouts, water skiers, and sailboards—just about anything that floats.

Closest to the city the water has its share of pollution,

but beaches nearer The Heads (as the entrance to the Harbour is known), including Lady Bay nude beach and those in Middle Harbour, are fed directly by the Pacific and are generally quite clean. Various foreshore green areas are protected as parts of Sydney Harbour National Park.

The **Harbour Bridge** divides Port Jackson into two sections. Its western side is mainly commercial, residential, and parkland, while east of the bridge, from east to west, are The Rocks, Sydney Cove, fringes of the Central Business District at Circular Quay on the cove, and the Opera House, as well as highly prized residential real-estate and parkland. For an overview of the city you might walk across the bridge on its pedestrian walkway via Cumberland Street in The Rocks. You can return to the city by train from Milson's Point Railway Station at the bridge's northern end. The athletically inclined might climb the 200 steps to a lookout perched on the bridge's southeast pylon; it is open from 10:00 A.M. to 5:00 P.M., Saturday to Tuesday.

All ferries and most harbor cruises start from Circular Quay, their regular routes taking them out of Sydney Cove past the cruise-ship passenger terminal.

Westbound ferries from Circular Quay go under the Harbour Bridge and pass the series of piers in Walsh Bay. Manly and other north- and eastbound ferries pass the eastern side of Harbour Bridge, then, in the middle of the harbour, **Fort Dennison**. The fort's round martello tower has crowned the tiny island since 1850, when, during the Crimean War between Britain and Russia, the fearful colony's cry was "The Russians are coming!" Most believe the island's other name, Pinchgut, described the condition of recalcitrant convicts dumped there and forced to survive on meager rations. Ferries visit the fort every day but Monday at 10:00 A.M., 12:15, and 2:15 P.M., departing from Wharf 6 at Circular Quay. Tel: (02) 251-5007.

At the northeastern side of the Harbour Bridge on Kirribilli Point, **Admiralty House** (1845) was the residence of successive admirals of the fleet before becoming the Sydney home of the Canberra-based Governors General, the British monarch's representatives in Australia. Next door, the smaller, rather less grand, late-Victorian Kirribilli House is the prime minister's Sydney home.

The **Taronga Zoo**, on Bradley's Head Road in the neighboring suburb of Mosman, has good Australian wildlife exhibits set against the city skyline views across the harbor. Here you can see those unique Australian creatures such as kangaroos, wallabies, koalas, wombats, and platypuses. Open daily from 9:00 A.M. to 5:00 P.M.; Tel: (02) 969-2777.

Farther north along the eastern Harbour shoreline, an increased swell indicates that you are passing the Heads, or, more accurately, the gap between North and South Head that forms the entrance to Sydney Harbour. Beyond the Heads, the resort and suburb of Manly—with harbor and ocean beaches—surrounds Manly Cove.

A ferry ride to Manly (see Sydney Beaches, below) reveals Port Jackson at its best. On weekends the boat wends its way through several racing courses with yachts often flying faster than the ferry. The 18-foot racers are particularly renowned for their colorful spinnakers and their ruthlessly hard-sailing crews.

If you're keen on sailing you can register to crew on a weekend race with a yacht that's short of a regular crew member. **Cruising Yacht Club** at Rushcutters Bay publishes a list of visitors who are available to crew; Tel: (02) 363-9731. The club also offers reciprocal membership to any yacht club member visiting Sydney. The dining room, overlooking the extensive mooring marina, welcomes visitors, who should contact the manager. If you would like to rent a boat, **Balmoral Marine Hire Boats** at 2 The Esplanade, Balmoral, rents out sailing boats, small motorcruisers, and runabouts; Tel: (02) 969-6006. **Eastsail** at D'Albora Marina, New Beach Road, Rushcutters Bay, offers motor launches and yachts; Tel: (02) 327-1166, and **Pacific Sailing School**, New Beach Road, Rushcutters Bay, offers beginning, advanced, and racing courses; Tel: (02) 326-2399. Owners of yachts for hire may require you to convince them of your competence.

When Port Botany took over much of Sydney's commercial shipping, the piers of Walsh Bay on the southwestern side of Harbour Bridge were preserved. Pier One became a tourist complex that's rather a mishmash. Pier Four, known as The Wharf, was given two theaters, plus all necessary backup, for the Sydney Theatre Company, and studios and rehearsal space for the Sydney Dance Company. The **Wharf Restaurant** at the end of the pier has a handsome harbor backdrop.

West of Walsh Bay, at the entrance to Darling Harbour, is Goat Island (base for the harbor firefighting fleet), and the Balmain waterfront, a semi-commercial area with tugboat berths and small ship-repair yards.

The northern shore of the Harbour's western section is mainly residential, and includes Hunters Hill, one of

Sydney's oldest and most attractive suburbs. It is renowned for its more than 200 elegant mid-Victorian homes, built from local stone by the Bordeaux-born Joubert brothers in the 1840s.

CENTRAL SYDNEY

Those much-publicized icons of Sydney, the Harbour Bridge (known to locals as "the Hanger") at Dawes Point and the white-cowled Opera House (opposite Dawes Point on Bennelong Point), mark Sydney Cove's twin extremities. Between these points, reclaimed land on the cove's southern foreshore forms **Circular Quay** (originally and more correctly named Semicircular Quay and now usually just called the Quay). As Sydney's main ferry terminal, the Quay is a place busy with tourists, buskers, and hucksters rubbing shoulders along the waterfront, and with souvenir shops, foreign exchange kiosks, and terrace cafés.

The Rocks, just west of Circular Quay, is the oldest surviving section of Sydney, the site of the original European settlement in Australia's first city. This is an especially popular area with visitors, where the old convict-built structures have found new life as restaurants and shops.

After the light and space of the harbor, many of Sydney's city streets seem meanly narrow, an impression heightened by the upward growth of the Central Business District. Here, office buildings and international hotels soar, although thanks to loud and insistent preservationists the commercial appetite for knocking down the old to build the ephemeral has been blunted.

The **Central Business District** (CBD) extends south from Circular Quay to the Central Railway Station, and encompasses prime shopping areas as well as the Queen Victoria Building, a hybrid shopping center, arcade, and architectural marvel. Food outlets—fast and sit-down—proliferate in this area.

Past conservation victories enable Sydney to offer something more than the usual holiday diversions. The center and some of the suburbs preserve vestiges of convict and free-settler colonial architecture, the styles running the gamut from utilitarian prisoners' dwellings to the excesses of Victoriana.

Macquarie Street, haunt of doctors and politicians, and much visited by those interested in Sydney's most striking old buildings, runs north–south, connecting Bennelong

Point and the Opera House with the Royal Botanic Gardens and, to the south, that other beautiful piece of public green space, Hyde Park.

Phillip Street, one block west of Macquarie, quakes under the Rule of Law; many lawyers have their chambers here, and there is an important grouping of courts in a glassy building fronting Queens Square.

Southwest of the southern end of Macquarie, between Park and Druitt streets, the **Town Hall** shares a city block with **St. Andrew's Anglican Cathedral**, mellow neighbors since the middle of the last century. The Town Hall's foyer and great hall have been recently (mid-1992) restored, marking Sydney's 150 years as a city. Visitors are welcome to look in any time from 9:00 A.M. to 5:00 P.M. unless some official event is in progress.

South from here, George Street's next block contains Sydney's major concentration of movie houses, though there's a smaller collection of them on Pitt between Market and Park. (**George** and **Pitt** streets are two of the Central Business District's main north–south streets west of Macquarie Street.) West of George Street and Town Hall is **Darling Harbour**—a redeveloped seaport that is now home to a fleet of museums, shops, restaurants, and convention and entertainment facilities. **Chinatown**—a partly pedestrian precinct—is concentrated largely south of Town Hall between George, Goulburn, Hay, and Harbour streets.

Southeast of Chinatown, **Central Station** is the starting point for intercity, interstate, and cross-country trains and a junction point for the reasonably comprehensive suburban rail system. Near its Eddy Avenue entrance, opposite Belmore Park, intercity and interstate buses arrive and depart (see Getting Around, below).

The Rocks

The Rocks, site of Australia's first settlement, is bounded by Sydney Cove, Dawes Point, Millers Point, and Observatory Hill. Within this area stood Australia's first jail compound, gallows, flogging frame, hospital, church, police station, bank, commercial wharf, and bond store (warehouse). Local riffraff and visiting seafarers caroused in the pubs, grog shops, and brothels here.

A jaundiced but almost certainly accurate view of The Rocks in its heyday is recorded in the observations of a health official who lamented, "How can you expect righteousness when one householder placed right in this street is using as his backyard the roof of his neighbor's house placed low in the street behind; or does it make for riches when the roadway narrows suddenly to a cart's width, and this man is growing roses in what should be the centre of the street?"

About 30 years ago Sydney's city fathers launched a competition to rebuild The Rocks. When a short list of contending models went on display, viewers were appalled that each entailed razing the whole area for high-density commercial and residential complexes. Residents, academics, and the building laborers union formed a solid front against what they saw as proposed desecration of the historic integrity of The Rocks, but developers persisted with plans to selectively tear down buildings steeped in history. Irate citizens demonstrated; scuffles led to arrests. Preservation of The Rocks became a passionate issue in Sydney, finally resolved in favor of a reasonable maintenance of the status quo. Many features of this cradle of Australia's Common Man remain intact. Despite its tourist focus, promotional cuteness has only superficially affected the convict-built stone houses, bond stores, and shops. While few old-time residents still live in The Rocks proper, adjacent Millers Point remains predominantly residential.

The northern end of George Street, once known as Sergeant Major's Row, has some fine old frontages along its western side, as well as a mélange of duty-free emporiums, restaurants,cafés, souvenir shops, and boutiques facing the Museum of Contemporary Art (see Museums and Galleries, below.)

One notable building, at 127 George Street, is the former **police station** built in 1888 on the site—along with Nurses Walk and Surgeons Court—of Sydney's first hospital. The station's sandstone façade, surmounted by a lion's head clenching a baton (night stick?) between its bared fangs, emphasized the power of the law at a time when The Rocks was far from law-abiding. Today, as **Australian Craftworks**, it sells works of craftspeople from all over the country.

Next door, the **Julian Ashton Art School**, opened in 1890, still holds life classes. In the same building, on the first floor, the **Aboriginal and Tribal Arts Centre** has a gallery full of authentic native art (see Shops and Shopping, below). Farther north, the rather upscale **Rockpool Restaurant** is on the site of the Old Chicago Hotel, a lively bar of the last century. The Orient Hotel, on the corner of Argyle Street, dates from the 1840s; its adjacent terrace houses boutiques and gift shops.

Between George Street and Harrington Street, at the northernmost end of Nurses Walk, is a notorious alleyway known as the **Suez Canal**. Here, in colonial days, dozens of drunken soldiers were lured, then bludgeoned and robbed by waiting hoodlums. Pubs were legion in the area, and those that remain still evoke a bit of colonial atmosphere. Farther down George Street is **Cadman's Cottage**, stone-walled and roofed with split shingles. Just north of Argyle Street, the house stands below the George Street level near the passenger terminal on what was a waterfront site before land reclamation. Built in the 1830s for the governor's coxwain John Cadman, this is Sydney's oldest city dwelling. Today it is open to the public and occupied by the National Parks and Wildlife Service. Beside it, well-worn stone steps lead to the former Seamen's Home at 104 George Street, now the new **Rocks Visitors Center**, which offers information about the area, an audio-visual presentation, and a brochure to help you explore the area on your own; Tel: (02) 247-4972.

At the Old Sydney Parkroyal Hotel, George Street forks left toward Millers Point. Every Saturday and Sunday this stretch is closed off for a street market, canopied in case of rain. Hickson Road, which goes straight at the fork, runs behind the original stone warehouses of Campbell's Bond, established by the colony's first substantial trader, Robert Campbell, who built a wharf opposite the site in 1800. Today a string of eateries and souvenir establishments, the converted warehouses are dominated by **The Waterfront** restaurant, which serves good seafood in a casual, outdoor setting that simulates the deck of a windjammer, complete with masts and sails.

Various harbor cruises start from landscaped Campbell's Cove Wharf beside the low-rise Park Hyatt Hotel, which arguably holds the best position in Sydney (an advantage reflected in its prices).

Curving to the extremity of Dawes Point, the foreshore is dominated by the towering pylon and southern span of the Harbour Bridge. The grassy climb to Lower Fort Street passes an imposing terrace and the 1820 Campbell residence, **Bligh House**.

The **Hero of Waterloo** pub (1815), at the corner of Lower Fort and Windmill streets, is older than the well-restored **Lord Nelson**, around the corner at Millers Point, but the latter claims to have held a continuous liquor license longer—since 1841. Both the Lord Nelson, which brews its own excellent beer, and the Hero of Waterloo have reproductions of early Rocks photographs, and both are good places to relax and enjoy a cool drink.

Argyle Place, at the southern end of Lower Fort Street, faces a village green and boasts a row of well-preserved early colonial cottages. At the eastern end of Argyle Place, **Holy Trinity**, commonly known as the Garrison Church when completed in 1855, was the place of worship for the Dawes Point Artillery Battery.

Above the village green, **Observatory Hill** is dominated by a mid-19th-century stone building still used for astronomical observations. The structure also houses a small exhibition of early astronomical equipment with hands-on displays.

Head down Argyle Street through the Cut, an opening through the cliff leading into Argyle Place that was hand-hewn by convict laborers and later widened by machinery. The stone building on the left at 16–18 Argyle Street was the bond store (warehouse) of astute ex-convict businesswoman Mary Reiby, who ruled the commercial scene of her day. It's now the **Argyle Arts Centre**, a conglomeration of gift and souvenir shops. Its cobbled courtyard, with towering walls and gantries once used to hoist wool bales, rum, and other products, gives a most authentic idea of early Sydney.

Rocks Walking Tours has been leading groups through the area since 1978: There are tours at 10:30 A.M., 12:30 P.M., and 2:30 P.M., Monday to Friday, and at 11:30 A.M. and 2:00 P.M. on Saturdays, Sundays, and public holidays. They take about an hour and three quarters, and start from 39 Argyle Street. Further information is available from the Rocks Visitors Centre; Tel: (02) 247-4972.

Sydney Opera House

Sydney's Opera House is strikingly situated on Bennelong Point, east of Circular Quay and opposite The Rocks on Sydney Cove. Begun in 1959 by Danish architect Joern Utzon, who won Sydney's international competition for his highly original design, the project was expected to be completed in five years at a cost of A$7 million.

One hundred and two million dollars and 14 years later the building was opened by Queen Elizabeth II. What went wrong was essentially a clash between the project's engineers and its designer over whether or not the design was actually buildable. Utzon said it was; the engineers said it wasn't, and urged compromise. Utzon criticized the New South Wales government of the day and quit the project.

A committee of local architects took over and amid a string of contretemps presented the city with a compromise. Utzon's low, sweeping, sail-like roofs became high pointed cowls, and the interior was much altered from its original concept. When the Opera House finally opened in 1973, however, it immediately became a symbol of Sydney. Many suggest that "performance complex" is a less impressive but more accurate name for the building, although nobody ever calls it anything but the Opera House.

Another uproar centered on which of the two main theaters should be assigned to opera and which to concerts. The symphony got the larger hall, leaving the smaller one, with a proscenium and orchestra pit many consider inadequate, for opera and ballet. The drama theater, while uninspiring and rather smaller than some might wish, has modern stage machinery and good sight lines. There is also a playhouse for small-cast plays, lectures, and seminars.

The **Bennelong Restaurant**, overlooking the southern, stepped approach to the Opera House, is open for dinner Monday to Saturday. The food is good, if expensive, and the atmosphere quite formal. There is a prix fixe pre-theater menu at about half the cost of the regular menu. The **Harbour Restaurant** on the northern broadwalk specializes in Asian-influenced seafood and is open for lunch, dinner, and pre-theater meals Monday to Saturday, while the **Forecourt** brasserie is open seven days from 9:00 A.M. "until late" on the lower concourse arcade. In the foyer, **Café Mozart** is open for pre- and post-performance light meals.

Guided tours of the theaters and foyers run continuously from 9:00 A.M. to 4:00 P.M. every day except Christmas Day and Good Friday. When productions allow, backstage tours of the complex, including rehearsal areas, are conducted on Sundays between 9:00 A.M. and 4:00 P.M. For general information, Tel: (02) 250-7111; box office bookings, Tel: (02) 250-7777; restaurants, Tel: (02) 250-7577; guided tours, Tel: (02) 250-7250.

Macquarie Street

A bronze statue of Lachlan Macquarie, governor of the colony of New South Wales from 1810 to 1822, stands near the Bridge Street corner of the street named after him. He seems to be clutching his greatcoat about him against the chilly southerlies that blow in August along Macquarie Street, which runs north from Hyde Park in the city center past the Parliament House, the State Library, the Royal Botanic Gardens, the pompous ex-government building strikingly preserved as part of the Inter-Continental Hotel, up to Sydney Cove and Circular Quay in the north.

Others did as much as Macquarie to shape this handsome city precinct, but his stamp on it—expressed through the work of Francis Greenway, the Colony's convict architect (he had been convicted of forgery)—is indelible. It begins at the southeastern end of the street where Greenway's simple Georgian-style **Hyde Park Barracks** building looks across Queens Square to his elegantly detailed St. James' Church. Today a museum, Hyde Park Barracks has changing historical displays and a permanent exhibition detailing the lives of past occupants—convicts, soldiers, immigrants, and officers of the courts—through artifacts, archaeology, and a sound-and-light show. There's also the opportunity for a gentrified taste of convict life with ▶ **bed and breakfast** accommodations at the museum. Overnight visitors sleep dormitory-style in hammocks, and wake for a dawn breakfast of damper, meat, and tea; Tel: (02) 692-8366. For the less adventurous, the café here serves more palatable light meals from 10:00 A.M. to 4:00 P.M. weekdays, 11:00 A.M. to 4:00 P.M. weekends and holidays.

North of the barracks, on the same side of Macquarie Street, is the columned and verandahed **New South Wales Parliament House**. One of the most striking of Greenway's buildings to survive, it was built as a hospital during Macquarie's administration by a trio of entrepreneurs in return for a three-year monopoly on the importation and sale of rum. Known as "the Rum Hospital," it was originally twice its present length. Its northern end served first as the New South Wales Parliament's entire home, now as its Macquarie Street wing. Visitors may look around and visit both parliamentary chambers, except on sitting days, when the visitors gallery is open. On sitting days, tours are offered Tuesdays and Wednesdays at 1:30 P.M., Thursdays at 9:00 A.M. During non-sitting periods (end of May to the beginning of September, and the end of November to mid-February) tours are conducted Mondays through Fridays at 10:00 A.M., 11:00 A.M., and 2:00 P.M. There is no charge and no appointment is needed; open from 9:30 A.M. to 4:00 P.M.

The Rum Hospital's southern end became the government mint, now the **Mint Museum**, housing a decorative arts collection including the Vickery collection, an excellent compilation of New South Wales postage stamps and an array of the colony's early coins. Its northern end was given over to the **State Library of New South Wales**, which received a much-needed extension in 1988 that liberated many volumes from the archives. The new wing, entered from Macquarie Street, seems at first to be all openness and light, thanks to the lavish use of glass in its construction, but most of the building is underground: Visitors enter on what is actually the eighth floor. Putting most of it below street level has kept the building in scale with the rest of Macquarie Street's historic structures, and aids in preserving the books. The new wing's Glasshouse Café and the bookshop are both popular.

When Macquarie asked Greenway to design an appropriately impressive Government House, the architect drew plans for a castle with romantically battlemented stables. He only got to build the latter, and it stands today, inside the Royal Botanic Gardens at the east end of Bridge Street, as the **New South Wales Conservatorium of Music**. Free lunchtime concerts are given here every Wednesday and Friday during the school year; Tel: (02) 230-1222.

North of the conservatory and closer to the harbor is the **Government House** Sydney finally achieved in the late 1830s. A flourish of turrets, battlements, and a generally Gothic air suggest Greenway's influence. Unfortunately, it's closed to visitors and only partly visible from the Botanic Gardens through the fence and shrubbery.

The **Royal Botanic Gardens**, open 8:00 A.M. to 5:00 P.M. daily, spreads for 75 acres from the shore of Farm Cove (named for the settlement's first foray into agriculture) to meet the 85 acres of parkland known as The Domain, which runs behind Sydney Hospital and the State Library and contains the Art Gallery of New South Wales (see Museums and Galleries). Formally set up by Governor Macquarie in 1816, the Botanic Gardens are the third-oldest such gardens in the Southern Hemisphere, after those at Rio de Janeiro and on Mauritius. About 95 bird species have been seen in the gardens; the ponds are a haven for native waterbirds and other species, and at night clouds of fruit-eating bats arrive from the North Shore. Some 7,000 different species of plants are nurtured here; native species are identified by blue labels. Plants of the tropics are displayed in the Arc and Pyramid glasshouses (Australian varieties in the Pyramid). **The**

Gardens Restaurant, overlooking the central ponds, is a delightfully sited luncheon spot, and the Visitors Centre has information about guided and self-guided tours; Tel: (02) 231-8128.

Mrs. Macquarie's Road runs in a double loop along the eastern side of the Botanic Gardens to Mrs. Macquarie's Point, separating Farm Cove and Woolloomooloo Bay, where newlyweds, still in wedding finery, often come to be photographed against the harbor backdrop. Mrs. Macquarie liked to sit at the point and watch the harbor, and it's very easy to find the seat, known as **Mrs. Macquarie's Chair**, that her husband had cut for her in the natural stone.

History buffs might enjoy the Macquarie Street Walk offered on Tuesday and Friday mornings by historian Anne Sullivan. The groups are small, and the talk informal and entertaining. Bookings are essential; Tel: (02) 327-2954.

At its southernmost end Macquarie Street runs into **Hyde Park**, which runs the length of five city blocks from Queens Square to Liverpool Street and has been part of the fun of Sydney since the city was founded. Today it comprises 40 acres of grass, ordered gardens, huge trees whose branches meet over a central walk, and long-beaked ibis scavenging among the pigeons and seagulls for scraps left by office workers lunching on the grass.

Darling Harbour

The renovation feat that converted part of Darling Harbour, across the CBD to the west from Hyde Park and southwest of The Rocks, and once the hub of the now defunct coastal cargo trade, into a bustling quarter with a convention center, five large exhibition halls, seemingly endless shops and food outlets, and public rambling and entertainment areas, was achieved in time for Australia's bicentennial year, 1988.

While some commercial shipping activities continue at the harbor end, the whole of Cockle Bay—that area of the harbor inland from Pyrmont Bridge—has become a recreation area for Sydneysiders. **Pyrmont Bridge** was an engineering marvel when it opened in 1902; its 230-foot swinging span is now a pedestrian walkway connecting the shopping and museum side (west) of Darling Harbour to the **Sydney Aquarium** (see Museums and Galleries) on the eastern (CBD) side. A classical **Chinese**

Garden, south of the aquarium and handy to Chinatown, was a bicentennial gift from China's Kwangtung province and is open daily from 9:30 A.M. to sunset.

Two maritime museums accent the salty tone. The **National Maritime Museum**'s soaring steel and glass space houses a collection of permanent exhibits detailing local shipping history from Captain Cook to the America's Cup (see Museums and Galleries). In the shadow of Pyrmont Bridge is the independent **Sydney Maritime Museum**, maintained by dedicated enthusiasts. Its fleet of old harbor vessels clustered around the 19th-century square rigger *James Craig* is in the throes of a restoration expected to last several years.

A monorail operates from various points in the central city to the heart of Darling Harbour (see Getting Around, below), or the energetic may walk, turning off George Street at Market Street, to Pyrmont Bridge. You might also walk from Liverpool Street, or from Chinatown via Harbour Street.

Chinatown

Chinese first came to Australia as contract laborers and servants to free settlers. When gold was struck they poured in by the thousands, many staying on after the lodes petered out. Sydney originally had small Chinatowns in The Rocks and near the Queen Victoria Building, then the central market. When produce trading moved to the Haymarket area, at the foot of George Street, the Chinese community moved with it.

Chinatown, southeast of Darling Harbour on the southern edge of the Central Business District, is bordered by Goulburn, Harbour, and Hay streets, and grew as a neighborhood where market workers and their families lived and played. Restaurants gradually opened to serve the Chinese community. It took Sydneysiders of the day— brought up on stolid British food—a long time to yield to the exotic cooking fragrances pervading Haymarket, but when they fell, it was (and still is) a love affair for life, keeping innumerable Chinese restaurants prosperous.

A few years ago Sydney's Chinese community—now mainly living in the suburbs—set about giving Chinatown a facelift. The main artery, **Dixon Street**, became fully pedestrian, complete with street lanterns and archways lauding Australian-Chinese friendship at either end.

Restaurant owners who had previously considered stark metal chairs and plastic-topped tables perfectly adequate blossomed forth with ceiling panels from Taiwan and dragons galore (a few diehard restaurateurs cling tenaciously to their plastic tables). Fortunately the changes are only superficial, and Sydney's Chinatown retains its reputation for some of the finest Chinese cuisine south of Hong Kong. While many restaurants here are Cantonese, migrants from Shandong, Szechwan, Shanghai, and Peking have brought their culinary marvels with them as well. Sydney's Chinatown is noisy but safe. To get there, walk or take a bus southward down George Street, alight at Hay Street, and turn right.

SYDNEY'S NEIGHBORHOODS

Like all great cities of the world, Sydney is a coalition of neighborhoods, each with its own personality. *Paddington/Woollahra* has appealing terrace houses, galleries, restaurants, and antiques shops. Raffish *Kings Cross* was a GI mecca during the Vietnam War; its sleazy red-light image contrasts sharply with demure *Elizabeth Bay* to the northeast on the harbor. Other neighborhoods include *Double Bay,* farther east of Elizabeth Bay along the harbor, known for its fashionable, expensive shopping area; the high-rise and elite *Darling Point;* and the marina enclave of *Rushcutters Bay* between Elizabeth Bay and Darling Point. The "best" address in town, ritzy *Vaucluse,* is farther east on the harbor's south side, near South Head. *Watsons Bay,* just past Vaucluse, leads to the harbor's spectacular South Head, and *Balmain,* on a peninsula just west of Pyrmont, is a renovated and gentrified formerly working-class suburb.

Paddington

Southeast of the city center, Paddington is Sydney's most vibrant neighborhood. A cross between New York's Greenwich Village and London's Earl's Court, Paddington teems day and night. Oxford Street and the neighborhood's side streets are lined with bookstores, pubs, art galleries, and the city's most unusual and interesting shops and boutiques. Paddington also has a large gay community.

From Hyde Park head east on Oxford Street as it climbs gradually to Taylor Square in **Darlinghurst**, and on to Paddington. **Taylor Square** is the center of Sydney's gay activity, colorfully demonstrated each year at the larger-than-life **Gay and Lesbian Mardi Gras** parade held along Oxford and Flinders streets to Anzac Parade. About half a million participants and onlookers attend the parade, which culminates in a dance party at the Royal Agricultural Society Showground in Moore Park. The parade is part of the Gay and Lesbian Mardi Gras festival, which runs annually throughout February and includes a full program of art exhibitions, a film festival, sports events, and plays at the Belvoir Street Theatre. For information contact the Sydney Gay and Lesbian Mardi Gras, P.O. Box 1064, Darlinghurst, 2010 N.S.W.; Tel: (02) 332-4088.

The main focus of Taylor Square—really just a junction of streets—is the austere sandstone Darlinghurst Court House (1888), which fronts old Darlinghurst Gaol (1822), now an arts and crafts technical college.

Oxford Street continues past Victoria Barracks, built for the British colonial garrison but still occupied by the Australian army's field and supporting unit command. Every Wednesday at 10:30 A.M. visitors may inspect the fine old Georgian sandstone buildings, where the cells of the convicts who built the barracks in 1848 are now used to display army memorabilia. Changing of the guard takes place at 12:30 P.M. (No tours from mid-December through January.) For information, Tel: (02) 339-3543.

At the top of the hill, next to the barracks grounds, Paddington's Italianate Town Hall can be seen as the formal entrance to a suburb of terrace houses, much restored as high-priced, rather trendy homes. Originally inhabited by solid burghers, the neighborhood declined and by the 1950s had long been working class and downright unfashionable. Some enterprising real-estate operators noted the fine cast-iron balconies and attractive façades and, perhaps with New Orleans in mind, began buying them up, inducing the resident toilers to move. Now almost every street in hilly Paddington has restored sandstone or elaborately painted houses beyond the financial reach of most new home buyers, and it has become synonymous with trendy bars, restaurants, galleries, and boutiques.

Opposite the Town Hall, now the Australian Film Institute's cinema, is **Juniper Hall**, a well-restored 1820 mansion built for gin distiller Robert Cooper, who not only supplied the colony with booze but is said to have sired 28 children. It's now a National Trust building and is open to the public from 10:00 A.M. to 4:00 P.M. every day but Monday. Beside it, Heely Street runs downhill to Fiveways, where that number of streets converge. The **Royal**

Hotel here is a corner pub of character with a pleasantly restored bar. Meals are served on the ironwork balcony.

Another popular local pub is the **London Tavern**, built in 1875 on William Street. Its Boar's Head Bar is a British-style snuggery and its trattoria serves medium-priced Italian dishes.

Oxford Street, which runs from the Central Business District to Paddington, has been touted as Sydney's equivalent of London's Kings Road, Chelsea. The comparison is not totally appropriate, but some of the shops have style, and, every Saturday morning for the last 17 years a market has been held in the grounds of the Uniting Church (see Shopping, below).

To the east, the Paddington sector of Oxford Street merges into Woollahra near Centennial Park. **Woollahra** is small and a bit more staid, with high-priced homes. Its main artery, Queen Street, is notable for boutiques and antiques shops.

Centennial Park, 530 acres bounded by Paddington/Woollahra, Bondi Junction, and Randwick, has a lot of birds, though at times there seem to be more bicycles here than anything else. Both cycling and horseback riding are popular, and there are tracks for both. Bicycles can be rented at three or four shops (all with the same rates) on nearby Clovelly Road, on the Randwick side. The cost is A$6 for an hour, A$10 for two hours, A$14 for three, including obligatory safety helmet (no deposit).

As for horses, two or three stables in the nearby showground charge about A$15 an hour for an escorted ride in the park. Centennial Park Horse Hire is one stable you might try; Tel: (02) 361-4513. Booking ahead is a good idea, and is essential on weekends. The **Centennial Park Café** is a good spot for brunch, lunch, or tea; Tel: (02) 360-3355.

Kings Cross

Kings Cross, centered around the junction of William and Victoria streets and Darlinghurst Road directly east of downtown and north of Paddington/Darlinghurst, is dominated by the Hyatt hotel's huge Coca-Cola sign. From World War II to Vietnam, GIs on R&R relished the unabashed rowdiness of "The Cross," with its open-air cafés next to strip joints, and prostitutes and transvestites announcing their availability. Despite this, The Cross has its more sober side, evidenced by a very good bookshop,

Clays at 103 Macleay Street, and the many people who have lived in the neighborhood for years. Visit the area for brunch on a Sunday morning and you will find a quaint, village atmosphere that is hard to reconcile with its sad, sleazy persona of the night. In recent years The Cross has developed into Sydney's backpacker capital, with cheap hostels and numerous cars sporting "for sale" signs.

Eastern Harborside Suburbs

From Kings Cross turn east onto Elizabeth Bay Road and the atmosphere changes; leafy streets and demure apartment blocks lead to a small harborside park in the heart of **Elizabeth Bay**. Built in 1839 for Colonial Secretary Alexander Macleay, **Elizabeth Bay House**, 7 Onslow Avenue, is notable for its distinguished façade, noble hallway, and spiral stairway. It has been beautifully restored and is open for inspection 10:00 A.M. to 4:30 P.M. Tuesdays through Sundays.

Continue downhill along Roslyn Gardens and Waratah Street to **Rushcutters Bay**, where a stretch of grass and old trees follows the bay's curve to the Cruising Yacht Club. Around Christmas, the ocean-going yachts that are to compete in the annual Sydney-to-Hobart race congregate here, preparing for their much-publicized departure on Boxing Day (December 26). A waterside walk along Beach Road and a short uphill climb leads to high-rise Darling Point, a basically unremarkable maze of streets.

Winding Greenoaks Avenue descends eastward from Darling Point to **Double Bay**, a fashionable suburb of boutiques, cafés and at least two remarkably good Chinese restaurants (see Dining, below). Knox, Bay, and Cross streets, plus New South Head Road between Bay and William streets, offer good window shopping, though there is little for the bargain hunter here.

The hills along New South Head Road between Double Bay and Watsons Bay make further walking out of the question—although runners in the thousands manage it in the annual 14-kilometer City to Surf race held on the second Sunday in August (see Sporting Life, below). The bus along New South Head Road (number 324 or 325 from Circular Quay; see Getting Around for details) goes through Rose Bay (pleasant harborside, but little more), and north to **Vaucluse**, possibly Sydney's "best address." Bus number 325 from Circular Quay stops near **Vaucluse**

House, one of the colony's first mansions, built by editor, lawyer, and explorer William Charles Wentworth. It is worth visiting for its period furniture and intriguing antiques; open 10:00 A.M. to 4:30 P.M. Tuesdays through Sundays. Its tearooms are highly recommended for their good food.

Dramatic **South Head** makes the effort of clambering up a rocky path worthwhile—the sea breaks over the rocky shoal beneath, and North Head towers on the other side of the harbor entrance. On weekends, particularly, boats of all kinds swarm between the Heads, creating a hazard for the occasional freighter carefully feeling its way among the chaotic small-boat traffic.

Balmain

Balmain is a gentrified suburb, west across the harbor from Sydney's Millers Point. It merits a morning stroll for its village atmosphere, terrace houses, and pleasant eating houses and pubs. It's also enjoyable getting there, with the choice of two ferry routes, the Hunters Hill or the Balmain service, both from Circular Quay, Wharf 5. The former is recommended for those who find hills punishing, as the Balmain service drops passengers at the rather steep eastern end of Darling Street, the suburb's main street. The Hunters Hill ferry turns left at the Bridge, passes—and sometimes stops at—Goat Island, skirts Snails Bay (there are some interesting old harborside houses here), to halt at Longnose Point. Louisa Road is the only street along this narrow peninsula, and it leads to Birchgrove Park. A stroll along Wharf Road, on the eastern side of the park, introduces more Victorian houses of character above a waterfront active with tugboat and barge services.

As you wander back toward Darling Street you'll see that the original village character of Balmain is reflected in the small maritime workers' homes that have been converted at considerable expense to middle-class dwellings.

Darling Street at Rowntree, with its cafés and agreeable small restaurants and pubs, is the heart of the suburb. The Saturday morning market on the grounds of Saint Andrew's Congregational Church on Darling Street at Curtis Road is a good place to find quality hand-crafted souvenirs. The walk downhill to the Balmain ferry is worthwhile, and, before you board, a stroll around the little park nearby affords some great views of Sydney's Central Business District.

MUSEUMS AND GALLERIES

The **Australian Museum**, at the corner of College and William streets on the east side of Hyde Park, was Australia's first museum, beginning in a small way in 1827. The present entrance building (1868) on College Street facing Hyde Park has an excellent museum shop selling Australiana and natural history books.

After many years of existing in a kind of 19th-century twilight, when it seemed to contain little more than a stultifying collection of stuffed birds on twigs, the museum has finally found the modern world. The well-presented natural history collection, displayed in a series of "permanent" exhibitions (which do change, but slowly) and short-term shows, reflects the physical terrain of the continent, aboriginal links with the land, the geographical region around Australia, and human evolutionary theory. There is a strong environmental theme. One of the most absorbing displays presents the life, arts, and customs of the Abelam people of Papua New Guinea, including a reproduction of an Abelam spirit house. Abelam elders were flown down to check out the accuracy of the details. Open daily from 9:30 A.M. to 9:00 P.M.

The **Sydney Aquarium**, on the eastern side of Pyrmont Bridge at Darling Harbour, has underwater acrylic tunnels that allow the visitor to get as close as possible to the bottom of the ocean without getting wet. Through them, you can follow a stream to the sea, inspect tidal pools and coral gardens, walk under the harbor, and see sharks, rays, and other local fish. Open daily from 10:00 A.M. to 5:00 P.M.

The **Powerhouse Museum**, at 500 Harris Street in Ultimo, on the western fringe of the Darling Harbour entertainment zone, is a recycling of two remarkable local treasures: the six-acre site of the long-defunct Powerhouse and the voluminous collections held by the cramped Museum of Technology, which previously had mostly been shut away in warehouses all over Sydney. The imaginative reincarnation of the Powerhouse site brought much of this material out into the light, including some of the oldest working steam engines in the world. It's a place illustrating social history, science, technology, and the decorative arts, and there's an accent on visitor participation. Open daily from 10:00 A.M. to 5:00 P.M.

The **National Maritime Museum**, in Darling Harbour, opened in 1991 in a soaring glass-and-steel structure next to Pyrmont Bridge. Six major exhibitions here detail aspects of Australian maritime history: the discovery and charting of Australia; whalers, sealers, and pearlers; passenger shipping from the convict transports, through passenger liners, to present-day boat people; the Australian navy; sport sailing, including the America's Cup and Sydney's 18-footers; and a gallery, funded by a bicentennial gift from the United States, commemorating maritime links across the Pacific. Open daily 10:00 A.M. to 5:00 P.M.

The floating collection, moored at two finger-wharves, includes a Broome pearling lugger; the *Kathleen Gillett*, a competitor in the first Sydney-Hobart yacht race; the World War II commando raider *Krait*; and a Vietnamese fishing boat, the *Tu do*.

The **Museum of Contemporary Art**, on Circular Quay West in The Rocks, opened late in 1991 and houses a collection of "art of the moment" that has been growing— mostly out of public view—since 1943, when a bequest to the University of Sydney began funding the purchase of the collection. Now containing 4,500 items, including works by Warhol, Hockney, Christo, Lichtenstein, Beuys, and Duchamp, the collection will continue to grow and be seen by a broader public in its new home, formerly the Maritime Services Board Building. This late Art Deco (1950s) building has been converted for the purpose, and will also feature temporary exhibitions; open daily 11:00 A.M. to 6:00 P.M. The museum's restaurant, whose entrance is on the harbor side of the building (the main entrance is on George Street), is catered by The Rockpool (see Dining, below), one of Sydney's best restaurants, and is very popular. You may encounter a line waiting to get in.

Nearby, at 18 Hickson Road, The Rocks, is the **Earth Exchange**, where you can walk through a volcano and an underground mine, and even survive an earthquake all in the cause of learning about Australia's geological and mining history. The Earth Exchange is open from 10:00 A.M. to 5:00 P.M. daily and the café on the top level has extraordinary harbor views.

The **Art Gallery of New South Wales**, on Art Gallery Road beside The Domain, is home to the largest and most comprehensive collection of Australian art, ranging from the early colonial period to mid-20th century. Its European section has old masters from the 15th to the end of the 18th century, French Impressionists, and 20th-century British and European works to around 1960. The Asian art collection includes prehistoric to modern works from China, Korea, Japan, India, and Southeast Asia. The gallery shop claims to have the largest selection of art books in Australia. The gallery restaurant, which has an outdoor section, serves light meals. Open daily 10:00 A.M. to 5:00 P.M.

The **S. H. Ervin Gallery**, at the National Trust Center on Observatory Hill (approach the center from The Rocks) is run by the National Trust, whose headquarters are here in a mid-19th-century building, the colony's first military hospital. The Ervin Gallery, located in a later addition, concentrates on changing exhibitions relating to Australian art and culture. Open 11:00 A.M. to 5:00 P.M. Tuesdays through Fridays; 2:00 to 5:00 P.M. on weekends.

Sydney's best-known commercial galleries include **Holdsworth Galleries**, 86 Holdsworth Street, Woollahra; **Macquarie Galleries**, 83 McLachlan Avenue, Rushcutters Bay; **Watters Gallery** (decidedly contemporary), 109 Riley Street, East Sydney; **Blaxland Galleries**, in Grace Brothers department store, 436 George Street, Sydney; **Robin Gibson Galleries**, 278 Liverpool Street, Darlinghurst; and **Coventry Gallery**, 56 Sutherland Street, Paddington. Aboriginal and Pacific art specialists include **Galleries Primitif**, 174 Jersey Road, Woollahra, and **Hogarth Gallery**, 7 Walker Lane, Paddington, which is associated with the **Aboriginal Tribal Art Centre**, 117–119 George Street. There's also an aboriginal art shop on the upper concourse level of the Opera House.

SPORTING LIFE

Spectator and participatory sports are close to the core of Sydney life. In winter, March to September, aficionados are most passionate about bone-jarring Rugby League football, and for the rest of the year it's cricket. The most important venues for both—the **Sydney Football Stadium** and the **Sydney Cricket Ground**—are side by side at Moore Park, southeast of the central city. Club matches in both sports are also played on fields throughout the suburbs. For information about Rugby League games, Tel: (02) 232-7566; for what's happening in cricket, Tel: (02) 360-6601.

Gambling on **horse racing** is popular, with flat racing at four main tracks. The closest to the central city is Randwick, near one of the city's most popular green areas, Centennial Park. Harness races are staged most Tuesdays and Fridays at Harold Park Paceway in Glebe, a western suburb. For racing information, Tel: (02) 660-3688.

Ferries follow the weekend **harbor-sailing races** of the quintessentially Sydney 18-footers, which evolved early this century as workingmen's racing yachts in reaction to the stately racers of the upper-crust Yacht Squadron. For information about the races, which are held on Saturdays in the warmer months, contact Rosman Ferries; Tel: (02) 955-3458.

Long-distance runners who plan ahead may wish to know that the 14-km **City to Surf** race from Sydney Town Hall to Bondi Beach is run the second Sunday in August; it's organized by the *Sun-Herald* newspaper; Tel: (02) 282-2833.

Sydney Beaches

Sydney's much-publicized beach scene is as good as it looks in the promos—with certain cautions mentioned toward the end of this section. The main ocean beaches, north and south from the Heads, are fundamentally for surfing, but some also have tidal pools for swimming.

OCEAN BEACHES

The most famous of Sydney's beaches is **Bondi**, located southeast of the city. Although large, it is nevertheless crowded on summer weekends and the southern end is reserved for surfers. Happily, it has extensive parking. The **Gelato Bar**, a long-established beachfront café on Campbell Parade near the Hall Street corner, is frequented by pastry connoisseurs from Bondi's large Jewish community. **Tamarama**, to the south of Bondi, is a small and trendy beach good for people-watching, but **Maroubra**, about 5 kilometers to the south, is where you'll find the serious surfers.

Northern beaches start with **Manly**, which has two beaches—one, harborside, for swimming, and an ocean beach for surfing. Manly has been a seaside resort for more than a century, trading on the slogan "Seven miles from Sydney, 1,000 miles from care." The sentiment still applies today; urban preoccupations seem to dissolve the moment you board the ferry at Circular Quay for the half-hour journey to Manly wharf on Sydney Harbour's northern extremity. Near the wharf people swim in the calm harbor water, though most prefer to walk the pedestrian plaza called **The Corso** to the Pacific surf beach fringed by towering Norfolk Island pines. Manly hosts a jazz festival at the beginning of each October, but its year-round attractions remain the surf and sand (and fish and

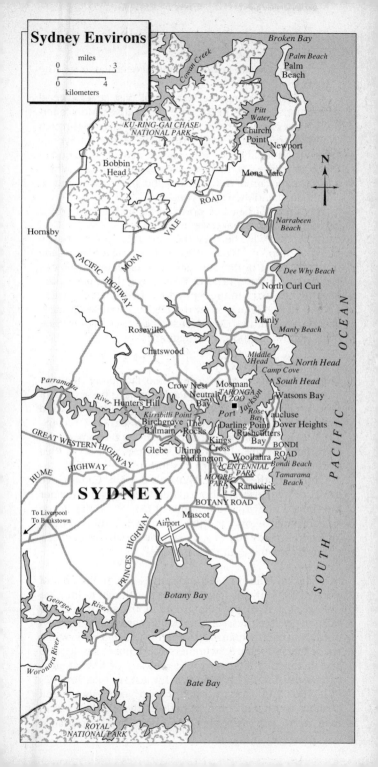

chips from **Ocean Seafoods** at the ocean end of The Corso).

A stroll east along the waterfront past several good sidewalk cafés leads to Fairy Bower (a cove). More energetic types can walk up North Head Scenic Drive through a military reserve to the North Head section of Sydney Harbour National Park. (You can also drive.) At the end of the road there's a pathway to the cliff's edge, which affords panoramic views across the harbor's mouth to South Head and the city beyond.

The string of beaches north of Manly are part of the surfing lexicon. If the waves aren't up at Queenscliff, Curl Curl, or Dee Why, perhaps they are at Long Reef, Narrabeen, Avalon, or Whale Beach. **Palm Beach** is at the northern point of the peninsula that ends in Barrenjoey Head, the southern head of Broken Bay. It's a good, safe beach, with extra interest provided by the fancy beachhouses here. Getting from the city to Palm Beach takes about one hour and 20 minutes by bus; see Sydney Side Trips, below, for more information.

HARBOR BEACHES

Balmoral, on the harbor's north side, facing the Heads, is a family beach. **The Bathers Pavillion** here has excellent food and fabulous views across Sydney Harbour, and through The Heads and on to the open sea; Tel: (02) 968-1133. The takeout fish and chips from **Bottom of the Harbour** here are always good. You can rent boats (see Sydney Harbour) and learn to windsurf here as well.

On the southern shore, **Watson's Bay** and **Camp Cove** north of Vaucluse are both family beaches, the former being well known as the home of Doyles on the Beach (see Dining, below) and the latter having some topless sunbathing. **Lady Bay** beach—a nude beach—is between Camp Grove and South Head itself.

Now the cautions. On surfing beaches stay in the area of water defined by the flags. They're positioned to indicate the safest part in prevailing conditions, and this is the portion under closest scrutiny by lifeguards (called lifesavers in Australia). Venturing too far out is dangerous. While shark attacks are rare, swimmers swept out to sea are not. The degree of pollution from stormwater or sewer outfall can be checked by phoning Beachwatch Hotline, Tel: (02) 901-7996. The tape-recorded report, covering coastal beaches north and south, is updated twice daily in summer, once daily in winter, and also warns of nuisance seaweed or stinging jellyfish, and lists beach closures caused by bad weather or dangerous currents.

GETTING AROUND

Sydney's Kingsford Smith International Airport is 8 km (5 miles) from the center of the city. Cabs meet inbound flights, and the fare to the city is about A$15. Airport Express buses operate from the international and domestic terminals to Circular Quay; the fare is A$5.

Visitors staying awhile in Sydney save with The SydneyPass, which is available for three-, five-, or seven-day periods and offers unlimited use of all buses and ferries, including harbor cruises, the Airport Express, and Sydney Explorer (but not suburban trains). It's sold at the Travellers' Information Service at the international terminal (which can also book accommodations), the Ansett Australia domestic terminal, Countrylink rail-travel centers, the Central Railway Coach Terminal, the Circular Quay ferry wharf, the Kings Cross Tourist Information Office, and the New South Wales Travel Centre. Three days, A$45; five days, A$65; seven days, A$75. For children under 16, all fares are A$10 less.

The Sydney Explorer bus operates seven days a week from 9:30 A.M. to 9:00 P.M., circulating at 20-minute intervals to 27 tourist attractions where passengers may leave or join. Without SydneyPass the bus costs A$20 for adults, A$15 for children; the fare is good for a full day's use.

You can also purchase a TravelPass weekly ticket that allows unlimited use of buses, trains, and ferries at significant savings from the regular prices; available from news agents, City Rail stations, and ticket machines at Circular Quay. FerryTen and MetroTen bus tickets allow ten rides for about half the standard price; buy them at State Transit bus depots, Circular Quay ticket offices, and Manly Wharf.

Public Transportation

The city has a reasonably good public transport system with bus services extending to the suburban limit and urban trains following a less extensive network. A monorail runs between the Entertainment Centre near Chinatown to Liverpool and Pitt streets to Darling Harbour; the fare is A$2. Long-distance coach (bus) services to New South Wales rural areas and to other states start from Eddy Avenue, at the lower colonnade below Central Station. The Travellers' Information Service, at the western end of the colonnade, sells tickets; Tel: (02) 281-9366. To reach Sydney's eastern neighborhoods by bus use the following routes: From Alfred and Pitts streets, Circular Quay, bus 311 goes to Elizabeth Bay and Kings Cross. Buses 324 and 325 pass through Kings Cross, Double Bay, and Rose Bay, but 325 deviates after Rose Bay to Neilsen Park and Vaucluse House; both terminate at Watsons Bay. For Darling Point, take bus 327 from the Quay. All these buses can be joined in the city on Pitt Street between the Quay and Hunter Street, Castlereagh Street between Hunter and Park, and along William Street leading to The Cross.

To the Beaches

Use the following bus routes for getting to the beach: For the **northern** beaches, bus 190 toward Palm Beach, from Wynyard Park (between York and Carrington streets at the northern end of the Central Business District), stops at all important northside beaches except Manly and Whale Beach. For Whale Beach change at Avalon to the 193. The 169 bus to Manly also starts at Wynyard Park, but a ferry is much more enjoyable. Manly ferries start from Wharf 3, Circular Quay, and take 30 minutes. Speedy Jetcats take 15 minutes from Wharf 2.

For **southern beaches**, bus 380 for Bondi starts from Alfred and Pitt streets, Circular Quay, and picks up passengers at stops along Elizabeth to Oxford Street, and along Oxford Street all the way to Bondi Junction. For Tamarama, take bus 380 to the Bondi Junction interchange, then transfer to bus 391.

To reach the **harbor beaches**, proceed as follows: For Balmoral, from Wynyard Park take bus 247 to Neutral Bay Junction interchange, then transfer to bus 257 to Balmoral. For Watsons Bay, Camp Cove, and Lady Bay, take bus 324 from Alfred and Pitt streets, Circular Quay, or board at any of the city pick-up points along Castlereagh to Park, then William Street to Kings Cross.

By Taxi or Car

Taxis are metered and plentiful, and maintain generally good standards. Roof lights indicate that they are available. Current rates start at A$1.70 and increase by A$1.05 per kilometer, but fare hikes are frequent.

Major rental car companies have desks at the airport and city offices (Avis, 02-902-9292; Budget, 02-339-8888; Thrifty, 02-380-5399). There are a number of rental car offices on William Street, just east of the CBD. Sydney driving manners are improving as police crack down on offenders. Traffic is on the left-hand side of the road, and at crossings—even where there's a stoplight—it's safer to look right and left before proceeding. Neglecting to fasten seat belts can bring a heavy fine. Furthermore, police alcohol patrols may stop drivers anywhere for breath-testing, and the penalty is severe for driving with a blood alcohol level above 0.5 percent.

Sydney's main routes eastward are William and Oxford streets. Both are uphill, but buses run along each and Cityrail operates to Kings Cross and Edgecliff Centre (for Double Bay), with the terminal at Bondi Junction. Trains operate on the City Circle every few minutes, from early morning until evening. Stops on the circuit are Saint James, Museum, Central Railway, Town Hall, and Wynard, making it a convenient and fast way of geting around the Central Business District.

The Sydney Harbour Tunnel, opened in late 1991, links the Warringah Freeway north of the harbor, with the Cahill Expressway on the south side, making it possible to bypass the central city on the east and easing peak-hour congestion on the Harbour Bridge. Both harbor crossings carry the same toll—A$2 at time of publication.

Ferries and Cruises

Sydney's State Transit controls all public transport in Sydney including ferry services. These operate from wharves 2, 3, 4, and 5 on Circular Quay. Manly is served both by a Jetcat, which makes the 7-mile trip in 15 minutes, and by a conventional ferry, which takes 30 minutes. Other services using conventional ferries operate with intermediate stops to the lower northside destinations of the Taronga Zoo at Bradleys Head Road, Mosman (a Zoo Pass ticket includes ferry to the wharf, bus to the zoo, and entry, all for about A$17), to Mosman itself, and to Neutral Bay.

A ferry operates to Watsons Bay on weekends and holidays, and inner-harbor services run to Balmain, Darling Harbour, and Hunters Hill. The Rivercat services Meadowbank, west of the Harbour Bridge, with a 33-minute crossing on weekdays and a slower (50 minute) ferry on weekends.

Sydney Ferries also operates daily cruises departing at 10:00 A.M., 1:00 P.M., and 8:00 P.M. The morning cruise goes west of the Harbour Bridge, the afternoon cruise concentrates on the eastern harbor and goes through The Spit to Middle Harbour, while the evening cruise features the night lights of Darling Harbour, the Central Business District, and Elizabeth Bay. The SydneyPass is valid on all regular services. For departure times, fares, and general information, Tel: (02) 13-1315.

Captain Cook Cruises and **Matilda Cruises** operate morning, afternoon, and lunch cruises. Captain Cook also offers sundown and dinner cruises, inspection tours of Fort Denison, and a Sydney Harbour Explorer plan that permits passengers to alight at a variety of stops around the foreshore and proceed on the next boat. Matilda Cruises uses the topsail schooner *Solway Lass* for lunch cruises and afternoon sailing. Captain Cook operates from Wharf 6, the Quay; Tel: (02) 251-5007. Matilda operates from the Quay and from the Aquarium Wharf, Darling Harbour; Tel: (02) 264-7377.

Sail on the Edge offers day (with barbecue lunch) and half-day (with afternoon tea) cruises of the harbor under sail. Trips depart from Campbells Cove in The Rocks; Tel: (02) 368-1244.

Bounty Cruises operates the sailing replica of H.M.S. *Bounty* (built for the De Laurentiis film version of *Mutiny on the Bounty*) for a coffee cruise, 1:00–3:00 P.M. on weekdays, for Sunday brunch, 9:30–11:30 A.M., and for a dinner cruise, 7:00–9:30 P.M. Saturdays. Departure is from Campbells Cove in The Rocks; Tel: (02) 247-1789.

The paddlewheeler **Sydney Showboat** operates morning, afternoon, lunch, and dinner cruises from Campbells Cove, The Rocks. Live jazz with lunch, cabaret with dinner; Tel: (02) 552-2722.

Walking Tours

Sydney is relatively flat and easy to walk, and comparatively safe if you stick to the populated areas and main streets. But if you'd prefer to walk with others **Kings Cross Walkabout Tours** (Tel: 02-356-3413) takes groups through that area, **Australian Pacific Tours** (Tel: 02-252-2988) covers the Opera House and Darling Harbour, and **Anne Sullivan** (Tel: 02-327-2954) conducts tours of Macquarie Street, the Circular Quay, and The Rocks.

Further Information

State Transit, the bus and ferry authority, has a map detailing routes of trains, buses, and ferries for the city center and environs, plus Airport Express and Sydney Explorer routes, available at its information office opposite Wharf No. 4 at Circular Quay. State Transit also has an information and sales desk at the international air terminal, on the arrival level. Water taxis operate on call anywhere on

Sydney Harbour with rates calculated from Circular Quay; Tel: (02) 955-3222.

For further bus and ferry information, Tel: (02) 13-1315. For train information, Tel: (02) 13-1500.

ACCOMMODATIONS

Sydney currently has an oversupply of accommodations, a situation that is expected to last until 1995. This has led to tariff fluidity, with few hotels charging published rates. Special deals abound, particularly if you make reservations through the New South Wales Travel Centre, at 19 Castlereagh Street, Sydney; Tel: (02) 231-4444. Many hotels have lower weekend rates; ask about them when booking.

Accommodations are listed in three categories: *expensive,* from A$250 per night for double room, double occupancy; *moderate,* from A$150; and *budget,* from A$80.

Many "boutique" hotels have varying degrees of character, and some have shared bathrooms. Only a few acceptable budget hotels are listed here. Unless otherwise stated, all accommodations mentioned have rooms with bath or shower, TV, phone, carpets, lounge chairs or a settee, and a desk or table. Minibars are not common, but most places have tea- and coffee-making equipment with teabags and coffee packets provided. If you're staying a week or more, renting an apartment with cooking facilities can save money. Accommodations are listed in main Sydney regions.

The telephone area code for all of Sydney is 02. When calling from outside Australia, omit the zero in the area code.

CIRCULAR QUAY AND THE ROCKS

Expensive

The ► **Regent of Sydney**, overlooking Sydney Cove, is modern and handsome. Most rooms have exquisite views of the Opera House and the flotilla on the harbor; telescopes are even provided in some rooms for harbor-watchers. The health club here has state-of-the art equipment, and the pool is one of the city's largest. The hotel's **Kables Restaurant** is highly rated for its imaginative use of Australian produce (see Dining).

199 George Street, Sydney 2000. Tel: 238-0000; Fax:

251-2851; in U.S. and Canada, Tel: (800) 545-4000. A$270–
A$375.

The ► **Park Hyatt**, in Dawes Point opposite the Opera
House, is a low-rise hotel nestled between the Harbour
Bridge and Circular Quay. Most of the 159 rooms have
harbor views, and every floor is serviced by both con-
cierge and butler. The ground level opens onto a boardwalk that overhangs the harbor, and there is a health spa
and rooftop juice bar as well.

7 Hickson Road, Sydney 2000. Tel: 241-1234; Fax: 256-
1555; in U.S. and Canada, Tel: (800) 233-1234. A$415–
A$600.

The ► **Observatory Hotel** is modeled on the historic
Sydney property Elizabeth Bay House (see Eastern Harborside Suburbs) and the mood is grand colonial. There's
a clubby bar and the Galileo restaurant here is reminiscent
of Harry's Bar in Venice. There's a pool, gym, and spa, and
views of Observatory Hill to Walsh Bay.

89-113 Kent Street, Millers Point 2000. Tel: 256-2222;
Fax: 256-2233; in U.S. and Canada (800) 237-1236. A$340.

The ► **ANA Hotel** incorporates a historic precinct
where three cottages have been preserved, one of which,
Lilyvale Cottage built in the 1840s, is now the hotel's
signature restaurant. The accommodations section has
been carefully renovated to include all modern conveniences.

176 Cumberland Street, The Rocks 2000. Tel: 250-6000;
Fax: 250-6250. A$300.

The ► **Old Sydney Parkroyal** is in the heart of The
Rocks; its rooms (some with views) are situated around
an atrium. The rooftop pool has great views of the harbor,
Opera House, and city skyline.

55 George Street, Sydney 2000. Tel: 252-0524; Fax: 251-
2093; in U.S. and Canada, Tel: (800) 835-7742. A$280.

The ► **Sydney Renaissance**, one block from the Circular Quay and close to the Stock Exchange and financial
district, is decorated with aboriginal artworks. Musicians
play in the late afternoon in the spacious, three-tiered
lobby, and guests have a choice of drinking at the Customs House Bar, with an authentic Aussie pub atmosphere, or the more sedate Bulletin Bar. The hotel's
restaurant, **Raphael's**, is highly regarded for its Pacific Rim
cuisine.

30 Pitt Street, Sydney 2000. Tel: 259-7000; Fax: 252-
1999; in U.S. and Canada, Tel: (800) 228-9898. A$195–
A$290.

Moderate

The ► **Stafford**, behind Nurses Walk in The Rocks, combines hotel and apartment accommodations. The modern hotel is built beside a collection of seven 1880s two-story terrace houses that contain 54 studio and one-bedroom apartments. Most have views of the harbor, the Opera House, and the city.

75 Harrington Street, Sydney 2000. Tel: 251-6711; Fax: 251-3458. A$170.

Budget

The ► **Russell**, a boutique hotel opposite Sydney Cove, was converted from an 1880s Port Jackson pub. It has a total of 30 rooms, each decorated in country-house style and much favored by Sydneysiders for one-night honeymoons.

143A George Street, Sydney 2000. Tel: 241-3543; Fax: 252-1652. Shared bath, from A$115; private bath, from A$190; Continental breakfast included.

The ► **All Seasons Harbour Rocks Hotel**, which backs onto Nurses Walk, is a three-level converted 1890s warehouse; only superior rooms have private bathrooms, and there is no elevator.

34–52 Harrington Street, Sydney 2000. Tel: 251-8944; Fax: 251-8900; in U.S. and Canada, (800) 423-2880. Shared bath, A$116; private bath, A$182.

MACQUARIE STREET AND CENTRAL BUSINESS DISTRICT

Expensive

The ► **Inter-Continental**, opposite the Botanic Gardens, has the most character of Sydney's hotels in terms of design, incorporating as it does the 19th-century sandstone Treasury Building, a gem of Victorian architecture. The glass-domed lobby, stuffed with leather sofas and oversized plants, has become a city-center meeting and conversation spot. Afternoon tea here is accompanied by a string quartet every day, and the hotel's **Sketches Bar and Bistro** features the works of some of Australia's premier artists. The **Treasury Room** restaurant offers fine dining in a grand Victorian setting (see Dining, below). Rooms in the central tower overlook the harbor, the Opera House, and the Botanic Gardens.

117 Macquarie Street, Sydney 2000. Tel: 230-0200; Fax: 240-1240; in U.S. and Canada, Tel: (800) 327-0200. A$285–A$350.

The ▶ **Sheraton Wentworth**, next to the Australian Airlines city terminal, is close to the financial district, the Central Business District, and most tourist attractions. The Garden Court restaurant here is highly rated for its discreet service and traditional menu.

61 Phillip Street, Sydney 2000. Tel: 230-0700; Fax 227-9133; in U.S. and Canada, Tel: (800) 325-3535. A$275; full breakfast included.

The ▶ **Hilton International**, in the heart of shopping land opposite the Queen Victoria Building, has a monorail station linking it to Darling Harbour and the Entertainment Centre. Its rebuilt Marble Bar is an extravagant, Rococo-style, early 1900s watering hole, and Juliana's nightclub frequently hosts internationally celebrated artists.

259 Pitt Street, Sydney 2000. Tel: 266-0610; Fax: 265-6065; in U.S. and Canada, Tel: (800) HILTONS. A$180–A$260.

HYDE PARK AREA

Expensive

▶ **The Park Lane**, an oasis of marble and elegant boutiques, is Sydney's newest luxury hotel. Its signature restaurant, **Gekko**, features an open kitchen that serves modern Australian fare with Asian overtones in a landscaped Australian native garden setting. The hotel has a skybridge to nearby department stores, and easy access to the monorail and just about every city attraction.

161 Elizabeth Street, Sydney 2000. Tel: 286-6000; Fax: 286-6565. A$310.

The ▶ **Sydney Marriott**, opened in 1992, overlooks Hyde Park. Its excellent rooftop recreational area includes a pool, a gym, a spa, a sauna, and an aerobics center.

36 College Street, East Sydney 2010. Tel: 361-8400; Fax: 361-8484; in U.S. and Canada, Tel: (800) 228-9290. A$260.

Moderate

The ▶ **Sydney Boulevard**, midway between Hyde Park and Kings Cross, has city- or harbor-view rooms, fabulous views from its 25th-floor bar and restaurant, and an Eastern-style bathhouse with therapeutic spa and massages.

90 William Street, Sydney 2000. Tel: 357-2277; Fax: 356-3786; in U.S. and Canada, Tel: (800) 835-SPHC. A$190.

The ▶ **Cambridge Inn**, off Oxford Street, offers small suites only, some with private balconies. It has a heated pool, sauna, and mini-gym, and its brasserie, featuring salads and char-grills, is a good spot for a meal even if you're not staying at the hotel.

212 Riley Street, Surry Hills 2010. Tel: 212-1111; Fax: 281-1981. A$170–A$185.

Budget

The ▶ **All Seasons Park Regis**, overlooking Hyde Park, occupies ten floors of a multi-story apartment building in the heart of the Central Business District. It features a rooftop pool, and its recently refurbished rooms are comfortable, though small.

Corner of Park and Castlereagh streets, Sydney 2000. Tel: 267-6511; Fax: 264-2252; in U.S., Tel: (800) 44-UTELL; in Canada, (800) 387-8842. A$85–A$110.

DARLING HARBOUR

Expensive

▶ **Hotel Nikko Darling Harbour,** on the city side of Darling Harbour, incorporates colonial buildings of the 1840s, including painstakingly restored sandstone warehouses. These buildings now incorporate the exclusive Takashi-maya department store, **Neo Pharaoh** nightclub, and **Kamogawa** restaurant, reputed to be the best Japanese restaurant in the city with tatami rooms, a ritualized *kaiseki* menu, and a *teppanyaki* bar (see Dining, below).

161 Sussex Street, Sydney 2000. Tel: 299-1231; Fax: 299-3340; in U.S., Tel: (800) NIKKO US. A$240–A$260, including breakfast.

Moderate

▶ **Novotel on Darling Harbour**, at 100 Murray Street, overlooks Darling Harbour from the west side, and has a tennis court, gym, pool, and sauna, as well as The 19th Hole, a high-tech golf driving range.

P.O. Box 600, Pyrmont 2009. Tel: 934-0000; Fax: 934-0099; in U.S. and Canada, Tel: (800) 221-4542. A$180–A$210, including breakfast.

The ▶ **Parkroyal at Darling Harbour** is at the southern end of the complex near Chinatown and has 295 rooms, three bars, and two restaurants. Its an easy walk to the retail section of the CBD.

150 Day Street, Sydney 2000. Tel: 261-4444; Fax: 261-8766; in U.S. and Canada, Tel: (800) 835-SPHC. A$230.

KINGS CROSS

Expensive

The ▶ **Hotel Nikko Sydney**, at Potts Point, is in the better end of Kings Cross. It has stunning skyline views, and its restaurant, **The Point**, currently enjoys the reputation of having one of Sydney's finest French menus (see Dining, below).

81 Macleay Street, Potts Point 2011. Tel: 368-3000; Fax: 357-4964; in U.S. and Canada, Tel: (800) NIKKO US. A$280, including breakfast.

The ▶ **Sebel Town House** attracts stars and their makers seeking peaceful surroundings and attention to their every whim. Its Celebrity Bar is good for spotting music-industry types; the Encore Restaurant serves dinner until late and snacks until 4:00 A.M. There's a rooftop pool, sauna, and gym.

23 Elizabeth Bay Road, Elizabeth Bay 2011. Tel: 358-3244; Fax: 357-1926; in U.S. and Canada, (800) 448-8355. A$195–A$280.

Moderate

The ▶ **Hyatt Kingsgate**, at the eastern end of William Street, has rooms with city and harbor views.

William Street, Kings Cross 2011. Tel: 356-1234; Fax: 356-4150; in U.S. and Canada, Tel: (800) 233-1234; A$230.

Budget

▶ **Clairmont Inn**, at 5 Ward Avenue, behind the main Kings Cross activity, is modern but cozy. It has an indoor pool, spa, and sauna.

5 Ward Avenue, Kings Cross 2011. Tel: 358-2044; Fax: 357-3730. A$77.

▶ **The Manhattan**, a busy tourist hotel in a refurbished Art Deco building, is located midway between Kings Cross and Double Bay. Rooms are spacious, and some have harbor views.

8 Greenknowe Avenue, Elizabeth Bay 2011. Tel: 358-1288; Fax: 357-3696; in U.S., Tel: (800) 44-UTELL; in Canada, (800) 387-8842. A$75–A$105.

DOUBLE BAY

Moderate

▶ **Peppers Cosmopolitan Double Bay** is an elegant hotel with a clublike atmosphere created by touches such as fireplaces and reading materials in the lounge, not to mention complimentary limo service to the CBD. Canopied four-poster beds add a dash of romance.

22 Knox Street, Double Bay 2028. Tel: 363-0777; Fax 327-3110. A$180.

Budget

▶ **The Savoy** is a boutique hotel in the heart of the cosmopolitan Double Bay neighborhood, surrounded by restaurants, elegant shops, and sidewalk cafés.

41 Knox Street, Double Bay 2028. Tel: 326-1411; Fax: 327-8464. A$85–A$100; Continental breakfast included.

APARTMENTS

Downtown

▶ **The York** is at the beginning of York Street close to the Harbour Bridge approach, the Quay, and the Central Business District. It has studio to three-bedroom apartments, a pool, a sauna, and a spa. The apartments have cooking facilities, but there's also a restaurant and bar on the premises.

5 York Street, Sydney 2000. Tel: 210-5000; Fax: 290-1487. A$150.

▶ **Metro Apartments Darling Harbour** is a new seven-story accommodation complex on the city side of Darling Harbour. It features split-level one-bedroom units with fold-out sofas in the sitting rooms.

132-136 Sussex Street (corner of King Street), Sydney 2000. Tel: 290-9200; Fax: 262-3032. A$120.

Kings Cross

▶ **Best Western Florida Motor Inn**, on a tree-lined dead-end street off Kings Cross, has 91 units (studios to two bedrooms) with fully equipped kitchens. The motor inn has a sauna.

1 McDonald Street, Potts Point 2011. Tel: 358-6811; Fax: 358-5951. A$95.

▶ **The Medina** is near Elizabeth Bay, midway between The Cross and Double Bay. Some of its studio units have balconies, and the rooftop garden offers views of the yachting haven of Rushcutters Bay.

70 Roslyn Gardens, Elizabeth Bay 2011. Tel: 356-7400; Fax: 357-2505. A$125.

Many more apartments are available in the city and inner suburbs; contact the New South Wales Travel Centre; Tel: 231-4444.

HOST HOMES

Another option is to stay in a private home and be treated as a family guest. For host home information contact ▶ **Home Hospitality**, 50 Rosemead Road, Hornsby 2007, Tel: 568-2331, Fax: 564-2607; and ▶ **Town and County Hosts**, 65 Buckland Street, Alexandria 2015, Tel and Fax: 310-2330.

DINING

Waves of immigration have assured Australia of splendidly varied food. Being definite about a particular place is hazardous, as new restaurants open—and close—with distressing rapidity. The following list includes only long-term survivors.

Sydney dines from about 7:00 P.M.; except at places catering to theatergoers and night owls, few kitchens are active after 10:00 P.M. Only in the most formal places, usually fine hotel restaurants, need men wear jacket and tie. Tipping is not rigorously based on a percentage of the bill, nor are service charges included; instead, the amount of a tip usually has to do with your personal reaction to the service.

While some excellent international chefs work in Sydney kitchens, a new local breed is cooking up some innovative dishes under the rubric of modern Australian cuisine, experimenting with the wide variety of fresh ingredients now available (renowned French chef Paul Bocuse claims that the selection at Sydney markets is almost equal to that in France) and keeping on the menu those dishes that please diners.

Australia is one of the few countries yet to suffer declining seafood quality because of pollution or overfishing, so few menus are without a choice of fish. Ocean perch, snapper (spelled *schnapper* in Sydney), and John Dory are among the best New South Wales fish, and whiting from South Australia, coral trout from Queensland, sea trout or salmon from Tasmania, and barramundi from the north appear on many menus. Farmed trout abound. Tuna, for sashimi and sushi, arrive at the market gleamingly fresh.

Australia has no true lobster—what you get are nipperless crayfish (the smaller ones taste better). Yabbies (hard-shelled freshwater shrimp) are plentiful, as are crabs of several species. A big mudcrab is a wonderful thing. Balmain "bugs" sound awful but are in fact slipper lobsters and taste delicious, while Tasmanian scallops are about the world's best, although outrageously expensive. Squid is plentiful, but beware the ubiquitous "calamari rings"—usually imported and rubbery.

Australian lamb is killed too late for its taste to match that of New Zealand lamb, and it's never as succulent as Greek baby lamb. Beef here is lean but seldom aged. It can be excellent as roast when treated well, though. Kangaroo is becoming more common on menus, as are crocodile, emu, buffalo, and venison—all farmed for the table, of course.

The telephone area code for Sydney is 02. When calling from outside Australia, omit the zero.

CENTRAL BUSINESS DISTRICT

Sydney's Central Business District denizens show keen interest in the lunch scene, haunting coterie hideaways in cellars, the specialty restaurants of a few top hotels, and some of the pricier Japanese and Italian eateries. **Kables,** on the mezzanine floor of the Regent of Sydney hotel, rates high. Service is impeccable and the restaurant's French-Canadian chef is passionate about modern Australian dishes. A specialty is pan-roasted fillet of farmed salmon on a purée of cucumber and potatoes with vermouth cream sauce. Lunch wounds the wallet less than dinner. For bookings, Tel: 238-0000. **Machiavelli Ristorante** is considerably cheaper. Servings are generous, the atmosphere cheerfully hectic, and the food aggressively Italian; the fellow at the next table might well be the state premier. Lunch and dinner Monday to Friday. At 123 Clarence Street, near Erskine; Tel: 299-3748.

Keisan, at the Holiday Inn Menzies Hotel at Wynyard, serves sushi, sashimi, and more substantial delicacies to grateful Japanese visitors and local aficionados. Medium range and popular for lunch; Tel: 299-1000.

Claudine's on Macquarie, opposite the Botanic Gardens at number 151, is a chic cellar with a reputation for substantial French cooking. Business executives and politicians gather for lunch, but the relaxed crowd at night is more interesting; Tel: 241-1749.

The Inter-Continental's **Treasury Room** combines good lunching—its chef, Tony Bilson, has been on the culinary cutting edge in Sydney for two decades—with Victorian decor. It is expensive, and reservations are recommended; Tel: 230-0200.

Sightseers breaking for a light lunch might consider **The Glasshouse Café** in the new wing of the State Library of New South Wales or the **Barracks Café** at Hyde Park Barracks. Both are on Macquarie Street and offer good value in interesting surroundings. Glasshouse Café, Tel: 223-4419; Barracks Café, Tel: 223-1155.

Around the Liverpool and George area, people are lured to **Capitan Torres**, at 73 Liverpool Street, for hearty Spanish food at moderate to low prices. Capitan Torres also has a tapas bar; Tel: 264-5574.

CHINATOWN AND DARLING HARBOUR

Chinatown starts one block south at Goulburn Street and Dixon Street. Part of Dixon Street is a pedestrian mall, and it is the neighborhood's backbone. The choice is overwhelming. **Yum Cha at the Golden Harbour**, at number 31, drags in crowds every day between 10:00 A.M. and 4:00 P.M., and on weekends from 9:00 A.M. to 4:00 P.M.; Tel: 212-5987. Other dim sum palaces in the district include **The Marigold**, seating 500 at 299–305 Sussex Street, Tel: 264-6744; **The New Marigold**, seating 600 in the Citymark Building at 683–689 George Street, Tel: 281-3388; and **The Regal**, seating 700 at 347 Sussex Street, Tel: 261-8988. For authenticity, variety, and good value, they are hard to beat.

Not far away, in Ultimo, is **The Restaurant**. Despite its uncompelling name and back-lane entrance at 88 Hacket Street, it is esteemed by Sydney's literati for its northern Italian cooking. Specialties include quail, milk-fed veal scallopine, and duck liver on a bed of fennel. It's medium to expensive; Tel: 211-5895.

Kamogawa, in the Corn Exchange Building (part of the Hotel Nikko at 177 Sussex Street, Darling Harbour, Tel: 299-5533) has *kaiseki ryori,* or banquet menus, which are presented with a reverence usually associated with the Japanese tea ceremony. *Teppanyaki,* a style of cooking done at your table, is also available.

CIRCULAR QUAY AND THE ROCKS

Neil Perry, the owner of the **Rockpool**, an elegant and quite expensive restaurant in an 1840s building at 107 George Street in The Rocks, is also the chef. His establishment is favored by an army of dedicated gourmets for its treatment of always-fresh local seafood. The salad of spiced baby octopus and Jerusalem artichoke is renowned; the oyster bar at the front of the restaurant is more casual and affordable; Tel: 252-1888. In the stone bond store (warehouse) at Campbell's Cove, the **Imperial Peking Harborside** produces notable northern Chinese and Cantonese dishes, with the emphasis on seafood. For harbor views, ask for a window table when booking; Tel: 247-7073.

On the western side of Circular Quay are Bilson's and No. 7 at the Park, good places to go for a celebration. **Bilson's**, on the upper level of the Overseas (shipping) Terminal, has fantastic views of the Opera House, with food and service to match; Tel: 251-5600. **No. 7 at the Park**, the signature restaurant of the Park Hyatt, is right on the water at Hickson Road. Appropriately, the menu emphasizes seafood; Tel: 241-1234. More casual, but still making waves on the food front, are **Merrony's**, at 2 Albert Street (Tel: 247-9323), and the **Paragon Café**, upstairs in the Paragon Hotel, at 1 Loftus Street (Tel: 241-3888). Bold, modern Australian fare is offered at both of these establishments, with hints of Asia, California, and the Mediterranean.

EAST SYDNEY AND DARLINGHURST

In the suburbs of Darlinghurst and East Sydney, just a 15-minute walk or a short cab ride east of the Central Business District, there are a number of good Italian restaurants. Among these are places such as **Beppi's**, located at the corner of Stanley and Yurong streets. Although in business for the past 38 years, Beppi's has a freshness of approach that many of its competitors would like to match; Tel: 360-4558. Other modish spots include **Tre Scalini**, at the corner of Yurong and Liverpool streets (Tel: 331-4358), and **La Colonna**, 117 Riley Street (Tel: 331-1559). At the bottom end of the market are such spaghetti institutions as **Bill and Toni's**, at 74 Stanley Street (Tel: 360-4702), and **No Names**, on Chapel Lane (Tel: 360-4711). There are no reservations, no tablecloths, and no other frills at these places.

An altogether different, though worthy, addition to this dining scene is **Riberries**, at 411 Bourke Street, in Darlinghurst (Tel: 361-4929). This is the place to sample the emerging Australian Bush cuisine: French-based fare using such wild ingredients as warrigal greens (similar to silverbeet), wattle seed (reminiscent of coffee bean), and sugarbag honey. The namesake berries with their clove scent turn up in the sticky date pudding, and witchitty grubs are on the menu, if you must.

Taylor Square, at the junction of Oxford, Bourke, and Flinders streets in Darlinghurst, has a couple of worthwhile cheap eateries, and a lively not-quite-cheap one, the **Taylor Square Restaurant**, where a clever young chef produces classic French and Italian numbers, plus some homey favorites. The restaurant, at 2 Flinders Street, doesn't take reservations; Tel: 360-5828 for hours. The **Balkan Seafood** restaurant at 215 Oxford Street, noted for charcoal-broiled seafood, is an overflow of the original **Balkan Restaurant** at number 209; Tel: 331-7570 for either. Strategically sited on the corner opposite the courthouse, **191 Oxford Street** is an open-fronted coffee shop with snacks.

A few blocks north, at the corner of Burton and Forbes streets, is **Dov**, a great coffee shop serving European and Mediterranean fare with Jewish influences; Tel: 360-9594. Sydney's only Kosher restaurant is the **B'nai B'rith Center** at 22 Yurong Street in East Sydney; Tel: 361-6035.

PADDINGTON

The town's leading restaurant critic rates the glitzy and expensive **Oasis Seros**, at 495 Oxford Street, highly enough for reservations to be essential. Specialties include salmis of pigeon braised with chestnuts and a checkerboard dessert of pineapple and aniseed sorbets; Tel: 361-3377.

Across the road at 10 Oxford Street is **Claude's**, one of the smallest and most expensive restaurants in Sydney. It's also one of the best, and advance reservations are essential. The owner/chef Damien Pignolet steadfastly refuses to take any credit cards or obtain anything more than a bring-your-own-liquor license; he prefers instead to concentrate on his elegant modern and classic regional French cooking. Tel: 331-2325. If the A$80 prix fixe menu here seems a bit steep, you can always head around the corner and sample Pignolet's cooking at his "day job"— the **Bistro Moncur** in the Woollahra Hotel on the corner of Moncur and Queen streets; Tel: 363-2782.

Lucio's, at 47 Windsor Street in Paddington, combines traditional Italian food with a touch of Sydney's artistic nostalgia: An earlier restaurant on the site was an artists' haunt, and a picture of old habitués at the entry includes Robert Hughes, the author of the best-selling book *The Fatal Shore*. Prices are moderate; Tel: (02) 380-5996 for reservations.

Darcy's, at 92 Hargrave Street, maintains a long tradition of food (Italian) and service that justifies its consistent support and permits maintenance of its considerable prices; Tel: 550-6650.

KINGS CROSS

Kings Cross has innumerable eating houses and most of the city's remaining coffee houses. Oldest (1950) is the minuscule **Piccolo Bar** at 6 Roslyn Street, home to a Runyonesque clientele of wrestlers, runners, and ladies with hearts of gold. Visiting celebrities like Pele, Dave Brubeck, and Louis Armstrong have also dropped in over the years. Owner-manager Joe Podesta knows the scene like few others; open from 11:00 A.M. to 6:00 A.M.

The stretch of nearby Victoria Street, from the fire station at the corner of Darlinghurst Road to the Liverpool Street intersection, has enough coffee houses to keep Sydney awake all night. **Formula 1** and **Tropicana Gelato** are on the odd-numbered side; **Andiamo, Morgans, Café Paradiso**, and the veteran **Bar Coluzzi, La Bussola**, and **San Remo** are on the even-numbered side. While usually geared to late-night trade, the stretch is crowded Sunday mornings for ritual brunch. While a tad tawdry, with some dreadful-looking characters sauntering by, The Cross is well patrolled, so if they pay due care and attention, late-night patrons can feel reasonably safe.

Bayswater Road, at the northern end of Victoria Street, has many restaurants that cater to all appetites. The **Bayswater Brasserie** at number 32 (Tel: 357-2749) is recognized as the benchmark for casual dining in Sydney. **The Last Aussie Fishcaf** at number 24 jumps (as do its customers) to a 1950s jukebox, but beneath the light-hearted façade is seafood of an exceptionally high standard; Tel: 356-2911.

At the western end of Bayswater, Darlinghurst Road heads north, becomes Macleay Street, and descends into toney Potts Point, where there are many bistros and brasseries. Among the pace-setters is the **Macleay Street Bistro** at 73A (Tel: 358-4891). The **Trianon Challis Avenue**, on a cross street (29 Challis Avenue), offers neo-classical French-based fare. Ask to sit on the vine-canopied terrace in warm weather; Tel: 358-1353.

The Point, the Hotel Nikko's brasserie on Macleay Street, serves moderate, prix fixe lunches and dinners with choices from a selective menu; wine is included in the luncheon price; Tel: 368-3000 for bookings.

DOUBLE BAY

Double Bay has what many consider Sydney's most stylish Chinese restaurant: **The Cleveland** at 63 Bay Street with its substantial and imaginative vegetarian menu; Tel: 327-6877. Its nearby, less expensive rival, **Imperial Peking**, is considered by some to match it; Knox and Bay streets, Tel: 326-1057. **Twentyone Espresso**, although not Chinese, is nostalgic for those reared on the pastries of Vienna and Budapest; 21 Knox Street; Tel: 327-2616.

Other eating places worth seeking out in this area include **Doyles On The Beach** seafood restaurant at 11 Marine Parade, Watson's Bay, for the view and for the generous helpings. It's moderate to expensive for what are often fairly standard fish and chips, but though the locals complain, there are still lines most lunchtimes and on spring and summer nights; Tel: 337-2007. You'd probably dine much more satisfactorily at **The Pier**, 594 New South Head Road, in the neighboring suburb of Rose Bay (Tel: 327-4187). The fish and chips here might be deep-fried fillets with sweet-potato straws, or steamed ocean trout with saffron noodles; quality is always high and the food complemented by the waterfront location.

Berowra Waters Inn is well out of town, but its top billing from the city's most important restaurant reviewer and its location on an arm of the Hawkesbury River make the effort worthwhile. The food is French-based in presentation and preparation, but uniquely Australian in its ingredient combinations. The prices are among the highest in Australia. Fly in with Aquatic Air (see North of Sydney in the Side Trips from Sydney section, below) and you'll pay even more, though the experience will be hard to rival. Landlubbers drive about an hour north up the Pacific Highway and take Berowra Waters Road from Berowra (or a taxi from Hornsby Railway Station) to Berowra Waters Wharf, where the restaurant's motor launch meets patrons and ferries them across the river to their destination. Reservations are essential; Tel: 456-1027.

While it's impossible to list even the majority of worthy eating houses, the *Sydney Morning Herald*'s *Good Food Guide* has nearly 200 pages of them, with ratings and maps. It modestly declares itself "Sydney's Food Bible" and has no competition.

NIGHTLIFE AND ENTERTAINMENT

In the 20 years since Queen Elizabeth II attended the **Opera House** opening, Sydney's performing arts and music scene has been transformed. Something is happening on Bennelong Point every night: opera or ballet in the

Playhouse; symphonies, chamber music, and recitals in the Concert Hall; productions by the Sydney Theatre Company in the Drama Theatre; and all manner of performances in the Rehearsal Room. Regular events on Bennelong Point include free entertainment on the broadwalk every Sunday morning and jazz in the afternoon at the **Forecourt** restaurant; for information, Tel: 250-7111; box office, Tel: 250-7777.

Sydney's venerable **Town Hall** reopened in 1992 after a multimillion-dollar restoration revitalized its long-faded Victorian grandeur. Events there have ranged from international jazz festivals, with stars like Ray Brown and Joe Williams, to comedy from Whoopie Goldberg and recitals by Isaac Stern and the late Andrés Segovia.

The city's three main commercial theaters are **The Royal**, in the MLC Centre on Castlereach Street, **Her Majesty's**, at 107 Quay Street, and the **Opera House Drama Theatre**. The **Seymour Centre**, near Sydney University in the inner western suburb of Camperdown, has three theaters and hosts many first-class visiting actors starring with locally cast companies. The **State Theatre** at 49 Market Street, once an Art Deco cinema, is used for special one-night performances from the likes of Christie Moore and Eartha Kitt and is home to the enthusiastically attended **Sydney International Film Festival**, held annually in June. For information, Tel: 660-3844.

Smaller but still important theaters noted for the high standard of their productions are the **Belvoir Street Theatre** in the Surry Hills area, the Sydney Theatre Company's **Wharf Theatre**, **Marian Street Theatre** in the northern suburb of Killara, the **Ensemble Theatre** at Kirribilli just north of the Harbour Bridge, and the **Footbridge Theatre**, associated with the University of Sydney. Fringe theaters include **The Stables** at Kings Cross, the **New Theatre**, and the **Voices Theatre Co-op**, both the last at Newtown.

There are two venues for comedy in Sydney. The **Comedy Store** at 278 Cleveland Street, Surry Hills, offers just a show, or dinner and a show, from Wednesday to Saturday; Tel: 319-5731. The **Harold Park Hotel**, Wigram Road, Glebe, features book, poetry, and script readings Mondays through Wednesdays, and comedy cabaret shows Thursdays through Saturdays; Tel: 692-0564.

The *Sydney Morning Herald* theater and entertainment listings carry information across the spectrum, from aspiring new groups to established performers. This paper's blue Metro section (Friday) and the Saturday listing are particularly detailed. Tickets may be bought from box offices, from Ticketek, which accepts credit-card phone bookings (Tel: 266-4800), or from the Halftix booth between Castlereach and Elizabeth streets in Martin Place, which sells half-price tickets for that evening's performances, from 12:00 noon to 5:30 P.M. weekdays and from noon to 5:00 P.M. on Saturdays (cash only). Travellers making flight reservations with Qantas have access to advance bookings for major ballet, opera, concert, and theater productions in Sydney, Melbourne, Brisbane, Adelaide, Perth, and Cairns. Travel agents have access to a full 12-month list of performances.

JAZZ

Sydney's jazz scene has been evolving since World War II. The presence of American GIs during the war helped get jazz started in the city, and since then Sydney has been treated to visiting jazz greats from Dizzy Gillespie to Gil Evans. But it would be unfair to credit the current buoyant scene to overseas influence alone. Many local men and women have kept things jumping and added an antipodean flavor to this always-developing musical form. James Morrison has international renown as a trumpeter, and groups like Galapagos Duck have received rave reviews in Europe. Still playing are veterans like pianist Judy Bailey, around town 40 years after she opened at Sydney's long-defunct jazz cellar El Rocco, as well as eminent clarinetist Don Burrows, pianist Dick Hughes (he played with Oscar Peterson during one of the latter's Sydney visits), pianist Julian Lee (whose style shows the influence of George Shearing), and George Golla, a guitarist in the Joe Pass class.

Permanent jazz venues include **The Real Ale Café**, 66 King Street, Tel: 262-3277; **Harbourside Brasserie**, Pier One, Walsh Bay, Tel: 252-3000; **Soup Plus**, George Street, between Market and King streets, Tel: 299-7728; **The Basement**, 29 Reiby Place, Circular Quay, Tel: 251-2797; **Round Midnight**, 2 Roslyn Street, Kings Cross, Tel: 356-4045; and **Parkroyal Hotel** at Darling Harbour (jazz at Sunday lunch only), Tel: 261-4444. All these places serve meals and drinks.

Jazz is lively on the pub circuit. Pubs with consistently good offerings are **Strawberry Hills Hotel** and the **Shakespeare Hotel**, both in Surry Hills; **Jacksons on George**, the **Paragon Hotel**, and **The Orient**, all at The Rocks; the **Cat and Fiddle** in Balmain; and the **Cockle Bay Bar** at Darling Harbour.

FOLK AND POP MUSIC

The folk music scene in Sydney is on and off. A few pubs feature folk singers. The **Rose, Shamrock and Thistle**, or Three Weeds, as it's affectionately known, hosts folk, soul, and soft-rock performers at 193 Evans Street, Rozelle; Tel: 555-7755. The best resource for what's going on in Australian folk music is **Folkways** at 282 Oxford Street, Paddington; Tel: 361-3980. The shop has a comprehensive selection of authentic aboriginal and bush music on cassettes and CDs.

Pop music of varying quality is a nightly phenomenon in many, many pubs. Currently popular venues in the city and near-suburbs include the **Phoenician Club**, at 173 Broadway, Ultimo, Tel: 212-5955; the **Nags Head**, 162 Saint John's Road, Glebe, Tel: 660-1591; and the **Pumphouse Brewery Tavern**, 17 Little Pier Street, Darling Harbour, Tel: 281-3967. Late-night dance venues include **The Cauldron**, at 207 Darlinghurst Road, **Neo Pharaoh** in the Hotel Nikko Darling Harbour, and **Rogues** at 16–18 Oxford Square; on Bayswater Road, Kings Cross, there are always crowds at **Studebaker's**, at number 33, and **Sugareef**, at number 20. Look in the *Sydney Morning Herald*'s blue Metro section on Fridays for listings, or in *What's On in Sydney,* a free brochure, available at most hotels, that covers much of the city's activities over a three-month period.

PUBS

Australia's reputation as a nation of beer swillers is changing. Growing health consciousness and random breath testing mean that you're more likely to encounter the average Aussie in a gym than a pub these days. That is not to say that they don't repair to the bar when there is something to celebrate, be it a promotion, a birthday, or simply the end of the week—they don't, however, do it as often as the stereotype would have you believe.

Pubs have had to counter this general decline in trade by a range of methods. In many cases music is the lure (see the jazz, folk, and pop music sections, above). Many of Sydney's young innovative chefs have honed their creative skillets in pub dining rooms as well. Memorable meals are to be enjoyed at the **Paragon Hotel** at Circular Quay; the **Phoenix Hotel**, at 1 Moncur Street, Woollahra; **Darley Street Thai** in the Botany View Hotel, at 597 King Street, Newtown; and the **Burdekin Hotel Dining Room** at 2 Oxford Street, Darlinghurst (its **Dugout Bar** is a good place for a pre-dinner cocktail).

At other hotels (pubs), mini-breweries are the attraction. The **Pumphouse Tavern** in Darling Harbour and the **Lord Nelson** at 19 Kent Street, The Rocks, offer "home brews" ranging from light lagers to dark ales. Pubs in the tourist precincts offer the chance to wet the whistle, catch up with some local color, and sample some cheap bar food billed as a counter meal. In The Rocks, the **Fortune of War**, the **Observer**, and the **Orient**, all on George Street, are such places, while in the beach suburb of Manly those with a thirst should head for the **Hotel Manly**, the **New Brighton**, or the **Steyne**.

Two pubs stand out as landmarks on the yuppie map of Sydney's places to see and be seen: **The Oaks** (a.k.a. "the bodyshop") at 118 Military Road in Neutral Bay (on the north side of the bridge) and the **Lord Dudley** at 236 Jersey Road in Woollahra (on the south side). Cheers.

SHOPS AND SHOPPING

Although the central city and main suburban shopping areas are cluttered with retailers, Sydney is nonetheless no bargain shoppers' paradise. Shipping costs make imported goods costly, and wage scales are not of the low kind that underpin bargain-hunters' haunts in less developed countries.

The best buys are obviously items specifically Australian—sheepskin and lambskin products, aboriginal print tee-shirts, stuffed koalas, Australian wool handknits, stockmen's raincoats, moleskins, and Outback-style hats (by Akubra and others)—all found in profusion in tourist shops in The Rocks and uptown.

Australiana

Years before a couple of internationally popular Australian movies alerted the world to Outback folk modes, R. M. Williams started his Bushman's Outfitters business to supply country people with practical garments— moleskins, work shirts, split-back raincoats suitable for sitting on horses, elastic-sided riding boots, and wide-brimmed hats for peering into the sun across vast distances. **R. M. Williams Bushman's Outfitters** shop at 389 George Street, between King and Market streets, opposite the Strand Arcade, is still at it. (Note: "moleskins" are trousers made of a closely woven cotton fabric, not the skins of small burrowing mammals!)

Adventurer Dick Smith publishes *Australian Geo-*

graphic magazines and has a chain of shops of the same name that stock quality Australiana, books, and outdoor equipment. There's an **Australian Geographic** shop in the city at 127 York Street, near the Queen Victoria Building (for which, see below).

Less obviously Australian, but still very good value, are the works of local artisans and craftspeople: handweavings; finely turned bowls, platters, and other useful objects in Australian woods, such as silky-textured huon pine, coachwood, and red river gum; blown glass pieces; hand-knitted and hand-woven wool garments; hand-dyed quilted jackets and silk garments; leather satchels; hand-plaited belts; handbags; gold and silver jewelry and jewelry with colored gemstones; quilts in modern and traditional patterns; stained-glass panels; and hand-painted wall hangings.

There are other arts and crafts outlets around, but it's hard to beat **Australian Craftworks**, at 127 George Street, The Rocks, for variety and quality. In this renovated 1882 police station the wares of 180 or so artists and craftspeople are for sale at any given time. Some of the displays are in the old jail cells. (There's an equally attractive and well-stocked branch of the store in the Old Corn Exchange Building, 151 Sussex Street, Darling Harbour.)

Aboriginal Tribal Art Centre, nearby at 117–119 George Street, has a large and varied collection of aboriginal and islander artifacts, including bark paintings and body ornaments from Papua, New Guinea, carvings from Arnhem Land in the Top End, dot paintings from the Northern Territory's Western Desert, and screen-printed clothing from the Tiwi people of Bathurst and Melville islands off Darwin.

The name **Ken Done** has become synonymous with his prints using sunny colors and motifs of reef, sea, and plants applied to resort wear and souvenir items from table linens to tee-shirts. Ken and his wife Judy have shops at The Rocks (123 George Street), at 77 Castlereagh Street, in the Queen Victoria Building, at Darling Harbour, and at 2 Waverley Street in Bondi Junction.

The Old Shopping Arcades

Sydney has two shopping places where the handsome surroundings are as enjoyable as finding something you want to buy: the **Queen Victoria Building**, three levels of shopping that fill the block bounded by George, Druitt, York, and Market streets, and the **Strand Arcade**, between George and Pitt streets, a few doors up from King Street.

The enormous QVB, as most people call the Queen Victoria Building, was built in 1898 as the city market in an incongruous style, with domes, pilasters, and stained glass. After having fallen into a confusion of usages, it was rescued in the early 1980s, grandly restored, and filled with well-presented shops and eating places. Its lowest level is linked with Grace Brothers department store (at the corner of George, Market, and Pitt streets) and Town Hall station.

The smaller-scale Strand Arcade is equally handsome in its way, with cast-iron balustrades, rich wood paneling, and a glass-domed roof that sheds soft, clear light at all levels. It opened in 1891 and now has about 80 tenants.

The Strand's Pitt Street end opens onto a block-long pedestrian mall that also has entrances to four other shopping arcades. None of these is as striking, but the newest, **Sky Garden**, has the kind of chic decor that attracts tenants like A. Testoni and Moda Pele. Emerging in Castlereagh Street, Sky Garden forms one end of a row of shops stretching to the MLC Centre. They include Hermès, Celine, and Louis Vuitton.

The **MLC Centre**, with entrances on Martin Place, Castlereagh Street, and King Street, contains the Theatre Royal in its lower depths, and has a range of boutiques.

The core of the central-city shopping area—along George, Pitt, and Castlereagh streets between Martin Place and Park Street—includes two **David Jones'** department stores facing each other diagonally across the junction of Castlereagh and Market streets. One is devoted mainly to women's fashion, presented in boutique style with featured designer labels, and the other to menswear, housewares, and an international food hall—including an oyster bar and a tempting but expensive chocolate department—in the basement.

Antiques and Bric-a-brac

Oxford Street, from the Victoria Street/South Dowling Street intersection near Paddington, has some pleasant oddities. **Mother of Pearl and Sons**, east of Taylor Square, specializes in unusual lamps and brassware. Oxford Street has a few antiques shops, but collectors should detour southward down South Dowling Street to the **Sydney Antique Centre**, at number 531, where old wares, large and small, antique and vaguely old, are on display from 50 or so dealers.

Head back to Oxford Street and walk east into Paddington. **Folkways**, at 282 Oxford Street, is a music store specializing in Australian music—from home-grown folk, jazz, and blues to hard-to-find bush ballads. There is one hip fashion shop after another in this area, as well as the books and tearoom of **New Edition Bookshop**. Opposite New Edition, the long-running **Paddington Market** is held every Saturday morning from 10:00 on the grounds of the Uniting Church. Begun as a distinctly hippie thing, it has developed commercially while retaining its New Age flavor. At the least it's a good shopping place for Australian theme tee-shirts, the used finery sought by the funky young, aromatic oils, and incense sticks. At best you may find good-looking jewelry, offbeat clothing, and attractive souvenir items, including modestly priced small ceramic statues of native creatures treated with understated humor by a ceramicist from Murrurundi in the Hunter Valley.

Oxford Street continues east into Woollahra, passing the more upscale **Woollahra Antiques Centre** on the way, at 160 Oxford Street opposite Centennial Park. Search out that curiously Australian invention, the milk jug cover—a delicately embroidered piece of gauze or cheesecloth weighted with beads and designed to keep flies at bay. Queen Street in Woollahra has a host of antiques and curio dealers. If it's antique Australiana you're after, specialists include **Appley Hoare Antiques** at 55 Queen Street, while **Anne Schofield Antiques** at 36 Queen Street has an excellent jewelry collection.

Books

Book fanciers looking for Australiana or seeking Australia through her early or modern writers will find the bookshop at the **State Library of New South Wales**, in the new wing on Macquarie Street, a useful source of novels, poetry by white Australian and aboriginal writers, and Australian classics.

The **Travel Bookshop** at 20 Bridge Street in the city center specializes in worldwide travel; however, it does carry a good range of Australian guides and maps, including maps of Sydney and environs.

Among the few antiquarian (or just plain old volumes) bookshops are **Tyrrell's**, at 328 Pacific Highway in Crows Nest; Tyrrell's is probably Sydney's oldest bookseller. **Bibliophile**, at 24 Glenmore Road in Paddington, sells old and rare books, maps, and prints; **Hordern House**, at 77 Victoria Street in Potts Point (Kings Cross), specializes in Pacific voyages and maritime and colonial art; **Tim McCormick**, at 55 Queen Street in Woollahra, deals in early Australiana.

Duty-Free Shopping

Duty-free stores downtown and in the suburbs offer potential bargains, but prices should be compared with those back home. Prices are generally lower in the city duty-free stores than at the airport. These days not all goods bought in duty-free shops before departing Sydney for overseas need to be taken from the shop in a sealed bag that must be kept intact until you've boarded your flight. Because of some confusing—but gratifying—official distinction between tax-free and duty-free goods, tax-free articles such as cameras, film, watches, and most electrical gadgets such as shavers and radios can be used as soon as purchased. Duty-free goods such as perfume, cigarettes, alcohol, and some jewelry must, however, be bought within ten days of departure and kept sealed until you board your plane. Go figure.

SIDE TRIPS FROM SYDNEY

By Charles Sriber, Helen Gordon,
and Kirsty McKenzie

The auto license plates in Australia may no longer proclaim New South Wales "The Premier State" in a reference to its place in Australian history as the nation's first European settlement, but the slogan still goes a long way in expressing that, in terms of visitor attractions, the state is second to none Down Under.

There is, of course, no east of Sydney, the capital of New South Wales, but west beyond the Blue Mountains the beginnings of the Outback, which seems to stretch endlessly across the continent, soon appear. Dry landscapes and the occasional tree, begging for water, are all that separate one rickety, dusty Outback town from another. **Dubbo,** some 335 km (200 miles) west of Sydney, is a major Outback center, servicing sheep, cattle, and grain farmers who seem immune to the heat, dust, and flies. No one blinks in Dubbo when a kangaroo bounds across a paddock. **Broken Hill,** 1,165 km (725 miles) northwest of Sydney, and built on the riches of silver mining until that went bust, straddles the New South Wales–South Australia state line and is a stop on the Indian-Pacific rail line that links Sydney with Perth.

Head south from Sydney along the Pacific coast and you'll drive through rain forests that provide natural air-conditioning from the heat and look as they must have in prehistoric times. The cities and towns south of Sydney—**Wollongong, Kiama, Nowra**—couldn't be duller, but the

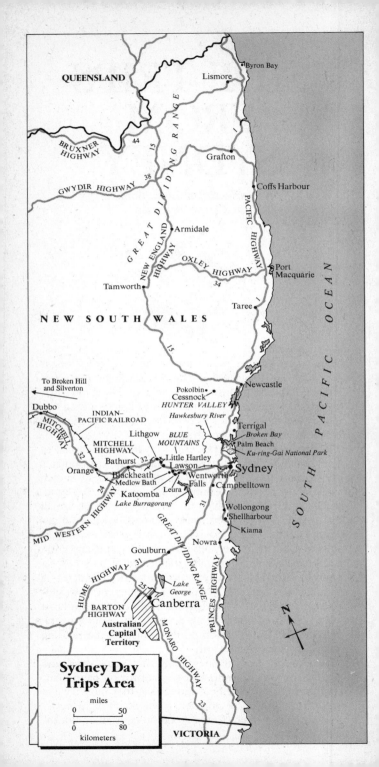

QUEENSLAND

Byron Bay

Lismore

BRUXNER HIGHWAY

GWYDIR HIGHWAY

44

15

38

Grafton

Coffs Harbour

NEW ENGLAND HIGHWAY

GREAT DIVIDING RANGE

Armidale

OXLEY HIGHWAY

PACIFIC HIGHWAY

Port Macquarie

34

Tamworth

Taree

NEW SOUTH WALES

15

1

To Broken Hill and Silverton

Pokolbin

Cessnock
HUNTER VALLEY

Hawkesbury River

Newcastle

Dubbo

INDIAN–PACIFIC RAILROAD

MITCHELL HIGHWAY

Lithgow

BLUE MOUNTAINS

Terrigal
Broken Bay
Palm Beach
Ku-ring-Gai National Park

32

MITCHELL HIGHWAY

Bathurst

32

Little Hartley

Lawson

Orange

Blackheath
Medlow Bath

Wentworth Falls

Sydney

24

Leura

Katoomba
Lake Burragorang

Campbelltown

MID WESTERN HIGHWAY

31

Wollongong
Shellharbour

Kiama

Goulburn

Nowra

HUME HIGHWAY

31

GREAT DIVIDING RANGE

1

Lake George

25

BARTON HIGHWAY

Canberra

Australian Capital Territory

MONARO HIGHWAY

PRINCES HIGHWAY

SOUTH PACIFIC OCEAN

N

23

Sydney Day Trips Area

miles
0   50

0   80
kilometers

VICTORIA

beaches on the coast here are perfect and much less crowded than those in Sydney.

On the northern coastal fringes of Sydney, **Palm Beach** is one of the city's posh neighborhoods, and its beach is a favorite of surfers. Nearby, about 45 km (26 miles) north of the city, is **Broken Bay**, which serves as the mouth of the **Hawkesbury River.** The river is one of Sydney's great recreational areas, to which boaters and picnickers flock on weekends.

Due north of Broken Bay are gentle farmlands reminiscent of New England, and the lush wine-growing regions of the Hunter Valley. Farther north, the town of **Tamworth** is Australia's Nashville, the nation's country-music capital. Fishing fans zero in on the northern coastal town of **Coffs Harbour**, where marlin and other sport fish are abundant in the deep waters off the coast. The Coffs Harbour Information Centre has a full list of the various types of day, weekend, and week-long fishing trips available; Tel: (066) 52-1522.

Byron Bay, north of Coffs Harbour on the coast near the Queensland border, is an appealing mixture of bohemians, artists, and "surfies." It is also the home of one of Australia's most famous exports, the actor Paul Hogan.

Full-day cruises on the Hawkesbury River and extended tours to Coffs Harbour, Broken Hill, and Dubbo can be booked at the Travel Centre of New South Wales at Martin Place in Sydney.

The day trips we suggest here, to the Blue Mountains, Hunter Valley, and Canberra, are just that—suggestions. It's a big state to explore, and there's adventure in New South Wales any direction you travel. We also include information on the silver-mining town of Broken Hill, in the far west of New South Wales. Broken Hill could be seen on a whirlwind day's flying tour out of Sydney, but an overnight trip is better for sampling the picture it provides of life in the New South Wales Outback.

MAJOR INTEREST

The Blue Mountains for scenery, nature, and hiking
Broken Hill, silver-mining Outback town
Hunter Valley wineries, dining, and hot-air
    ballooning
Canberra, Australia's capital

WEST OF SYDNEY
The Blue Mountains

When Sydney sizzles, many people head for the relative cool of the Blue Mountains, 100 km (60 miles) to the west of Sydney and visible on a clear day from such perches as Centrepoint Tower in the city. The faint, hazy blueness of the mountains when seen from a distance comes, experts opine, from the vaporish emanations of the leaves of countless eucalyptus trees, causing some refraction of the light and making the distant hills appear blue. The mountains are an easy day trip by train or rental car. Once in the mountains, however, you will need a car to get around. Several rental-car firms, including Budget, have outlets in **Katoomba**, the largest town in the mountains.

The Blue Mountains are the place to escape for solitude. Over the years, parts of the region have been "tarted up," as the Aussies say to explain the billboards and neon signs announcing another guesthouse, restaurant, or tourist attraction. But most of the region is pure, ecologically perfect, and little changed since it was formed 180 million years ago.

That leaves plenty of room to commune with nature, which is why bushwalking is the number one sport in the Blue Mountains. The region is the wilderness area closest to Sydney, and for vacationers who do not intend to travel to other regions of the country, a trip here for a bushwalk is an excellent way to sample the Aussie bush. If you've only a day to spare, Sydney Nature Tours takes small groups by train to the lower mountains, and accompanies them on a seven-mile guided hike that culminates in a picnic lunch at **Red Hands Cave** decorated by aboriginal artists hundreds of years ago. There's a swim in a rock pool on the way back; Tel: (02) 519-9360.

Bushwalks
There are some 100 separate and well-marked trails in the Blue Mountains. A map available at the Blue Mountains Tourist Authority at Echo Point in Katoomba is a must; Tel: (047) 82-0756. Most bushwalks are designed for those in average shape; few are longer than four hours in duration. The easiest walk is the 10- to 20-minute stroll from the tourist information office in Katoomba along **Echo Point** to the **Queen Elizabeth Lookout**, which provides an excellent view of the **Three Sisters**. An an-

cient aboriginal legend has it that these rock formations were formed when three sisters were turned to stone by a witch doctor because they wanted to marry men of a different tribe. Unfortunately, the witch doctor died before he thought to turn them back into people, and to this day no one has figured out how to undo his curse. Echo Point (so named for its impressive echo) is also the starting point for the one-and-a-half-hour round-trip trek down the 860-step **Grand Staircase** into Jamieson Valley.

The steps descend into a quiet glen of ferns, trees, flowers, and moss-covered rocks. For those with abundant energy to follow it, the trail winds around a cliff and comes out at Katoomba Falls, but hikers can stop before that and take a mountain-railway car back to the top. This **Scenic Railway**, a converted mine trolley that once carried coal miners to the now defunct mine gouged out of the cliff base, is a favorite (though hair-raising) trip of visitors to the Blue Mountains. Be aware that the last trip out of the mine is at 4:50 P.M. every day; to miss this means a long climb back up the cliff. More challenging walks are the three-and-a-half-hour trek along Federal Pass at Katoomba and the eight-hour hike along the Giant Staircase to the Ruined Castle, both rock formations. Again, these two bushwalks are designed for those in average shape; the time estimated for both is for round trips.

Scenic Drives

Numerous scenic drives through the mountains have been mapped out as well. Signs along the roads point them out and all are equally spectacular; just turn down any marked road for magnificent mountain views.

On many of the roads there are well-marked scenic lookout points, and none is less compelling than another. The limestone caves of **Jenolan**, on the western side of the mountains about 75 km (47 miles) past Katoomba, are one of the state's oldest attractions; nine caves are open for inspection. Accommodation here is available in the Tudor-style ▶ **Jenolan Caves House**, managed by the Peppers group.

Throughout the mountains are old country towns that date to the days in the last century when settlers made their way inland. Most picturesque is **Leura**, about 10 km (6 miles) east of Katoomba. Most of the buildings on the town's one main street date to the 1920s or earlier and have been classified as landmarks by the National Trust. The few shops on this short street sell antiques, crafts, and gifts.

DINING IN THE BLUE MOUNTAINS

There are many restaurants scattered about the Blue Mountains, but few are memorable. Most serve adequate food at moderate prices. In Katoomba, the **Clarendon**, 68 Lurline Street, serves good Aussie-style home cooking and turns itself into a dinner theater on Saturday nights. Nearby, **Steaks Down Under**, 122 Katoomba Street, lives up to its name.

Also worth a try are **18 Govett's Leap Road**, Blackheath (Tel: 047/877-4507), and **Table Manners**, 54 Waratah Street, Katoomba (Tel: 047/82-4465). The chef at **Darley's** restaurant, a Katoomba country house built around a century-old mansion called Lilianfels, built his following at one of Sydney's leading small restaurants. The **Leura Hotel** on Fitzroy Street serves lunch and dinner seven days a week and opens its garden bistro on warm days. **La Sala**, 128 The Mall in Leura, is a bistro-style restaurant with an Italian accent. Expect a splendid performance on the plate and at the table by co-owner and entertainer Reg Livermore.

The most enticing restaurant, though it doesn't necessarily serve the best food, is at the ▶ **Hydro Majestic Hotel** in the little town of Medlow Bath, a few miles west of Katoomba. The hotel stands on the edge of an escarpment above the Megalong Valley; views from the restaurant's bay windows are splendid. The 55-room hotel itself, which opened in 1904, has been renovated. It's a great spot to visit to understand what a major resort the Blue Mountains were for Sydneysiders 50 years ago.

STAYING IN THE BLUE MOUNTAINS

Most accommodations in the mountains are guesthouses or motels, with guesthouses being more appealing for an overnight stay. Some have fireplaces and cozy parlors and a restaurant, and rates are generally moderate. Accommodations are hard to come by on Saturday nights from June to August. Many establishments insist on a two-night reservation on weekends during this time, and offer special discounts on weekdays.

In Katoomba, the ▶ **Katoomba Mountains Lodge**, set in magnificent grounds, provides satisfactory lodging, as does the ten-room ▶ **Balmoral House**, set on a five-acre property at 196 Bathurst Road. The ▶ **Mountain Heritage Country House Retreat** here has Old World charm, a pool, a restaurant, a cocktail bar, and breathtaking views; ▶ **Lilianfels** is a new hotel at Echo Point that is well worth its expensive rates. Comfortable accommodation is available at the pleasant ▶ **Fairmont Resort** in Leura. ▶ **Cleo-**

patra Country Guesthouse in Blackheath combines good food, magnificent gardens, and accommodation; it has one apartment, two rooms with private baths, and two attic rooms with shared facilities. Cleopatra offers midweek and weekend packages combining accommodation and meals, or you can merely—if that's the word—dine here and estimate its towering reputation at prices on the high side of moderate. Bring your own wine, but be sure to book well in advance. Another quaint small guesthouse is ▶ Pegum's, on Honor Avenue in Lawson.

If you prefer to fend more for yourself, there is ▶ Jemby-Rinja Lodge at Blackheath, with six-bed cabins or pole-frame tree-houses for two tucked away in bushland. Bed linen may be rented. (Horticulture lovers might enjoy the cool country garden at Mount Tomah, 20 km/12 miles north of Lawson off Bells Line Road. The gardens of Mount Wilson, also off Bells Line Road, are well known for their autumn and spring displays; call the Glenbrook Tourist Association for more information; Tel: 047/39-6266.)

▶ Crystal Lodge is the only health resort in the Blue Mountains. The staff at this redone mansion in Katoomba indulges guests in beauty therapy, t'ai chi, and hypnosis and allows them to soak in herbal baths and bob in a flotation tank. They'll also plan bushwalks. Only vegetarian food is served in the restaurant.

More information about a day trip or longer jaunt to the Blue Mountains can be obtained in Sydney at the New South Wales Travel Centre, 44 Martin Place, Tel: (02) 231-4444; or by calling the Blue Mountains Tourist Authority on the Great Western Highway in Glenbrook; Tel: (047) 39-8013.

Broken Hill

Contrasting starkly with the fertile coastal strip of New South Wales, the state's far western district is much dryer and browner, and is rather forbidding. Its city, **Broken Hill**, grew out of the 1883 lucky strike of German-born boundary rider Charles Rasp, who detected what he thought were tin deposits on a ridge near the border with South Australia. It turned out to be silver and lead, part of an ore deposit claimed to be the world's biggest.

Rasp formed a syndicate, pegged out a sizable claim, and founded the Broken Hill Proprietary Company Limited (BHP), still Australia's biggest. Rasp's rich lode is far from exhausted, and mining continues here today, but without the company that started it; BHP ended its mining interests in the city of Broken Hill in 1939.

Unremarkable architecturally, Broken Hill is an interesting community, shaped by isolation (it is 1,170 km/727 miles by road from Sydney), the aridity of the surrounding countryside, and the Barrier Industrial Council, which made it a 100-percent union town. In the early days, most houses were built of corrugated iron, despite summer temperatures that often exceeded 100 degrees F. Temporary structures, these houses could be moved when mines closed and work beckoned elsewhere. Most, however, have proved permanent. The green of the city, so at odds with the surroundings, is the result of local conservation schemes and a dam on the Darling River, 70 miles away.

Despite a population of fewer than 30,000, Broken Hill has spawned a considerable artists' colony of generally mature traditionalists known as the Brushmen of the Bush. Their prolific output is reflected in the presence of many private art galleries here in addition to the municipal gallery, home to an elaborately crafted silver tree. The best known of the private galleries is **Pro Hart**, at 108 Wyman Street, which takes its name from the famous painter of folk themes, whose work is represented in major Australian galleries.

The Broken Hill Flying Doctor base at the Broken Hill Airport (Tel: 080/88-0777) uses the bush radio network to maintain contact with remote homesteads and keeps its aircraft ready for emergency takeoff. It is open for tours on weekdays at 10:30 A.M. and 3:30 P.M., and on weekends at 10:30 A.M. Children far from any local school get their lessons from the daily School of the Air, which also operates from the base. Visitors are welcome to call in and listen to the school or crosstalk between members of isolated country homesteads, who have formed firm friendships with people they have never met. Reservations must be made the day before at the Tourist Information Centre on the corner of Blende and Bromide streets; Tel: (080) 87-6077.

Several mines in the area are open for inspection. **Delprat's**, where production has been discontinued, is probably the most interesting; visitors are taken in a cage lift down 400 feet of mine shaft. For reservations, Tel: (080) 88-1604.

Silverton, 25 km (16 miles) northwest of Broken Hill, is a colorful town with a pub and jailhouse that are often used in films (such as *Mad Max II* and *A Town Like Alice*) and TV commercials. Camel-back tours of the town leave from outside the pub. After the tour you might drop in for a drink, a cup of homemade soup, and some Aussie humor with publicans Innes and Colin McLeod. Although Silverton was once a thriving mining town of 3,000 inhabitants, only a handful of people live here today.

Mootwingee National Park, 130 km (85 miles) northeast of Broken Hill, is starkly beautiful and has aboriginal sites rich in carvings, paintings, and caves. **Kinchega National Park**, about 110 km (68 miles) southeast of Broken Hill, encompasses the Menindee Lakes, home to multitudes of waterbirds. The park, as well as other out-of-town attractions such as **White Cliffs** opal mining town, are on the itinerary of Silver City Tours; Tel: (080) 87-6956. Crittendon Aviation delivers the mail and supplies to far-flung bush properties; you can join them, subject to space on the aircraft, most days of the week; Tel: (080) 88-5702. Information on the far western area of the state is available from the New South Wales Travel Centre, 44 Martin Place, Sydney; Tel: (02) 231-4444.

STAYING AND DINING IN BROKEN HILL

Although the possibilities here are limited, you're a long way from anywhere else. The ▶ **Old Willyama Motor Inn** has comfortable rooms, a pool and a spa, and an excellent room-service menu from its restaurant, Mr. Pickwick's. Casual counter meals are served in most of the town's pubs; try the **Palace** or the **Royal Exchange** for a quick bite. More formal dining can be enjoyed at the **Apollyon** in the Daydream Motel at 77 Argent Street; Tel: (080) 88-3033.

NORTH OF SYDNEY

There are also day-trip possibilities to the north of Sydney. For anyone with an interest in walking in natural bushland, the 40,000 acres of **Ku-ring-Gai Chase National Park**, between Middle Head and the yachtsmen's retreat Broken Bay, offers clean air, native flora, and small fauna. The Ku-ring-Gai Wildflower Garden is a good spot in spring to see native species such as flannel flowers and the waratah, New South Wales's emblem, in bloom. The National Parks and Wildlife Service's **Kalkarri Visitor Centre** here, which has its own native wildlife park, can get you started on a variety of signposted walks, and volunteer guides may be available to tell about the surroundings. For information on these bushwalks and directions how to get there, Tel: (02) 457-9853.

THE HAWKESBURY RIVER

The northern boundary of Ku-ring-Gai Chase National Park is formed by a maze of bays and inlets where the Hawkesbury River enters the Pacific Ocean at Broken Bay. The easternmost inlet, which forms the Palm Beach peninsula, is a yachting haven called **Pittwater**, which you explore by chartering a boat from **Pittwater Yacht Charter** at Lovett Bay, Church Point, at the southern end of the inlet; Tel: (02) 997-5344. Crews are available if you're not a sailor. To venture into Broken Bay, there are cruisers for hire from **Skipper-a-Clipper** in Akuna Bay, Tel: (02) 450-1888; or houseboats from **Holidays Afloat** at 65 Brooklyn Road, Brooklyn (northwest of Church Point); Tel: (02) 985-7368. If all this sounds too hands-on, there are two-, four-, or six-night cruises on the 60-cabin **Hawkesbury Explorer**; Tel: (02) 247-5458.

If time is short it's a good idea to hop the Palm Beach ferry for a quick circuit around Pittwater, from the wharf at **Palm Beach**; Tel: (02) 918-2747. Or, if you have a full day to spare, head for the Brooklyn wharf and join Australia's last riverboat postman as he delivers the mail and supplies; Tel: (02) 985-7566.

Your budget allowing, **Aquatic Air** has a treat in store with their seven-seater flying boat trip from Rose Bay near Sydney to Palm Beach; Tel: (02) 974-5966. There's a flight scheduled daily (A$100 round-trip), but on weekends they operate a shuttle service on demand. The 15-minute flight affords a fabulous gull's-eye-view of the city and northern beaches, and both Sydneysiders and visitors make use of the service to take lunch at one of Palm Beach's many informal restaurants (courtesy coach provided). Recommended eateries include the **Careel Bay Café**, Tel: (02) 918-8101, and **Beach Road Restaurant**, Tel: (02) 974-1159.

For a land-based exploration of the Hawkesbury River basin join **Hawkesbury 4WD Bush Treks** for half or full-day tours (Tel: 045/73-1280), or take a 4WD wilderness tour from **Shannon Park**, a farmstay on Sydney's northern extremity about an hour's drive from the city. They'll pick you up from city accommodations; Tel: (045) 75-0273.

The Hunter Valley

The Hunter Valley, three hours' drive north of Sydney beyond the mouth of the Hawkesbury, is one of the country's two major wine-producing areas, the other being South Australia's Barossa Valley (for which, see the Adelaide and South Australia chapter, below). In truth, only a small portion of the Hunter is given over to wine producing, but it was Australia's first established wine region, and for visitors the vineyards and wineries, some of which have been in business for a century or more, are all that matter. Among the most renowned of the wineries are Tyrrells, McWilliams Mount Pleasant, Lake's Folly, Lindeman's, Wyndham Estate, Rothbury Estate, Brokenwood, Richmond Grove, Draytons, Tullochs, and Oakvale.

The trip to the Hunter Valley is rather like a trip out of San Francisco to the wine-growing areas of Napa and Sonoma. Like those regions, the Hunter is rich in wineries that open their doors for tours, tastings, and purchasing. Hidden country inns and appealing restaurants round out the valley's allure for those who care to venture beyond Sydney for a weekend. The winery region is too scattered for walking; a car, bicycle, or tour is necessary (see Getting Around, below).

The valley's location between the Pacific Ocean and the Great Dividing Range provides the perfect Mediterranean climate for grape growing. Australians, like the Americans and unlike the French, name their wines by grape type (varietal), and in the Hunter several types can be relied on to produce excellent wines. For white wines, Hunter growers are famous for Sémillon and Chardonnay. The Sémillons produce a fine dry wine, while the Chardonnays yield a respectable white "Burgundy." For red wines, the best buys from the Hunter are Pinot Noir and Cabernet Sauvignon. The red "Bordeaux" produced from the Cabernet Sauvignon grapes grown in the Hunter are especially good, and some are being exported overseas. There are other good wine types produced in the Hunter Valley, but it's hard to go wrong with these four. Growers at each winery, however, are more than glad to comment on further options.

Cessnock is the main town in the vineyard region of the valley; most of the wineries open to the public are within a few miles of it. The **Hunter Valley Wine Society**, 4 Wollombi Road, has information and maps to the wineries and is open seven days a week.

The most famous producer in the Hunter Valley is **Tyrrells**, which is one of the few Australian wineries still operated by the original family; it has been in business for some 130 years at the same location on Broke Road. The family has to some degree resisted the advances of the high-tech world of mass production, still using wooden casks to mature their wine, and hand presses. Tyrrells is open 9:00 A.M. to 5:00 P.M. every day but Sunday.

McWilliams Mount Pleasant, another producer that has been in business for more than a century, is just outside Cessnock on Marrowbone Road. The McWilliams name is well respected for its quality Pinot Noir. Guided tours of the winery are conducted every day but Sunday. **Lake's Folly** is a relative newcomer to the Hunter, having opened for business in 1963, but it has already established itself as a top producer of both Chardonnay and Cabernet Sauvignon wines. The winery, on Branxton Road, is open weekdays. Two other popular wineries are **Lindeman's Winery** on Debeyers Road near Broke Road, and the smaller **Rothbury Estate** on Broke Road.

STAYING AND DINING IN THE HUNTER VALLEY

▶ **Casuarina Country Inn** and ▶ **Peppers Guest House** are among the top wine-region accommodations. The former is noted for the cooking of Swiss-born owner/chef Peter Meier, who is rated among the state's top cooks. Peppers Guest House won the 1991 National Tourism Award for being the best independent hotel in Australia. ▶ **Carriages Guest House**, in Pokolbin, shares similar standards and makes a point of its regional antique furniture. It organizes horse-drawn carriage tours of the wineries. ▶ **The Convent at Pepper Tree** was indeed once a convent, transported from Coonamble, New South Wales, and rebuilt at Pokolbin as the guest house component of an attractive complex that includes a winery as well as **Robert's** restaurant, specializing in cuisine *au feu de bois,* or cooked over a stove fuelled by wood and vine clippings.

Several other restaurants in the vineyard region can also be recommended. **Blaxlands** and **Arnold's**, adjacent restaurants opposite Rothbury Estate on Broke Road, serve modern Australian cuisine at moderate prices, about A$75 for two without wine. **Pokolbin Cellars**, located in the Hungerford Hill Wine Village on Broke Road, is another winery open to the public for tours, tastings, and purchasing. Its restaurant offers moderately priced French meals. The entire Hungerford Hill Wine Village complex, which also features a quaint antiques shop, is worth a visit. Drive back into Cessnock to find restaurants that serve non-French, less expensive meals.

Like its Sonoma counterpart, and like wine-producing regions in France, the Hunter Valley is a popular haunt for **hot-air ballooning**. Balloon Aloft operates its hot-air machines from North Rothbury and sends its balloons up in the early morning for scenic flights over the valley; Tel: (049) 38-1955 or (008) 02-8568.

More information about the Hunter Valley is available at the Travel Centre of New South Wales in Sydney (Tel: 02/231-4444) or from the Cessnock Tourist Information Centre (Tel: 049/90-4477). The staff will be happy to map out the best route to Cessnock.

CANBERRA

Locating a nation's capital away from its established major cities is an understandable compromise, and few locations could have been more neutral in concept than that of Canberra, seat of Australia's federal government. When the Australian colonies defused their rivalries sufficiently to agree to federation, counterclaims by Sydney and Melbourne to be the federal capital prompted wiser heads to seek a neutral site. When federation became a fact on January 1, 1901, the choice fell on a spot about midway between the two contending cities, a sheep-farming region with an aboriginal name roughly translating as "meeting place." What could be more suitable?

In 1908 an international competition for an appropriate design plan for the new capital—to be called Canberra—was won by Chicago architect Walter Burley Griffin. He visualized a city arranged in concentric circles set around a parliament house and with an artificial lake and much open space and parkland. The city's realization was slow in coming: Burley Griffin died in 1937, and it was not until 1960 that Canberra began to take its present form. From a government gulag of civil servants, diplomats, politicians, and disgruntled journalists, it grew to acquire considerable culture and some mildly invigorating nightlife.

Completion of a few quality hotels, with their attendant restaurants and cocktail bars, helped, and the city now boasts 250 restaurants and 70 clubs, discos, concert halls, and theaters. It remains a green, clean city, and it finally got its lake, named after Burley Griffin, which effectively divides the city in two.

Canberra is an easy trip by car, bus, plane, or train from Sydney. A car is the best idea, because Canberra sprawls

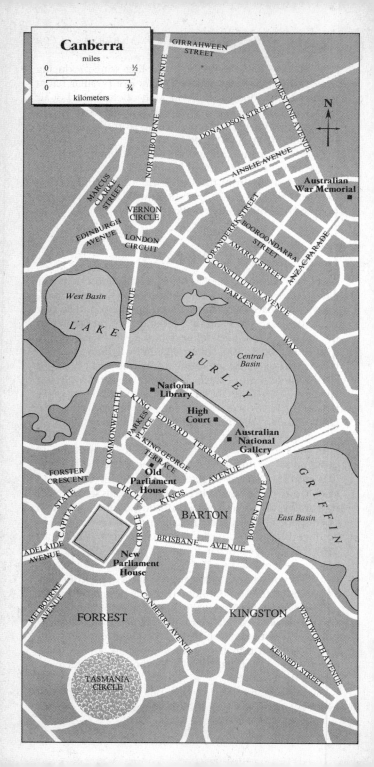

Canberra

miles

0		½

0		¾

kilometers

N

GIRRAHWEEN STREET

NORTHBOURNE AVENUE

LIMESTONE AVENUE

DONALDSON STREET

AINSLIE AVENUE

MARCUS CLARKE STREET

EDINBURGH AVENUE

VERNON CIRCLE

LONDON CIRCUIT

Australian War Memorial ■

CORANDERRK STREET

BOOROONDARRA STREET

AMAROO STREET

ANZAC PARADE

CONSTITUTION AVENUE

PARKES WAY

West Basin

L A K E

B U R L E Y

Central Basin

AVENUE

■ **National Library**

High Court ■

COMMONWEALTH AVENUE

KING EDWARD TERRACE

PARKES PLACE

KING GEORGE TERRACE

Australian National Gallery ■

FORSTER CRESCENT

■ TERRACE
Old Parliament House

STATE CIRCLE

CAPITAL CIRCLE

KINGS AVENUE

BARTON

BOWEN DRIVE

G R I F F I N

East Basin

New Parliament House

BRISBANE AVENUE

ADELAIDE AVENUE

MELBOURNE AVENUE

FORREST

CANBERRA AVENUE

KINGSTON

WENTWORTH AVENUE

KENNEDY STREET

TASMANIA CIRCLE

and it is often too cold, too hot, or too wet to walk around without handy transportation. There are city buses and cabs.

The new **Parliament House** on Capitol Hill at the end of Commonwealth Avenue, opened to celebrate Australia's Bicentennial in 1988, was designed by a New York architectural firm that won an international competition, the same way Burley Griffin got the job to design the old Parliament House. Its controversial design, an unimposing bunkerlike profile beneath a towering flagpole, creates mixed reactions, but members of its twin chambers find it heaven compared with the original Parliament House, which they had long outgrown.

The spacious, echoing halls are lined with paintings of former members of parliament, and anyone is welcome to spend a few minutes in the public galleries of the House of Representatives or the Senate chamber. The sessions are open to the public almost every day of the year.

The **Australian War Memorial** at the northeastern end of Anzac Parade forms the northern end of a line of sight that extends from New Parliament House, up Federation Mall, past Old Parliament House, and across the lake and Anzac Gardens. Opened during World War II, it chronicles the nation's participation in all its wars from colonial campaigns in Africa up to Vietnam. Of particular interest are the Gallipoli exhibition, which retells the story of Australia's most famous and deadly World War I conflict, and a Japanese submarine, captured in Sydney Harbour during World War II. **Blundell's Cottage**, the preserved homestead of the original sheep farm purchased as the site of Australia's first federal capitol, is at the southern end of Anzac Parade.

On the opposite side of the lake, the **Australian National Gallery**, on King Edward Terrace next door to the High Court, is perhaps the most appealing exhibit for non-Australians. Displayed here is a superb collection of paintings by Australian artists and other works by artists from around the world (including Jackson Pollock's *Blue Poles*). The gallery is particularly strong in post–World War II artists. Also on King Edward Terrace, the **National Library** stages significant exhibitions on aspects of Australian life, based on historic documents and material from its archives. On McCoy Circuit in Acton, a five-minute drive west of the city center, the **National Film and Sound Archive** traces the development of Australia's considerable reputation in filmmaking. The adjacent **National Sci-**

ence Centre displays robotic dinosaurs and hands-on scientific exhibits. The Canberra Explorer Bus visits all of the above destinations, departing from the Jolimont Tourist Centre, 67 Northbourne Avenue.

STAYING AND DINING IN CANBERRA

Most accommodations in the city fall into the motel category, but there are some full-service hotels: the ▶ Capital Parkroyal, ▶ Lakeside International, and ▶ The Pavilion. (Accommodations are generally cheaper on the weekends.) The most exclusive—and charming—hotel in the city is the ▶ Hyatt Canberra. A magnificently restored building not far from the new Parliament House, the Hyatt is notable for the harmonious marriage of one of the capital's oldest hostelries with a sympathetically executed extension maintaining Art Deco touches; the addition of the new building has created 250 deluxe rooms. The archival pictures in the Speakers Bar give an insight into early Canberra, and many people enjoy relaxing in its lounges for an afternoon as they sip drinks or coffee. Be aware, however, that the Hyatt has prices to match its charm.

Several restaurants in Canberra are noteworthy. The Oak Room at the Hyatt Hotel Canberra is a place of luxurious formality and impressive, if expensive, food; reservations are essential; Tel: (06) 270-1234. The Charcoal Restaurant, at 61 London Circuit in the city center, serves thick steaks, has a good Australian wine list, and accepts major credit cards; Tel: (06) 248-8015. Canberra's young professionals hang out at the Fringe Benefits Brasserie, 54 Marcus Clarke Street. The restaurant is so named because it is a fairly typical expense-account establishment. It, too, serves grilled steaks and chops and is happy to accept most credit cards; Tel: (06) 247-4042. For upmarket Chinese food downtown, Ruby, at 18 Woolley Street in Dickson (about a 10-minute drive north of the city center; Tel: 06/249-8849), serves Cantonese seafood, while The Great Wall, at 133 Marcus Clarke Street (Tel: 06/247-5423), specializes in the steamed dishes of Shanghai.

For a reasonably priced lunch with atmosphere, Mirrabook in the National Art Gallery's sculpture garden offers a casual outdoor setting enlivened with Japanese-designed fog sculpture billowing over a small, reedy artificial lake. The mist is man-made, but the effect of this extraordinary exhibit, ethereal. It is closed between the June long weekend and early October; Tel: (06) 273-2836. Young people will enjoy a late-night drink at **Graphix Brasserie** on Jardine Street in the Kingston shopping center, a few minutes from Parliament House.

Complete tourist information can be obtained from the Sydney office of the Canberra Tourist Bureau at Wingello House, 1–12 Angel Place, Sydney; Tel: (02) 233-3666. Otherwise, once in the capital, visitors should stop at the Canberra Tourist Bureau in Jolimont Centre, Northbourne Avenue, for a map and other information about the city; Tel: (06) 245-6431.

GETTING AROUND

The Blue Mountains

There are about a dozen trains a day between Sydney's Central Station and Katoomba in the Blue Mountains, but it's probably a good idea to rent a car in Sydney to explore the mountains fully. The drive from city to mountains is no more than 100 km (60 miles). If you do want to rent a car in Katoomba try Cales, at 60 Wilson Street; Tel: (047) 82-2917.

The Blue Mountains Adventure Company leads cycling tours to out-of-the-way places via 21-speed mountain bikes. You'll need to be reasonably fit to join them; Tel: (047) 82-1271 or (018) 210-743.

Horseback riding is also popular in the Valley; Werriberri Trail Rides offer rides by the hour, day, and overnight with tent or pub accommodation and mounts to suit all levels of experience; Tel: (047) 87-9171. The Explorer Bus tours Katoomba and Leura's highlights, including Echo Point, Leura Cascades, Everglades Gardens, the Scenic Railway, and several good bushwalk starting points. Tours begin at Katoomba Railway Station; Tel: (047) 82-1866 (weekends and public holidays only). The Blue Mountains Tourist Authority has a pamphlet detailing scenic drives throughout the mountains and foothills area; ask for it at their Echo Point information center.

The Hunter Valley Region

Trains also run between Sydney and Newcastle and Cessnock near the Hunter Valley wine region. Again, a car is needed to get around to the various wineries and vineyards, so it is smarter to rent a car in Sydney and make the three-hour drive up the Pacific coast to the Hunter Valley. If you don't care to drive that distance, there are car-rental agencies in Newcastle.

Bikes may be rented from the Pokolbin Village Guest

House and the Pokolbin Resort. Top Hat Tours provides chauffeur-driven tours of the wineries; Tel: (049) 90-1699. Hunter Vineyard Tours (Tel: 049/91-1659) or Hunter Valley Four-Wheel Drive Tours (Tel: 049/38-5031) operate half- or full-day tours of the region. You may rent a car at Cessnock Auto Port, 188 Vincent Street, Cessnock, Tel: (049) 90-1278; or Hunter Valley U-Drive, 329 Maitland Road, Cessnock, Tel: (049) 90-4951.

Canberra

There are several flights daily from Sydney Airport to Canberra operated by Ansett Airlines, Australian Airlines, and Eastwest Airlines. A car can be rented at the Canberra Airport. If you prefer, several trains a day leave Sydney Central Station for Canberra. The quickest is the Canberra XPT, Australia's fastest train, which operates twice daily in both directions. The trip takes about five hours and costs under A$50 one way in first class and A$33 one way in economy. There is also daily express bus service between Sydney and Canberra that costs about A$30 one way. The trip takes four and a half hours.

A comprehensive public transportation network is in place for getting around the rest of New South Wales. From Sydney, trains, buses, and planes travel to most cities and population centers in the state. Trains and buses are often slow because, once out in the country, they tend to stop at every wide place in the road. However, they provide close-up views of rural Australia and might be considered by travellers who aren't in a hurry.

If you have limited vacation time you can get out into the country with Eastwest Airlines, which flies from Sydney Airport to such outposts as Dubbo; Hazelton Airlines services Broken Hill. Schedules make it possible to turn visits to these country towns into day trips.

Travel agents can book most domestic transportation in Australia before your trip, but there is usually no problem, especially on trains, buying tickets on the day you're travelling.

ACCOMMODATIONS REFERENCE

The rates given here are projections *for 1994. Where a range of rates is given, the lower figure is the low-season rate, the higher figure the high-season rate. Unless otherwise indicated, rates are for double room, double occupancy. As prices are subject to change, always double-check before booking.*

▶ **Balmoral House.** 196 Bathurst Road, **Katoomba,** N.S.W. 2780. Tel: (047) 82-2264. A$130–A$200.

▶ **Capital Parkroyal.** 7 Binara Street, **Canberra,** A.C.T. 2601. Tel: (06) 247-8999; in U.S., (800) 835-7742; in California, (800) 252-2155; in Canada, (800) 251-2166; Fax: (06) 257-4903. A$120–A$185.

▶ **Carriages Guest House.** Halls Road, **Pokolbin,** N.S.W. 2320. Tel: (049) 98-7591. A$110–A$150.

▶ **Casuarina Country Inn.** Hermitage Road, **Pokolbin,** N.S.W. 2320. Tel: (049) 98-7888; Fax: (049) 98-7692. A$130–A$180.

▶ **Cleopatra Country Guesthouse.** Cleopatra Avenue, **Blackheath,** N.S.W. 2780. Tel: (047) 87-8456; Fax: (047) 87-6092. A$330–A$450.

▶ **The Convent at Pepper Tree.** Halls Road, **Pokolbin,** N.S.W. 2320. Tel: (049) 98-7764; Fax: (049) 98-7323. A$190–A$295.

▶ **Crystal Lodge.** 19 Abbotsford Road, **Katoomba,** N.S.W. 2780. Tel: (047) 82-5122. A$160–A$170.

▶ **Fairmont Resort.** 1 Sublime Point Road, **Leura,** N.S.W. 2780. Tel: (047) 82-5222; in U.S., (402) 398-3200; Fax: (047) 84-1685. A$180–A$233.

▶ **Hyatt Canberra.** Commonwealth Avenue, **Yarralumla,** A.C.T. 2602. Tel: (06) 270-1234; Fax: (06) 281-5998; in U.S. and Canada, (800) 233-1234. A$145 (if booked through A.C.T. Tourism Commission; Tel: 06/245-6464). A$290.

▶ **Hydro Majestic Hotel.** Great Western Highway, **Medlow Bath,** N.S.W. Tel: (047) 88-1002; Fax: (047) 88-1063. A$128–A$220.

▶ **Jemby-Rinja Lodge.** 336 Evans Lookout Road, **Blackheath,** N.S.W. 2785. Tel: (047) 87-7622; Fax: (047) 87-6230. A$90–A$98.

▶ **Jenolan Caves House.** Jenolan, N.S.W. 2790. Tel: (063) 59-3304; Fax: (063) 59-3227. A$88–A$253.

▶ **Katoomba Mountains Lodge.** Lurline Street, **Katoomba,** N.S.W. 2780. Tel: (047) 82-3933. A$42–A$74.

▶ **Lakeside International.** London Circuit, **Canberra,** A.C.T. 2601. Tel: (06) 247-6244; Fax: (06) 257-3071; in U.S., (800) 44-UTELL; in Canada, (800) 387-8842. A$115–A$330.

▶ **Lilianfels.** Blue Mountains, Lilianfels Avenue, **Katoomba,** N.S.W. 2780. Tel: (047) 80-1200; Fax: (047) 80-1300. A$215–A$285.

▶ **Mountain Heritage Country House Retreat.** Lovel Street, **Katoomba,** N.S.W. 2780. Tel: (047) 82-2155; Fax: (047) 82-5323. A$135–A$165.

▶ **Old Willyama Motor Inn,** 30 Iodide Street, **Broken**

Hill, N.S.W. 2880. Tel: (080) 88-3355; Fax: (080) 88-3956. A$80.

▶ **The Pavilion.** Canberra Avenue and National Circuit, **Canberra**, A.C.T. 2063. Tel: (06) 295-3144; Fax: (02) 295-3325; in U.S., (800) 783-9929. A$185 weeknights; A$145.

▶ **Pegum's.** Honor Avenue, **Lawson**, N.S.W. 2780. Tel: (047) 59-1844; Fax: (047) 59-2086. A$175–A$220, breakfast and dinner included.

▶ **Peppers Guest House.** Ekert Road, **Pokolbin**, N.S.W. 2321. Tel: (049) 98-7596; Fax: (049) 98-7739. A$160–A$291.

QUEENSLAND
THE GREAT BARRIER REEF AND OUTBACK

By Len Rutledge

Len Rutledge, a resident of Queensland for more than 20 years, has run his own newspaper in Cairns and produced the longest-running syndicated travel column in Australia. He publishes a tourism magazine in Townsville and writes for publications throughout the Pacific area and Europe. He is the author of several guidebooks.

Queensland, the "Sunshine State," attracts more travellers than anywhere else in Australia, except for Sydney, the major gateway to the country. First and foremost in Queensland, of course, is the Great Barrier Reef and its resorts. Also contributing to the state's appeal are the incredibly good weather, the great and uncrowded beaches, and the interesting fauna and flora. The Outback areas of Northern Queensland and such remote places as Cooktown add even more to the appeal of Queensland.

Queensland covers an immense geographical area. In the south, near the coast, is the city of Brisbane. South of Brisbane is the Gold Coast; north of the city is the Sunshine Coast. North of the Sunshine Coast is the southern end of the Great Barrier Reef; then, continuing north, comes the Central Great Barrier Reef area, whose most important city is Townsville. In the coverage below, we make a detour at Townsville to explore the Outback in this region, then return to the coast, going up to the Northern Great Barrier Reef area around the city of Cairns, where, again, there's a detour into the Outback. Finally, we reach the Cape York Peninsula—the northern

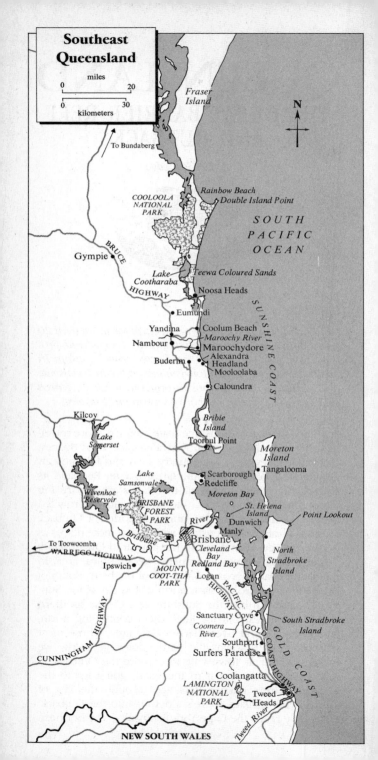

tip of Queensland and the closest point in Australia to Papua New Guinea.

MAJOR INTEREST IN THE BRISBANE AREA

Brisbane
Queen Street Mall
Queensland Cultural Centre
Mount Coot-tha and Botanic Gardens and
     Planetarium
Lone Pine Koala Sanctuary

Gold Coast
The surf beaches
Downtown Surfers Paradise
Sea World, Dreamworld, and W. B. Movie World
     amusement parks
Currumbin Sanctuary

Sunshine Coast
The surf beaches
Noosa Heads
Small inland towns
Fraser Island (spectacular sand island)

MAJOR INTEREST ON THE GREAT BARRIER REEF

Coral viewing
Marine life
Diving
Staying on the reef

MAJOR INTEREST IN
THE SOUTHERN REEF REGION

Island resorts
Rockhampton Victorian cityscapes
Whale-watching cruises
Capricorn Coast's quiet beaches
Inland gem fields and cattle country

MAJOR INTEREST IN
THE CENTRAL REEF REGION

Townsville
Great Barrier Reef Wonderland
Sunshine
Flinders Mall and Flinders Street East for shopping

Around Townsville
Magnetic Island
Whitsunday and other island resorts
Sailing the Whitsundays
Deep-sea fishing
Mission Beach (for peace and tranquillity)
Charters Towers and the Outback

MAJOR INTEREST IN
THE NORTHERN REEF REGION

Cairns
Galleries for aboriginal and New Guinean art
Seafood and tropical fruit

Around Cairns
Trips to the Great Barrier Reef
The Marlin Coast beaches
Green and Fitzroy islands
Kuranda Railway and Village
Port Douglas
Cooktown for frontier town atmosphere
Scuba-diving and Marlin fishing

Cape York
Wilderness adventure

BRISBANE, THE GOLD COAST, AND THE SUNSHINE COAST

Queenslanders are different from other Australians. You notice it as soon as you cross the border, but the farther north or west you go the more obvious it becomes. Maybe the tropical heat slows people down; perhaps the magnificent beaches make people less interested in the office; or it could be that they are all slightly mad to want to live in a state that others say is years behind the rest of Australia.

Some derogatorily call Queensland the "deep north," others think of it as paradise—but there's no denying that Queensland has become Australia's vacation playground.

Brisbane is Queensland's capital and the state's largest city. The nearby Gold Coast is the major holiday center, luring about three million visitors each year. The Sunshine Coast just up the shore, however, is emerging as a major competitor. Together, these three areas of southeast Queensland constitute the third-largest population center in Australia.

BRISBANE

Brisbane is the hardest Australian city to characterize. This, the third-largest city in the country, is still labeled by many as a large country town (but some people say the same about Melbourne). Others see it as nothing more than a gateway to Queensland's other attractions. They are wrong; Brisbane today is a modern subtropical city with an appealing blend of old and new, a thriving commercial heart, and a lifestyle and climate envied by inhabitants of Australia's other major cities.

The telephone area code for Brisbane is 07.

The City Center

The center of Brisbane is bordered on two sides by the loops of the Brisbane River, whose banks are slowly being developed to include parks and walkways that make for a pleasant contrast to the generally undistinguished high-rise buildings that form the central core. The city is set in undulating countryside about 20 miles upriver from Moreton Bay. Town planning was not high on political leaders' priority lists until fairly recently, so much of the suburban area is a hodgepodge of development, lacking in broad thoroughfares and other amenities. Even in the city center on the river's north side the main streets are too narrow, and the Brisbane City Council seems to be undecided as to whether to carry on with further downtown freeway development or to encourage a traffic-free area. In the past it's done both, so a long stretch of riverbank is dominated by an elevated freeway that leads commuters to midtown traffic chaos.

But this doesn't mean that central Brisbane is entirely unattractive. The **Queen Street Mall**, which converted Queen Street into a pedestrian walkway, has been nicely developed and recently extended to three blocks. Downtown remains a major shopping area, best explored by walking. Start at the huge Myer Shopping Centre on the

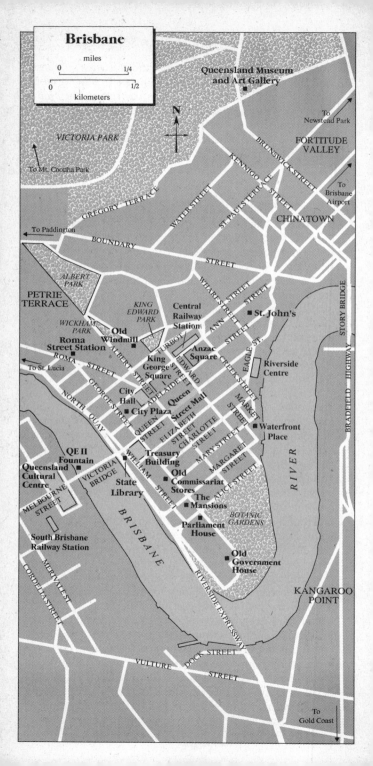

Queen Street Mall, then walk northeast along the mall. Two blocks away on Ann Street, next to St. John's Cathedral, is the **Deanery**, the site of the proclamation in 1859 declaring Queensland a separate colony from New South Wales. Close by is Anzac Square, with its eternal flame of remembrance of Australian troops killed during World War I, just opposite the Central Railway Station.

Next you might walk through King Edward Park to the **Old Windmill** and Wickham Park. The Old Windmill, originally used to grind grain, dates from 1829, making it one of the city's oldest buildings. South of the Old Windmill is King George Square and the Neoclassical City Hall. Take time to visit **City Hall** and use the elevator to reach the lookout area at the top of the clock tower. Try to avoid being there on the hour; the clock chime can be deafening. While in the building visit the **City Hall Art Gallery and Museum** to see some interesting items from Brisbane's recent and more distant past; Tel: 225-4355. Now walk via City Plaza shopping center to the Italian Renaissance–style Treasury Building at Queen and George streets, currently being transformed into Brisbane's first casino.

George and William streets contain numerous government offices, including the state's **Parliament House** (1868) and the **Old Government House** (1862). Just opposite here, the **Botanic Gardens** provide 45 pleasant acres for strolling and relaxing.

A National Trust "Historic Walks" brochure will throw more light on the sites of historical interest in the city. It's available from Old Government House, some hotels, and other visitor information centers. General city information is available from a kiosk in the Queen Street Mall, near the Hilton International Brisbane hotel; Tel: 229-5918.

If you do not want to see Brisbane on foot, the Brisbane City Council offers a Citysights Tour on an open, trolley-style bus that allows you to stop off at about 20 locations and reboard a later bus; Tel: 225-4444. Sunstate Day Tours has tours covering Brisbane, the Gold Coast, and the Sunshine Coast; Tel: 236-3355. Superior Tours has limousine service for that extra-special tour; Tel: 368-3857; Fax: 368-3287.

The best views of Brisbane can be seen from the *Kookaburra Queen II,* a beautiful paddle steamer, which departs from the Pier at Waterfront Place and offers morning tea, lunch, and dinner cruises; Tel: 221-1300.

The city provides plenty of shopping opportunities.

The **Myer Centre** on the Queen Street Mall, for example, is one of Australia's largest city-center shopping developments. **Queensland Aboriginal Creations** at 135 George Street is a good place for original handicrafts and artifacts; **M. E. Humfress and Co.** at 26 Market Street has excellent fur, leather, and sheepskin goods; and the **Proud Australian** in The Pavilion, Queen Street Mall, has a particularly wide range of Australian-made gifts.

For those with more expensive tastes, the **Town Gallery** on Queen Street has a good collection of art by distinguished Australian artists; **The Treasure House** in the Myer Center; and **The Rock Shop** at 193 Adelaide Street offers excellent Australian opals and other gems.

DINING AND NIGHTLIFE IN BRISBANE

Brisbane doesn't boast such renowned restaurants as do Melbourne, Sydney, and Adelaide, but the city does have several good places to eat. Of the hotel restaurants, **Denisons** at the Sheraton, with its Queensland-influenced cuisine, historic **Siggi's** at the Heritage, **Victoria's** at the Hilton, and **Eight Plates** at the Brisbane City Travelodge are all excellent.

Allegro in Central Station Plaza serves good food accompanied by live classical music. It is not open Sundays; Tel: 229-5550. **Pier Nine Seafood Restaurant** (Tel: 229-2194) on Eagle Street and **Michael's Riverside** (Tel: 832-5522) at the Riverside Centre (a shopping and office complex on Eagle Street) both provide sophisticated dining overlooking the Brisbane River. For something a little more relaxed, try the courtyard of **Faces** (Tel: 369-0039), a B.Y.O. establishment with European food indoors or alfresco on Given Terrace, Paddington (2 km/1¼ miles northwest of the city), or **Jimmys on the Mall** in the Queen Street Mall for good seafood in a casual atmosphere.

Seafood is excellent everywhere in Queensland, but many of the names on the menu will appear strange to non-Australians. Shrimps are known as banana prawns, while Moreton Bay bugs are a type of bay lobster. Among the unusual species offered are barramundi, a delicious perch; coral trout and coral cod from the Great Barrier Reef; and mud crab or sand crab.

Cat's Tango on Hawken Drive in St. Lucia (5 km/3 miles southwest of the city center) offers impromptu entertainment, including belly dancers, palm readers, and gypsy violinists, together with good food and friendly service; Tel: 371-1452. **Crazies Comedy Restaurant** on Caxton

Street, Petrie Terrace, invites you to an outrageous night of entertainment where you often become part of the comedy. It's bizarre but fun.

For action into the early morning hours, the **Chill Bar** on Mary Street, the **Jazz and Blues Bar** at the Brisbane City Travelodge, and **Some Place Else** at the Sheraton are all satisfactory. For more contact with the locals try **Rosie's Tavern** (Tel: 229-4916) on Edward Street; **Fridays** (Tel: 832-2122) at the Riverside Centre on Eagle Street, with three restaurants, four bars, and a nightclub featuring live music seven nights a week; or **The Underground** (Tel: 236-1511) on Petrie Terrace, with a deejay and the latest hits from Wednesday to Sunday and live music in the cocktail bar on Fridays, Saturdays, and Sundays.

The **Warana Festival**, Brisbane's annual fun and culture fest, takes place for two weeks every September. There is a parade through city streets and special theatrical, cultural, and sporting events throughout the city and suburbs. For further Festival information, Tel: 846-2333.

STAYING IN BRISBANE

The ▶ **Hilton International Brisbane**, rises 25 stories above the Wintergarden Shopping Centre on Elizabeth Street. The marble lobby on the fourth floor has the tallest atrium in Australia, and the hotel offers several bars and restaurants, a pool, gymnasium, health club, sauna, spa, and tennis court. One of Brisbane's best hotels, the ▶ **Sheraton Brisbane Hotel & Towers** has a car entrance on Turbot Street and a pedestrian entrance on Anzac Square. All 440 rooms have nice city views, and there is an understated elegance about the whole operation. The reputable ▶ **Mayfair Crest International Hotel** is a long-time favorite with plenty of facilities and an excellent location on King George Square. Right next to Waterfront Place is Brisbane's newest luxury hotel, the ▶ **Heritage**. The riverfront location is appealing and the hotel's decor, particularly in public areas, is rich and sophisticated. You may be able to get an attractive room rate before word spreads and occupancy climbs.

Southside

The south bank of the Brisbane River is an area in transition. The huge **Queensland Cultural Centre** is a superb permanent facility, while much of the remaining riverbank has been transformed into **South Bank Parklands**, a dining and recreation area with much appeal. Access from the city center is via Victoria Bridge from the Queen Street Mall or by train to South Brisbane Station.

The Cultural Centre has several components. The **Queensland Art Gallery** houses a wide-ranging Australian and European collection that includes classical and contemporary pieces; the **Performing Arts Complex** comprises a series of auditoriums and other facilities for classical and popular performing arts and exhibitions; the **Queensland Museum** has displays emphasizing the natural, human, and technological history of Queensland. Two cafés at the Centre, the bistro-style **Lyrebird Restaurant** and the delightful **Fountain Room**, provide good dining options. The complex has been completed with the opening of the **State Library**. Guided tours are available daily at 10:00 A.M., noon, and 2:00 P.M.; admission for adults costs A$5. For more information, Tel: 840-7830.

Not far from the Cultural Centre on Melbourne Street is **Squirrels**, a charming restaurant serving vegetarian cuisine, while the **Cordelia Street Antique and Art Centre**, located in an old church, features some of the best antiques in Brisbane and is open Wednesday to Sunday; Tel: 844-8514.

Fortitude Valley and Newstead

The Fortitude Valley area immediately north of the central city once rivaled downtown as a shopping district and for some time was the major nightlife area. Today there are a few department stores here, a multistory market, and a renovated Chinatown with some good restaurants (in the Chinatown Mall, the **Emperor's Palace** and the **Golden Palace** offer reasonable prices and authentic food). The city's exhibition grounds here spring to life for the Brisbane Show, a regional fair held for one week each August. There is still nightlife, although some of it borders on the seedy.

For shopping in Fortitude Valley there is **The Potters' Gallery** on Brunswick Street for unusual quality pieces by local and visiting artists (open Wednesday to Sunday). **McWhirters Marketplace** on Brunswick Street is a huge, three-level complex of markets, food outlets, shops, and artists' studios and workshops.

Newstead Park, a pleasant and historic riverside area, is just a little farther north of Fortitude Valley. Newstead House here, built in 1846, is the oldest home in Brisbane. On Chester Street the beautiful and equally historic **Rose-ville Restaurant** serves lunch and tea Tuesday to Friday and dinner Tuesday to Saturday. Newstead's relaxed **Breakfast Creek Boardwalk Tourist Complex** probably has Bris-bane's best seafood. The neighborhood also offers other dining options as well as shops selling books, antiques, and arts and crafts. Try the **Breakfast Creek Wharf Seafood Restaurant** (Tel: 252-2451) for freshly prepared seafood at reasonable prices. The nearby **Breakfast Creek Hotel** is a real Brisbane institution, a public bar where beer is served from wooden kegs, with great steaks and a garden for eating and drinking.

Around Brisbane

Mount Coot-tha, a little less than 8 km (5 miles) west of the city center and the highest point in the suburban area, has many hiking trails, lookouts, and facilities. The **Sum-mit Restaurant** at the lookout has good food and affords a dazzling view at night; Tel: 369-9922. Around the foothills are the **Mount Coot-tha Botanic Gardens** and the **Sir Thomas Brisbane Planetarium**, which together have de-veloped into one of Brisbane's most popular attractions. Bus 39 departs for Mount Coot-tha from Ann Street (near Albert Street in Brisbane) hourly from around 9:00 A.M. until 5:00 P.M. The Gardens have a large collection of native Australian plants and a superb tropical display dome in which tropical plants grow all year. There is also an excellent Japanese garden. The Planetarium is Austra-lia's largest.

Mount Coot-tha is part of the **Brisbane Forest Park**, which comprises 65,000 acres of natural bushland con-taining deep gorges, majestic tree ferns, forest, and small villages. There is a wildlife display area, restaurant, crafts shop, and information center, all at park headquarters, 60 Mount Nebo Road. Bush Ranger Tours has a four-hour night tour—giving you the chance to see nocturnal animals—every Friday, and morning tours on Saturdays and Sundays; Tel: 300-5381.

At the **Lone Pine Koala Sanctuary**, 11 km (7 miles) southwest of the city center, you can cuddle koalas, hand-feed kangaroos, and watch wombats, emus, and platypuses. The sanctuary has developed into a major attraction for overseas visitors, who will have limited opportunities to see these animals in the wild. The koala colony is claimed to be the largest in the world. The best way to get there is with Koala Cruises, whose boat departs from North Quay at 1:00 P.M. every day; Tel: 229-7055, or with Mirimar Cruises, whose boat departs at 10:30 A.M.; Tel: 221-0300.

The **Australian Woolshed** on Samford Road in Ferny Hills (12 km/7½ miles northwest of the city) offers sheepshearing displays and ram parades at 11:00 A.M. and 2:00 P.M. daily; Tel: 351-5366. The **Early Street Historic Village** in Norman Park (6 km/3½ miles east of the city) is a collection of buildings from Queensland's early days set in an attractive environment; Tel: 398-6866.

Among the **Moreton Bay Islands** east of Brisbane, **North Stradbroke Island** has good beaches, dramatic headlands, and freshwater lakes. Car ferries run from either Cleveland or Redland Bay (20 km/12 miles southeast of Brisbane) to Dunwich on the island approximately every hour. There are various accommodations on the island, with the ▶ **Anchorage Village Beach Resort** probably the best choice.

St. Helena Island is a tiny national park where you can see the ruins of St. Helena prison, which operated on the island from 1867 until 1932 and was one of Queensland's harshest penal settlements. Day trips operate from the Breakfast Creek area just north of Newstead in Brisbane on Saturdays and Sundays and from Manly (25 minutes east of the city by train) daily; Tel: 393-3726.

On the western side of largish **Moreton Island** is the ▶ **Tangalooma Moreton Island Resort**, once an old whaling station. Accommodation at the resort, in low-rise Mediterranean-style lodges with balconies and kitchens, is good, but many visitors prefer merely to take the day trip from Brisbane. The resort catamaran leaves Pinkenba near the mouth of the Brisbane River at 9:30 A.M. Tuesday through Friday and at 9:00 A.M. Saturdays and Sundays. Tel: 268-6333 for information on free bus connections to Pinkenba from Brisbane. You can also reach Bulwer on the northern end of the island by passenger and vehicular ferry from the Scarborough Boat Harbour at the northern end of the Redcliffe Peninsula.

Bribie Island, one hour north of Brisbane by bus, is reached by a bridge from mainland Toorbul Point to the southern end of the island. Upwards of 8,000 people call this island, with its good surfing and calm channel toward the mainland, home.

THE GOLD COAST

The Gold Coast's extensive surf beach and its many months of sunshine would be enough to pull many tourists to the area. Of course, that's how it all began, but the attractions have increased to such an extent that for many visitors the beach hardly matters. In its place are shopping, dining, nightclubbing, golfing, boating, and gambling. Most of these man-made attractions reflect the massive growth that has transformed an area of sand dunes and swamps into one of arcades, hotels, and golf courses.

Many companies operate bus transfers and tours from Brisbane to the Gold Coast. For full details, check with the Queensland Government Travel Centre at 196 Adelaide Street, Brisbane; Tel: 221-6111.

The Gold Coast is both a region and a city. (The Gold Coast municipality, incorporating the major centers of Coolangatta, Burleigh Heads, Surfers Paradise, and Southport, stretches up the coast from the New South Wales border; the Gold Coast region, loosely speaking, includes adjacent tourist areas as well.) It extends 30-odd miles from the Coomera River in the north to the Tweed River in the south. Its undisputed center is Surfers Paradise.

Surfers Paradise

"Big, brassy, bright, but barely beautiful" sums up the town of Surfers Paradise, 80 km (50 miles) south of Brisbane via the Pacific and Gold Coast highways. This is where the bodies are brownest, the bikinis are smallest, the shops are swankiest, and the action is coolest. Along the strip high-rise apartment blocks, hotels, and vacation rentals jostle for space as in Waikiki and Miami Beach. On the wide sandy beach, beautiful bodies soak up the sun while the more energetic enjoy the surf.

At street level there is color and movement in a kaleidoscope of neon signs, take-out food places, designer boutiques, tourist joints, and tacky souvenir shops. But just as you might be about to dismiss this town as a second-rate international beach resort, take a walk down Orchid Avenue in late afternoon or early evening and suddenly a more sophisticated, elegant, cosmopolitan Surfers Paradise will emerge.

The main part of Surfers Paradise consists of a three- or

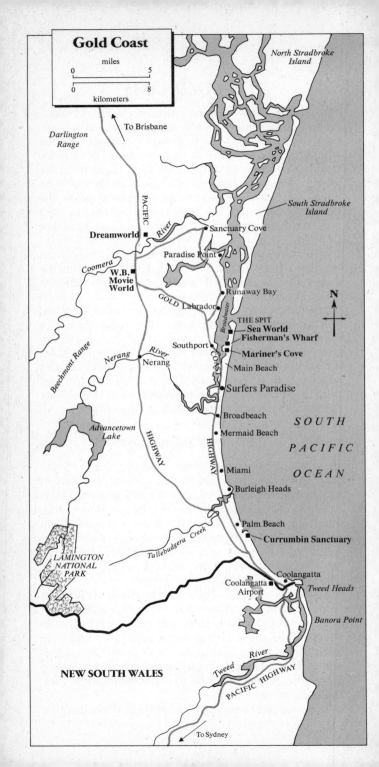

four-block stretch between the surf beach and the Nerang River. The central spine is the Gold Coast Highway linking Brisbane with New South Wales to the south. In downtown Surfers the traffic on the highway is nonstop, the sidewalks can be crowded, and the vacation spirit mixes uneasily with the commercial hustle.

SHOPPING AND DINING IN SURFERS

Some relief comes in the arcades that lead from the highway toward the beach. Here you will find the best shops (especially duty-free), take-out food, and souvenirs. Many shops are open seven days a week, once a rarity in Australia. The newest arcade and one of the best is **The Galleria** surrounding the high-rise ANA Hotel. Nearby are the **Forum** and the **Dolphin Arcade**. Each contains clothing stores, restaurants, fast-food outlets, souvenir shops, and so forth, and there are all the usual designer-label boutiques, jewelry, souvenirs, and Australian fashions. These are places for browsing and personal discovery, not for guidebook recommendations. The other major complex is **Paradise Centre**, which has 120 specialty shops, a supermarket, more than 30 places to eat, five bars, and the Ramada Hotel.

Down one side of the Paradise Centre, Cavill Avenue turns into Cavill Mall, with outdoor restaurants and a few garden areas, and this in turn leads directly to the beach. Midway, **Orchid Avenue** leads off to the left. Here the pace is slower, the streetscape more appealing, the outdoor cafés more inviting. Have a drink by the Forum fountain and watch a good cross-section of the world shuffle by. **Raptis Plaza,** which fronts both Cavill Mall and The Esplanade, has further shopping and dining choices.

This whole area is packed with restaurants. At **Daniel's** on Orchid Avenue—Daniel's has some of the best steaks you'll find anywhere—the food is served on handmade pottery, and the furniture is handcrafted (Tel: 075/70-1366); **Danny's**, in Tiki Village on Cavill Avenue, has outstanding Italian food and live Latin music (Tel: 075/38-2818); **The Loft** on Thomas Drive, Shevron Island, features elegant, affordable dining and the chance to bring your own favorite wine for dinner every night but Sunday. There are another hundred or so restaurants in Surfers Paradise, and it's hard to make a serious mistake.

STAYING IN SURFERS PARADISE

An array of accommodations presents itself here. The ▶ Ramada Hotel, the ▶ ANA Hotel (ANA stands for All

Nippon Airways), and the ▶ **Gold Coast International** are all fine modern, high-rise hotels with good rooms, excellent restaurants and bars, and satisfactory service. A newer establishment is the 265-room ▶ **Surfers Paradise Travelodge** on the Gold Coast Highway toward Broadbeach to the south. It's a smart, friendly, family-oriented resort that boasts Queensland's only revolving restaurant. Alongside these choices are scores of high-rise vacation apartments that have full cooking facilities and are ideal for those staying a few days. There is a huge range of less expensive motels and guesthouses as well. Despite this, accommodation can be very tight at Christmastime and during midyear school holidays (June and September). Prices also rise frighteningly at these times. There are several general booking services for all types of accommodations. Two you might try are Gold Coast Accommodation Service, on the Gold Coast Highway (Tel: 075/92-1414), and Accommodation Bookings Gold Coast, on Hanlan Street, Surfers Paradise; Tel: (075) 38-5269.

North from Surfers

Main Beach, Southport, and The Spit are immediately north of Surfers Paradise. **Southport** was the first town on the Gold Coast, and it's still more of a real town than most of the other areas. It lacks the excitement of Surfers Paradise and pretty much goes about its own business, although the new Southport Mall and the nearby Australia Fair complex offer some shopping opportunities.

The town of Southport is sheltered from the ocean by a long sand promontory called The Spit, which runs north from Main Beach. Between The Spit and the mainland is a bay called the Broadwater. This area has recently undergone major development. Leading the way is **Sea World**, a huge aquatic amusement center that is the largest man-made attraction on the Gold Coast. There are dolphin and water-ski shows, a monorail, roller coasters and other rides, as well as places to eat. For theme-park addicts it's one of the best around. Tel: (075) 88-2222. Adjacent is the low-rise ▶ **Nara Resort Hotel**, which seems to cater mainly to a midmarket Australian and Japanese clientele.

Nearby, the ▶ **Gold Coast Sheraton Mirage Hotel** sets the standard by which all other Gold Coast hotels are judged. This stylish property has a prime beachfront location and its own shopping and marina complex. While it's somewhat removed from the Surfers Paradise action, a ten-minute limousine ride can fix that. Mariner's Cove and Fisherman's Wharf add further attraction to this area with their shops, outdoor eateries, and boardwalks.

Power boats and other sports equipment can be rented from several outlets along this section of waterfront. Trips operate from here to the family-oriented ► **Tipplers Tourist Resort** on **South Stradbroke Island** for lunch and swimming, and farther north to Dunwich on North Stradbroke Island (see Around Brisbane, above). These waters are excellent for fishing; flathead and whiting are best from December to March, while bream, snapper, and tailor are caught from May to August.

Naturally, this area is big on seafood restaurants. **Grumpy's Wharf**, on The Spit opposite the Sheraton Mirage Hotel, has a casual atmosphere and great water views (Tel: 075/32-2900). **Holy Mackerel**, on Marine Parade, Southport, claims to be the oldest restaurant on the Gold Coast and is highly recommended (Tel: 075/33-1017). Two other places that usually get rave reviews are **Omeros Seafood Restaurant** at Marina Mirage, Main Beach (Tel: 075/77-0085), and **Cav's Steak House** on Frank Street, Labrador (Tel: 075/32-2954). Both are relaxed and casual—in fact, it's hard to find a formal restaurant in these parts.

Farther north along the wide tidal Broadwater you come to the towns of **Runaway Bay** and **Paradise Point**, where there are several large marinas. This is real watersport territory—the warm, calm water is perfect for water-skiing, jet-skiing, catamaran sailing, sailboarding, parasailing, fishing, paraflying, and cruising.

Farther north again is **Sanctuary Cove Resort**, aiming to become Australia's top address. The development includes the low-rise ► **Hyatt Regency at Sanctuary Cove**, which sprawls in colonial splendor through gardens and around man-made lakes with a refined yet casual elegance. Sanctuary Cove has exclusive residences for 1,400 families, a top marina, and extensive sporting facilities, including two golf courses. This undoubtedly ranks among Australia's top resorts, even though there is no beach.

About 3 km (2 miles) west of Sanctuary Cove on the Pacific Highway, **Dreamworld**, a Disneyland-like theme park, has an Australian atmosphere that's popular with families. For kids of all ages, nothing here beats it. Tel: (075) 73-3300. Close by is **W. B. Movie World**, Australia's answer to Universal Studios; the most visited attraction in the Gold Coast region; Tel: (075) 53-3891.

South from Surfers

The surf-pounded sand strip runs south from Surfers Paradise for 25 km (15 miles) through Broadbeach, Mermaid Beach, Miami, Burleigh Heads, and Palm Beach to Coolangatta. None of the other centers, by itself, can rival Surfers Paradise, but together they offer an impressive variety of attractions and accommodations.

Broadbeach, 3 km (2 miles) south of Surfers Paradise, marks the end of the beachfront high-rise clutter. There is a great beach, two surf lifesaving clubs that provide beach-patrol services, the **Pacific Fair Shopping Centre**—the largest shopping complex on the coast—and the ▶ **Conrad International Hotel and Jupiters Casino**. The Conrad is built on its own island in the Nerang River and is a complete holiday center in itself. There are four licensed restaurants, a 24-hour casino with more than 100 gaming tables, a 1,000-seat showroom featuring girls and feathers, a nightclub, pool, spas, tennis courts, and a full gymnasium and health club. It is an unusual mixture of the sophisticated and the laid-back.

The Conrad Hotel is huge by Australian standards, and the casino is one of the most open and relaxed in the country. Patrons can arrive by road or by an up-to-date, mile-long monorail that links the casino with the ▶ **Pan Pacific Gold Coast Hotel** and the superb three-level **Oasis** shopping center at the beach in Broadbeach. Inland from here are some of Australia's most expensive houses, built on artificial cays along waterways that ultimately connect with the Nerang River and the Broadwater. Half-day cruises operate throughout the region from the Nerang River jetty at the end of Cavill Avenue in Surfers Paradise.

Development south from here is more spread out, and some areas are even rather scruffy. **Burleigh Heads** provides the next cluster of high rises, overlooking a lovely surf beach and rocky promontory. There is a small national park here with hiking paths and picnic tables. Just south of Palm Beach is **Currumbin Sanctuary**, owned by the National Trust of Queensland. The well-known lorikeets (a type of parrot) feed in the early morning and late afternoon, but there are so many varieties of birds and animals that a visit anytime is a delight. Adult admission, A$12; Tel: (075) 98-1645.

The highway continues south past the Gold Coast Airport to **Coolangatta** on the New South Wales border. This is a pleasant town with a good beach and lots of surfing. There is little artificial sophistication, and so some people prefer it to the hype of Surfers. **Oskar's Seafood Restaurant**, on Marine Parade overlooking the beach, is rated as one of the best in Queensland; Tel: (075) 36-4621.

The ▶ **All Seasons Greenmount Beach Resort**, situated on a headland overlooking the beach, provides some of the best accommodations in these parts. Along this whole stretch of highway there is a huge choice of motels, serviced apartments, and vacation rental properties at bargain prices. Except for school vacation times, advance booking is not usually necessary at most of them.

INLAND FROM SURFERS

The hinterland area to the west of the coastal resorts has long been overshadowed by the beach, but now it is being seen as a major attraction. Within 25 miles of the coast you can be at 4,000 feet in beautiful mountain country with huge beech trees, waterfalls, and charming Old World–style resorts. Bus tours to these areas, which include Mount Tamborine, Canyon Lookout, the Natural Arch, and Beechmont Plateau, operate from all areas of the Gold Coast. If you want to stay longer, adequate accommodations in a mountain setting are available at the ▶ **Binna Burra Mountain Lodge** or at ▶ **O'Reilly's Rainforest Guest House**, on the edge of the **Lamington National Park**, a large plateau with rain forest, excellent birdlife, and lovely scenery.

THE SUNSHINE COAST

The Sunshine Coast north of Brisbane claims to be the fastest-growing region in Australia. Its attractions are the beach, the weather, and the relatively unspoiled nature of the area. Unfortunately there are already signs that this will become all-too-equal competition for the neon-lit Gold Coast. If that happens, the Sunshine area will have lost much of its original charm.

The Sunshine Coast is about 45 miles long, with several seaside centers separated by fairly sparse development. But already the gaps are closing. Before too long it will be a continuous ribbon of development joining Caloundra, Maroochydore, Coolum, and Noosa. Each of these towns has its devotees, but sophisticated visitors will head for Noosa or the Hyatt Regency at Coolum.

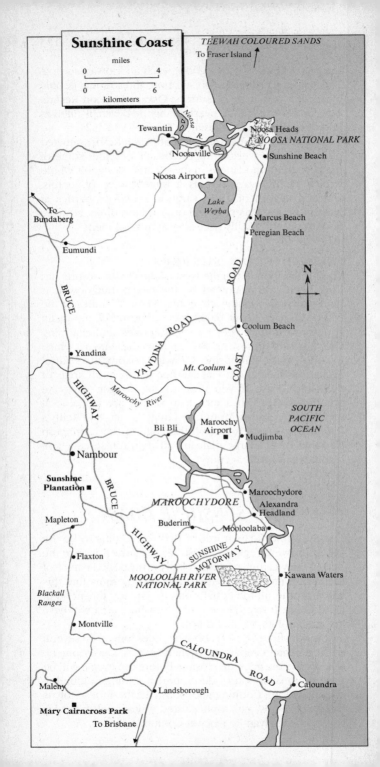

Noosa

Noosa roughly covers the small towns of Tewantin, Noosa-ville, Sunshine Beach, and Noosa Heads, but if you want to be in the center of things only **Noosa Heads** will suffice. Here you will find the best shopping, the best restaurants, the widest choice of upscale accommodations, and the only real sophistication.

Sophistication is, of course, relative. No Australian beach resort has the elegance of parts of the French Riviera or the West Indies, but Noosa Heads at least has some interesting architecture, a genuine subtropical atmosphere, a small collection of "beautiful people," and a nice understatement that implies that there are things happening but that you will have to search for them yourself. **Hastings Street** is where you must be, the place to be seen. But let's put Noosa into perspective: You can walk the length of Hastings Street in five minutes. The entire Noosa *area* has a population of fewer than 30,000.

Anyone staying longer than a day will need no help with shopping hints. Wander up and down Hastings Street and you will find many charming boutiques, souvenir shops, and restaurants. Shops welcome browsers. Casual wear abounds; sandals, hand-printed cottons, and original jewelry are all excellent buys here. The natural beauty of the Noosa environment has attracted many artists, and their work is for sale in local galleries.

Noosa's restaurants have a well-deserved reputation. One of the nicest is **Touche Noosa** upstairs next to the Sheraton Noosa Resort; its casual but chic atmosphere, food, wine list, and service are all excellent; Tel: (074) 47-2222. Also worth trying is **Pavilions** at the Netanya Noosa Resort; Tel: (074) 47-4722. Both restaurants have good international menus with some local seafood and grill specialties. If you are really into seafood, **Roser's** is the place to go; Tel: (074) 47-3880. The menu is straightforward but interesting and the wines are reasonably priced. All three restaurants are on Hastings Street, all are moderately priced, and all accept diners in casual clothes. The **Rolling Rock Nightclub** in Bay Village, Hastings Street, opens seven nights a week for late action; Tel: (074) 47-2255.

STAYING IN NOOSA

Accommodations in Noosa are good and reasonably priced, except for a few weeks at Christmas and during the September school holidays. The best resort hotel is the ▶ **Netanya Noosa Resort**, which has a beachfront position on Hastings Street. There are one- and two-bedroom suites and penthouses with private balconies, saunas, and full kitchen facilities. The ▶ **Noosa International Holiday Resort** is larger but still very attractive. Most units have two bedrooms and two bathrooms and a fully equipped kitchen and laundry. The disadvantage is that it's a ten-minute walk to the beach, but the two pools, three spa pools, and two saunas are some compensation, and there is a courtesy bus service.

The newest and largest hotel in Noosa is the ▶ **Sheraton Noosa Resort** on Hastings Street. The hotel does not have a beachfront site, but the rooms surround an attractive pool and recreation area. The hotel is rapidly becoming the center of sophistication for the area.

Noosa also has a good range of self-contained apartments. The spectacular ▶ **No. 1 Hastings Street**, which cascades down a steep hill, and the cheaper but still excellent ▶ **Seahaven Beachfront Resort** and the ▶ **Ocean Breeze Resort** are all on Hastings Street as well. They offer restaurants, bars, barbecue facilities, pools, and—of course—the beach.

AROUND NOOSA

Noosa Heads is famous for its beach and the adjacent **Noosa National Park** and **Sunshine Beach**. The national park has walking trails through rain forest and open grasslands, while Sunshine Beach is said to have the best and most consistent waves on the Sunshine Coast. For many, however, the **Noosa River** and lake system are the biggest attractions here. Enthusiasts can rent a boat, canoe, or houseboat for fishing or sightseeing, but most visitors will be content to take a tour; these come in several shapes and sizes. The *Everglades Water Bus* runs a six-hour cruise with barbecue lunch on the Noosa River and Lake Cooroibah, as well as a shorter afternoon cruise; Tel: (074) 47-1838. Cooloola Cruises runs similar cruises; Tel: (074) 49-9177. Both tour operators pick up guests at their hotels.

Another popular tour runs to the **Teewah Coloured Sands,** an expanse of glorious beach lined by 200-foot cliffs of differently colored sands, immediately north of Noosa across the Noosa river. Day tours by four-wheel-drive vehicles—including lunch, a swim, and a visit to one of the freshwater lakes—operate each day. These also travel the beach to Double Island Point or continue on to **Rainbow Beach.**

FRASER ISLAND

Those not put off by a long day might consider making the 12-hour round-trip to Fraser Island, about 100 km (60 miles) north of Noosa. Fraser Island—the world's largest sand island, and now protected from sand-mining and timber-cutting after a bitter struggle—has superb beaches, towering sand dunes, and clear freshwater lakes and streams. Tourism is strictly controlled, and each tour operator is restricted to a certain area. All, however, will show you the beaches, the pristine rain forest, and the lakes. Fishing is great, but swimming can be dangerous. Visitors often see dingoes (native dogs) and brumbies (wild horses). The cost of the full day runs to about A$85. For those with time and a love of the outdoors, a few days at the ► **Eurong Beach Tourist Resort** here might be worthwhile. You can arrange a four-wheel-drive transfer from the Sunshine Coast or a flight to the small private airfield. Alternatively, you could try the new ► **Kingfisher Bay Resort** on the western side of the island. There is a vehicular barge and a high-speed catamaran from Urangan Boat Harbour, Hervey Bay.

Elsewhere on the Sunshine Coast

Noosa is neither the largest center nor the only holiday spot in this part of Australia. The coast region stretches south from Noosa for about 40 miles and inland to the Blackall Ranges, encompassing a variety of attractions from large-scale beach resorts to inland hill towns, natural rain forests, and mountains.

Caloundra, at the southern end of the beach strip, is a family-oriented vacation town with several good beaches. The ► **Oasis** on Landsborough Parade provides rooms and villas in lush tropical gardens, while the nearby **Reflections Restaurant** (Tel: 074/91-0333) has excellent seafood. Horse-racing enthusiasts will enjoy Corbould Park racecourse here.

The name **Maroochy** covers the three centers of Maroochydore, Alexandra Headland, and Mooloolaba. Mooloolaba, the southernmost, is about 16 km (10 miles) north of Caloundra. These towns have grown dramatically in recent years and now have good shopping, entertainment, and accommodations options. The beach is still the prime attraction here, however; it's good for both surfing and swimming. **The Wharf**, a multimillion-dollar tourist facility along the lines of San Francisco's Fisherman's Wharf, provides good eating and shopping choices. **Un-**

derwater World oceanarium, with its excellent 80-meter-long Plexiglas underwater tunnel, is right next door; Tel: (074) 44-8488.

Fronds on the Esplanade, Mooloolaba (Tel: 074/44-1573) and **La Terrasse** at 57 Cotton Tree Esplanade, Maroochydore (Tel: 074/43-3924), are two good restaurants in the area. There are cruises on the Maroochy River, and a visit to **Nostalgia Town** on David Low Way provides a laugh at the past and an opportunity to go on some ingenious fun rides (Tel: 074/48-7155). **Fridays on the Wharf** (Tel: 074/44-8383) at Mooloolaba and **Galaxy** at the Alexandra Hotel in Maroochydore are popular nightclubs for the young at heart. The ► **Novotel Twin Waters Resort** at Mudjimba, just north of Maroochydore, provides good, medium-priced low-rise accommodation around a large man-made lake with adjacent recreation facilities including an excellent golf course.

Coolum Beach, 12 km (7½ miles) north of Mudjimba, is a small center that was thrust into the limelight with the opening of the ► **Hyatt Regency Coolum**. This is the largest and most prestigious resort on the coast and the first all-suite health spa and resort complex in Australia. The low-rise resort sprawls around a championship golf course and through attractive bush. The Hyatt Regency has more than a mile of ocean frontage, eight swimming pools, a tennis center, and a marvelous health and spa center, together with restaurants, shops, and craft activities for guests.

INLAND ATTRACTIONS

Inland from the coast are several attractions. **Buderim**, a delightful little hillside town that affords dramatic views of the coast, is 7 km (4 miles) from Alexandra Headland. Try **Burnetts on Buderim** (Tel: 074/45-3003) for lunch, and visit the **Buderim Festival Centre**, housed in the old ginger factory on Burnett Street. You can watch glass blowing, pewter, pottery and lapidary artists at work; Tel: 074-455-221.

Sunshine Plantation, which for a long time was the biggest draw in this region, has been bypassed by the new Sunshine Motorway, so it's struggling to keep its million-visitors-a-year tag. It's a strange combination: pineapple farm, rain forest area, tourist attraction, and educational facility. Try the fresh tropical-fruit parfaits, sundaes, and drinks.

The Ettamogah Pub, on the Bruce Highway near the turnoff to Caloundra, is part of **Aussie World**, an amuse-

ment park with a decidedly Australian theme. Apart from
the beer, you can enjoy country entertainment in a huge
barn, buy Aussie food and souvenirs, and try some fun
rides. From here you can make a picturesque circuit
through the **Blackall Ranges**. The drive offers splendid
natural rain-forest and mountain scenery combined with
galleries, antiques shops, fine restaurants, rural retreats,
and crafts stores. It's a quiet but thoroughly delightful area.

Continue south on the Bruce Highway to Landsborough, then turn west and climb the mountains to
Maleny, the largest center in the ranges. The town itself is
of some interest, but the surrounding countryside and
the accommodation opportunities have even more appeal. ▶ **Maleny Lodge Guest House** offers bed-and-
breakfast accommodation in a charming historic home;
▶ **Solothurn Rural Resort** in Maleny has nine self-
contained cottages and facilities for horseback riding,
swimming, and tennis. Stop at the **Mary Cairncross Park**
to see spectacular views of the Glass House Mountains.

Drive north from here to the delightful village of
Montville. Modern buildings have been integrated with
restored old cottages to maintain a true village atmosphere. Arts and crafts abound and there is a historical
walk to keep the visitor in touch with the past. This is
the creative heart of the Sunshine Coast, and there are
myriad galleries, studios, crafts cottages, fine restaurants,
and tearooms—it is special. **Pottinger's Restaurant** (Tel:
074/42-9407), **Mistys Mountain Restaurant** (Tel: 074/42-
9264), and the **Camphor Cottage** are all great places for
lunch in the main street of the village.

Only a few miles north is **Flaxton**, where there are more
tearooms, restaurants, and bed-and-breakfast accommodations. Call in at the **Flaxton Gardens** restaurant and tearoom for refreshments and interesting pottery and crafts.
The **Flaxton Inn** and the **Flaxton Barn** have similar offerings. The views around Flaxton are delightful. Now go
north to **Mapleton**, another small village with tearooms
and cottage crafts. Stop for a meal or a drink at the **Mapleton Tavern** and visit the lily ponds just beside the main
street. You now have the option of driving for 15 km (9
miles) on a narrow track through mature forest to Yandina
or taking the paved road to Nambour. Both have appeal.

Nambour is a working town settled in 1860, with
sugarcane trains crossing the main street and a sweet
smell of prosperity. This is the real world, content to do
without the hype of some of the coast. A wide range of
tropical produce is grown in the surrounding area.

Yandina, about 8 km (5 miles) farther north on the Bruce Highway, is home to Australia's only ginger processing factory. At the ginger factory, you can take a tour of the plant and eat in the restaurant or picnic on the lawns. Garden-lovers will enjoy a stop at the nearby Fairhill Native Plants botanic garden. Another 8 kilometers (5 miles) along the highway brings you to **Eumundi,** a small town rich with history, art, and culture. The Imperial Hotel is a good place to try the local Eumundi beer. **Eumundi Antiques** and **Eumundi Gallery** are two shopping options in the main street, and the Saturday morning Eumundi crafts market is justly famous for its quality merchandise at attractive prices.

THE
GREAT BARRIER REEF

The Great Barrier Reef is one of Australia's best-known attractions, yet few visitors have an accurate picture of what the reef is like and even fewer appreciate the problems associated with seeing it. The Great Barrier Reef is a 1,200-mile-long chain of coral reefs paralleling the Queensland coast; most of the reef is below the water's surface except at the lowest of tides. The reef is a sensational underwater attraction whose mysteries and beauty are only now being opened to human exploration. Fortunately, development of reef-viewing facilities has been rapid, so that under normal weather conditions everyone who wants to experience this unique environment can now do so, whether or not they swim and scuba dive.

The Reef

The Great Barrier Reef is a huge coral system built by billions of tiny marine animals, each just a few millimeters in size. The living coral polyps excrete limy skeletons; when the animals die, their skeletons remain. New polyps grow on their dead predecessors, and in this way a reef is slowly built.

Coral requires warm, clean, salty water for proper growth, and the outer edge of the Australian continental shelf provides near-perfect conditions. This is where the reef is best and viewing most spectacular. The reef has few islands. Coral cannot live above water, but sometimes dead coral rubble and coral sand will accumulate inside a reef and rise above water level. Over time this can become colonized, first with grass, which attracts seabirds, then later with shrubs and trees, which grow from seeds carried by the birds.

Unfortunately the tourism industry isn't always precise with its terms, so a place referred to as a "reef island" isn't necessarily a coral cay. In fact, most of the popular resort islands are continental-type islands, that is, the tips of offshore mountain ranges. Some of these have fringing reef that can be quite spectacular, but these reefs aren't the Great Barrier Reef.

The first thing you see on the reef is coral. It comes in a bewildering variety of shapes, sizes, and colors. Many visitors are initially disappointed that there is so much "dead" coral everywhere. This is due in part to the staghorn corals that make up the largest proportion of coral on the reef. The staghorns provide shelter to fish and other animals, but unfortunately they are easily broken by storms and human beings.

As you approach the outer edges of the reefs, however, you see more spectacular pieces of coral: delicately colored ferns, huge lumps of brain coral, and some of the soft corals that don't actually take part in the building process but add their beauty to the underwater garden.

The Great Barrier Reef would be no more than a giant breakwater for the Pacific Ocean were it not for the prolific marine life that inhabits all reefs. The fish come in an extraordinary variety of colors and shapes, and some have rather strange behavior patterns. For visitors they represent the second major reef attraction, and the development of semi-submersible vessels and underwater observatories means that the fish can now be seen much more easily than in the past.

Colors are of immense value to reef fish as warning or camouflage. Many have vivid bands, spots, or patches that break up their outline and confuse predators. Some reef fish can even change color to match their surroundings. Other fish have intimate relationships with larger creatures: Some small wrasse fish are cleaners, taking parasites from larger fish; even eels and huge manta rays visit these "cleaning stations" for service. Certain intrepid species live within the poisonous tentacles of the giant anemone in complete safety. Reef visitors can often witness all this fascinating activity. In some parts visitors can see giant groupers, amazing fish that can seem almost tame and will swim with divers and wait to be fed. They can grow up to ten feet in length and weigh almost 900 pounds.

Then there are the numerous colorful shells. One of the most common is the ringed money cowrie, while the most interesting is undoubtedly the giant clam. At least 50 species of cowries inhabit Australian reef waters, along with many varieties of sand-dwelling volutes.

Gateways to the Reef

The Great Barrier Reef starts just south of the Tropic of Capricorn and runs north almost to Papua New Guinea. The main reefs are 150 miles off the coast from Rockhampton at the southern end, but as you travel north the distance from the coastline to the reef lessens. By the time you reach Port Douglas the reef is only about 15 miles offshore. While it is possible to reach the reef from many coastal centers, it's probably best to head for one of the following towns:

Townsville, the research capital of the reef, is becoming a major tourist center as well. The city is home to the Great Barrier Reef Marine Park Authority, the Australian Institute of Marine Science, James Cook University, and the Great Barrier Reef Wonderland. From Townsville you have the choice of day trips to Kelso Reef and several other points where coral viewing is possible. (See the Central Great Barrier Reef section below.)

Cairns was the first center to take advantage of the tourist appeal of the Great Barrier Reef, and more day-visitors go to the reef from here than from any other mainland city. Visitors have a choice of going to Fitzroy Island, a continental-type island with good fringing reef; to Green Island, a true coral cay with visitor facilities; or to one of two outer reefs where tour operators keep pontoons and semi-submersible vessels. The pontoons are anchored rafts that have no facilities for staying overnight. (See the Cairns and Northern Great Barrier Reef section below.)

Brisbane, though hundreds of miles south of the Great Barrier Reef, is an important gateway because of its access to the cities of Bundaberg and Gladstone, which in turn are gateways to Lady Elliot Island and Heron Island, the two southernmost reef islands (for which, see the Southern Great Barrier Reef section below).

Staying on the Reef

There are only three alternatives at present if you wish to stay *on* the Great Barrier Reef: Lady Elliot Island and Heron Island, both in the Southern Reef; and Green Island, near Cairns in the Northern Reef. All are coral cays that have limited, moderately priced accommodation. (For additional details, both on access towns and on these island resorts, see the individual reef sections below.)

Visiting the Reef

For those who are short on time or have special interests, other facilities exist for visiting the reef.

Day trips on fast catamarans are available to various reefs and cost around A\$90. Most include lunch, coral viewing from glass-bottomed boats or semi-submersible vessels, swimming, and snorkeling. Some offer scuba-diving opportunities at additional cost. Daily trips operate from the Whitsunday Islands, Townsville, Mission Beach, Cairns, and Port Douglas, while boats operate from Mackay, Bundaberg, and the town of Seventeen Seventy several days a week, and from Great Keppel Island, Orpheus Island, and Lizard Island for guests at those resorts. The largest boats carry up to 350 passengers.

Extended cruises are also available. The *Elizabeth E II* cruises from Mackay, visiting some of the Whitsunday Islands and the Great Barrier Reef on a four-day itinerary; Tel: (079) 574-281. Roylen Cruises has a somewhat similar cruise with a five-day itinerary; Tel: (079) 55-3066. Both leave Mackay Harbour on Monday mornings. These operations cater to about 40 passengers per cruise.

The *Coral Princess* cruises from Townsville to Cairns and back (four days, three nights each way); this catamaran stops at several inshore islands and resorts but also visits reefs and cays on the Great Barrier Reef. Departure from Townsville is on Tuesdays, and from Cairns on Saturdays. The maximum number of passengers that can be accommodated is 54; a one-way trip costs around A\$980. Tel: (077) 21-1673 or, for reservations, (008) 079-545 (toll free).

Diving the Reef

The Great Barrier Reef provides some of the best diving in the world, and there are plenty of opportunities to use the facilities of local professionals. This local knowledge is essential: The warm, clear water may look perfect, but there are currents, the coral is sharp, and there are other dangers as well.

Fortunately most island resorts now have trained dive masters, and most dive tours are excellently run. Charter-boat operators are familiar with the reef and know its dangers. Australia has a good diving safety record, and most operators will require a diving-oriented medical certificate together with an acceptable diving qualification before you will be permitted to rent gear or enter the water.

Many resorts run basic-training courses that allow you to shallow-dive with a group to see a little of the reef. The courses last about two hours and cost A$40–A$60. Some resorts and a number of mainland centers provide facilities for full accreditation, which will take five to seven days. Diving tours operate from several centers along the coast. Those from Townsville north are considered the best, but Heron Island in the south and Lizard Island in the far north are also very popular.

Virtually all of the Great Barrier Reef is a marine national park controlled by the Great Barrier Reef Marine Park Authority. There are a number of rules regarding where you can go and what you can do, so check with local divers. If you intend to camp on a privately owned island, get the owner's permission. If the island is government-owned, obtain a permit from the National Parks and Wildlife Service, P.O. Box 42, Kenmore, Qld. 4069; Tel: (079) 36-0511. (Receiving permits can take several weeks.)

Spearfishing in scuba gear is generally prohibited, and minimum sizes apply to about 50 species of crabs and fish. Some animals, such as turtles, clams, dugongs (sea cows), and triton shells, are completely protected and illegal to hunt.

Tanks and weight belts are universally available on a rental basis from resorts and gateway city dive operators.

Weather

The weather plays a vital part in the enjoyment of the Great Barrier Reef. Few visitors want to battle with rain, high winds, or huge seas to reach a suitable vantage point. Divers hope for clear skies and light winds so that visibility will be at its best, while sailors want small seas and consistent breezes.

During the Great Barrier Reef's winter (June to

September) the southeast trade winds blow parallel to the Queensland coast. The winds are dry, mild (10–20 knots), and constant. Cruising yachts sail northward, spinnakers flying.

In summer (December to March) the northeast monsoons, saturated with moisture after their long Pacific voyage, deluge the reef and coast with sudden, heavy showers. Thunderstorms are common, and there is the occasional cyclone. Rain can last for three or four days, then there can be a week of fine weather. At this time the humidity is high and southern Australians stay away. Many visitors from the Northern Hemisphere are less disturbed by this weather, especially if they're coming from the northeastern United States or Canada in the middle of a cold winter.

The transition periods of April to May and October to November are often warm, sunny, and languid.

There are considerable weather differences within the reef region. Records indicate that over the past 80 years the Cairns region has had more cyclones than other areas of the coast, yet in recent years the number has been small. Cairns also has more rainy days than most other areas, and this can be a problem for short-term visitors.

All of Australia's tropical coastline has a problem with marine stingers. These jellyfish (Portuguese men-of-war) are found close inshore between November and April each year. Some inflict a painful sting, while one variety can be fatal. Understandably, locals avoid ocean swimming while stingers are around, and you should too. Swimming is safe in filtered rock pools and also inside netted areas in the water off many beaches.

THE SOUTHERN GREAT BARRIER REEF REGION

The Great Barrier Reef reaches its southern extremity at Lady Elliot Island, offshore from Bundaberg. A group of reefs and islands runs north to just above the Tropic of Capricorn, then there is a big gap until the central reef region around Townsville. Relatively speaking, the southern reef region is small, stretching a mere 120 miles

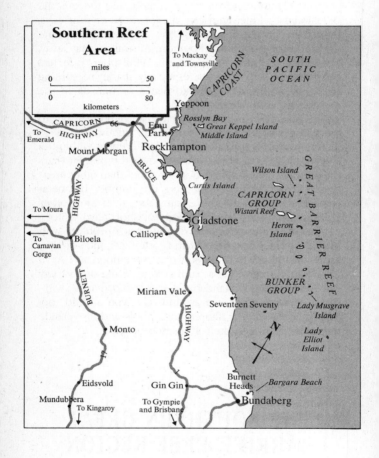

along the coast. It is an important tourist region, however, because this section of reef lies closest to the big population centers farther south. The coastal cities of Bundaberg, Gladstone, and Rockhampton are gateways to individual islands, while at the same time they go about their business as regional industrial and commercial centers.

The Islands and Reefs

Lady Elliot Island is the southernmost coral cay on the Great Barrier Reef. It is a low sand and coral island about 104 acres in area that takes roughly two and a half hours to circumnavigate on foot. Parts of the island are barren while other areas have dense tree and grass cover. Many birds inhabit the island, particularly from October to May. The number of people who can visit at any one time is limited by the marine park authority, so the island never feels crowded. In the past the island has been underdeveloped, so it has often been overlooked, but recent improvements in accommodations have brought it into prominence. The island is 190 miles north of Brisbane and 55 miles northeast of Bundaberg. Flights are available from Brisbane to Bundaberg, with a transfer to Lady Elliot Island by Whiticker Air. Flight time is 25 minutes.

Accommodation at ▶ **Lady Elliot Island Resort** is provided in comfortable cabins with private bathrooms or safari tents, and meals are served in the dining room or on a terrace overlooking the reef. There is a store and a dive shop. Snorkeling and diving equipment is available for rent, and you can dive straight off the beach. The atmosphere is casual and relaxed.

Lady Musgrave Island (due east of Seventeen Seventy) does not have accommodations, but this is the destination of the one-day reef cruises that operate four days a week from Burnett Heads Boat Harbour near Bundaberg (Tel: 071/52-9011) and from the town of Seventeen Seventy (Tel: 079/749-188). It takes just over two hours to reach the island, the lagoon, and the fringing reef from Burnett Heads and about an hour and fifteen minutes from Seventeen Seventy.

Heron Island is known worldwide by divers for its clear waters and variety of dives, but you don't have to partake in the sport to enjoy this lovely coral cay. It can be walked around in half an hour, is alive with birdlife, and is shaded by pandanus (screw pines) and coconut palms. It is also home to green turtles and loggerhead turtles, which lay their eggs here from November to March. The island is about 40 miles offshore, with launch and helicopter connections from Gladstone. The launch costs around A$120 round trip, the helicopter around A$320. As is the case with most Queensland islands, the accommodations on Heron Island have recently been expanded and improved, however there is still limited luxury accommodation available.

The ▶ **Heron Island Resort** has the usual facilities: dive shop, beach, semi-submersible vessel, fishing trips, pool, tennis court, bar, and entertainment. It offers a range of prices. Nearby ▶ **Wilson Island** has been opened up as an adjunct to the Heron Island Resort, for those who crave being farther from civilization. Accommodation is in eight canvas bungalows, and there are a small dining area and shared bathroom facilities.

Wistari Reef was the destination for a daily reef trip from Gladstone Marina by Wistari Reef Adventures, but it did not operate during 1992 or 1993 because of poor economic conditions. It is likely to start again when tourist demand increases. There is a day trip to Erskine Island from Gladstone Marina (Tel: 079/736-730).

Great Keppel Island, a continental-type island far west of the Great Barrier Reef, is reached by air from Rockhampton or by launch from Rosslyn Bay (A$24 round trip). The main resort, ▶ **Great Keppel Island Resort,** is owned by Australian Airlines and was once heavily promoted as a young people's enclave, but now it is also visited by families and people of all ages. The accent, however, is on organized activities, and for participants there is never a dull moment: swimming, snorkeling, fishing, sailing, parasailing, sailboarding, golf, tennis, squash, archery, spas, and bars. The newer accommodation is upscale and stylish; so, too, is the Admiral Keppel Restaurant and Neptune's Nightclub, with its resident band and cabaret show.

▶ **Wapparaburra Haven,** also on Great Keppel Island, offers a less expensive alternative, with cabins and camping facilities and a kiosk for food and basic necessities.

The Mainland

BUNDABERG TO GLADSTONE

Bundaberg, the access point to Lady Elliot Island and launch site for day trips to Lady Musgrave Island, is a major sugar-producing center. The city of about 45,000 is famous for its rum distillery. You can tour the distillery as well as several sugar mills; for something different, visit **Tropical Wines** on Gin Gin Road, which produces dessert-style wines from fresh Queensland fruit. The Historic Museum, the Botanical Gardens, the Hinkler House Museum, Fairymead House, and the Bundaberg Steam Railway are clustered together on a site between the winery and the city. This is a good place for a luncheon stop at the restaurant or at one of the barbecue facilities or for a picnic on the lawns. The **Bacchus** on Takalvan Street is considered the city's best restaurant.

Bundaberg is also known for its whale-watching cruises, which operate mid-August to mid-October. These aim to bring you close to humpback whales, which frequently give awesome displays of breaching and fin- and tail-slapping. The city's love affair with these creatures finds its focus in a spectacular six-story environmental wall mural by Wyland, the U.S. artist internationally famous for his "whaling walls."

Bargara Beach, 13 km (8 miles) north of the city, provides some of the last surf on the route north. The ▶ **Don Pancho Beach Resort** here offers good facilities and access to the beach and a golf course. Nearby **Mon Repos Environmental Park** has a famous turtle rookery, where between mid-January and late March thousands of young turtles hatch and head for the sea.

Gladstone is not everyone's idea of a great city to visit. It is one of the busiest ports in Australia, exporting coal and aluminum and importing bauxite, and is significant to visitors primarily because it is the departure point for Heron Island. It is also home to the **Tondoon Botanic Gardens**, which specializes in native Australian plants and offers 136 acres of meandering pathways and hiking trails. There is a range of moderately priced motel-style accommodations in town, with the ▶ **Country Plaza International** being one of the best in the central city. **Swaggy's Australian Restaurant** at 56 Goondoon Street is a good place for a meal.

ROCKHAMPTON

North of Gladstone and situated astride the Tropic of Capricorn, Rockhampton is a solid city of 55,000 with many reminders of its past as a gold-rush town; today cattle ranching is the big industry. Quay Street has one of Australia's best Victorian commercial streetscapes; more than 20 buildings here have National Trust classification. A National Trust walking-tour brochure is available from hotels and visitor-information outlets.

Right in the center of the shopping and business area is the moderately priced ▶ **Duthies Leichhardt Hotel**, a well-known favorite with 120 rooms. Three streets away, the ▶ **Country Comfort Inn** is a medium-rise building with views to the river that is now regarded as the best accommodation in town. Those wanting history should try the beautiful old ▶ **Criterion Hotel**, which is reasonably priced but fairly basic in facilities. It is one of the original hotels on the riverbank.

Rockhampton has always been a "civilized" town, so it's no surprise to find that the **Pilbeam Theatre/Art Gallery** complex on Victoria Parade is one of the best around. The gallery has an excellent collection of 1970s and 1980s paintings by Australian artists as well as some very fine ceramics. Also worth seeing are the **Botanical Gardens**, with a koala sanctuary, south of town on Spencer Street, and the **Dreamtime Cultural Centre**, Australia's largest aboriginal cultural center, on the Bruce Highway in North Rockhampton; Tel: (079) 36-1655.

INLAND FROM ROCKHAMPTON

There are several places to visit just outside Rockhampton; bus tours operate from the city. Some 38 km (24 miles) southwest on the Burnett Highway is **Mount Morgan**, an old mining town with a huge gold and copper open-cut mine 990 feet deep. The mine has operated off and on for more than a hundred years. Mine inspections take place at 9:30 A.M. Monday to Friday; Tel: (079) 38-1550. There is also an excellent historical museum; Tel: (079) 38-2122. About 30 km (19 miles) north of Rockhampton on Highway One, the **Berserker Range** has several limestone caves and a heritage museum; guided tours are available. Some 260 km (161 miles) inland on the Capricorn Highway is the attractive town of **Emerald**, and some 50 km (31 miles) farther on are the sapphire, topaz, and amethyst gem fields of Central Queensland. Visit the **Miners Heritage Walk-In Mine** at Rubyvale, the gem fields' largest underground hand mine. For those who have no luck, rough and cut sapphires are available for sale. Between Rockhampton and Emerald you will see evidence of the huge open-cut coal mines that dot this area, providing Australia with large amounts of export dollars.

A distance of 230 km (140 miles) south of Emerald is **Carnarvon Gorge**, a spectacular oasis between towering sandstone cliffs in the Carnarvon Range National Park. The most developed area of Carnarvon has a camping area at the gorge entrance and a tourist resort nearby. Walking trails lead to aboriginal rock art sites, spectacular lookouts, and sheltered fern-clad ravines. There are sealed roads to this area but no regular tours. Much farther west from Emerald (420 km/260 miles), at **Longreach**, is the **Stockman's Hall of Fame**, a museum dedicated to the Outback pioneers that has attracted visitors who have more time and a particular interest in the country. While in this region you might also visit **Winton**, home of "Waltzing Matilda," 180 km (111 miles) west of Longreach on the Landsborough Highway.

THE CAPRICORN COAST

Yeppoon is the major center for the 24-mile stretch of beach to the northeast of Rockhampton known as the Capricorn Coast. This area has long been popular with local vacationers looking for wide, sandy beaches and a quiet, relaxed time. Accommodations and restaurants in this area are adequate rather than spectacular; at most times of the year you should select accommodation by cruising along the coast road until you come upon something that appeals to you.

Yeppoon has been thrust into prominence by the construction of the ▶ **Capricorn International Resort** just north of the town. This reasonably priced, Japanese-owned resort is built on 20,000 acres of parkland and wildlife sanctuaries and has restaurants, nightclubs, a swimming pool, spa, sauna, two 18-hole golf courses, and nine miles of beach. At present, guests are Australian and Japanese, with a handful of other international visitors. There are water-sport facilities together with golf, lawn bowls, and tennis in this area.

Two good scenic drives north and south of Yeppoon are well marked. From **Rosslyn Bay** you can visit Great Keppel Island and the nearby **Middle Island Underwater Observatory**, where there is excellent coral viewing from inside a windowed enclosure that extends both above and below the water; Tel: (079) 39-4191. The ▶ **Rosslyn Bay Inn Resort**, near the departure point for the Great Keppel Island ferries, has better-than-average facilities.

THE CENTRAL GREAT BARRIER REEF REGION

This region has become one of the most popular and fastest-growing tourist areas in Australia. Here you'll find some of the best sections of the Great Barrier Reef, lovely islands, good beaches, tropical rain forest, Outback country, and Australia's sunniest city, Townsville. This is the beginning of North Queensland—where the pace is slower, time has less meaning, and there's a feeling of friendliness now missing from much of the rest of the world.

Australian aboriginals have lived here for thousands of years, but Western knowledge of the area started with Captain Cook, who sailed the coast here in 1770, naming many islands, capes, and bays. There are more black faces here than in most areas of the country. They come from three distinct groups: aboriginal people now living within the general community; Torres Strait islanders, who have left their small, isolated islands and settled on the mainland; and South Seas islanders, who are mainly descendants of forced laborers brought in to work the sugar fields in the late 1800s. There is also a large Italian population that first arrived after World War I to work on the sugar farms. Italians now own the majority of the area's sugar industry.

TOWNSVILLE

Townsville (population 125,000) is the "big city" of North Queensland; you have to travel 1,400 km (870 miles) south to Brisbane to find anything larger. Townsville is undergoing significant growth these days, with a lot of development not yet completed, and the town seems to be in the process of redefining its personality as a tourism and commercial center. High-rise towers cluster next to century-old colonial buildings, and palm trees and bougainvillaeas jostle with rental signs and fast-food outlets. Pleasure craft and a ship repair yard fight for control of Ross Creek.

Visitors come to Townsville for the weather and the reef. The city has a perfect warm-to-hot winter climate

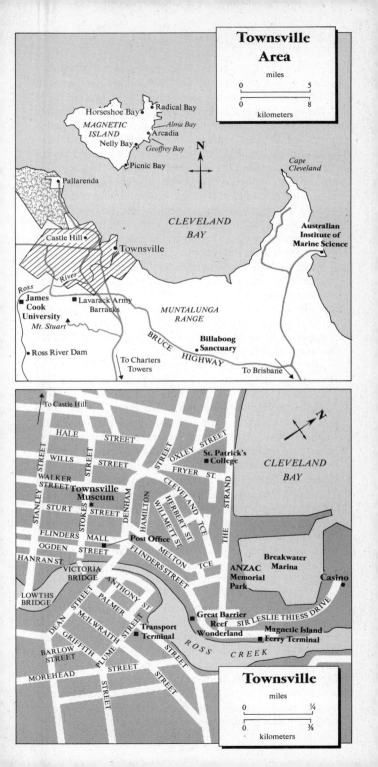

Townsville Area

miles
0 — 5
0 — 8
kilometers

MAGNETIC ISLAND

Horseshoe Bay • Radical Bay
Alma Bay
• Arcadia
Nelly Bay • *Geoffrey Bay*
• Picnic Bay

N

• Pallarenda

Cape Cleveland

CLEVELAND BAY

Castle Hill •
• Townsville

Australian Institute of Marine Science

Ross River

■ **James Cook University**
■ Lavarack Army Barracks
Mt. Stuart

MUNTALUNGA RANGE

• Ross River Dam

BRUCE HIGHWAY

■ **Billabong Sanctuary**

To Charters Towers   To Brisbane

Townsville

miles
0 — ¼
0 — ⅜
kilometers

To Castle Hill

HALE STREET
WILLS STREET
WALKER STREET
STANLEY STREET
WILLS STREET

OXLEY STREET
■ St. Patrick's College
FRYER ST.

CLEVELAND TCE

Townsville Museum
STURT STREET
STOKES STREET
DENHAM STREET
HAMILTON
HERBERT ST.
WILLMETT ST.

CLEVELAND BAY

FLINDERS MALL
■ **Post Office**
OGDEN STREET
HANRAN ST.
MELTON TCE

THE STRAND

FLINDERS STREET

Breakwater Marina

ANZAC Memorial Park

• **Casino**

VICTORIA BRIDGE
LOWTHS BRIDGE
ANTHONY ST.
PALMER STREET
DEAN STREET
McILWRAITH STREET
GRIFFITH STREET
BARLOW STREET
PLUME STREET
MOREHEAD STREET

■ **Transport Terminal**

■ **Great Barrier Reef Wonderland**

SIR LESLIE THIESS DRIVE

Magnetic Island Ferry Terminal ■

ROSS CREEK

(April to October) with clear days and balmy nights. Sunshine is guaranteed; in fact Townsville receives more sunshine hours than any other large city in Australia.

Flinders Mall is the perfect introduction to Townsville. The two-block pedestrian precinct is crowded with palms and tropical trees, fountains, street-side chess and backgammon games, benches, children's playground equipment, and an amphitheater. Here too are the main stores, fashion boutiques, and shopping arcades, the boardwalk food fair (in a delightful location along the banks of Ross Creek), the Visitor Information office, and the **Perc Tucker Art Gallery**, with its good collection of paintings, sculptures, and other works by North Queensland and international artists and craftspeople.

Flinders Mall leads to **Flinders Street East**, a nicely preserved tourist precinct with restaurants, art galleries, souvenir shops, and nightclubs. Old-style lampposts, many beautifully restored buildings from the late 19th century, some dripping in fancy iron lacework, and tropical landscaping add to the appeal. At the far end is the **Great Barrier Reef Wonderland** complex.

The aquarium at Great Barrier Reef Wonderland is operated by the Great Barrier Reef Marine Park Authority. The facility includes a huge walk-through seawater tank, complete with waves and tides, that holds a living coral reef and associated marine environment. Because of the fragile nature of this environment the achievement is remarkable, and it is one of the most spectacular views of living coral that you can see. You should also see the Great Barrier Reef film at the adjacent Omnimax Theater. Then you can visit the Great Barrier Reef itself with sufficient knowledge to appreciate fully what you see.

Flinders Mall, Flinders Street East, and the Great Barrier Reef Wonderland are the best areas in which to shop. Many stores here are open more often than the five-and-a-half-day Australian norm. Among the items sold here are aboriginal artifacts, coral, artworks, and tropical beachwear.

Castle Hill, which dominates the central city, has a lookout providing spectacular views. There is a walkway from Stanley Street to the hilltop, but it is a hot climb in the middle of the day. City tours include it on their itineraries, or you can take a taxi. The nearby **Townsville Environmental Park** between the airport and Pallarenda is best reached by bicycle or taxi. It is recognized as one of the world's most important waterbird sanctuaries, while **Billabong Sanctuary** 16 km (10 miles) east on the

Bruce Highway is an attractive home for tropical wildlife, including crocodiles and koalas. There is a daily half-day tour from the city. The rapidly developing **Townsville Palmetum** near James Cook University has the world's most comprehensive collection of palms. And don't miss the Sunday-morning **Cotters Market** in Flinders Mall; it's North Queensland's largest arts-and-crafts market, and you will be amazed by the variety of offerings.

Staying and Dining in Townsville

The ► **Sheraton Breakwater Casino/Hotel**, on the waterfront, is the city's best hotel. The 200-room hotel overlooks the Pacific Ocean, Magnetic Island (for which, see below), and the Breakwater Marina. Nearby are a ferry terminal for the Magnetic Island catamaran, an overwater restaurant, and the departure points for reef, diving, and sailing trips. Some of Townsville's other good hotels are along a nearby section of beach. Best are the high-rise ► **Townsville Ambassador** and the low-rise ► **Townsville Reef International**. Both have lush gardens, pools, and excellent bars and restaurants. Located on Flinders Mall, the high-rise, mid-priced ► **Townsville Travelodge Hotel**, has a rooftop pool and observation area.

The best restaurant in town is probably **Melton's** at the Sheraton. Jackets are not mandatory, but most male patrons wear them, with or without ties. Other fine hotel restaurants are **Cassis** on the roof of the Townsville Ambassador, **Flutes** in the Reef International, and **Palmer's** at the beautifully restored Australian Hotel in South Townsville. Dress at these restaurants is definitely relaxed.

North Queensland is famous for tropical fruits and seafood. Most menus include dishes based on these products, while some restaurants specialize in them. You can almost always find good fresh prawns, Moreton Bay "bugs" (i.e., lobsters), mud crabs, and two local fish, barramundi and coral trout. **Ancient Mariners** on Flinders Street just west of the mall (Tel: 077/72-3324) and **Admiral's** on Sturt Street at Blackwood Street (Tel: 077/21-1911) are two very popular all-you-can-eat seafood smorgasbords where there is some music and atmosphere—but the emphasis is on quantity. **Banana's Rock Café** (Tel: 077/71-2799) and **Luvit Pancake Parlor** (Tel: 077/21-1366), both on Flinders Street East, are noisy and fun, while the nearby **Metro Eastside** (Tel: 077/72-2709) serves good vegetarian food.

The city has a collection of good French, Chinese,

Italian, Greek, Malay, Mexican, and other ethnic restaurants as well. Some of the better ones are the **Dynasty Restaurant** on Flinders Street East for classic Chinese seafood cuisine (Tel: 077/72-7099), **L'Escargoterie** on Palmer Street near Victoria Bridge for French provincial cooking (Tel: 077/72-3435), and **Hog's Breath Cafe** on Flinders Street East for excellent Australian steaks (Tel: 077/71-5747).

Several places feature contemporary Australian rock music. Best are the **Dalrymple Hotel**, the **Seaview Hotel**, and the **Rio Rock** at the Cri Tavern, while the top discos are the **Bank** and **Illusions**—both on Flinders Street East— and **Elizas** at the Crown Hotel in South Townsville. **Portraits Wine Bar** on Flinders Street East and the **Sheraton Lobby Lounge** are popular quieter spots for talking, drinking, and dancing, while the **Quarterdeck** overlooking the marina is a great place for an early evening cocktail.

MAGNETIC ISLAND

Magnetic Island was one of Australia's best-kept secrets, but several major resort developments have changed that. The island, opposite Townsville in Cleveland Bay, is larger than many along the coast and has a permanent population of about 2,500. Many of the residents commute to Townsville daily by catamaran (20 minutes). The island was named in 1770 by Captain Cook, who thought his ship's compass was affected by the rocky promontories. No one since has agreed.

There are fine beaches, good walking trails through the bush, and several little resort towns on Magnetic Island's eastern side. The island has two well-priced hotels, three or four nice family resorts, a multitude of self-contained holiday units, and a variety of other accommodations.
▶ **Arcadia Resort Hotel**, on the beach at Geoffrey Bay, and
▶ **Latitude 19 Resort**, about half a mile inland from Nelly Bay, are two well-kept properties with good rooms, swimming pools, bars, restaurants, and other vacation facilities.

One of the joys of Magnetic Island is being able to move from bay to bay as whim dictates. There is a good bus service with helpful drivers who will stop almost anywhere, or you can hire small MiniMoke vehicles (which carry four people), mini-motorcycles, or bicycles. Sporting facilities include a nine-hole golf course, bowling, tennis, horseback riding, and, of course, all types of water sports. There are lifesaving clubs at Picnic Bay and Alma Bay (Arcadia), which provide beach lookouts and patrols on weekends.

Two companies operate catamaran services to the island from downtown Townsville about every 90 minutes. There is also a car ferry to the island that operates several times daily.

THE CENTRAL REEF

Running more or less parallel to the coast, the Central Great Barrier Reef stretches from Mackay north to Mission Beach. Most access to the reef is from Townsville, the Whitsunday Islands, Mackay, and Mission Beach.

Seeing the Central Reef

The most visited reef in this region is **Kelso Reef**, which is linked to Townsville by a high-speed catamaran (90 minutes) or helicopter (20 minutes). Coral viewing can be done in a glass-bottomed boat or by snorkeling or scuba diving. Similar day trips to the reef are offered by the M.V. *Quickcat* from Clump Point just north of Mission Beach and by various boats on different days from the Whitsundays and Mackay. The cost is about A$95.

There are some other trips that, though they don't actually go to the Great Barrier Reef itself, still give you a chance to see some good coral. From Townsville there are trips to Orpheus Island for coral viewing and island exploring, and there's an occasional trip to Great Palm Island (see Other Islands, below, for both). The cost runs from A$50 to A$75.

In the Whitsundays area there is an underwater observatory on **Hook Island**, which is worth visiting if you are not keen on snorkeling or diving but still want to see something of the reef. Boats operate from Shute Harbour and from some of the islands.

Diving the Central Reef

Firms in the Central Reef area offer three types of diving expeditions: coastal reef dives, shipwreck dives, and outer reef drop-offs. It's important to understand what type of dive is being offered by the numerous operators.

It's possible to dive the coastal reefs and some wrecks on day trips, but the outer reefs require extended tours. Experts rave about the diving on the outer reef wall, where drop-offs plunge 165 feet or more, and where water clarity is outstanding. This is where you can get

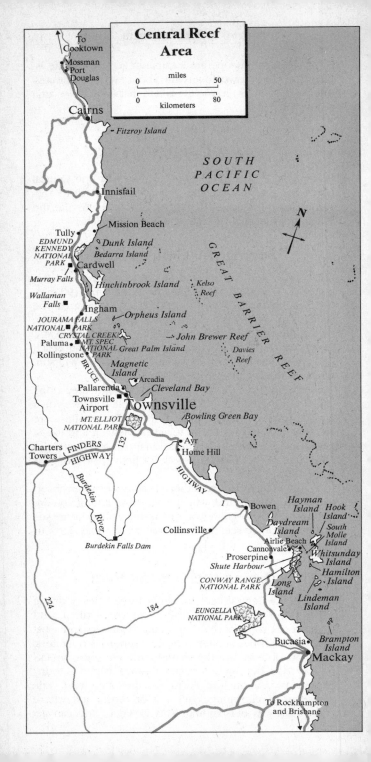

some brilliant underwater photographs if you own or rent the right equipment. Most of the dive boats offer rental gear and some even have on-board photographic processing equipment.

Diving day trips are available from Townsville to Kelso Reef, to Orpheus Island, and to the *Yongala* wreck. The *Yongala* is considered by many to be the best wreck dive on the reef because of the abundance of sea life there. The 4,000-ton ship sank in 100 feet of water in 1911 during a heavy storm, with the loss of 120 lives. Unfortunately the wreck is in fairly exposed waters, so winds and strong tides can affect comfort and water clarity. On a good day, however, this may be the ultimate dive experience.

A number of extended trips are also possible. The Dive Bell takes the 66-foot M.V. *Hero* out on overnight and extended trips, Pro-Dive has *Running Free* doing two-night trips, and Mike Ball Dive Expeditions operates M.V. *Watersport* and M.V. *Supersport*. All boats provide cylinders and weight belts, with other gear available for rental. Dive trips are usually heavily booked, so plan ahead. (**Dive Bell**, 141 Ingham Road, Townsville 4810; Tel: 077/21-1155. **Mike Ball Dive Expeditions**, 252 Walker Street, Townsville 4810; Tel: 077/72-3022. **Pro-Dive**, Great Barrier Reef Wonderland, Townsville 4810; Tel: 077/21-1760.)

Learning-to-dive facilities here are excellent. Short, hold-hands courses are available at some of the resorts. Full-certificate courses are also readily available; these give you a qualification that is recognized all over the world. Mike Ball Dive Expeditions has a dive center in Townsville that has been widely acclaimed. **Sun City Watersports** uses a 50-meter pool for initial training, then takes you to the reef for further experience; Tel: (077) 71-6527.

Fishing

The reef is a fisherman's paradise, both for the variety of fish and for the near-certainty of a good catch. Reef fishing trips depart daily from Townsville, less frequently from other centers, and can last for 8, 12, or 15 hours. Some are little more than drinking binges, but others are for serious fishermen. Local travel agents will be happy to provide details and make recommendations, or you might try **Challenger Charters**, Tel: (077) 72-4857.

There is also a rapidly growing **game-fishing** industry based in Townsville. The Cape Bowling Green fishing grounds offer marlin, sailfish, and other large game fish. Most boats are light tackle, and several world records have been posted. Good catches have been made as early as March, but the best season appears to be from June to November. There are several fishing competitions in the August-to-October period. Visitors can hire a game-fishing boat complete with crew, tackle, bait, meals, and drinks for about A$1,000 a day for up to eight passengers. Sometimes a single seat may be obtained on a charter or regular trip; try Australian Pacific Charters; Tel: (077) 71-2534.

THE WHITSUNDAY ISLANDS

The 70-odd islands of the Whitsunday group and Whitsunday Passage, which separates them from the mainland, are probably the best and most beautiful places in Australia to spend a vacation on water.

Most of the islands have been declared wholly or largely parkland, and many have fringing reef. All are within 30 miles of Shute Harbour near Proserpine, which is about halfway between Townsville and Mackay to the south. Shute is the jumping-off point for island cruises and yacht rentals. The islands are not on the Great Barrier Reef, but they provide facilities for getting to it.

The principal mainland center for this region is **Airlie Beach** (next to Shute Harbour), a small, attractive waterfront town with a rapidly growing tourism infrastructure. Airlie Beach is three hours south of Townsville by bus (services are operated by all major companies). There is a small airport with some commuter flights.

Air access to the islands is via Ansett Airlines to **Hamilton Island**. Direct flights operate from Brisbane, Sydney, and several northern and western centers.

Whitsunday Islands Resorts

Each of the Whitsunday Islands resorts—one resort complex on each of six islands surrounding Whitsunday Island, although none on that island itself—has a specific niche in the marketplace.

The ▶ **Hayman Resort** on **Hayman Island** is very upscale, sophisticated, and expensive. No costs have been spared to make this a luxury resort. There is an air of elegance, of good living, of indulgence. Food, service, and facilities are excellent; if you have reached the top,

Hayman is for you. This 230-room resort has splendid furnishings, tropical gardens, a huge man-made swimming lagoon, and a choice of four fine restaurants.

Most visitors get to the resort by the launch (40 minutes) that leaves from near the Hamilton Island airstrip, but you can also travel via Airlie Beach or by seaplane from Townsville.

▶ **Hamilton Island Resort** is more difficult to define. It started out upscale, changed direction, and now caters to a midrange-to-luxury clientele. This is by far the largest resort off the Queensland coast, with high-rise and low-rise buildings, a marina, a deer park, an airport, a nice beach, a huge pool, a shopping village, and a throbbing nightlife. Development is ongoing. Hamilton guests come in a variety of ages, backgrounds, and interests. The island is diverse enough to satisfy all—except those looking for peace and quiet. The resort has seven restaurants of varying standards, as well as fast-food outlets and a supermarket. All accommodations have been built within the last ten years.

You can fly directly to Hamilton Island from many southern cities, or use the high-speed catamaran from Shute Harbour (30 minutes).

▶ **South Molle Island Resort**, now operated by Ansett Airlines, is one of the older establishments, but extensive rebuilding has kept it in good condition. The island has long stretches of beach, good water-sport facilities, walking trails, a large swimming pool, and a small golf course. Restaurants emphasize quantity rather than quality, but prices are reasonable and guests enjoy the relaxed, friendly atmosphere.

Prices here are much lower than on Hayman and much of Hamilton, so the island attracts family groups, young people, and middle-class Australians looking for sun, sea, and excitement. There is nightly entertainment and a resident band. A launch runs to South Molle from the Hamilton Island airstrip or from Shute Harbour (20 minutes).

Daydream Island is one of the smaller resort islands, and is home to the ▶ **Daydream Island Travelodge Resort**, which opened in 1991. The resort has been split into two, with day-trippers and the beach club at one end of the island and the main resort at the other. A coastal boardwalk and a mountain trail link the two sections. Marketed to a wide clientele—singles and families alike—it offers extensive water-sport facilities, a choice of restaurants and bars, tennis courts, a gymnasium, and several pools. There are several nice beaches here, and boats operate regularly from Shute Harbour (15 minutes) and from Hamilton Island.

Long Island is the only island with more than one resort. The ▶ **Long Island Palm Bay Hideaway** has recently been upgraded but still provides basic accommodation for those who are seeking an island without frills or expensive entertainment. Cabins are available with small kitchens and ceiling fans; meals may also be eaten in a communal dining room. There is a spa, a pool, and a nice beach. A little over a mile away, the ▶ **Radisson Long Island Resort** caters to an adult clientele in a village atmosphere. It offers two pools, a spa, sauna, gym, tennis and basketball facilities, and a range of accommodations in the mid-market category.

The ▶ **Lindeman Island Resort** is the longest operating of the resorts and the most southerly in the Whitsunday group. Bought in 1991 by the Club Méditerranée group, it has since added and changed facilities to match other Club Med properties around the world. There are plenty of activities and good dining in two restaurants and at the poolside barbecue area. During the day guests can avail themselves of golf, tennis, and water sports, while at night a disco operates on the beach. The island is reached by air from Mackay or Proserpine or by boat from Hamilton Island or Mackay.

Whitsunday Mainland

Airlie Beach, a small, attractive waterfront town, is the principal mainland center in this region and, together with adjoining **Cannonvale**, offers reasonable shopping and restaurant facilities as well as many good accommodations from which to choose. The area is quite attractive, with timbered mountains, extensive water views, and pretty settlements. **Conway Range National Park** is nearby, with lush rain forest and walking trails.

Major resorts at Airlie Beach include ▶ **Whitsunday Terraces**, in a central elevated position overlooking the town; ▶ **Coral Sea**, a small property on the waterfront; ▶ **Club Crocodile**, the newest and largest of the resorts on a site a little bit farther from town; and ▶ **Whitsunday Wanderers**, a particularly popular choice for families. Whitsunday Terraces is the most expensive of these resorts; the others grow less expensive in the order in which they're listed.

Shute Harbour, a 15-mile bus ride from Airlie Beach, is the departure point for numerous nautical day trips. Most operations are well run, and you can visit just one or a number of islands in a day. There is a growing number of other good water-based attractions here, such as yacht and motor cruises that go nowhere in particular. Boats call at a deserted beach, give you time for some snorkeling, and generally just offer a relaxed day in the sun. At least half a dozen of these trips leave the Shute Harbour jetty every day, so telephone around when you get there to see which suits you best. Try the *Apollo* (Tel: 079/46-6922) or the *Gretel,* a former America's Cup contender (Tel: 079/46-6224).

Sailing

Shute Harbour is the center of Australia's bareboat yacht-charter business simply because the Whitsunday area provides the ideal weather, temperature, and attractions to keep "boaties" happy.

Bareboat chartering in the Whitsundays is less than 20 years old, yet facilities are outstanding. It's not yet possible, however, to equate the Whitsundays with the Bahamas, the Riviera, or the Aegean; the Whitsundays' attraction is their solitude and the large number of uninhabited islands, with a sprinkling of resorts.

Three types of charters are available. Absolute novices can charter a boat complete with skipper, who will do most of the work and take you to the best fishing, snorkeling, and sightseeing locations. If you're keen the skipper will also teach you how to handle the boat yourself and let you have some practice.

For those able to sail but who need a little help, some companies have flotilla cruises during the peak season where you travel in a group with an experienced skipper close by. It's good moral support, and it can be fun being with people who enjoy a similar lifestyle.

Then there are the true bareboat charters, where you cruise without help at your own pace wherever you wish to go. All you need is food and a chart to get back to your starting point at the end of the rental period. Some skill and experience help, but generally the weather and sea conditions are kind. Motor cruisers are available for those who prefer motorized transport.

Major companies in the charter business here are **Australian Bareboat Charters**, Shute Harbour (Tel: 079/46-9381); **Cumberland Charter Yachts**, Airlie Beach (Tel: 079/46-7500); **Hamilton Island Charters**, Hamilton Island (Tel: 079/46-9900); and **Whitsunday Rent-a-Yacht**, Shute Harbour (Tel: 079/46-9232).

There are also sailing opportunities on large crewed vessels. Many of these run as day trips, but others extend for longer periods. You can choose among the romance of a brigantine, the luxury of a world-cruising yacht, or the excitement of a famous racing yacht. Trips are available for three, five, six, or seven nights departing from Shute Harbour or Hamilton Island. You should check **Margherita** (Tel: 079/46-6224), **Rogue II** (Tel: 079/46-6665), and **Reef Enterprise** (Tel: 079/46-7228) before making a decision.

The Hamilton Island Race Week in April and the Whitsunday Fun Race in September draw competitors and spectators from Australia and overseas.

OTHER ISLANDS IN THE CENTRAL REEF AREA

Apart from the Whitsundays there are other islands in the Central Reef region popular with visitors. All provide sunshine, sand beaches, clear water, relaxation, and good facilities.

SOUTH OF TOWNSVILLE

Brampton Island, about 72 km (45 miles) south of Whitsunday Island, is mountainous, with lush forests and fringing reef. The island is a national park, and its ▶ **Brampton Island Resort** is low-rise, casual, and mid-market. There are many water and land-based sports facilities on the island for windsurfing, catamaran sailing, tennis, and volleyball. The resort also offers evening entertainment and a choice of restaurants and bars.

The Mainland

The island is reached by air (15 minutes) or launch from **Mackay**, a small city surrounded by sugarcane some 400 km (250 miles) south of Townsville. Mackay is the region's commercial center, and it has Australia's largest bulk-sugar loading terminal, as well as a major coal-loading port south of the city. Regular boat trips to the reef and southern Whitsunday Islands depart from Mackay, and there are some nice beaches north of the city. The ▶ **White Lace Motel** provides some of the best accommodation in the city, but don't expect anything particularly grand.

For a beach-resort atmosphere try ▶ **Kohuna Village**

Resort at Bucasia, 15 minutes north of the city. A series of *bures* (individual hut/villas) is perched right on the beachfront here. Each *bure* is tastefully decorated and has its own bathroom and kitchen facilities. A festive family atmosphere prevails at Kohuna Village.

NORTH OF TOWNSVILLE

No resort exists on **Great Palm Island**, and in fact you cannot stay overnight at present. The island is run by an elected council, and considerable debate continues to wage about the desirability of developing tourism; the main interest on the island is its 3,500 aboriginal inhabitants. Access is by air from Townsville (20 minutes), with several flights daily.

Orpheus Island is about 90 km (56 miles) north of Townsville and is connected to it by seaplane service (20 minutes). ▶ **Orpheus Island Resort**, small and exclusive, has won several industry awards for excellence. Expensive and stylish, it is a place for enjoying good food and wine, relaxing on the beach, around the pool, or in the spa, and meeting others who, like you, want to escape reality for a short while. Many are from overseas and come here for the privacy, rather than for the type of activities offered at other resorts.

Hinchinbrook Island 208 km (129 miles) north of Townsville off of Cardwell, is North Queensland's biggest island and one of the most spectacular, with high mountains, thick forests, and narrow channels winding through mangroves. Most of the island remains untouched by development. The small ▶ **Hinchinbrook Island Resort** is on the northern end, connected to Cardwell on the mainland by speedboat (30 minutes) and to Townsville by seaplane (30 minutes). Accommodation is in individual cabins scattered on the hillside, with a central pool and bar/restaurant area—and a great beach. Guests are encouraged to simply enjoy the beauty and solitude of this island: There are no telephones, radios, or television sets. Most guests are Australian couples or families who enjoy the outdoors and are not seeking hectic nightlife.

Bedarra Island, north of Hinchinbrook, is exclusive. It has two small luxury resorts: ▶ **Bedarra Bay** and ▶ **Bedarra Hideaway**, where no children or day-trippers are allowed; most guests are couples from Melbourne and Sydney or visitors from the United States and Europe. Each resort takes a maximum of 32 guests; both are operated by Australian Airlines. The resorts provide excellent facilities and cuisine as well as peace and privacy for those who can afford it. Access is by launch from Dunk Island, its neighbor to the north.

Dunk Island provides one of the prettiest venues of any of the resorts. Rain forest, good beaches, and a hillside national park combine to form an idyllic setting. It was on Dunk that E. J. Banfield lived and wrote *The Confessions of a Beachcomber* early this century. The island environment is remarkably little changed today. The ▶ **Dunk Island Resort** has been extensively redeveloped in recent years, and refurbishing continues. Dunk can accommodate 400 people—and often does. It is extremely popular with the southern Australian package vacationer looking for an upscale vacation; there are growing numbers of international visitors, however. The tariff is all-inclusive, except for a few sports such as game fishing and target shooting. Two lovely beaches, two pools, two restaurants, several bars, and activity centers mean that the resort never feels crowded. The bayview villas on the beachfront are the best accommodations.

Access to Dunk Island is by air from Townsville or Cairns (40 minutes), boat from Clump Point near Mission Beach (30 minutes), or water taxi from Mission Beach (10 minutes).

THE NORTH QUEENSLAND OUTBACK

A great deal of mystery, intrigue, and romance has been attached to life in the Australian Outback. As far as visitors are concerned, the Outback is anywhere inland where there are few people. You can be on the edge of the Outback only 80 km (50 miles) inland from Townsville. All the ingredients are there: isolation, great wildlife, old mining towns, huge cattle properties, and Outback characters.

Some people call this the real Australia. Certainly the people, the country, and the lifestyle are "real"—but they're as foreign to the average Australian as to the overseas visitor. It's fascinating, it's intriguing, but it's a life few would want to live. In other words, it's something for a short visit.

You can rent a car or camper van in Townsville and drive into the Outback, but for most people the environment is too strange and daunting for that. You will probably want to take a tour with locals who know the country and can make you feel comfortable.

Charters Towers

This town of about 7,000 people, 120 km (75 miles) southwest of Townsville on the Flinders Highway, is the largest and most interesting local remnant of a past era. From 1872 to 1916 it was a fabulously rich gold-mining city, with a peak population of about 35,000 and the nickname "The World." Today, beautiful old buildings, several museums, and a restored stock exchange are reminders of those days. You still occasionally see "ringers" (local cowboys) on horseback and hitching horses to posts in the main street, just as they did a hundred years ago. The 1980s saw gold fever return to Charters Towers, but this time it was big companies developing recently discovered deposits. Plans are in the works to re-create an area of old goldmining activity, but at present visitors cannot actually see mining at close hand.

Charters Towers is accessible from Townsville on day trips, offered by several companies on different days of the week.

TOURING THE OUTBACK

For those with the time, **Australian Explorer Tours** operates a three-day/two-night Outback and rain forest tour, which visits Charters Towers, then heads north into the wonderful country of the Great Basalt Wall and the upper reaches of the Burdekin River. You can see loads of wildlife, visit working cattle stations, stay in bush camps, see Australia's highest single-drop waterfall, and travel through delightful rain forest. Departures are from Townsville on Sundays; bookings are essential. (Australian Explorer Tours, c/o The Travel Co., Denham Street, Townsville 4810; Tel: 077/71-5024.)

Another way to experience the Outback is by arranging a stay at a Queensland farm; see the Accommodations Reference section, below, for more information.

UP THE COAST FROM TOWNSVILLE

The Bruce Highway northward from Townsville to Cairns passes through interesting country. The drive can be made in about four hours, but there are numerous sites clearly marked along the way that can extend the time to several days. Although the road parallels the coast, for most of its length it is several miles inland, so the beach suburbs north of Townsville are bypassed. At **Rolling-stone**, 50 km (31 miles) from Townsville, there is good safe river swimming; a side road leads 6 km (3½ miles) off the highway to Balgal Beach, where there is excellent fishing.

Approximately 15 km (9 miles) farther north, a road to the left climbs the rain forest–covered ranges to the **Crystal Creek/Mount Spec National Park**, with its bushwalks, swimming holes, lookouts, and village of Paluma (20 km/12 miles off the highway). Some 20 km farther along the highway a sign indicates **Jourama Falls National Park**, a very popular river swimming spot 6 km (3½ miles) off the highway.

Ingham, 120 km (75 miles) northwest of Townsville, is a sugar-producing town with a heavy Italian influence. Almost half its population is made up of Italian immigrants who once worked as cane cutters, but who now own most of the farms. Inland is Wallaman Falls and beautiful rain forest, while on the coast **Forrest Beach** and **Taylors Beach** have good swimming.

The Bruce Highway now climbs high above the coast, providing a spectacular view of rugged Hinchinbrook Island and the mangrove-flanked passages of Hinchinbrook Channel, then continues into the vacation center of **Cardwell**.

Stop and look at the National Parks Information Centre near the jetty at Cardwell and consider a boat trip either to the Hinchinbrook Island Resort or through the Hinchinbrook Channel to the mangrove boardwalks. Just north of Cardwell, the **Edmund Kennedy National Park** has interesting mangroves, huge paperbark trees, swamps, and boardwalks, but it also has many mosquitoes. **Murray Falls** is another pleasant detour 15 km (9 miles) off the highway.

Tully, the wettest place in Australia, will drench you (it gets 14 feet of rain a year), while nearby **Mission Beach** provides solitude and tranquillity. The almost five-mile-long beach is fringed with coconut palms and rain forest, and although there are three excellent resorts and a range of other accommodations along this beautiful stretch of coastline, at times you may be entirely alone.

CAIRNS AND THE NORTHERN GREAT BARRIER REEF REGION

Cairns, in so-called Far North Queensland, is the most northerly Queensland city. It has recently been engulfed by world tourism, and some of its citizens aren't quite sure they like all the consequences.

Cairns has gained high-rise hotels, a major international airport, a greatly expanded tourism infrastructure, and a wide range of expensive but generally tacky visitor-oriented clothing, jewelry, and souvenir shops; it has lost much of its slow pace, its isolation, and its small-town gregariousness. Cairns is nonetheless widely perceived to be more relaxed and casual than Townsville, and to have more of a holiday atmosphere about it. Cairns—and Far North Queensland in general—has its own lifestyle, quite different even from that of southern Queensland.

Those Queensland natives who knew Cairns, Port Douglas, and Cooktown ten years ago are sad to see the passing of an era. Those who nowadays come here for the first time find an area attuned to visitors and generally able to fulfill their expectations. And yet these towns, especially Cooktown, are still a very, very long way from St-Tropez.

Nothing, however, has yet changed the region's lovely wet, green rain forests, its clear water and extensive reefs, or its wide, sandy beaches, where you can still find peace and solitude.

CAIRNS

Cairns (pronounced "Cans") is one of the fastest-growing cities in Australia, and the growth is almost entirely due to tourism. About eight years ago the Australian government built a modern international airport in the city, and shortly afterward the state of Queensland decided to market it heavily as the northern gateway to Australia from North America and Asia. The airport has been hugely successful (it has indeed become the major north-

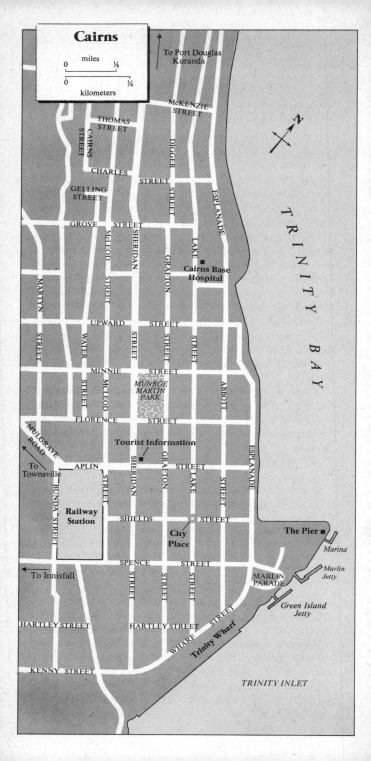

ern gateway into Australia) and international tourism into the region has boomed. Accommodations, day tours, restaurants, shopping, car rentals, and reef facilities have all mushroomed to meet demand.

A pattern that has repeated itself around the world quickly emerged. Locals respond to the initial demand by building mediocre facilities in a hurry; local governments adopt a liberal attitude to town planning and building regulations; and then international developers move in, pushing real-estate prices sky-high. That's Cairns today. Despite recent fluctuations in tourist numbers Cairns continues to grow, and there are indications that future development may be of a higher standard. The Hilton International Cairns, the Cairns International, the Matson Plaza, the Radisson Plaza, and the Holiday Inn have all raised both building and service standards and set Cairns on the road toward becoming a desirable international destination.

The Cairns region has far more of interest than the city of Cairns itself, but many visitors base themselves in the city and sightsee on day trips. The only real alternatives are to stay at one of the beach resorts north of town, or at Port Douglas, even farther north.

The annual **Fun in the Sun Festival** is held in October, offering a street parade, a fair, and some sporting and cultural events. May to October has the best weather, but this is also the peak season, when accommodation can be tight.

Exploring Cairns

Central Cairns is built on flat land between the railway station and the shoreline. There are wide streets with huge shade trees and sidewalks for strolling. The center of Cairns is **City Place**, a small pedestrian precinct that was formed by closing a street intersection and converting the legs into cul-de-sacs. The main retail shopping area comprises the two blocks toward Trinity Bay and two blocks south toward Trinity Inlet.

Visitors are inevitably drawn to the waterfront, so walk down Shields Street to the **Esplanade**. You may be disappointed to find that the water here is very shallow and there is no beach; at low tide the mangrove mud stretches for hundreds of yards, but the numerous water birds are some compensation. The Esplanade has been largely taken over by the backpackers who flock to the city for the warm weather. It's a real cosmopolitan scene—

everyone is relaxed and happy—and the backpackers have encouraged a series of cheap eateries.

Head south on the walkway that runs along the shore toward the inlet. To your left is the Pier complex, with its many shops and restaurants, and the low-rise ▶ **Radisson Plaza Hotel** in a delightful waterfront setting; to the right is the ▶ **Pacific International Hotel**, once the premier hotel in Cairns.

Ahead is the site where in 1876 Cairns started as a small port for the gold and tin mines in the interior. Later this rowdy area was known as the Barbary Coast, and no genteel visitor ventured here after dark. Most of the sleaziness has now gone—along with, unfortunately, many of the fine old buildings with wide wrought-iron balconies.

Turn left onto Marlin Parade and walk to Marlin Jetty. During the 1970s and 1980s Cairns was an important center for big-game fishing, but recent seasons have not been as good. The reef waters northeast of the city have produced huge fish, some weighing more than a thousand pounds. The season lasts from September to November, and despite the high cost many boats are booked well in advance. At other times of the year you can see their sleek lines bobbing against the jetty; one look shows you that game fishing is a multimillion-dollar industry here. (For details see Northern Reef and Marlin Fishing, below.) The paddlesteamer S.S. *Louisa* departs mornings and afternoons from Marlin Jetty for a desultory and uneventful trip along the mangrove-lined estuary (Tel: 070/31-3065). M.V. *Terri-Too* operates a similar program (Tel: 070/31-4007), and Sunlover Cruises operates a dinner cruise on a catamaran (Tel: 070/31-1055).

Overlooking this area is the high-rise ▶ **Hilton International Cairns** on a lovely waterfront site. Just across the road is the very stylish ▶ **Cairns International Hotel**; it's not on the waterfront but is right next door to a major shopping complex.

This is also the location of a cruise-liner terminal and retail/office complex called **Trinity Wharf**. On the ground floor is a bus terminal now used by all express operators, and upstairs are several restaurants. This is also the departure area for daily boat cruises to Green Island, Michaelmas Cay, Hastings Reef, and Fitzroy Island, and for charter boats for fishing, snorkeling, and diving trips to the Outer Reef. The wharf area is naturally a great place for seafood restaurants; **Tawny's** on Marlin Parade (Tel: 070/51-1722), the ever-popular and moderately priced **Barnacle Bill's** on the Esplanade (Tel: 070/51-2241), and **Barra's** in the conservatory on Abbott Street (Tel: 070/31-4343) are three of the best.

A walk north along Lake Street will lead you back to City Place. On the way you pass several arcades and shopping centers full of giftware and fashion shops, as well as a number of small eating places. The **Cairns Museum**, which contains aboriginal artifacts and other exhibits pertaining to northern Queensland, is housed at City Place.

Cairns must have some of the best restaurants of any provincial city in Australia, but many close early and there is a disappointing lack of good open-air dining. To some extent this is due to Cairns's climate; from December to May it is very hot and wet. Seafood and tropical fruit are the two local specialties, and these are extensively used, even at so-called international-style restaurants such as **Verandahs** (Tel: 070/510-011) on Shields Street and **Dundee's** (Tel: 070/510-399) at Sheridan and Alpine streets. **Creme de la Creme**, a small French restaurant at 14 Lake Street, has reasonable prices and offers excellent service (Tel: 070/52-1220). **Yamagen** at 40 Village Lane offers exquisite Japanese food (Tel: 070/31-6688), and **Charlies on the Esplanade** provides an excellent seafood buffet at very reasonable prices (Tel: 070/51-5011).

Nightlife has not grown apace with the recent tourism development, so Cairns is not the place for a wild night-time vacation. The cocktail bar at the Hilton is busy early in the evening, while the Pier Marketplace offers the chance to see aboriginal and Pacific Islander dance. **Ribbons** at the Hilton and the **Canoe Club** in the Pier market-place next to the Radisson are two of the better discos.

Shopping in Cairns

It's as a visitor shopping center that central Cairns excels. There are souvenirs of substance at **Australian Aspect** on Wharf Street and **Australian Craftworks** on Village Lane next to the Cairns International Hotel; **Presenting Australia** in the Pier marketplace has some exclusive hand-painted resort wear, aboriginal art, jewelry, and crafts; the **Australian Bush Trading Co.** on Spence Street has clothing and souvenirs; while **Crocadilliacs** at 81 Lake Street has the largest range of tee-shirts and swimwear in the area. There are many shops where you can buy opals, including **Opal Lovers** at 121 Abbott Street and **The Sapphire and Opal Center** at 129 Abbott Street.

The laid-back lifestyle of the Cairns region suits artists;

examples of their work can be seen in many galleries. **Editions Gallery** on Village Lane, the **Lake Street Gallery** at 44 Lake Street, the **Pier Gallery** at the Pier marketplace, and the **Pottery Place** at 171 Newell Street are good possibilities. Bargains are often available at the **City Place Art Markets** held each Friday and Saturday from 10 A.M. to 2 P.M. The art of other cultures is also sold in galleries here: **Gallery Primitive** at 26 Abbott Street has Australian aboriginal and New Guinean artifacts; the **Niugini Gallery** at 55 Lake Street specializes in artifacts and village handicrafts from Papua New Guinea; and **The Asian Connection** at 51 Abbott Street combines the art of Papua New Guinea with that of Indonesia, Thailand, India, and China.

For locally produced arts and crafts, visit the market at **Rusty's Bazaar** on Grafton Street on Saturday morning or the **Mud Markets** every weekend at the Pier, where local craftspeople bring pushcart shops to the central plaza and sell paintings, handicrafts, jewelry, carvings, glassware, and many other things.

Cairns is in the wet tropics, so it's not surprising that there is lush tropical growth in some parts, for example in the **Centenary Lakes/Flecker Botanical Gardens/ Whitfield Range Environmental Park** region about 3 km (2 miles) northwest of the city center. These sites, which are more or less contiguous, combine lakes, formal gardens, parkland, and mountain walks. Don't visit in the rain or during the mosquito-breeding season (December to March), but otherwise the area is a delight. While out this way you might also wish to visit the **Royal Flying Doctor Visitor Centre** on Junction Street to learn more about how this airborne medical service helps the Outback.

▶ **Cairns Colonial Club**, 4 km (2½ miles) north of the city center, is a popular resort for middle-class Australian and international visitors. It is in the middle of a flat residential area and is not close to any beach, but there is a huge pool, a bar, a restaurant, and free transport to and from the city center and the airport.

AROUND CAIRNS

While Cairns receives much publicity, it is actually the Cairns *region* that visitors rave about. The combination of reef, islands, rain forest, and lush rolling farm country is enchanting.

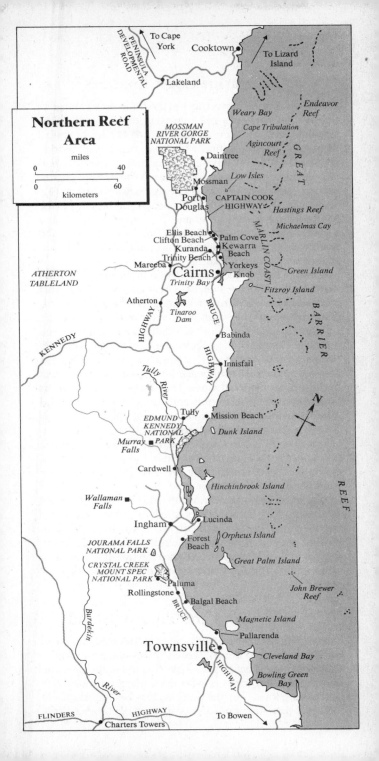

The Marlin Coast Beaches

For some people Cairns City has the huge disadvantage of having no beach. It's not until you travel north to the Marlin Coast, between 20 and 35 km (12 to 22 miles) from Cairns, that you find white-sand beaches and swimmable water. Each of these beaches and residential areas has developed its own character. Visitors can choose among Yorkeys Knob, Trinity Beach, Kewarra Beach, Clifton Beach, Palm Cove, and Ellis Beach; the beaches to the north are most appealing, and Palm Cove is the major tourist center. All the local communities have shops and resorts or other accommodations, and regular bus service connects each to Cairns.

Some of the best accommodation in the area is at **Palm Cove**, at the large ▶ **Ramada Great Barrier Reef Resort** with its huge free-form swimming pool surrounded by giant trees, and the small, exclusive ▶ **Reef House Resort**, which offers expensive lodging in a delightful setting. The Paradise Village Shopping Centre here will meet ordinary needs, and it's all set amid huge paperbark trees, palms, and the beautiful beach. In this same area you will find the large ▶ **Palm Cove Travelodge Resort**, with its ten swimming pools, tennis and squash courts, golf, and other activities just a short distance from the beach.

The ▶ **Kewarra Beach Resort** is another excellent bungalow development with a touch of the exotic—and a gorgeous crescent beach. The huge lobby and open restaurant add to the beachfront site. Most guests are Australian couples or families.

As with all of northern Australia, these inviting beaches are plagued by dangerous box jellyfish from November through April. To combat the menace, five stinger-resistant floating net enclosures have recently been built along the coast, and these have proved to be effective. It is unwise to swim without protection, so use the enclosures or your hotel's pool.

Green Island and Fitzroy Island

About 15 miles offshore from Cairns is **Green Island**, a true coral cay with a small, recently rebuilt resort—the ▶ **Green Island Reef Resort**—catering to families and the hundreds of day-trippers who flock there on tours. The beaches are lovely and the water is clear, but unfortunately the coral that surrounds the island has been extensively damaged and is now generally in poor condition. Tour operators now go to Michaelmas Cay or one of the nearby reefs as part of a Green Island/reef day trip.

Fitzroy Island, a larger, mountainous, and well-treed resort island near Cairns, offers some good mid-range accommodation at the ▶ **Fitzroy Island Resort** and reasonably good coral just offshore. A trip here can be combined with a visit to Green Island in a day.

Boats of several companies leave the Cairns foreshore at various times; the largest operator is Great Adventures (Tel: 070/51-0455). Other options include Big Cat (Tel: 070/51-0444) and Reef Jet (Tel: 070/31-5559).

Several cruising yachts operate day trips to reef waters. They leave from the Marlin Jetty or the Pier Marina. Of particular note is *Ocean Spirit* (Tel: 070/31-2920), claimed to be the world's largest sailing catamaran.

Kuranda Railway and Village

One of the best excursions available from Cairns is the Kuranda train trip along a century-old rail line that rises from sea level to the cool Atherton Tableland, a plateau ranging in elevation from about 2,000 to 3,000 feet. The one and a half hours it takes to reach Kuranda is full of top sights, 15 tunnels, 40 gorges, and great anticipation. Trains leave at 8:30 and 9:00 A.M. from Cairns Railway Station and from the Freshwater Connection (10 km/6 miles out). Two tips: It is worth paying the extra fare to be on the commentary train, and on the trip up the best views are from the seats on the right-hand side.

Kuranda railway station, with its tropical flowers and ferns, is pretty, but the adjacent little village is an even greater delight. There is a particularly colorful Sunday-morning market at Kuranda and a smaller version Wednesdays through Fridays. The **Heritage Rainforest Market**, houses a small museum of local historical material and a café. Next door is the **Australian Butterfly Sanctuary**, with a huge walk-through enclosure containing up to 2,000 of the colorful creatures, notably the electric-blue Ulysses and the Australian Birdwing, the country's largest butterfly (guided tours on the hour; Tel: 070/93-7575). Nearby, the **Kuranda Wildlife Noctarium** displays nocturnal animals of the rain forest in their active, natural state. The various species coexist and interact just as they do in the wild. There is also a river cruise and the opportunity to rent canoes on the Barron River, which flows past the village. Finally, don't miss the

Tjapukai Aboriginal Dance Theatre; this is one of the few places in Australia to see aboriginal dance blended with modern theater technique. The one-hour performance, daily at 11:00 A.M. or 1:30 P.M., is excellent; Tel: (070) 93-7544.

Kuranda has some casual restaurants, the usual tourist shops, and some outstanding local art at the **Kuranda Gallery** and at the **Wild Art Gallery**, both on the main street. Good, reasonably priced accommodation is available at the ▶ **Kuranda Rainforest Resort**. If you don't want to stay you can catch an afternoon train back to Cairns, and there are also regular buses.

Inland from here the **Atherton Tableland** offers an escape from the coastal heat, with some of Australia's most stunning waterfalls and several interesting lakes and other sights. A number of operators in Cairns offer tours of the tableland, so check around for price and availability.

For action seekers, the one-day **whitewater rafting** trip on the Tully River, 150 km (93 miles) south of Cairns, is excellent. Two companies operate similar trips from Cairns and Townsville: Raging Thunder (Tel: 070/51-4911 or, toll-free, 008/07-9092) and Raft & Rain Forest (Tel: 070/51-7777 or 008/07-9039).

PORT DOUGLAS AND CAPE TRIBULATION

The Captain Cook Highway north of Cairns, from just south of Ellis Beach, runs right along the coast, passing lovely beaches and dramatic scenery. Between Cairns and Port Douglas there are two zoos: **Wild World**, which has birds, reptiles, kangaroos, and crocodiles, and **Hartley's Creek Zoo**, which stars Charlie the Crocodile. Other places worth seeing along the road are **Vic Hislop's Shark Show**, for anyone fascinated by these creatures (Tel: 070/55-0117), and the nearby **Paradise Palms Golf Course**, which claims to be the most exclusive public course in Australia. You will find it difficult to get on the course some weekends; Tel: (070) 59-1166. Those with the nerve can experience free-fall at the **A. J. Hackett Bungy Jump Centre**; Tel: (070) 31-1119.

Port Douglas was once a sleepy backwater in a delightful location. Now it has been "discovered," and visitors have flooded in, forcing many of the locals to leave. It's still a very pretty town, with nice country pubs and one of the best beaches around, but Port Douglas has changed—it's impossible to build A$300 million worth of resort development in a town of 600 people and expect it to remain the same.

Staying and Dining in Port Douglas

Although it has swept away the old Port Douglas, the ▶ **Sheraton Mirage Resort** is in fact a masterpiece of resort design and could well be the best hotel on the Queensland coast. It is expensive, but you'll receive much in return. The resort offers swimming, golf, tennis, a gymnasium, and water activities of various types, yet it's also possible to find a quiet corner and make believe you are in your own tropical paradise. The rooms are huge, and they sprawl through tropical gardens and around a large lagoon swimming pool.

The nearby ▶ **Radisson Royal Palms Resort** is pleasant and less expensive but lacks a beach. At ▶ **Club Tropical**, overlooking the water near the center of town, you can choose an excellent room with Asian, Mediterranean, Old World, or modern decor. The food at **Oskars Seafood Bar and Grill** at Club Tropical is outstanding.

For many years Port Douglas has had at least two well-publicized expensive restaurants: the **Nautilus Restaurant** (Tel: 070/99-5330) and **Sassi at Island Point** (Tel: 070/99-5323). Both still exist and each has retained its delightful setting, and they have been joined by **Danny's** on Wharf Street, which specializes in alfresco lunches; **Macrossans** at the Sheraton Mirage for fine dining; and **D.J.'s** at Marina Mirage for dining and nightclubbing.

Excursions from Port Douglas

Port Douglas has developed into a departure point for cruises, due largely to great work by the **Quicksilver Connections Company**; Tel: (070) 99-5500. This outfit has a daily trip to **Low Isles**, a small coral cay surrounded by 50 acres of reef; a daily trip to **Agincourt Reef**, where there is a pontoon, an underwater observatory, and a semi-submersible vessel; and daily wave-piercer catamaran service from Cairns. All these trips are excellent. The Low Isles trip costs A$63, Agincourt A$108; fares are slightly higher with Cairns pickup.

Also worth doing is the **Bally Hooley Express** rail tour from Port Douglas, which takes you in old railway cars pulled by a retired cane-hauling locomotive through sugarcane farms to Mossman, a pretty "sugar town." The **Rainforest Habitat** on the main Port Douglas Road is an environmental attraction that features a three-acre walk-in aviary with rain-forest landscaping, pools, waterfalls, some 65 species of native birds, and 20 butterfly species.

North to Cape Tribulation

After Port Douglas the road continues north through sugarcane fields to Mossman, then farther on to the village of Daintree. To the west of Mossman is the **Mossman River Gorge** and **Daintree National Park**. The beautiful river and waterfalls of the gorge make it one of those rare places of great natural grandeur; locals enjoy the swimming holes. You can stay in the forest at the modern and exclusive ▶ **Silky Oaks Lodge**, which provides chalets in a delightful setting. Just before Daintree a gravel road leads to the Daintree Ferry, where there are tours on the river to see rain forest and what most people hope to see: crocodiles.

After passing the ferry landing the road continues at a reasonable standard to **Cape Tribulation**, a virgin promontory named by Captain Cook as he ran his ship onto the Endeavour Reef. The area is being rapidly developed, some say spoiled, but there is still untouched beach, rain forest, and fresh mountain streams. Tours run to Tribulation from Cairns and Port Douglas, and if you are confident enough you could drive this far in a conventional vehicle, although the rental companies may insist that you travel no farther than the ferry. For an organized tour, contact Australian Pacific Tours (Tel: 070/51-9299) or Tropic Wings Tours (Tel: 070/35-3555). There are several smaller "environmental" operators as well.

▶ **Crocodylus Village**, just south of Cape Tribulation at Cow Bay, while not luxurious, provides a suitable environment for the night, while ▶ **Coconut Beach Rainforest Resort**, at Cape Tribulation, suits the demands of a more upscale clientele and has won several tourism and environmental awards.

North of here the road deteriorates rapidly. Despite massive opposition from conservationists and the general public, the state government and local council bulldozed a goat track through primeval forest, causing severe destruction to the region and probably damage to the nearby reef. The road, which was negotiable only by four-wheel-drive vehicles, is now totally impassable for many months of the year, although it is sought out by adventure travellers in the dry winter months.

COOKTOWN AND LIZARD ISLAND

Cooktown, 340 km (210 miles) north of Cairns by a lonely road (or by airplane), was Australia's first, if transient, British settlement. After James Cook had a close encounter with the Great Barrier Reef in 1770, he beached his ship for repairs where Cooktown now stands. The repairs took six weeks, so Cook and his naturalist, Joseph Banks, had plenty of time to study the flora and fauna of the strange new land. It was here that Cook named the kangaroo, and the majority of specimens that he took back to England came from the Cooktown area.

Little happened from then until 1873, when James Mulligan discovered gold in the nearby Palmer River. It turned out to be one of the richest gold rushes in history. By 1885 Cooktown's population exceeded 35,000, including about 18,000 Chinese. Now the gold is gone. A few years ago the population was down to 800, but it is growing again. Cooktown is slowly discovering tourism.

Cooktown is a place to visit for atmosphere. There are some things to see, but just walking along the main street and sitting in a local pub are the best ways to appreciate that this is a frontier town different from just about anywhere else in the world. Everything in Cooktown is done at half pace, which is the pace the visitor should work at, too.

Among the sights is the **James Cook Historical Museum** in the Sir Joseph Banks Gardens. The exhibit is nothing very special, but the building (which was once a Catholic convent school) is interesting because of its age and architectural style. Another old-time building worth seeing is what is now the Westpac Bank on the main street. On the edge of town the old cemetery contains many memories, and the Chinese Shrine is another striking reminder of a past era. So too are the **Botanic Gardens**, originally established in the 1870s and recently restored. You can ride or walk to the top of Grassy Hill and stand where Cook did as he looked out to sea, searching for a way through the reefs to open water.

One of the most surprising finds in Cooktown is the ▶ **Sovereign Hotel**. The original building, now gone, was built in 1874, but in 1987 the Sovereign was transformed into a small resort, with tropical gardens, a pool, a cocktail bar, a restaurant, and spacious quarters. It just might tempt you into staying the night—or a month. Bear in mind that Cooktown is not East Hampton, Muskoka, or St-Tropez; it's laid-back and quaint yet still very rough around the edges.

Lizard Island, some 60 miles north of Cooktown, is the most northerly of the coastal island resorts. The ▶ Lizard Island Lodge is expensive and luxurious, and the many beaches and clear water are wonderful. The marine life here is spectacular. For the marlin-fishing season (from August through December) you need to book months ahead to get a room (the maximum number of guests is 64). At present there is no regular connection from Cooktown to the island, although there are daily flights from Cairns. Occasionally there is an aerial Cairns/Lizard Island/Cooktown/Cairns day tour, which will give you glimpses of this wide area but can't possibly do justice to a region that to be truly appreciated requires time for you to adjust to the pace, the ambience, and the isolation.

THE NORTHERN REEF: SCUBA-DIVING AND MARLIN FISHING

James Cook was a superb navigator and consummate seaman. He sailed from England to Tahiti, circumnavigated and charted New Zealand, and sailed 1,800 miles along the eastern coast of Australia before running aground on the northern section of the Great Barrier Reef.

Since that time the Great Barrier Reef has become the graveyard for more than 500 ships. Now, however, thousands of visitors safely visit the reef each day. Fast boats travel daily from Cairns and Port Douglas to platforms above the reef, where underwater observatories or semi-submersible submarines provide excellent viewing. Current costs are about A$95 for the day.

Scuba-diving trips are also abundant. **Haba Dive** operates daily dive trips to the reef from Port Douglas. In Cairns, **Down Under Dive** operates daily to the reef in a fast catamaran. For something a little different, **Rum Runner** operates a four-day, three-night dive/sail trip to the outer Great Barrier Reef for up to 14 divers. All these boats carry diving equipment, compressor, and radio, and provide all meals. (Haba Dive, Tel: 070/99-5254; Down Under

Dive, Tel: 070/31-1288; Rum Runner, Tel: 070/31-4077.) Scuba courses are available from beginners to assistant instructor standard. **Deep Sea Divers Den** claims to be Australia's largest dive school and operates three catamarans from Cairns that you can sleep on; Tel: (070) 31-5622. The **Peter Tibbs Scuba School** (Tel: 070/52-1266) is another operation with a good reputation—an important consideration, as there have been several unfortunate accidents off Cairns in recent years that have tarnished the reputations of some other operators.

Cairns is the gateway to the great black-marlin fishing grounds of the Coral Sea. These days about 95 percent of the big fish are tagged with a plastic capsule that helps the fishery authorities plot populations and migrations. After fishermen are photographed alongside their catch, the fish are released. Marlin fishing is expensive; boats nudge A$1,500 a day, and that's usually for only four to six passengers. Bottom fishing is much cheaper, and boats are available to take up to 30 passengers. Lines, bait, and other necessities are provided. For information, contact the Cairns Game Fishing Club (Tel: 070/51-5979).

For the really keen fisherman a visit to ▶ **Bloomfield Wilderness Lodge** south of Cooktown will be a great experience. The lodge is open from May to January and provides opportunities to fish for both bottom and open-sea species.

CAPE YORK

From Cairns a huge, harsh, and lonely triangle of land points north toward Papua New Guinea. This is Cape York Peninsula, one of the wildest, least developed areas of Australia outside of the deserts.

This area is anything but desert, however. The eastern highlands, which are part of the Great Dividing Range, extend along the eastern side of Cape York Peninsula to within 120 miles of its tip. Monsoonal rains between December and April, and other rains during the year, keep most rivers here flowing constantly. Rain forests cover the eastern slopes and lowlands, while the swamps and low country to the west are flooded for several months each year.

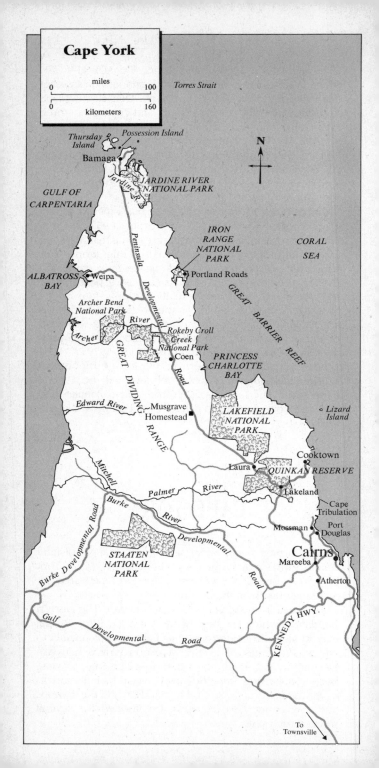

Visitors are attracted to this region for a variety of reasons. One is simply that it remains a challenge. Roads are poor and facilities are sparse, but the sense of achievement in penetrating the area—then returning to civilization—is great. Cape York excursions aren't for would-be adventurers, but for the truly bold.

The Road to the Cape

The journey from Cairns to Cape York along the Peninsula Developmental Road is still one of Australia's great road (or track) adventures. The distance of about 1,000 km (600 miles) will take three or four days in good weather but can take months during the December-to-May wet season. During the wet season access is not possible in a conventional vehicle, and those inexperienced with four-wheel-drive vehicles would be foolish to try even in the best of machines.

Fortunately there are numerous tour companies that offer trips to Cape York. Some use normal four-wheel-drive landcruiser-type vehicles, others special vehicles such as Unimogs. Some excursions are one-way with the other leg done by air, while others are 12- to 14-day round trips by road from Cairns. A few of the better Cape York tour operators in Cairns are **Australian Pacific Tours**, Tel: (070) 51-9299; **Oz Tours Safaris**, Tel: (070) 55-9535; and **Wild Track Adventure Safaris**, Tel: (070) 31-4565.

The road north from Cairns leads inland to Mareeba, then north toward **Lakeland**. Lakeland Downs was the vision of a millionaire who dreamed of producing corn, sorghum, and other crops on 75,000 acres of cleared country. But the country refused to be tamed, and a fortune was lost. The township survived the bad times, and today it's the gateway to Cape York Peninsula, with a hotel/motel, trailer park, store, and service station.

The craggy Palmer Range north of here is an impressive sight. This is Quinkan country, named after the aboriginal people who were driven out by whites some 120 years ago. They left huge cave paintings that tell a wonderful story that has amazed anthropologists. The **Quinkan Reserve** area has restrictions, but visitors are welcome to use the walking tracks that lead to some of the cave-art sites.

The next town is **Laura**, founded in the 1870s to serve the gold-rush track from Cooktown to the Palmer River; it's now a small settlement with a resident population of about 100. Camping sites and basic hotel accommodations are available. To the north stretches the **Lakefield National Park**, a vast area of rain forest, paperbark woodland, swamp, mangrove, open grassy plains, and mud flats. In the wet season the rivers overflow and join to form massive lakes. In the dry season there is still enough water to support a wealth of wildlife: Water birds, crocodiles, parrots, kangaroos, wallabies, and dingoes are all common. Crocodiles ensure that swimming here can be distinctly and dramatically unhealthy.

After driving through Lakefield you rejoin the main track at **Musgrave Homestead**, now a roadhouse with some accommodations but originally a telegraph station opened in 1887 on the Overland Telegraph Line, which extended right up the spine of Cape York Peninsula and eventually, by submarine cable, to Thursday Island off the peninsula tip. The small town of **Coen** farther north is a relative oasis of civilization; it has a school, a few shops, a hotel, a police station, and so on.

From here north it is a slow grind. The track deteriorates, and each creek-crossing seems harder than the last. For visitors, though, the sense of achievement continues to increase with the true wilderness experience of Cape York.

The country now changes from bloodwood to ironbark scrub to heath; to the east is the wonderful rain forest of **Iron Range National Park**. Incredible ten-foot-high "magnetic" anthills (they all point in the same direction) dot the countryside. In parts you can find palmlike pandanus plants providing food for the flocks of cockatoos. There are also pitcher plants that trap unsuspecting insects, and more than 50 varieties of orchids.

After three days' hard driving you will be relieved to find the town of **Bamaga** and finally to see the waters of Torres Strait. Bamaga dates to 1946, when a group of black islanders moved to the mainland from their overcrowded island off the coast of Papua New Guinea. It is now a small but progressive town with schools and even a small college; there is little of interest to the visitor, however. Tourism has reached this area via an old World War II airfield, originally built by the United States Army Air Corps but now partially reopened as Bamaga's airport. Remote, undeveloped **Thursday Island** is less than two hours away by speedboat.

The aboriginal-run ► **Pajinka Wilderness Lodge**, with its attractive units, bar, restaurant, and swimming pool, is linked by bus to Bamaga, about 30 km (19 miles) away. The nearby ► **Punsand Bay Private Reserve** is primarily suited to the fisherman, the adventurer, or anyone seeking to experience nature close at hand. The tip of Cape York is a short drive from Bamaga. This is the most northerly part of mainland Australia, and one steeped in history. Malays, Chinese, Dutch, Spanish, Portuguese, and Japanese all visited this area, but it was left to Captain Cook to raise the British flag on Possession Island in 1770 and claim the whole of eastern Australia for Britain.

GETTING AROUND

Brisbane has Australia's most modern domestic air terminal, and the city is accessible from anywhere in Australia. The International Airport has good connections from New Zealand, North America (via Continental and Qantas from San Francisco and Los Angeles), Asia, and Europe (British Airways). A bus service operates to city hotels; taxis are also available for about A$18.

There are express trains to Brisbane from Sydney, and intrastate rail services from many parts of Queensland. All major bus companies have express services to Brisbane, operating in and out of the Transit Centre on Roma Street. Brisbane has an electric rail network and an extensive bus system.

Rental cars are readily available at the airport and the Transit Centre; driving from here to the Gold and Sunshine coasts is easy. There are good bus connections to these areas, and day tours are also available.

The Gold Coast airport at *Coolangatta* is served by direct flights from Sydney, Melbourne, and some other southern ports. The Sunshine Coast airport has limited services. Transport within the Gold Coast area is excellent, with various tourist bus services linking most attractions; in the Sunshine Coast area, transportation is more limited. Hotels and motels are the best sources of current information. Taxis are available everywhere.

Bundaberg, Gladstone, and *Rockhampton* all have air service from Brisbane. These cities are on the east-coast rail and road network, so there are good train and bus connections from both north and south, but watch out for times, because some services arrive very early in the morning. Rental cars are available in all three cities. A taxi ride from each airport to the center of each town costs about A$9.

Though each center offers some day and extended tours, there are no organized tours that cover this region completely. Lack of facilities usually means lack of demand, so it's clear that touring the region is not high among local priorities. More common is a flight to one of the gateway centers, then a stay on one of the islands or in the Yeppoon area.

You can fly to *Townsville* from almost anywhere in Australia, with direct services from Brisbane, Sydney, Cairns, Mount Isa, and Alice Springs, among others. International services from Indonesia are offered by Garuda Airlines. A good, cheap airport-to-city bus connection passes many hotels and motels. Rental cars are available from four companies at the airport and from city depots. Mackay has air services from Brisbane and Townsville. Townsville, Mackay, Bowen, and Cardwell are served by the Sunlander and Queenslander air-conditioned trains from Brisbane. Townsville is also the terminus for the Inlander train from Mount Isa, west in the Outback. All the major express-bus companies have several daily services through the region.

Cairns has become the most important northern gateway into Australia, with direct flights from North America (via Qantas and United), New Zealand, Papua New Guinea, Japan, and Southeast Asia. It is also a major hub for the domestic air network, with flights to southern capitals, Alice Springs, Ayers Rock, and Darwin. There is an airport shuttle bus that travels past many of the major hotels and motels.

Cairns is the northern terminal for the east-coast railway and all east-coast bus systems. And because it is the northernmost sizable city on the east coast, it is also the starting or finishing point for several one-way tours that travel to and from Brisbane, Sydney, or Melbourne.

This is a good place to rent a car, because traffic is light and it's easy to find your way around. Cars are available at the airport and downtown. All the majors are there plus several "cheapie" operators. It's also possible to hire a four-wheel-drive vehicle or camper-van. The tourist office has several maps to help you find your way around the area.

A bus service runs to Kuranda and on to several towns in the Atherton Tableland. There is also a bus to *Port Douglas*.

A large number of tours are available from Cairns. Your hotel will be pleased to advise you on destinations and companies.

ACCOMMODATIONS REFERENCE
The rates given here are projections *for the 1994 high season—Easter, June to September, and Christmas to*

mid-January. Unless otherwise indicated, rates are for double room, double occupancy. As prices are subject to change, always double-check before booking.

Brisbane

▶ **Anchorage Village Beach Resort.** East Coast, Point Lookout, **North Stradbroke Island**, Qld. 4183. Tel: (07) 409-8266, toll-free (008) 077-008; Fax: (07) 409-8304. A$88–A$132.

▶ **Heritage.** Edward and Margaret streets, **Brisbane**, Qld. 4000. Tel: (07) 221-1999; Fax: (07) 221-6895. A$300.

▶ **Hilton International Brisbane.** 190 Elizabeth Street, **Brisbane**, Qld. 4000. Tel: (07) 231-3131; in U.S., (800) 445-8667; in Canada, (800) 268-9275; Fax: (07) 231-3199. A$255.

▶ **Mayfair Crest International Hotel.** King George Square, **Brisbane**, Qld. 4000. Tel: (07) 229-9111; in U.S., (800) 44-UTELL; in Canada, (800) 387-1338; Fax: (07) 229-9618. A$75–A$99.

▶ **Sheraton Brisbane Hotel & Towers.** 249 Turbot Street, **Brisbane**, Qld. 4000. Tel: (07) 835-3535; in U.S. and Canada, (800) 325-3535; Fax: (07) 835-4960. A$250–A$320.

▶ **Tangalooma Moreton Island Resort. Moreton Island**, Qld. 4025. Tel: (07) 268-6333; Fax: (07) 268-6106. A$195.

Sunshine and Gold Coasts

▶ **All Seasons Greenmount Beach Resort.** 3 Hill Street, **Coolangatta**, Qld. 4225. Tel: (075) 36-1222; Fax: (075) 36-1102. A$75–A$95.

▶ **ANA Hotel.** 22 View Avenue, **Surfers Paradise**, Qld. 4217. Tel: (075) 79-1000; in U.S. and Canada, (800) HOLIDAY; Fax: (075) 70-1260. A$185.

▶ **Binna Burra Mountain Lodge. Lamington National Park**, Qld. 4211. Tel: (075) 33-3622, toll-free (008) 074-260; Fax: (075) 33-3658. A$196–A$290 (all meals included).

▶ **Conrad International Hotel and Jupiters Casino.** Gold Coast Highway, Broadbeach Island, **Broadbeach**, Qld. 4218. Tel: (075) 92-1133; in U.S., (212) 697-9370 or (800) 223-1146; Fax: (075) 92-8219. A$200.

▶ **Eurong Beach Tourist Resort.** Fraser Island, Qld. 4650. Tel: (071) 27-9122; Fax: (071) 27-9179. A$80.

▶ **Gold Coast International.** Gold Coast Highway, **Surfers Paradise**, Qld. 4217. Tel: (075) 92-1200; Fax: (075) 92-1180. A$175–A$205.

▶ **Gold Coast Sheraton Mirage Hotel.** The Spit, Sea

World Drive, **Southport**, Qld. 4215. Tel: (075) 91-1488, toll-free (008) 074-443; in U.S. and Canada, (800) 325-3535; Fax: (075) 91-2299. A$375–A$550.

► **Hyatt Regency Coolum.** P.O. Box 78, Warran Road, **Coolum Beach**, Qld. 4573. Tel: (074) 46-1234; in U.S. and Canada, (800) 233-1234; Fax: (074) 46-2957. A$260.

► **Hyatt Regency at Sanctuary Cove.** Casey Road, **Hope Island**, Qld. 4212. Tel: (075) 30-1234; in U.S. and Canada, (800) 233-1234; Fax: (075) 77-8234. A$240–A$290.

► **Kingfisher Bay Resort.** Fraser Island, Qld. 46500. Tel: (07) 221-1811; Fax: (07) 221-3270. A$170–A$180.

► **Maleny Lodge Guest House.** 58 Maple Street, **Maleny**, Qld. 4552. Tel: (074) 94-2370; Fax: (074) 94-3407. A$98.

► **Nara Resort Hotel.** The Spit, **Main Beach**, Qld. 4215. Tel: (075) 91-0000; Fax: (075) 91-2375. A$190–A$250.

► **Netanya Noosa Resort.** 75 Hastings Street, **Noosa Heads**, Qld. 4567. Tel: (074) 47-4848; Fax: (074) 47-3914. A$160–A$220.

► **Noosa International Holiday Resort.** Edgar Bennett Avenue, **Noosa Heads**, Qld. 4567. Tel: (074) 47-4822; Fax: (074) 47-2025. A$100.

► **Novotel Twin Waters Resort. Mudjimba**, Qld. 4564. Tel: (074) 48-8000, toll-free (008) 072-277; Fax: (074) 48-8001. A$170–A$180.

► **No. 1 Hastings Street. Noosa Heads**, Qld. 4567. Tel: (074) 49-2211, toll-free (008) 072-211; Fax: (074) 49-2001. A$165.

► **Oasis.** Landsborough Parade, **Coloundra**, Qld. 4551. Tel: (074) 91-0333; Fax: (074) 91-0300. A$59 room, A$105 villa.

► **Ocean Breeze Resort.** 6-8 Hastings Street, **Noosa Heads**, Qld. 4567. Tel: (074) 47-4977; Fax: (074) 47-2170. A$117–A$145.

► **O'Reilly's Rainforest Guest House. Green Mountains**, Qld. 4275. Tel: (075) 44-0644; Fax: (075) 44-0638. A$198–A$270 (all meals included).

► **Pan Pacific Gold Coast Hotel.** Surf Parade, **Broadbeach**, Qld. 4218. Tel: (075) 92-2250, toll-free (008) 074-465; Fax: (075) 92-3747. A$125–A$180.

► **Ramada Hotel.** Paradise Centre, Gold Coast Highway, **Surfers Paradise**, Qld. 4217. Tel: (075) 79-3499; Fax: (075) 92-0026; in U.S., (800) 228-2828; in Canada, (416) 485-2692 (call collect). A$130–A$180.

► **Seahaven Beachfront Resort.** 13 Hastings Street, **Noosa Heads**, Qld. 4567. Tel: (074) 47-3422, toll-free (008) 072-013; Fax: (074) 47-5260. A$70–A$200.

► **Sheraton Noosa Resort.** Hastings Street, **Noosa**

Heads, Qld. 4567. Tel: (074) 49-4888; Fax: (074) 49-2230. A$224–A$370.

▶ **Solothurn Rural Resort.** Reeseville Road, **Maleny,** Qld. 4522. Tel. and Fax: (074) 94-2438. A$110.

▶ **Surfers Paradise Travelodge.** Gold Coast Highway, **Surfers Paradise,** Qld. 4217. Tel: (075) 92-9900; Fax: (075) 92-1519. A$165.

▶ **Tipplers Tourist Resort.** Tipplers Parade, **South Stradbroke Island,** Qld. 4216. Tel: (075) 77-3311; Fax: (075) 77-3746. A$90.

The Southern Great Barrier Reef Region

▶ **Capricorn International Resort.** Farnborough Road, **Yeppoon,** Qld. 4703. Tel: (079) 39-0211; Fax: (079) 39-5666. A$110.

▶ **Country Comfort Inn.** 86 Victoria Parade, **Rockhampton,** Qld. 4700. Tel: (079) 27-9933; Fax: (079) 27-1615. A$87–A$96.

▶ **Country Plaza International.** 100 Goondoon Street, **Gladstone,** Qld. 4680. Tel: (079) 72-4499; Fax: (079) 72-4921. A$85.

▶ **Criterion Hotel.** Quay Street, **Rockhampton,** Qld. 4700. Tel: (079) 22-1225; Fax: (079) 22-1226. A$40–A$44.

▶ **Don Pancho Beach Resort.** Kelly's Beach, **Bargara,** Qld. 4670. Tel: (071) 59-2146; Fax: (071) 59-2788. A$55–A$65.

▶ **Duthies Leichhardt Hotel.** Corner Denham and Bolsover streets, **Rockhampton,** Qld. 4700. Tel: (079) 27-6733; Fax: (079) 27-8075. A$75.

▶ **Great Keppel Island Resort.** Via **Rockhampton,** Qld. 4700. Tel: (079) 39-5044; Fax: (079) 39-1775; in U.S., (800) 551-2012 or (800) 445-0190. A$150–A$190.

▶ **Heron Island Resort.** Via **Gladstone,** Qld. 4680. Tel: (079) 78-1488; in U.S., (800) 551-2012; Fax: (079) 78-1457. A$250–A$498 (meals included).

▶ **Lady Elliot Island Resort.** Via **Bundaberg,** Qld. 4670. Tel: (071) 52-2322, toll-free (008) 072-200; Fax: (071) 53-1285; in U.S., (213) 465-8418. A$500 (meals included).

▶ **Rosslyn Bay Inn Resort. Rosslyn Bay,** via Rockhampton, Qld. 4700. Tel: (079) 33-6333; Fax: (079) 33-6297. A$70.

▶ **Wapparaburra Haven. Great Keppel Island,** via Rockhampton, Qld. 4700. Tel: (079) 39-1907; Fax: (079) 39-3464. Tents A$24; cabins A$75.

▶ **Wilson Island.** Via **Gladstone,** Qld. 4680. Tel: (072) 68-8224; Fax: (072) 68-8220. A$150 (meals included).

The Central Great Barrier Reef Region

▶ **Arcadia Resort Hotel.** 7 Marine Parade, Arcadia Bay, **Magnetic Island**, Qld. 4819. Tel: (077) 78-5177; in U.S., (213) 465-8418; Fax: (077) 78-5939. A$45–A$65.

▶ **Bedarra Bay** and ▶ **Bedarra Hideaway. Bedarra Island**, via Townsville, Qld. 4816. Tel: (070) 68-8233; in U.S., (800) 551-2012 or (800) 445-0190; in Canada, (800) 235-8222; Fax: (070) 68-8215. A$800–A$958 (meals, drinks, and sporting facilities included).

▶ **Brampton Island Resort.** Via **Mackay**, Qld. 4740. Tel: (079) 51-4499; Fax: (079) 51-4097. A$140.

▶ **Club Crocodile Resort.** Shute Harbour Road, **Airlie Beach**, Qld. 4802. Tel: (079) 46-7155; Fax: (079) 46-6007. A$55–A$119.

▶ **Coral Sea Resort.** 25 Ocean View Avenue, **Airlie Beach**, Qld. 4802. Tel: (079) 46-6458; Fax: (079) 46-6516. A$105.

▶ **Daydream Island Travelodge Resort. Whitsunday Passage**, via Shute Harbour, Qld. 4802. Tel: (079) 46-9200, toll-free (008) 075-040; Fax: (079) 48-8499. A$160.

▶ **Dunk Island Resort.** Via **Townsville**, Qld. 4816. Tel: (070) 68-8199; Fax: (070) 68-8528. A$265–A$464.

▶ **Hamilton Island Resort. Whitsunday Passage**, Qld. 4803. Tel: (079) 46-9999, toll-free (008) 075-110; in U.S. and Canada, (800) 268-1469; Fax: (079) 46-8888. A$195–A$285.

▶ **Hayman Resort. Hayman Island**, Qld. 4801. Tel: (079) 46-9100, toll-free (008) 075-025; in U.S., (800) 4-ANSETT or (800) 6-ANSETT; in Canada, (800) 268-6370; Fax: (079) 469-410. A$350–A$590.

▶ **Hinchinbrook Island Resort.** Via **Townsville**, Cardwell, Qld. 4810. Tel: (070) 66-8585, toll-free (008) 777-021; Fax: (070) 66-8742. A$380–A$480.

▶ **Kohuna Village Resort.** Bucasia Beach, via **Mackay**, Qld. 4750. Tel: (079) 54-8555; Fax: (079) 54-6080. A$82.

▶ **Latitude 19 Resort.** Mandalay Avenue, Nelly Bay, **Magnetic Island**, Qld. 4819. Tel: (077) 78-5200, toll-free (008) 079-902; in U.S., (213) 465-8418; Fax: (077) 785-806. A$75.

▶ **Lindeman Island Resort.** Via **Mackay**, Qld. 4741. Tel: toll-free within Australia (008) 801-823; in U.S., and Canada (800) CLUB-MED. A$200.

▶ **Long Island Palm Bay Hideaway. Whitsunday Passage**, Qld. 4741. Tel: (079) 46-9233, toll-free (008) 334-009; Fax: (079) 46-9233. A$127–A$167.

▶ **Orpheus Island Resort.** Via **Townsville**, Qld. 4850. Tel: (077) 77-7377; in U.S. and Canada, (800) 235-8222; Fax: (077) 77-7533. A$530–A$880 (meals included).

▶ **Radisson Long Island Resort. Long Island,** Qld. 4741. Tel: (079) 46-9400, toll-free (008) 075-125; Fax: (079) 469-555; in U.S. and Canada (800) 333-3333. A$150.

▶ **Sheraton Breakwater Casino/Hotel.** Sir Leslie Thiess Drive, **Townsville,** Qld. 4810. Tel: (077) 22-2333; in U.S. and Canada, (800) 325-3535; Fax: (077) 72-4741. A$105–A$245.

▶ **South Molle Island Resort. Shute Harbour,** Qld. 4802. Tel: (079) 46-9433; in U.S., (800) 4-ANSETT or (800) 6-ANSETT; in Canada, (800) 268-6370; Fax: (079) 46-9580. A$260–A$320 (meals included).

▶ **Townsville Ambassador.** 75 The Strand, **Townsville,** Qld. 4810. Tel: (077) 72-4255; Fax: (077) 21-1316. A$105.

▶ **Townsville Reef International.** 63/64 The Strand, **Townsville,** Qld. 4810. Tel: (077) 21-1777; Fax: (077) 21-1779. A$92.

▶ **Townsville Travelodge Hotel.** Flinders Mall, **Townsville,** Qld. 4810. Tel: (077) 72-2477, toll-free (008) 079-903; Fax: (077) 21-1263. A$85–A$120.

▶ **White Lace Motel.** Nebo Road, **Mackay,** Qld. 4740. Tel: (079) 51-4466; Fax: (079) 51-4942. A$69.

▶ **Whitsunday Terraces Resort.** Golden Orchid Drive, **Airlie Beach,** Qld. 4802. Tel: (079) 46-6788, toll-free (008) 075-062; Fax: (079) 46-7128. A$99–A$122.

▶ **Whitsunday Wanderers Resort.** Shute Harbour Road, **Airlie Beach,** Qld. 4802. Tel: (079) 46-6446, toll-free (008) 075-069; Fax: (079) 46-6761. A$90–A$99.

Cairns and North

▶ **Bloomfield Wilderness Lodge.** Via **Cooktown,** Qld. 4871. Tel: (070) 33-2002; Fax: (070) 60-8200. A$260 (includes all meals).

▶ **Cairns Colonial Club.** 18-26 Cannon Street, **Manunda,** Cairns, Qld. 4870. Tel: (070) 53-5111; in U.S., (800) 551-2012; Fax: (070) 53-7072. A$99–A$150.

▶ **Cairns International Hotel.** 17 Abbott Street, **Cairns,** Qld. 4870. Tel: (070) 31-1300; Fax: (070) 31-1801. A$195.

▶ **Club Tropical.** Wharf Street, **Port Douglas,** Qld. 4871. Tel: (070) 99-5885, toll-free (008) 079-069; Fax: (070) 99-5868. A$235–A$285.

▶ **Coconut Beach Rainforest Resort. Cape Tribulation,** via Cairns, Qld. 4870. Tel: (070) 98-0033; Fax: (070) 98-0047. A$230 (bed-and-breakfast).

▶ **Crocodylus Village.** Cow Bay, **Cape Tribulation,** Qld. 4870. Tel: (070) 98-9166; Fax: (070) 98-9131. A$45.

▶ **Fitzroy Island Resort.** Via **Cairns,** Qld. 4870. Tel:

(070) 51-9588; Fax (070) 52-1335. A$260 double, villas; A$65 double, backpackers.

▶ **Green Island Reef Resort**. Via **Cairns**, Qld. 4870. Tel: (070) 51-4644; Fax: (070) 51-3624; in U.S., (714) 675-7306 (call collect). A$130.

▶ **Hilton International Cairns**. Wharf Street, **Cairns**, Qld. 4870. Tel: (070) 52-1599; in U.S., (800) 445-8667; in Canada, (800) 268-9275; Fax: (070) 52-1370. A$200–A$310.

▶ **Kewarra Beach Resort**. Kewarra Road, Kewarra Beach, **Cairns**, Qld. 4879. Tel: (070) 57-6666; Fax: (070) 57-7525. A$199–A$272.

▶ **Kuranda Rainforest Resort**. Kennedy Highway, **Kuranda**, Qld. 4872. Tel: (070) 93-7555; Fax: (070) 93-7567. A$77.

▶ **Lizard Island Lodge**. Via **Cairns**, Qld. 4870. Tel: (070) 60-3999; in U.S., (800) 551-2012 or (800) 445-0190; Fax: (070) 60-3991. A$874 (meals included).

▶ **Pacific International Hotel**. 43 The Esplanade, **Cairns**, Qld. 4870. Tel: (070) 51-7888; in U.S., (800) 44-UTELL; Fax: (070) 51-0210. A$185.

▶ **Pajinka Wilderness Lodge**. Via **Bamaga**, Qld. 4876. Tel: (070) 31-3988; toll-free (008) 80-2968; Fax: (070) 31-3966. A$200 (all inclusive).

▶ **Palm Cove Travelodge Resort**. **Palm Cove**, Qld. 4879. Tel: (070) 59-1234; Fax: (070) 59-1297. A$210.

▶ **Punsand Bay Private Reserve**. Via Bamaga, **Punsand Bay**, Qld. 4876. Tel: (070) 69-1722. A$70–A$180.

▶ **Radisson Plaza Hotel**. Marlin Parade, **Cairns**, Qld. 4870. Tel: (070) 31-1411; in U.S., (800) 333-3333; Fax: (070) 31-3226. A$200–A$265.

▶ **Radisson Royal Palms Resort**. Davidson Street, **Port Douglas**, Qld. 4871. Tel: (070) 99-5577; Fax: (070) 99-5559. A$140.

▶ **Ramada Great Barrier Reef Resort**. Corner Veivers Road and The Esplanade, **Palm Cove**, Qld. 4871. Tel: (070) 55-3999; in U.S., (800) 228-2828; in Canada, (416) 485-2692 (call collect); Fax: (070) 55-3902. A$155–A$170.

▶ **Reef House Resort**. Williams Esplanade, **Palm Cove**, Qld. 4871. Tel: (070) 55-3633; Fax: (070) 55-3305. A$177–A$225.

▶ **Sheraton Mirage Resort**. Davidson Street, **Port Douglas**, Qld. 4871. Tel: (070) 99-5888; in U.S. and Canada, (800) 325-3535; Fax: (070) 98-5885. A$400–A$480.

▶ **Silky Oaks Lodge**. Finlay Vale Road, **Mossman**, Qld. 4873. Tel: (070) 98-1666; Fax: (070) 98-1983. A$350.

► **Sovereign Hotel**. Charlotte Street, **Cooktown**, Qld. 4871. Tel: (070) 69-5400; Fax: (070) 69-5582. A$42–A$132.

Station and Farm Holidays

Some Queensland farms and stations are now welcoming visitors looking for an unusual vacation. They offer you the chance to drive a tractor or ride a horse, muster sheep or cattle, feed calves, lambs, and chickens, and do things for fun that country people call work. A couple of suggestions are:

► **Lorraine Outback Sheep Station**. A 120-square-mile sheep station with plenty of Australian wildlife 550 km (340 miles) west of Rockhampton. Day trips are available to the Stockman's Hall of Fame in Longreach. Tel: (076) 57-1693; Fax: (076) 57-1796. A$122 including dinner and breakfast.

► **Planet Downs Resort**. Excellent amenities in modern buildings with central restaurant, bar, and sports facilities, surrounded by a 400-square-mile cattle property, 250 km (155 miles) west of Gladstone. P.O. Box 420, Zillmere, Qld. 4034; Tel: (07) 265-5022; Fax: (07) 265-3978. A$720, all inclusive.

NORTHERN TERRITORY

THE RED CENTRE AND THE TOP END

By Chris Brockie

Chris Brockie worked on Australian cattle stations until an automobile accident forced him to find less rugged work in journalism, first with the Australian Broadcasting Corporation and then as bureau chief for two major newspaper groups. Originally a New Zealander, he has lived and worked mostly in the Australian Outback, particularly the Northern Territory, since 1972; he now lives in South Australia and is a freelance writer. He has also returned to his original trade of cooking and is second chef at a deluxe motor inn.

For many years only the hardiest and most intrepid traveller visited the Northern Territory. This was partly due to its inaccessibility—the tyranny of distance is Australia's greatest natural enemy—and partly because Territorians did not see tourism as a viable industry. After all, if Australians didn't want to visit, then surely nobody from overseas would either.

All this has changed. Territorians now realize that the benefits they took for granted do interest others. The same spirit of adventure that attracted the early explorers and travellers is what attracts today's visitor to this timeless land.

MAJOR INTEREST

The Red Centre
Historic Alice Springs
Natural grandeur of Palm Valley
Uluru National Park: Ayers Rock and the Olgas
Ayers Rock Resort
Aboriginal culture

The Top End
Darwin's relaxed lifestyle
Bathurst and Melville islands; the Tiwi people
Natural beauty and wildlife of Kakadu
    National Park
Sailing and fishing at Nhulunbuy
Katherine Gorge

Born of "bloody hard yakka" ("bloody" is the Great Australian Adjective; "yakka" is an aboriginal word for hard work that has become an Australian colloquialism), the Northern Territory has evolved from a pioneering cattle-raising region to a mining-oriented land where tourism is the second-largest industry. In fact, Territorians have a philosophy that goes something like this: "If you can't dig it up and sell it to them, get them to come and look at it."

The Territory's early colonial roots are essentially British, yet many see in it what Hollywood once portrayed as the American West. It is now often referred to as "The Last Frontier," and it is big. Covering roughly 487,627 square miles, it is about twice the size of Texas and just over five times the size of the United Kingdom.

It is not until you near Katherine in the north of the territory that you become aware that it really consists of two areas as distinct as fire and water: the Red Centre, which bakes under a blazing sun that heats the iron-red sands to searing temperatures, and the Top End, a well-watered tropical wonderland.

In between is the Barkly Tableland (running east into Queensland) and the small mining town of Tennant Creek, guarded by the Devil's Marbles and by the sometimes huge termite (white ant) mounds.

The Territory's vastness and increasing popularity among domestic and international travellers have led to a proliferation of short and extended tours. It is thus suggested you seek a copy of the Australian Tourist Commission's *1993–94 Northern Territory Holiday Planner,* which lists more than 500 tours ranging from half-day town visits to several days of wilderness adventure to photographic and aboriginal culture tours. A copy of the Commission's *Come Share Our Culture* brochure is another asset if you're interested in aboriginal tours.

THE RED CENTRE

The Red Centre, a spectacular area of rugged mountain ranges and inviting oases, takes its name from the predominant color of the land here. A blazing sun hangs ominously overhead, turning the earth a sunburned brown that attracts and holds incredible heat. During the summer, humidity is low, water scarce, and temperatures often rise into the low hundreds, occasionally reaching 120 degrees F. Yet in the winter (especially during July and August) night temperatures can fall below freezing.

Although tourism is the most obvious facet of Central Australia's economy, the area is also a major supplier of beef cattle, oil, and natural gas.

ALICE SPRINGS

Alice Springs, the hub of the Red Centre, lies about halfway between Darwin and Adelaide, almost at the geographical center of Australia. An ideal touring base, it has undergone tremendous growth and development in recent years that, depending on whom you talk to, has or has not led to a loss of character. Many of the old hotels, known colloquially as pubs, have been demolished, replaced by modern facilities that provide comfort and luxury but have none of the flavor of the area's pioneering heritage.

Just as Alice Springs is today the center of Northern Territory tourism, it was once the starting point of exploration for the expanding colonies. Exploration began earlier, but it was not until John McDouall Stuart began exploring the interior in the early 1860s that it began to open up.

Although the Territory was annexed to South Australia in July 1863, the Red Centre remained terra incognita until 1870, when Charles Todd, South Australia's postmaster general, began the Overland Telegraph line from

Adelaide to Darwin. His work would lead to the discovery of a spring in the dry Todd River that would be named after his wife, Alice, and become one of the pleasantest spots in the area.

Now constituting a historic reserve, Alice Springs' original buildings have been restored; the **Old Telegraph Station**, for example, is an ideal spot to relax. Take an afternoon off from touring and indulge in the Aussie culinary pastime, barbecuing, which is easily done here on the gas cookers set among the tall ghost gums (white-barked eucalyptus trees) lining the Todd River. Ingredients for your barbecue—lean Centralian beefsteaks, sausages, wine, breads, and other tasty morsels—can be ordered from your hotel kitchen in a hamper.

The telegraph station became operational in 1872, yet it wasn't until 1889, when the South Australian government sent people northward looking for suitable railheads, that the site where Alice Springs now stands was established as a settlement. Originally called Stuart, the town was located two miles south of the telegraph station. The first train arrived only in 1929; until then camels were the major mode of transport.

There are constant reminders of this camel connection. The train from Adelaide, **The Ghan**, is named in memory of the cameleers, many of whom were Afghans, who plied the route before the railway was built. In 1980 The Ghan's original narrow-gauge line was replaced by a standard-gauge railway.

At **MacDonnel Siding**, about 10 km (6 miles) south of Alice Springs (turn right onto Norris Bell Avenue and travel 500 meters), the Ghan Preservation Society has established a working museum where diesel and steam locomotives and passenger and dining cars from the old Ghan have been restored. About 19 miles of the old track remain, and the society now runs excursion trips to Mount Ertiua Siding, where an area with picnic and barbecue facilities has been developed. Building the railway took over 300,000 hours, including 130,000 hours of work by inmates from the Alice Springs Gaol.

Apart from the one-and-a-half-hour train ride ($A17 per adult), the society, in conjunction with the Camp Oven Kitchen, runs a four-and-a-half-hour trip (A$49 per adult), which includes a dinner of traditional damper (unleavened bread cooked in coals), soup, and roast beef (see Dining and Nightlife below).

Alice Springs hosts an annual **Camel Cup** race meeting, usually held the second Saturday in May at Blatherskite

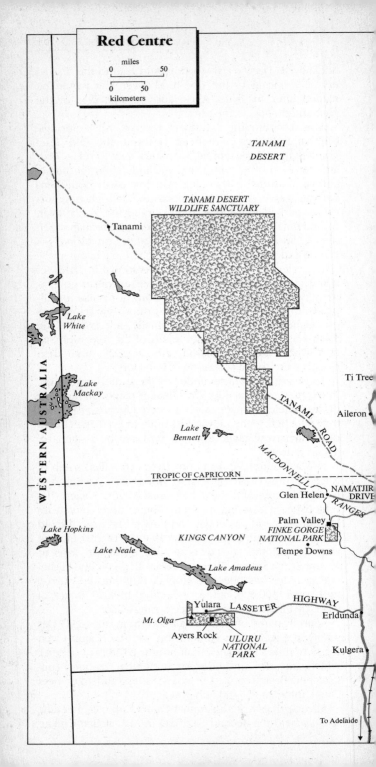

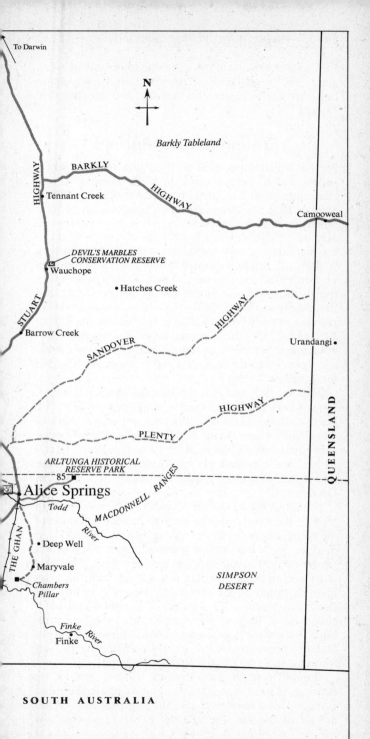

Park on the outskirts of town. Now an international event, since 1987 it has spurred especially keen competition between teams from Alice Springs and Virginia City, Nevada.

Around in Alice Springs

For an enlightening look at The Alice, as the town is called, and to help yourself imagine some of its lost character, spend a couple of hours on the **Heritage Walk**. Start in Todd Mall (the pedestrian continuation of Todd Street) at what was Alice Springs' first mission hospital, Adelaide House. Opened in 1926, the hospital became an accommodation and convalescent house for Outback women and children from 1939 until 1961. Next move on to Hartley Street, where you will find, among other things, the Old Court House (1928), the Residency, and the old Stuart Gaol (1908)—the oldest building still remaining in the town area. The **Residency** was built from 1926 to 1927 for John Charles Cawood, Alice Springs' first government resident, or administrator. It is now owned and operated by the Museums and Art Galleries Board of the Northern Territory.

Between 1926 and 1931 the Territory was administered in two parts, north and south of the 20th parallel, called North Australia and Central Australia, respectively. Each of these had a Government Resident and a four-man advisory council. It was not until 1931 that the "North Australia Act" was repealed and the Northern Territory came under the control of a single administrator, based in Darwin.

The **Royal Flying Doctor Service** (RFDS) was set up in 1928 by the Reverend John Flynn to provide a "mantle of safety" to isolated areas throughout Australia. When Flynn died in 1951 the service covered about five million square miles. The Alice Springs base opened in 1939, and is located in Stuart Terrace, just a short walk from the main shopping center. Visitors can view a short film that details the history and activities of the RFDS and see a collection of historic photographs and other memorabilia. Tours of the base last about 30 to 45 minutes and are available between 9:00 A.M. and 4:00 P.M. Monday through Saturday, and 1:00 P.M. and 4:00 P.M. on Sundays.

The only way for many Outback children, isolated by distance, to receive an education is through regular radio contact with a teacher at the Alice Springs base of the **School of the Air**. The crackle of radio conversations helps you to realize that more than six hundred miles may separate teacher and student. The school is on Head Street next to the Braitling School and is open to visitors between 1:30 and 3:30 P.M. on weekdays.

Other places worth visiting in Alice Springs are **Panorama Guth,** at 65 Hartley Street, which houses a 360-degree painted panoramic landscape of the Central Australian landscape as well as artifacts from the early pioneering days; **Diorama Village,** east of the town center on Larapinta Drive, depicting the legends and myths of the aboriginal people; **Pitchi Richi Sanctuary,** a large outdoor museum featuring birds, flowers, and sculpture located south of the city on Old South Road; and **Olive Pink Flora Reserve,** a botanic garden that focuses on Central Australia's plant life. Although Alice Springs has no public transport, all these places are within easy walking distance of the town center and can be seen comfortably in a day.

Shopping in Alice Springs

Shopping is relaxed here and confined mainly to Todd Street and the pedestrian Todd Street Mall. **Aboriginal Arts Australia** on Todd Street, set up by the Australian government to help market traditional aboriginal arts and crafts, has a large variety of traditional and contemporary works, ranging from bark and sand paintings to carvings, weavings, and **didgeridoos**—traditional aboriginal musical instruments up to six feet long and about two inches in diameter. Usually made from hollow tree branches, they are played by blowing and sucking air through them.

Most other gift and souvenir shops around town offer traditional aboriginal works as well, along with some fine examples of locally produced pottery, textiles, and other handicrafts. One of the most exciting shops is **Walkabout Clay Crafts** in Todd Street Mall, which features delicately painted jewelry adaptations of traditional art created by local aboriginal artisans using only the four traditional aboriginal colors: black, white, red, and yellow.

The art of Central Australian aboriginals is well represented among a dozen or so galleries. However, while some of the material is relatively inexpensive, anyone seeking a piece of genuine aboriginal art can expect to part with several thousand dollars. The **CAAMA Shop** at 91 Gap Road features works by aboriginal artists and musicians. Another outlet, **Papunya Tula Artists** at 78 Todd Street, is owned and operated by aboriginals and has some excellent artworks.

Dining and Nightlife in Alice Springs

Many of Alice Springs' better restaurants are at hotels, but **Flynns on the Mall**, open seven days a week for breakfast, lunch, and dinner, provides quality inexpensive meals in a café-style setting. Flynns is run in conjunction with the **Retreat Restaurant**—part of the Territory Motor Inn on Leichardt Terrace—which offers perhaps the best dining in Alice Springs.

For more traditional cuisine, step back into the culinary wonders of the early pioneers with a menu of beef, buffalo, and barramundi (an Australian lungfish) at the **Overlander Steakhouse** on Hartley Street. Another alternative is dinner in the bush: The **Camp Oven Kitchen** offers the chance to wine and dine on a three- or four-course dinner cooked beneath the stars on an open campfire (Tel: 089/53-1411).

One of Alice Springs' newer restaurants, situated near the Coles supermarket complex on Railway Terrace, the **Residence Restaurant** is housed in a National Heritage Trust building that served as the home of Alice Springs' postmasters between 1932 and 1977. (The restaurant is named after the old Residency building on Hartley Street.) It has four dining rooms—each named for a postmaster—catering to up to 50 people.

Alice Springs' nightlife revolves around pubs and clubs. Most have some form of live entertainment at one or another time during the week. The most notable and enjoyable may be **The Old Alice Inn**, formerly the Todd Tavern, in Todd Street Mall. The inn has five bars, including the upscale Maxim's Bar and Restaurant, Melba's Piano Bar, and Dimensions Nitespot. **Dimensions** is undoubtedly the favorite among Alice Springs' younger visitors.

At the other end of town is the **Alice Junction Tavern** at the Heavitree Gap Tourist Resort. Here jazz lovers are entertained Saturday to Wednesday, and on Friday nights and late Saturday nights the disco lovers have their turn. There is country-and-western music Saturday evenings and Sunday afternoons.

Staying in Alice Springs

The Northern Territory's diverse nature has been re-created, probably unwittingly, in the range of available accommodations. But because The Alice is more a base for further exploration than a destination in and of itself, it makes little difference which hotel you choose.

If after a day touring the dusty Outback you need a little extra style and comfort, try the ▶ **Melia Alice Springs Hotel** or ▶ **Lasseters Hotel Casino** along Barrett Drive. (Lasseters, as its name implies, is also a licensed gambling casino with opulent decor and strict dress standards.) These hotels are expensive, but recommended; they have great meals, from formal dining to café snacks.

Among other hotels in town a popular choice is the refurbished 102-room ▶ **Frontier Oasis Resort**, which offers a relaxing atmosphere with fine meals. The ▶ **Vista Alice Springs**—located opposite the casino and a member of Vista International Hotels—provides comfortable rooms and quick access to the golf course.

With few exceptions, hotels and motels provide airport transportation.

AROUND ALICE SPRINGS

Château Hornsby, 15 km (9 miles) south of Alice off the Stuart Highway, is the Territory's first and only commercial winery. On Sundays, Tuesdays, Wednesdays, and Fridays you can ride a camel to dinner here from The Alice through Frontier Camel Tours (Tel: 089/53-0444; Fax: 089/55-5015). For about an hour you trek down the Todd River on camelback, swaying with each step but enjoying the different perspective this mode of transport gives of the surrounding country. At the winery you are given a tour of the cellar and a wine tasting before sitting down to dinner. The tour and dinner take about five hours and cost A$69. At the end of the night you are returned to your hotel by minibus.

Chateau Hornsby is an experience not to be forgotten, especially when the entertainment is provided by the world's leading master of a uniquely Northern Territory instrument, the Fosterphone. Five nights a week Ted Egan plays his Fosterphone (a carton of Foster's lager tuned by drinking the carton's contents), sings, and tells yarns in an outlandish fashion. Join in for a chorus of his popular "Oh They've Got Some Bloody Good Drinkers in the Northern Territory."

The **Stuart Auto Museum**, just a few minutes out of town off the Ross Highway, houses a fine collection of fully restored antique automobiles. It also has a large collection of motorbikes, as well as motoring memorabilia.

PARKS AND GORGES

There are many gorges and parks within a short drive of The Alice that require a half to full day to explore. However, it is not until you travel more than 100 km (60 miles) from town that you find the more spectacular sights: Chambers Pillar, Palm Valley, Kings Canyon, Arltunga, and Glen Helen. From a lonely wedge-tailed eagle gliding the thermals above you to the fragile plant life of Palm Valley and Kings Canyon, the area around The Alice will make you aware of how minuscule your place in the world is.

Chambers Pillar, discovered in 1869 by explorer John McDouall Stuart, lies about 150 km (93 miles) south of Alice Springs; you need a four-wheel-drive vehicle to get there along the Maryvale Station Road. Sitting atop a domed hill, the cream-colored pillar is about 495 feet in circumference and some 165 feet tall. Since its discovery this lonely sentinel has been a landmark to explorers and adventurers. The aboriginals have various names for it, one of which is "Idracowra"; all the names mean "place of the adulterous male."

Palm Valley, 155 km (96 miles) west of Alice Springs and accessible only by four-wheel-drive vehicle, is part of the 89,000-acre **Finke Gorge National Park**. *Livistonia mariae* palms, thousands of years old and found nowhere else in the world, take you back in time as you walk among the rock pools. Some 30 of the 300 plant species here are considered among the world's rarest. There are no amenities here except for barbecue and toilet facilities. Allow at least a full day for the return trip. Camping is allowed.

Some 320 km (200 miles) southwest of The Alice is an almost biblical setting: **Kings Canyon**, a living natural-history museum where a multitude of plants—including one species that's a living fossil—grow among the rugged landforms and pools of water. There are no facilities in the canyon proper. However, just 7 km (4 miles) away in the Watarrka National Park is ► **Kings Canyon Frontier Lodge**, which offers both motel-style and lodge-style accommodation, a restaurant, café, and general store in a comfortably rustic setting.

Even at **Arltunga**, amid the rugged MacDonnell Ranges 110 km (68 miles) west of The Alice, where the atmosphere is more modern, you feel like a bit player on the mammoth stage of history. A little more than 100 years ago gold was discovered here, but, as at many goldfields, the yield soon petered out. Sitting amid the excavated rubble you can almost hear the long-dead miners chipping away at the rock in search of an elusive dream, or the battery crushing the gold-bearing ore brought in from the diggings. And if this doesn't work, take a walk among the recently restored stone buildings.

If you can't hear the history in the wind, the locals will relate and embellish it as you sit at the bar of the **Arltunga Hotel**. Described as the loneliest pub in the scrub, the bar is a place where it's not uncommon for stockmen from surrounding cattle stations to be found drinking and telling tales of their exploits.

Just 130 km (80 miles) west of Alice Springs along the paved Namatjira Drive is the **Glen Helen Gorge Nature Park**, where the tranquil (sometimes mighty) Finke River squeezes between majestic sandstone walls at the start of its meandering journey into the Simpson Desert.

On the outskirts of the park is the ► **Glen Helen Lodge**, an ideal spot to spend a few days while exploring the Serpentine, Ellery, Ormiston, and Glen Helen gorges. The lodge's restaurant **Cloudys** (where wild dingoes may be heard howling during dinner) has won several Territory and national awards for its cuisine. Towering over the lodge is the impressive Mount Sonder. Nearby, visitors can swim in the chilly waters of the Finke River, the world's oldest river. Regular helicopter flights over the gorges and to the top of Mount Sonder leave from the front lawn of the lodge.

Outback Tours

While it's possible to drive to these places yourself, it's best to take one of the specially organized tours from Alice Springs. These are usually for small groups, and the guide is often the owner/operator—someone who has lived and worked in the area for years.

Frontier Camel Tours offers a two-and-a-half-day camel tour along the Finke River for about A$385 per person, which includes an overnight stop at the lodge and dinner at Cloudys; Tel: (089) 53-0444; Fax: (089) 55-5015.

For a more relaxed and personal tour, try either of these firms: **Tailormade Tours** or **Sahara Luxury 4 Wheel Drive Tours**. Tailormade Tours (Tel: 089/53-0881; Fax: 089/52-5483) is able to organize chauffeur-driven limousine and luxury-class four-wheel-drive tours starting at around A$140 per person; Sahara (Tel: 089/52-2134; Fax: 089/53-2414) offers a similar service catering to no more than six people at a time.

ULURU NATIONAL PARK

Uluru National Park, which includes Ayers Rock and the spectacular group of rounded mountains called the Olgas, has been one of the most controversial areas in Australia since it was returned to the traditional aboriginal owners in October 1985. The 520-square-mile national park bearing the aboriginal name for Ayers Rock has been leased back from its traditional aboriginal owners and is managed by the Australian National Parks and Wildlife Service. Entry fees are as follows: adults (16 years of age and over), A$10; A$40 for a family or group of four or more adults. The pass is valid for five days and, depending on individual operators, may be included in specific organized tours. There is no camping allowed in Uluru National Park; campers will need to park their bedrolls at Ayers Rock Resort; see below.

Ayers Rock Resort

For almost a decade the Northern Territory's only true resort town—just outside the park boundary—was known as Yulara. A self-sufficient township (the Territory's fourth-largest community) and a self-contained destination capable of accommodating up to 5,000 visitors a day, it's now officially known as Ayers Rock Resort. It was designed to be environmentally friendly by Sydney architect Philip Cox, and does not tower over the surrounding countryside. In fact, when driving to the resort you'd swear it wasn't there.

About 500 km (310 miles) southwest of Alice Springs, Ayers Rock Resort is a comfortable four to five hours away from The Alice by car, or 45 minutes by air. The drive down passes through the heart of Australian cattle country, studded with grazing horses and Brahman, Hereford, and shorthorn cattle and dotted with groves of shady desert oak. It is serviced regularly and directly by most major and secondary airlines and bus companies. And for people driving up the paved Stuart Highway from South Australia in search of a relaxing holiday mingled with the Outback experience, the resort is closer than Alice Springs.

A conglomeration of vacation facilities have been improbably constructed in the middle of the Outback near Ayers Rock and the Olgas. Here you'll find every amenity you expect of a resort, including shops and its own pub, the **Ernest Giles Tavern**. The pub, which is frequented by visitors, is also the local watering hole for the resort's workers.

Accommodation ranges from the international-class ▶ **Sails in the Desert Hotel** to the more moderate ▶ **Desert Gardens** to the ▶ **Outback Pioneer Hotel**—and down to the camping ground. Stylish dining here is restricted to the Sails and Desert Garden hotels. Typical menus include excellent Australian seafood brought in fresh daily along with more unusual (even to many home-grown Aussies) foods like kangaroo-tail soup and emu fillets stuffed with crocodile meat.

The resort is not short on the elegance befitting its resort status, with V.I.P. Chauffeur Cars offering privately escorted tours with fully trained, uniformed chauffeurs in late-model air-conditioned limousines 24 hours a day; Tel: (089) 56-2283; Fax: (089) 56-2150.

Almost one million people (60 percent of whom are from overseas) visit here annually. A multimillion-dollar, two-stage expansion of the resort began a few years ago to service them. The first stage included a new medical center and a 20-shop commercial center; the second stage includes conference facilities, a new restaurant, a health club, and hotel expansion.

The Olgas

Thirty kilometers (19 miles) from Ayers Rock Resort, the Olgas—which the aboriginals call Kata Tjuta, "place of many heads"—look like three dozen giant upturned caramel puddings tinged red and gold. The entire range is more than four miles long by three miles wide. Mount Olga, at almost 2,000 feet high, is the tallest of the domes. In aboriginal legend Mount Olga is the home of the giant serpent Wanambi, who lives in a cave below. When angry the monster blows gusts of wind through the gorges; when happy Wanambi changes into a rainbow, spreading himself across the more than 30 magnificent domes.

Like Ayers Rock, the Olgas are steeped in aboriginal myth, with everything having its origins in the Dreamtime, the aboriginal creation myth. The Olgas are more spectacular, more eerie, more visually interesting than Ayers Rock.

Consider the ironic luxury of being driven around the Outback in a limousine. You can even arrange a formal dinner at the Olgas—try wining and dining and being served at a portable table complete with crisp white linen and polished silverware and illuminated by gas lamps as the sun drops behind the jumbled Olgas. Make arrangements through V.I.P. Chauffeur Cars; Tel: (089) 56-2283; Fax: (089) 56-2150.

Ayers Rock

Ayers Rock is the ultimate attraction here. People came to Ayers Rock long before the multimillion-dollar resort was built. It was—and still is—a challenge. Like Mount Everest, it has to be climbed because it is there. The aboriginals say—and some Europeans agree—that a profound spiritual aura emanates from within this, the world's largest monolith.

About a 20-minute drive from the resort, the rock is an awesome sight. It rises 1,143 feet above the ground, is almost two and a quarter miles long and one and a half miles wide, and has a base circumference of nearly nine miles. It sits like a gigantic Baked Alaska, and some speculate that it stretches 16,250 feet underground.

Geologists believe the rock is some 600 million years old and was formed during the Cambrian period before being pushed skyward through an inland sea during massive earthquakes that occurred about 460 million years ago. During the Cretaceous period, about 100 million years ago, Ayers Rock is thought to have been an island in a huge lake, the water gouging bays and caves from the rock. The waters slowly receded (aboriginal myth has it that Tiddalik, the biggest frog ever known, drank all the fresh water, turning the lush, green land into what is now the dry, barren heart of Australia), and the rock has remained unchanged for 40 million years, except for a constant process of "spalling," the flaking and peeling of the rock face through erosion.

Depending on the time of day, the prevailing weather, and the season, the rock changes color from brilliant reds and flaming oranges to purple, mauve, and even black. Sunset is often the best time of day to watch the changing spectrum. There are free, regular tours by park rangers, usually lasting about an hour. At different times through the week teams of aboriginal and non-aboriginal rangers conduct a special two-hour tour—the Liru Walk—when they give both aboriginal and Western cultural interpretations of the rock and surrounding park.

The dangers that confront visitors to the Territory cannot be stressed too often. In recent years, both at the Olgas and at Kings Canyon, there have been several deaths of people ill-prepared for the elements. All these deaths could have been avoided—some victims died of thirst, others from being unable to withstand the often grueling climbs. At least a liter of water per person should be taken on short walks, and four liters a day should be drunk in hot weather.

Climbing Ayers Rock is also dangerous: Sufferers of heart conditions (including high blood pressure and angina), asthmatics, and those who fear heights or are prone to dizziness should not make the climb. If you are generally unfit, or have doubts, do not attempt it.

There is ample evidence of those who have lost their lives on Ayers Rock; memorial plaques are fixed permanently to the rock at the place where the climb starts. There is also an emergency alarm at this site, activated by opening the door of the alarm box. The alarm then sounds for 30 seconds on every UHF radio within the park and resort. The system allows for a two-way conversation with a park ranger who will assist in co-ordinating the emergency response. Ayers Rock is often closed during the middle of the day. While the temperature may be a "cool" 100 degrees F in the shade, the temperature on the rock can easily be 113–122 degrees F, and heat stress can kill.

The Aboriginal Culture

For thousands of years Uluru has been home to the Pitjantjatjara, Yunkantjatjara, and Ngaanyatjara people, and as with all other aboriginal groups their relationship with the land is complex. It is encompassed in the Dreamtime, essentially the framework of all life. The aboriginals believe that before the Dreamtime the world was a truly featureless place. However, over time the earth produced animals that thought like humans, and whose adventures and travels changed the landscape into a three-dimensional historical record.

For the aboriginals, all things, living and nonliving, are related. For example, southwest of Ayers Rock there is a stand of desert oaks that, according to aboriginal myth, are the Liru (poisonous snake men) creeping up on the Kunia (carpet snake men). The pockmarks on the southern face of the rock are said to be where the Liru spears hit as they chased the Kunia; the deep ridges on the top of the rock are the tracks made by the fleeing carpet snake men.

Uluru is said to be the center of all existence, and it is not unusual for non-aboriginals visiting for the first time to feel an inexplicable religious and spiritual aura emanating from the rock.

With World Heritage status, Uluru is totally protected as an area of national and international importance. It is Australia's first Aboriginal National Park, and since the park was turned back over to aboriginal control some dramatic changes have been made to protect the local inhabitants and the fragile natural milieu.

In 1986 the small Mutitjulu community near the rock was closed to the public. As one publication aptly put it, ". . . with rapidly increasing numbers of tourists they were being mistaken for one of the park's attractions. Dozens of buses would arrive every day to see them and their homes and to photograph them as if they were a rare species of wildlife."

A basic understanding of the aboriginal culture can be gained instead in a visit to the **Maruku Arts and Craft Centre,** just behind the park's entry station, where you can view *Uluru,* a film made by the local Mutitjulu, which tells the history of their land and the importance of Tjukurpa—existence itself.

Because of the complex issues that surround the park and its traditional owners, there are some rules that must be adhered to, although many non-aboriginals, particularly Australians, resent them.

Most aboriginals do not like their photographs to be taken because, they say, they lose their inner spirit if photographed. At Uluru there is a policy of *Don't Even Ask.* Also, if you have plans to sell or publish any photographs taken within the park, formal permission *must* be obtained, in advance, from the Australian National Parks and Wildlife Service. Commercial photography is defined as any photography for anything other than private use. (The same conditions apply to Kakadu National Park.) Commercial photographers can obtain assistance in making their applications through the Northern Territory Tourist Commission.

One of the greatest crimes against the traditional owners is entering a sacred site. These are clearly marked within the park and are protected under Northern Territory and Commonwealth legislation.

Australian aboriginal culture is complex, and gaining an understanding of it is not an easy task. The effort, however, is worth your while. Begin your exploration of aboriginal culture in Alice Springs, at the recently opened **Strehlow Research Centre.** The works of one of Australia's most controversial researchers and anthropologists, Theodor George Henry Strehlow, are featured here in a superbly designed exhibit incorporating the earth, wind, and fire theme of the Aranda people. Tel: (089) 51-8000; Fax: (089) 51-8050.

If you have more time to spare, consider taking a guided aboriginal tour. **Desert Tracks Pitjantjatjara Tours** offers eight-day trips that incorporate sleeping in swags (bedrolls) and learning about aboriginal culture. The guide starts each tour with the words, *Palya. Ngalya pitjala nyawa ngayuku ngura. Pulkara nintiriwa yaaltji anangu maru tjutangku manta kanyilpai* ("Welcome. Come and visit my country. Learn how aboriginal people look after this country.") Travel comfort is minimal, but you become part of the community and are rewarded by the total experience. The camp is at Angatja—372 miles southwest of Alice Springs (including 125 miles of dirt road) just over the border in South Australia. The area is restricted under the Pitjantjatjara Land Rights Act of South Australia, and therefore professional photographers, writers, and journalists on the trek may have special conditions placed on them. The content of the trek may change depending on the Angata people's ceremonial obligations. The tours are limited to 200 people divided among ten tours a year, 20 people per tour. The cost for the tour is A$1,925, and includes translators, aboriginal guides, and teachers. Reservations (or rather applications) must be made well in advance and paid in full 30 days before departure. Desert Tracks has the exclusive right to take groups into the area; Tel: (089) 52-8984; Fax: (089) 52-3117.

A large portion of the area surrounding Uluru, excluding Ayers Rock Resort, is aboriginal land to which entry is prohibited without a permit. For information on arrangement of permits, see Getting Around, at the end of this chapter.

THE TOP END

Whatever you do, don't leave behind the insect repellent, sunscreen, sturdy walking shoes, and sun hat you've been carting around the Red Centre when you head into the

Top End. The flies and sun are just as fierce here as they are in the Centre, despite the difference in climate.

The Top End summer—October through April—is called the "Wet." The air is hot and humid and the average rainfall is between 40 and 52 inches. And because of its high humidity and temperatures—in the mid-to-high 90s F—it is referred to by locals as the "suicide season."

Winter here is the "Dry," when little if any rain falls. Humidity is low and temperatures average 86 degrees F. Most visitors prefer to come during the Dry, but the Wet provides more interesting and enduring memories, especially at Kakadu and at Katherine Gorge.

Unlike the Centre, where the prolific wildlife is often hiding from the searing heat, the Top End is a large walk-through botanical and zoological garden.

DARWIN

When the aircraft cabin begins to feel steamy (it's the plane's air conditioner struggling to adjust to the high humidity outside), you know you're coming into Darwin.

Settlers didn't actually succeed in establishing a permanent settlement here until the fifth try. That was in 1869, when Palmerstown was founded. The harbor was called Port Darwin after Charles Darwin, who was aboard the H.M.S. *Beagle* when it explored the harbor; the town was officially renamed Darwin in 1911.

Darwin was almost forgotten until 1872, when the Overland Telegraph from South Australia began operations. Darwin's importance soon increased because the telegraph was the main communications link between Australia and Britain in those days, and Darwin was the access point for the link with mainland Asia.

Still considered Australia's Asian gateway, Darwin today is a multicultural city; more than 40 nationalities make up the population, and the city has a distinctively Asian quality. A walk through the **Smith Street Mall** in the city center on a Saturday morning is ideal for buying bargain-priced sarongs and other Asian-style crafts from the street vendors.

Darwin is unlike any other Australian city, for its history has been turbulent. In 1942 the Japanese bombed Darwin 60 times. Cyclones, a fact of life for Top End residents, have frequently ravaged the city, the worst time being on Christmas Eve, 1974, when Cyclone Tracy's 174-mph winds roared in from the Timor Sea and flattened more than 90 percent of the city, injuring more than 150 people and killing 65.

Such is the character of Darwinites that after evacuation most returned to pick up their lives and rebuild the city, and it has since become a modern metropolis. Development is a key word in the vocabulary of most Territorians: Some hate it, while others welcome it, but regardless of the arguments development is ongoing. Several new multimillion-dollar projects include the State Square (a new Legislative Assembly and Supreme Court precinct) and a Galleria shopping complex in the city center.

The business and commercial center is built on a peninsula on the north side of Darwin's port, dotted with high-rise buildings and surrounded by leafy suburbs and lush, tropical gardens. Despite the modernization of this once rugged outpost (described in the 1930s as "a corner of hell") the city proper retains a relaxed atmosphere and is a welcome change for those driving up through the Outback from Alice Springs.

Unlike Alice Springs, which draws its physical character from the harsh Outback, Darwin's ambience is casual, relaxed, and friendly. Its inhabitants are very fond of drink. So wide is the range of beer available that ordering becomes an exercise in remembering the primary colors: Blue is for Foster's lager, green is Victoria Bitter, white is Carlton Draught, and cold gold is Castlemaine XXXX ("Four X," supposedly so named because Australians can't spell "beer"). Sinking a tinnie (a can of beer) is a real pastime in Darwin, the climate providing the common excuse.

Darwin's worship of beer has led to the Beer Can Regatta each June, where rules two and three state: "Thou Shalt Build Thy Craft of Cans" and "Thy Craft Shall Float by Cans Alone." Drowning is prohibited and it is decreed that everyone "shall have a bloody good time."

Many visitors to the Top End use Darwin as a touring base, taking advantage of the multitude of single-day tours to outlying attractions. But don't neglect Darwin itself; the city has its own ample array of attractions and it is small enough to walk around.

Exploring Darwin

Begin by strolling along The Esplanade from **Lyon's Cottage** at the corner of Knuckey Street and The Esplanade—a charming bungalow built in 1925 from local stone. Continue southeast down The Esplanade to the former

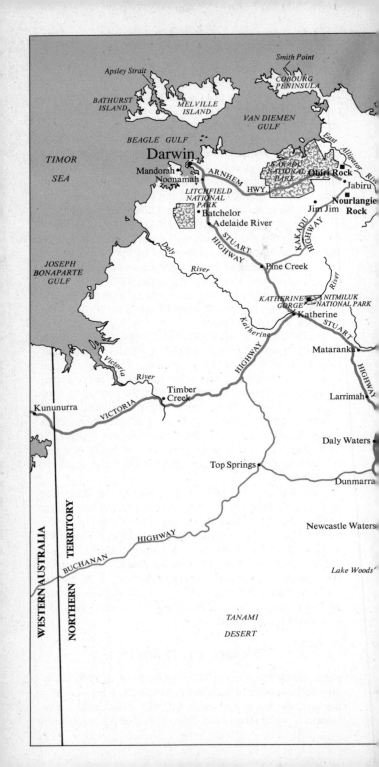

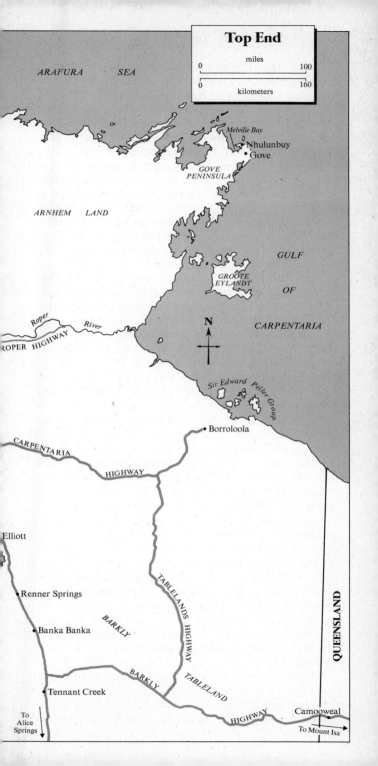

Admiralty House, now an art gallery, the **Old Post Office**, and **Government House**, built in 1870 and today known as "Seven Gables." Turning north onto Smith Street you will see **Christ Church Cathedral**. Constructed in 1902, the church was destroyed by Cyclone Tracy and its ruins have since been incorporated into a stunning new cathedral. Across the way is **Browns Mart**. Although now a small, popular theater, Browns Mart began as a mining exchange before becoming a fruit and vegetable market. It is also said to have been a well-patronized brothel in earlier years. Across the road is the old **Town Hall**, built in 1883. Continue north into the Smith Street Mall where, apart from two or three restored buildings—The Commercial Bank and The Victoria Hotel—you are in the heart of Darwin's shopping center.

If you do not want to walk around Darwin, **Keetleys Tours** will pick you up at your hotel in the morning and take you on a four-hour tour, stopping at sights mentioned above and others, including the Northern Territory Museum of Arts and Sciences and the East Point Military Precinct; Tel: (089) 81-4422; Fax: (089) 41-1341 (see below).

Australian Frontier Cruises also gives you an opportunity to relax in comfort aboard its superb launch, the *Billy J.,* with a two-and-a-half-hour morning cruise or a 90-minute sunset cruise. Most enjoyable, though, is a combination of the sunset cruise and *corroboree* (aboriginal dance performance), which, for around A$42 gives you the 90-minute Sunset Cruise from Fisherman's Wharf (starts at 6:00 P.M.) and then transfers you to the Gunya Amphitheatre for a pleasant buffet meal and the corroboree; Tel: (089) 41-0744; Fax: (089) 81-3173.

Because Darwin is a coastal settlement, many of its activities and attractions center around water. For an unusual experience try hand-feeding fish: On the foreshore off **Doctor's Gully** (just west of the waterfront Esplanade), high tide is feeding time for thousands of fish as they swarm in to dine on bread, octopus, squid, and other treats. Visitors are welcome to participate, although fish are sometimes reticent to take tidbits from strangers (over the years the fish have come to trust one woman who feeds them so much that some will roll over to be scratched).

No visit to Darwin would be complete without spending some time at the **markets**. Perhaps because of the large Asian population—for whom markets are the usual way of conducting business—Darwin has established a reputation as having the most diverse markets in Australia. There are plenty to choose from: Mindil Beach Market, opposite the casino (see Staying in Darwin, below), is open Thursday nights; Parap and Winnellie markets are open Saturdays, and on Sundays there is the flea market at Rapid Creek. The markets offer bargain-priced goods ranging from quality handmade garments and silkscreened fabrics to locally produced handicrafts, many with Asian and aboriginal motifs. You'll also get a chance here to taste some of the finest Asian foods available in Australia.

Darwin's remoteness attracted not only adventurers and speculators—today called entrepreneurs—but also thieves, vagabonds, and other unsavory characters. North of the city center, at the corner of East Point Road and Ross Smith Avenue, stands **Fannie Bay Gaol**—once remote but now surrounded by suburbs. The jail was used for almost a century, until 1979, when Berrimah Prison was finished. Its gallows (they were modeled on those at England's Newgate Prison) were built in 1952 to hang two convicted murderers. Fannie Bay has reopened as a museum. After the Japanese bombed Darwin, many of Fannie Bay's prisoners, some convicted of murdering Japanese pearlers, were set free. Again, following Cyclone Tracy in 1974, many inmates were pardoned. Interestingly, not one prisoner attempted to escape the prison after Tracy's ravages. Many worked alongside the other shocked survivors to rebuild the shattered city. Like the Territory, Fannie Bay Gaol was unconventional.

Darwin's **Northern Territory Museum of Arts and Sciences**, also at Fannie Bay, houses a wide range of historical items relating to the Northern Territory in addition to extensive displays from around Southeast Asia. The museum's art gallery has a large selection of works by Australian artists. **Indo-Pacific Marine**, also at Fannie Bay, is one of the world's few living coral aquariums.

The **East Point Military Precinct** is a museum well worth visiting, for it gives an interesting and perceptive view of the role Darwin played in the defense of Australia during World War II. It was refurbished in 1992 for the 50th anniversary of the bombing of Darwin.

Staying in Darwin

If you're into lounging by the pool, the comfortable, moderately priced, and relaxing ▶ **Darwin Frontier Hotel,** in the city center off Daly Street, is the place to stay. Its rooftop restaurant affords superb views of the surrounding parklands and the Darwin skyline across the harbor, and its swimming pool is set in a tropical garden.

For a more stylish approach either the ► **Melia Darwin Hotel** or the uniquely designed ► **Beaufort Darwin**, both in the heart of the city, should do. Both are ideally suited to the business traveller or the vacationer, with sauna/spa facilities and swimming pools. These hotels stand out for their decor and their dedication to service, making guests feel totally pampered. Both have good restaurants and coffee shops. The Beaufort's excellent dining facilities include **Siggi's**, for international cuisine, and the less formal **Rafferty's** grill and oyster bar.

The ► **Diamond Beach Hotel Casino** at Mindil Beach (west of the city) is quite upscale, with superb views of the Botanic Gardens and a relaxing two-mile-long beach; it of course has licensed gaming floors.

For something with more of the rugged charm of "old Darwin" the 70-room ► **Hotel Darwin** on the corner of The Esplanade and Herbert Street—about halfway between the former Admiralty House and the Old Post Office—is worth considering. Overlooking the beach, it is comfortable and air conditioned but has managed to retain the charm of a steamy, tropical hotel.

If you plan on staying in Darwin for a week or more consider the ► **Marrakai Luxury Apartments**. These self-contained units are often used by visiting businesspeople as a home away from home. The complex has a swimming pool and sauna/spa facilities but no restaurant.

Dining and Nightlife in Darwin

Dining out plays an important role in Darwin's social life, and the city's restaurant options reflect its ethnic diversity. Epicures may knock the extension of the so-called Aussie cuisine into exotica like buffalo and crocodile as tasteless and even a bit pretentious, but don't worry if you'd rather indulge in classic French food, Italian or Greek fare, or Asian cookery—Darwin has it all.

Charlie's Restaurant used to be (officially) called the Olympic, but for years locals have known the place as Charlie's because of its popular owner/chef, Charlie Cagnetti. The restaurant, at the corner of Knuckey Street and Austin Lane, offers some of the best Italian food in Darwin. Friendly and relaxed, it's open for lunch and dinner; reservations are strongly recommended; Tel: (089) 81-3298.

Another place serving quality food is **Christo's On The**

Wharf, on Mitchell Street next door to the Sheraton. The Greek fare, particularly the seafood, is simple but exquisite; Tel: (089) 81-8658.

If you like watching your food being prepared, try **Night Tokyo** on Smith Street, a traditional Japanese *teppanyaki* restaurant, where cooking is performance art; reservations are essential; Tel: (089) 81-7484. Another good Asian eatery is the Mongolian **Ghengis Khan Restaurant** on East Point Road in Fannie Bay. Here you select your food from the display, then watch the chefs prepare it; Tel: (089) 81-3883.

You may, however, want to eat Australian. **Gabby's Bar and Bistro** in Cavenagh Street gives you the "true flavor of the Territory" with its crocodile and buffalo dishes.

For scenic views, take a sunset cruise around the harbor on the *Billy J;* Tel: (089) 41-0744.

For jazz buffs the **Casino**, the **Travelodge**, the **Atrium Hotel**, and the **Hotel Darwin** are the places to head. If you're interested in art, have a meal at the Esplanade Gallery's **Garden Café** on the corner of Knuckey Street and The Esplanade. Here you can enjoy a light, relaxing meal while viewing a variety of Territory landscapes.

For rock, discos, and piano bars there are **Fannies Nightclub**, the **Victoria Hotel**, and **Squires Tavern**, respectively, and the very popular **Hot Gossip Entertainment Complex** in Cavenagh Street, where you can dance the night away at **Scandals** or enjoy the more sophisticated atmosphere of **Whispers Cocktail and Piano Bar**. The Melia has provided an English-pub environment at what is appropriately called **The Pub**.

Another choice for nighttime entertainment is the **Darwin Travelodge**, with its spacious, varied bistros. On most nights between May and October you can relax here poolside at a traditional Aussie barbecue while being entertained by a corroboree.

AROUND DARWIN

Litchfield Park, just a two-hour drive south of Darwin, is the Top End's newest park attraction, covering 162,000 acres. Here along the Tabletop Range are four large waterfalls cascading through pockets of rain forest. The park is one of the Top End's better areas for bushwalking. Before setting out make sure to obtain a copy of at least one of the following topographical maps: 1:100,000 scale Reynolds River Sheet No 5071; or 1:50,000 scale sheets No 5071-1, 2, 3, and/or 4.

There are no accommodation facilities in the park itself. If you intend to spend time here you should consider stopping at the ▶ **Rum Jungle Motor Inn** at Batchelor, 24 km (15 miles) east of the park. The inn is a welcome stop even if you are not visiting the park, thanks to its tropical surroundings and the availability of parachuting and trail riding.

If crocodiles really interest you and you want a closer look, **The Crocodile Farm** is worth a visit. The farm is about a 30-minute drive south of Darwin along the Stuart Highway. Australia's first commercial croc farm, it has more than 7,000 of the reptiles, from hatchlings a few inches long to 13-foot giants. About 30 American alligators are also on view, enabling visitors to see the differences between the two species.

The Top End has many beautiful and secluded beaches, some quite close to Darwin. Many have grassy areas shaded by tall trees. At **Casuarina Free Beach** it is quite legal to bathe in the buff. The Diamond Beach Casino overlooks the popular **Mindil Beach**, which stretches along the coast west of the city for several miles; you can rent boats here for an hour or longer. Other popular Darwin beaches are **Vesteys**, **Casuarina** (different from the free beach), **Nightcliff**, and **Fannie Bay**. All are north of Mindil Beach and within easy reach of the city center by bus.

Top End beaches can be dangerous for the unwary. Sharks as well as crocodiles inhabit the coastal waters. Perhaps the most dangerous creatures, however, are the sea wasps, jellyfish that infest much of Australia's tropical coast during the Wet. Although it's not absolutely necessary during the Dry (it may draw a bit of a giggle from some people), you might want to wear a pair of nylon pantyhose when swimming in Australia's warmer waters. Divers often wear them to protect their legs from jellyfish stings. If wearing pantyhose is not for you, keep a small bottle of vinegar handy. Rubbing vinegar on the sting helps prevent the jellyfish barb from continuing to inject toxin, which can kill within minutes if left untreated.

Ignore warnings at your own risk. Celebrating the finish of the Wet in 1989, swimmers ignored official warnings about the presence of box jellyfish—as sea wasps are also known—which resulted in several people being stung, including a young boy who was hospitalized. During the Wet, many water sports such as windsurfing and parasailing are totally discouraged.

CROCODILES

A word about crocodiles; they are endemic in the Top End. There are two species, the freshwater crocodile, which is usually harmless unless provoked, and the more dangerous saltwater crocodile. Crocodiles can move quickly: When food entices them, the crocodiles slip menacingly from the mud banks into the water, then, often without warning and with jaws snapping, leap high out of the water to snatch their meal and quickly disappear. A two-and-a-half-hour cruise aboard the *Adelaide River Queen* along the Adelaide River outside of Darwin gives you a firsthand look at the crocodiles in their natural environment. (Tours leave from The Pavillion at the Adelaide River Bridge. You may be picked up at your hotel in Darwin, or drive the 64 km/40 miles southeast to The Pavillion yourself; Tel: 089/88-8144.)

Crocodiles can even jump into boats. Do not swim in waters marked with croc signs, and be watchful when moving around riverbanks—ignoring these warnings can be fatal. Unlike many other dangerous species found throughout the Territory, such as snakes and spiders, saltwater crocodiles are not likely to retreat from danger.

Visitors can now take out insurance against crocodile attack. The Northern Territory Insurance Office has, for a small fee, introduced "croc cover," although for anyone to collect, the attack has to be fatal.

The most infamous, yet the most beloved, of Territory crocs, Sweetheart, a 16½-foot-long, 1,716-pound monster, is preserved at the Northern Territory Museum of Arts and Sciences in Darwin. Renowned for attacking boats, Sweetheart died in 1979 (he accidentally drowned after being captured for relocation to a quieter part of the Finniss River). So popular is the Sweetheart legend that the Diamond Beach Hotel Casino has named a bar after him and has a six-foot neon replica lazing in a giant cocktail glass overlooking the gaming floor.

BATHURST AND MELVILLE ISLANDS

A short 80-km (50-mile) plane ride north of Darwin aboard Air North's "Gooney Bird" (a DC-3) will take you to Bathurst and Melville islands, home of the Tiwi people.

Unlike the aboriginal communities of the Red Centre, which are essentially off limits, those of the Top End show an intense desire to share their culture with others. As at other aboriginal communities, individual visitors must have entry permits.

Darwin-based **Tiwi Tours** and **Australian Kakadu Tours** both provide an opportunity to visit the islands for half a day or as long as three days. You will have a chance to mingle with the people and, if you like, to buy some fine examples of northern Australian aboriginal arts and crafts.

Tiwi Tours offers half-day and full-day tours of both islands, while Australian Kakadu Tours offers one-, two-, and three-day tours that supply an aboriginal guide to help you hunt and gather traditional foods. Visiting both islands means you'll have to cross the narrow Apsley Strait from Bathurst Island to Melville. Be prepared to get wet; the trip is often made in an open boat. For Tiwi and Australian Kakadu tours, Tel: (089) 81-5144; Fax: (089) 81-5391.

Tiwi means "people," "we the people," or "we, the chosen people." Their culture differs from that of the mainland aboriginals, and until the late 1800s the Tiwi had little contact with the mainland. On both islands you will find yourself becoming, albeit for a short time, part of the community. The openness of the Tiwi is such that you are welcome to join in whatever they are doing; you need only ask.

You will also find yourself absorbed in the islands' history and hear lighthearted tales, like the one about the bishop who had 150 wives.

On a more serious note, the Tiwi were the first Australians to feel the wrath of the Japanese during World War II, when bombers strafed the islands on their way to bomb Darwin. Australia's first Japanese P.O.W. was captured on Melville Island by a Tiwi, Matthias Ulungura, after crash-landing there.

The Tiwi are renowned for their colorful screen-printed fabrics, which have graced the covers of many international fashion magazines. Clothes and fabrics manufactured by the Tiwi are sold throughout Australia under the labels Tiwi Designs, Jilmarra, and Bima Wear.

On Melville Island, where a large Caribbean pine plantation has been established, you can swim at **Taracumbie Falls**—no crocodiles here—before heading off in a minibus along the often dusty track to Milikapiti, where you visit an aboriginal burial site, with its colorful, carved *pukamani* poles. The islands so capture the imagination that you may feel a little like Gauguin in Tahiti. And you certainly won't want to leave.

KAKADU NATIONAL PARK

An Australian politician once remarked that much of the three-million-plus-acre Kakadu, 250 km (155 miles) east of Darwin, was nothing but "clapped-out buffalo country." This World Heritage area has suffered degradation by feral buffalo and other introduced animal and plant species, but Kakadu is still beautiful. It is as rich in aboriginal history as it is in mineral wealth—and many interests are eyeing that mineral wealth.

Kakadu is home to about a third of all the bird species in Australia, more than 20 species of frogs, some 45 species of fish—28 of which can be found in the Magela and Nourlangie creeks alone—saltwater and freshwater crocodiles, and countless other species of animals (including many insects) and plants. To appreciate Kakadu takes time, to understand it would take centuries. Kakadu is waterfalls cascading (though not always) from the ancient rock formations of the Arnhem Land Escarpment; it is a storybook of aboriginal history and mythology; it is tidal flats and estuaries surrounded by mangrove swamps; it is fishing for barramundi in the billabongs (water holes) and rivers; it is grassy plains and rain forests filled with birds, insects, reptiles, and other animal life; it is indeed a World Heritage environment. (A real and constant threat to Kakadu looms, however, as poisonous cane toads move west from northern Queensland, and a Brazilian water weed has been introduced that is beginning to choke some of its river systems.)

Such is the nature of Kakadu that several specialized tours are available catering separately to the photographer, the bird watcher, or the fisherman. There are also several companies offering half- and full-day aerial tours.

For the adventurous (and physically fit), one group of operators provides a number of refreshingly novel ways to get to know Kakadu. **Adventure Terra Safaris**—comprising Dial-A-Safari, Bushranger Tours, and Breakwater Canoe Tours—offers adventures ranging from two-day (about A\$190) to seven-day safaris (about A\$980), to longer tours, lasting up to 15 days, that combine canoeing and overland travel in the Territory. The people at Adventure Terra Safaris are recognized as pioneers in organizing "wilderness" journeys in the Northern Territory and are justifiably proud of their excursions; Tel: (089) 41-2899, 24 hours; toll-free within Australia, Tel: (008) 89-1127; Fax: (089) 41-2833.

Like Uluru, Kakadu is managed by the Australian National Parks and Wildlife Service and entry fees are now charged. The fee (at time of publication) was A$10 per adult or A$40 maximum per family, and is valid for two weeks. Children under 16 are admitted free. There are also various other charges within the park for camping and some of the displays.

The Wet leaves a lasting impression on visitors. Toward the end of the season, much of Kakadu becomes an almost sheer carpet of green and gold and pink as lilies and grasses flower, and huge flocks of water birds begin moving about in search of food. Unfortunately much of the park becomes inaccessible as the large floodplains become inland seas. The two largest of these are Magela and Yellow Waters, with Magela often extending for 80 square miles. It is interesting to see traditional enemies, such as snakes and mice, sharing the same branch as they take shelter from the floods.

Two popular sites within the park are **Jim Jim Falls** and **Twin Falls**. The falls are at their peak during the Wet, when they can be best appreciated from the air. The water cascades in a raging torrent, its mist and spray painting ghostly images in the gorges. In the Dry the water slows to a mere trickle, but access is relatively easy to both falls at this time. There is a one-half-mile walk over rocks to get to the base of Jim Jim Falls, but to reach the bottom of Twin Falls you must paddle on a surfboard or rubber air mattress for six miles.

Road conditions within the park vary, and despite the apparent closeness of a site it may take hours to reach. During the Dry it takes only 45 minutes to drive the 40 km (25 miles) to the East Alligator area from the park's headquarters, yet it takes three to four hours to get to Jim Jim Falls, 70 km (43 miles) from the Kakadu Highway.

Geologically, Kakadu's age ranges from more than 100 million to more than 200 million years old—depending on what rocks you happen to sit on. For the aboriginals it is as old as life itself, the Dreamtime.

The aboriginals have no recorded history as we know it: There are no books written by the tribal elders to teach the younger generation their history; for them history is recorded in the mind and handed down in song and dance, or by drawings. At **Ubirr** (Obiri Rock), just outside the eastern perimeter of Kakadu, journey back to . . . when, nobody knows—but it is thought that the oldest paintings here may date back at least 20,000 years, making them possibly the most ancient artworks known. **Nour-**

langie Rock, farther south, is another ancient rock art "gallery" well worth a visit. Here, however, there are also more recent works—as recent as 1982—that still employ the traditional methods. The best time to see these masterpieces is in the early morning or late afternoon, when it is cool. (Actually, that is the best time to do almost everything in the Northern Territory.)

From the ancient to the nuclear: That is another face of Kakadu. The A$350-million Ranger uranium mine here is Australia's largest, and the world's second-largest, producer of the ore. Kakadu Air Services has set up an information center at Jabiru Airport—Jabiru Township was established east of Kakadu park to service the Ranger, Nabarlek, Jabiluka, and Koongarra mines—and offers free tours of the Ranger mine. The tour provides an interesting view of the mine's operations and an opportunity to find out about the mine, uranium, land ownership, conservation, and other issues from the mine operators' perspective.

There are several camping spots within the park, with standard accommodation at either the ▶ Gagudju Lodge Cooinda, via Jabiru, or the ▶ Frontier Kakadu Village on the Arnhem Highway. Or, you can stay inside a crocodile, or rather an architect's version of one: the ▶ Gagudju Crocodile Hotel at Jabiru Township, a hotel shaped like a giant crocodile.

Access to Kakadu from Darwin is via the paved Arnhem Highway, which turns east off the Stuart Highway 35 km (22 miles) south of Darwin. Over the years tourism has inspired significant upgrading of the roads into Kakadu from Darwin. If you intend to drive yourself, contact Destination Australia for more information; Tel: (03) 650-5560 or, toll-free within Australia, (008) 33-1373.

ARNHEM LAND

East of Kakadu National Park stretches the vast expanse of Arnhem Land. Proclaimed an aboriginal reserve in 1931, much of Arnhem Land remains virtually unexplored by Europeans, and it has long been basically off limits to the general public. It is now, however, slowly being opened up to visitors. Destination Darwin offers a limited but interesting range of tours into the area; Tel: (089) 48-0788 or (089) 41-3882; Fax: (089) 48-0766 or (089) 41-3881.

Tours commence at several departure points—Darwin, Smith Point on Coburg Peninsula (see below), and the town of Jabiru just east of Kakadu—and fly you via light aircraft to the isolated Mudjeegarrdart airstrip in the remote northwest corner of Arnhem Land. From there, you are transported by four-wheel-drive wagon to the **Umorrdul** aboriginal rock art sites, which date back more than 20,000 years. You can also spend time with your aboriginal guides spearing for crabs along the coast of the Van Diemen Gulf. The area, a virtually untouched wilderness, is home to the Gummulkbun aboriginal people and an abundance of wildlife, including both native and introduced species. Wild pigs and Timor ponies roam freely across the open wetlands. It's a photographer's delight, but, as at all aboriginal reserves, strict rules apply, even when you're part of an approved tour. Guests are forbidden to bring alcoholic beverages into the area, although liquor may be available within the confines of a camp. Photography is prohibited in some areas; your guides will let you know when picture-taking is and is not allowed.

There's another way to have a look at the area—one that doesn't involve roughing it at all (just the opposite, in fact). The accommodations at ▶ **Seven Spirit Bay**, a self-contained vacation hideaway, are luxurious. Seven Spirit, which lies inside Gurig National Park and Coburg Marine Park on the Coburg Peninsula, is expensive, but the price includes all activities and meals (it does not include transportation or alcohol). The Coburg Peninsula pokes itself like a gnarled finger into the waters of the Van Diemen Gulf; the setting is extremely isolated—600 miles northeast of Darwin and accessible only by boat or light aircraft—but at Seven Spirit you'll be treated like royalty. The camp's 24 "habitats" (they don't call them "rooms," here) stand in a garden setting; each has two double beds and a detached private bathroom. Despite its remoteness and the obvious difficulty in getting supplies here, Seven Spirit has truly excellent food. No effort is spared when it comes to taking care of guests: There's even a darkroom for camera buffs. And there's plenty of opportunity for capturing images of wildlife, including Banteng cattle, Timor ponies, and the elusive Sambar deer that wander this wilderness.

Nhulunbuy

Some 650 km (400 miles) east of Darwin, at the far northeastern point of Arnhem Land, is the Gove Peninsula, and the town of Nhulunbuy (also called Gove), which sits on the small Melville Bay.

When bauxite mining began here in the early 1970s, on land leased from the Arnhem Land Reserve, a support town was needed. Today, Nhulunbuy is a thriving community of about 3,800 people. It is roughly two hours by jet from Darwin; driving to Nhulunbuy is not recommended, as the only road in is from Katherine (see below) and requires considerable experience with Outback conditions to negotiate. There are, however, a few charter operators that will take you here by boat from Darwin. These include Coral Divers (Tel: 089/81-2686) and Fathom Five Pro-Charters (Tel: 089/85-4288). Because rates and availability are continually changing it is recommended that you contact a tour operator well in advance. Permits for road access are required; contact the Northern Land Council; Tel: (089) 20-5100.

Like many areas of the northern coast the peninsula was once visited by fishermen from Macassar, Indonesia, searching for trepang (bêche-de-mer, or sea slugs). Until European settlement, those Malaysian fishermen were often the only contact Top End aboriginals had with the outside world.

Although Nhulunbuy is small and isolated, some say it is the ideal place to live. An oasis of palms and tropical plants, the township is surrounded by white, sandy beaches, mangrove swamps, and tropical forest. Much of the immediate countryside is flat. As in Darwin, there are two seasons, the Wet and the Dry. During the coolest months, June and July, the temperature averages about 77 degrees F, and in November and December it rises to about 90 degrees F. Nhulunbuy's weather is monsoonal, and, as at Darwin, venomous jellyfish infest the water during the Wet, making swimming impossible.

One of the most popular places to stay in Nhulunbuy is the quiet ▶ Hideaway Safari Lodge. Virtually opposite the airport and well out of town, it is very tranquil. It has only ten rooms and is often used as a transit point for extended tours of the region, but the service is so personal, making you feel like part of an extended family, you may decide to stay longer. More centrally located, however—in fact, right in the heart of the township—is the ▶ Gove Resort Motel (formerly the Walkabout Hotel).

Sailing and Fishing

Just off the coast the Arafura Sea meets the Gulf of Carpentaria, and the township is a magnet for yachts sailing around Australia or, for that matter, around the world. Drinking at the yacht club on Melville Bay (Tel:

089/87-1172) can be as rewarding as sailing with these people, to whom the town of Gove is a supply depot. The club is just a short drive from the town center. As is the case with most licensed clubs in Australia, you must be signed in by a member or pass as a bona fide traveller. If you want to spend some time here, the locals will see to it that you get in. As you sit on the verandah drinking the inevitable tinnie, gaze seaward and dream of big marlin.

In recent years, usually in November, Gove has hosted the Northern Territory's **Gove Game Classic**, a fishing competition that attracts game fishermen from around Australia. The Classic promotes the developing marlin grounds off Truant Bank, about 37 miles off the coast from Nhulunbuy. The first marlin was not taken here in competition until 1984, but reports of marlin in the area are frequent, including the story of a 2,860-pound body—headless and gutted—found in the hold of a Taiwanese fishing boat. The fishing season for black marlin and sailfish is short, November through December, and charter boats operating from Gove are hard to come by. However, with sufficient lead time (at least three months) you will probably be able to secure one.

Personalized charters can be arranged through Lady Sariah Charters in Nhulunbuy. The firm will organize your charter and provide all equipment plus airport/accommodation transfers. You must provide your own alcohol, however, and fishing lures are available on a replace-if-lost basis. From A$660 a day per person, with a maximum of six people per charter; Tel: (089) 87-2832.

KATHERINE

Author Neville Shute brought recognition to Central Australia, particularly Alice Springs, with his book *A Town Like Alice*. Like other parts of the Northern Territory, Katherine, 300 km (186 miles) "down the Track" (the Stuart Highway) from Darwin, has also been immortalized in print—in Mrs. Aeneas (Jeannie) Gunn's book *We of the Never-Never,* published in 1908 and made into a film in 1981 (see Bibliography, above). A remarkable woman, Jeannie Gunn was the wife of the manager of Elsey Station and the first white woman to set foot in the area.

Like Alice Springs, Katherine began life as a repeater station for the Overland Telegraph. Katherine and Alice Springs are similar in many other ways. They are both centers of the large pastoral industries in their regions, and both have a large aboriginal population. Katherine is in a significant grain-growing region but, unlike The Alice, has not yet had its frontier spirit altered by tourism. Because this is one of Australia's fastest-growing areas, however (the establishment of the nearby Tindall Royal Australian Air Force Base is a major factor), this is changing, evidenced by the increasing number of regional tours now available.

Set on the banks of the Katherine River—named by John McDouall Stuart in 1862 after Katherine Chambers, the daughter of one of his expedition's backers—Katherine was one of the territory's earliest settlements. The single most popular attraction here is **Katherine Gorge**, actually 13 gorges, 32 km (20 miles) northeast of town within the Nitmiluk National Park. Several companies offer cruises of two to four hours in duration. Frontier Katherine Gorge Cruises (Tel: 089-71-1123) offers a four-hour cruise for A$35 per person.

As you cruise through the first of the gorges in specially designed flat-bottomed boats, past sloping, tree-lined banks, you may feel a little disappointed, wondering what all the fuss is about. But beyond the rock barrier that separates the first from the second gorge (you have to change boats) the mood changes. Here the sides are vertical, rising a sheer 300 feet, and the gorge takes a series of 90-degree turns. Normally the near-three-mile cruise of both gorges ends at the next rocky bar; however, it is possible to go farther into the system.

Because of the land barriers between the gorges, boats have to be carried across them during the Dry and left for use—until the Wet, when they are retrieved before the Katherine River turns into a torrent of angry water.

The best way to get to Katherine is to pick up a rental car, preferably a four-wheel-drive vehicle for off-road exploration, in Darwin. Have it reserved to pick you up at your hotel or at the airport. Access to Katherine from Kakadu is via the partly paved Kakadu Highway, which comes out at Pine Creek, 90 km (56 miles) north of Katherine.

After spending a day exploring Katherine Gorge, drive 100 km (60 miles) farther south to Mataranka to stay at the ▶ **Mataranka Homestead Tourist Resort**, 7 km (4 miles) off the Stuart Highway on the Roper Highway. Mataranka was established in 1916 as an experimental cattle station; a replica of the Elsey Station homestead has been built here. Nearby are the **Mataranka Thermal Pools**, where the water is a constant 93 degrees F. A swim in the pools is relaxing and refreshing despite the Territory's hot weather. Mataranka is surrounded by a forest of towering paperbark trees and cabbage palms.

GETTING AROUND

Getting to the Territory poses few problems. Most visitors, even those headed first to Darwin, come in from the south—that is, from Sydney, Melbourne, or Adelaide—and through Alice Springs, by air, road, or rail.

Darwin has the Territory's only civilian international air facilities, which mainly service Southeast Asia.

Australia's two major domestic airlines, Ansett and Australian, have regular daily flights to Alice Springs and Darwin from major southern cities and secondary ports. Darwin is also serviced daily with regular flights from Alice Springs and major Southeast Asian cities.

You can expect a flight of between two and three hours from the major southern cities to Alice Springs and another two hours to Darwin. Ansett and Australian Airlines have regular flights to Ayers Rock. Katherine is serviced by flights from Darwin and Alice Springs.

If you have time it is worth considering rail or road transport into the Territory. The only direct rail line into the Northern Territory is The Ghan from Adelaide, South Australia. In Queensland you can catch The Sunlander from Brisbane to Townsville, connecting there with The Inlander west to Mount Isa. From there you finish your trip to Darwin by bus.

The Ghan

Unlike its infamous narrow-gauged predecessor, which took up to a week to reach Alice Springs from Adelaide, The Ghan takes just 22 hours and has such facilities as a dining car and sleepers. A trip on The Ghan is a self-contained adventure where the confinement, along with the common interest of travelling to the Northern Territory, leads to a sharing of personal experience with people from diverse cultures and backgrounds. Many lifelong friendships have been forged after a cross-country journey aboard The Ghan.

To travel on The Ghan is to experience one of the great train journeys of the world. With its colorful history The Ghan is legendary among train buffs. The Ghan has the plushly, romantically furnished Stuart Restaurant and two licensed lounge cars, the Oasis Car and the nonsmoking

Dreamtime Lounge. On-board entertainment includes poker machines, computer games, and a piano bar. Amenities include a hair salon and a souvenir shop. Reservations can be made by calling Australian National Railways; in Adelaide, Tel: (08) 231-7699; in Alice Springs, Tel: (089) 52-1011; elsewhere in Australia (toll-free), Tel: (008) 888-417.

Despite fervent efforts by the Northern Territory government in recent years, Alice Springs and Darwin are still not connected by rail.

Driving

There are three main roads into the Territory: the Stuart Highway from Adelaide, the Barkly from Brisbane via Mount Isa in Queensland, and the Victoria from Western Australia via Kununurra (for which see the Western Australia chapter). Driving gives you the freedom to visit areas of interest as well as the advantage of staying at each place as long as you wish.

In Darwin the Automobile Association of the Northern Territory has an agency at 79 Smith Street. The association provides road information Monday through Friday and can arrange international driving permits; Tel: (089) 81-3837.

The long distances involved—for example, over 1,000 km (600 miles) from Adelaide in South Australia to Alice Springs—can be dangerous if you are unaccustomed to this type of driving. Also, breakdown problems are compounded by the distances, sometimes over 200 km (125 miles) between roadhouses (garages). Unfamiliar road conditions, wandering livestock, kangaroos, and road-trains (massive road transporters hauling up to three trailers laden with livestock or other freight) all pose additional driving dangers. Also, about two-thirds of the Territory's roads are unpaved; on these you should drive at half the normal highway speed.

Before leaving on a trip contact the local police station for information on road conditions; some tracks may be closed or restricted to four-wheel-drive vehicles. Also inform someone of your destination and likely time of arrival. Once there, telephone to let them know you have arrived.

The major bus companies—Greyhound, Stateliner, Ansett Pioneer, and Bus Australia—have regular service linking the Territory with all important towns.

Aboriginal Land Permits

For information and arrangement of permits to enter aboriginal lands, contact the following: Alice Springs/Tennant Creek Regions; Central Land Council, 33 Stuart Highway, P.O. Box 3321, Alice Springs N.T. 0871. Tel: (089) 52-3800. Darwin, Nhulunbuy, Katherine Regions; Northern Land Council, 9 Rowling Street, P.O. Box 42921, Casuarina N.T. 0800. Tel: (089) 20-5100. Melville or Bathurst Islands Region; Tiwi Land Council, Hgui, Bathurst Island via Darwin N.T. 0822. Tel: (089) 47-1838.

ACCOMMODATIONS REFERENCE

The rates given here are projections *for 1994. Unless otherwise indicated, rates are for double room, double occupancy. As prices are subject to change, always double-check before booking.*

A 5 percent "tourism marketing duty," funds used by the government to promote the region as a tourist destination, is payable on all Northern Territory accommodation. Every effort has been made to ensure that the duty has been calculated in the prices given below. However, when making reservations, it is advised that you ask whether the quoted price includes this amount.

▶ **Beaufort Darwin**. The Esplanade, **Darwin**, N.T. 0800. Tel: (089) 82-9911; Fax: (089) 81-5332; in U.S., (800) 44-UTELL; in Canada, (800) 387-1338. A$205.

▶ **Darwin Frontier Hotel**. Buffalo Court, **Darwin**, N.T. 0800. Tel: (089) 81-5333; Fax: (089) 41-0909. A$110.

▶ **Desert Gardens Hotel**. Yulara Drive, **Yulara**, N.T. 0872. Tel: (089) 56-2100; Fax: (089) 56-2156; in U.S., (800) 44-UTELL; in Canada, (800) 387-8842. A$200.

▶ **Diamond Beach Hotel Casino**. Gilruth Avenue, **Mindil Beach**, N.T. 0800. Tel: (089) 46-2666; Fax: (089) 81-9186. A$190.

▶ **Frontier Kakadu Village**. Arnhem Highway, **Kakadu National Park**, N.T. 0886. Tel: (089) 79-0166; Fax: (089) 79-0147. A$110.

▶ **Frontier Oasis Resort**. 10 Gap Road, **Alice Springs**, N.T. 0870. Tel: (089) 52-1444; Fax: (089) 52-3776. A$89.

▶ **Gagudju Crocodile Hotel**. Flinders Street, **Jabiru**, N.T. 0886. Tel: (089) 79-2800; Fax: (089) 79-2707; in U.S., (800) 44-UTELL; in Canada, (800) 387-1338. A$168.

▶ **Gagudju Lodge Cooinda**. **Jim Jim**, N.T. 0886. Tel: (089) 79-0145; toll-free within Australia (008) 023-181; Fax: (089) 79-0148; in U.S., (800) 44-UTELL; in Canada, (800) 387-8842. A$80–A$110.

▶ **Glen Helen Lodge.** Namatijira Drive, Western Mac-Donnells, via **Alice Springs**, N.T. 0870. Tel: (089) 56-7489; Fax: (089) 56-7495. A$72.

▶ **Gove Resort Motel.** Westal Street, **Nhulunbuy**, N.T. 0880. Tel: (089) 87-1777; Fax: (089) 87-2322. A$110.

▶ **Hideaway Safari Lodge.** Prospect Road, **Gove**, N.T. 0880. Tel: (089) 87-1833; Fax: (089) 87-2627. A$95.

▶ **Hotel Darwin.** 10 Herbert Street, **Darwin**, N.T. 0800. Tel: (089) 81-9211; Fax: (089) 81-9575. A$85.

▶ **Kings Canyon Frontier Lodge.** Kings Canyon, Watarrka National Park, N.T. 0870. Tel: (089) 41-0744, reservations agent; Tel: (089) 56-7442, lodge; Fax: (089) 56-7410. A$140.

▶ **Lasseters Hotel Casino.** Barrett Drive, **Alice Springs**, N.T. 0870. Tel: (089) 52-5066; Fax: (089) 53-1680. A$100.

▶ **Marrakai Luxury Apartments.** 93 Smith Street, **Darwin**, N.T. 0800. Tel: (089) 82-3711; Fax: (089) 81-9283. A$200 including daily service; A$175 with weekly cleaning service, minimum 7-night stay.

▶ **Mataranka Homestead Tourist Resort. Mataranka**, N.T. 0852. Tel: (089) 75-4544; Fax: (089) 75-4580. A$58–A$74.

▶ **Melia Alice Springs Hotel.** Barrett Drive, **Alice Springs**, N.T. 0870. Tel: (089) 52-8000; Fax: (089) 52-3822. A$205.

▶ **Melia Darwin Hotel.** 32 Mitchell Street, **Darwin**, N.T. 0800. Tel: (089) 82-0000; Fax: (089) 81-1765. A$205.

▶ **Outback Pioneer Hotel.** Yulara Drive, **Yulara**, N.T. 0872. Tel: (089) 56-2170; Fax: (089) 56-2320. Dormitories (40 beds) A$18; cabins A$80; double rooms A$175.

▶ **Rum Jungle Motor Inn.** 220 Rum Jungle Road, **Batchelor**, N.T. 0845. Tel: (089) 76-0123; Fax: (089) 76-0230. A$78.

▶ **Sails in the Desert Hotel.** Yulara Drive, **Yulara**, N.T. 0872. Tel: (089) 56-2200; Fax: (089) 56-2018; in U.S. and Canada, (800) 325-3535. A$230–A$260.

▶ **Seven Spirit Bay.** P.O. Box 4721, **Darwin**, N.T. 0801. Tel: (089) 79-0277; Fax: (089) 79-0284. A$720.

▶ **Vista Alice Springs.** Stephens Road, **Alice Springs**, N.T. 0870. Tel: (089) 52-6100; Fax: (089) 52-1988; in U.S., (800) 44-UTELL; in Canada, (800) 387-8842. A$116.

TASMANIA

By Mike Bingham

*Mike Bingham, a longtime resident of Tasmania and a
member of the Australian Society of Travel Writers, is the
travel editor of* The Mercury, *Tasmania's largest newspaper, and of its sister publication,* The Sunday Tasmanian.

The island of Tasmania, the smallest and most remote
of Australia's states, has long traded on its history—
particularly its beginnings as a British penal settlement—
to attract visitors. In recent times, however, there has
been a realization that the island's greatest appeals are its
natural beauty and laid-back lifestyle. The island is compact (26,000 square miles, about the size of the Republic
of Ireland) but has Australia's most varied scenery and a
relaxed pace of life. Unlike that in the rest of Australia, the
scenery in Tasmania changes rapidly, and the contrasts
are frequently spectacular. Less than an hour separates
sandy beaches from craggy mountains, or a city from
impenetrable wilderness.

MAJOR INTEREST

Surviving remnants of the colonial past
Wilderness areas and adventure tours

Hobart
Sullivans Cove's shops and restaurants
Battery Point's winding streets
Views from Mount Wellington

Tasmania outside Hobart
Old Port Arthur prison settlement
Richmond historic village
Maria Island

Penny Royal World in Launceston
Cradle Mountain–Lake St. Clair National Park
South West National Park
Farm and colonial cottage accommodations

Tasmania was discovered by the Dutch explorer Abel Tasman in 1642, but that discovery was ignored by his countrymen, and Tasman's voyage was rated a failure. It was another 130 years before the next European arrived, and not until 1803 that the British established a settlement on the site of present-day Hobart in the south of the island; even then they did so only to block any attempt by French explorers to claim it for France, as well as to gain another dumping ground for convicts.

More than half the convicts sent to Australia between 1788 and the 1860s, when transportation ended, were landed in Tasmania, or Van Diemen's Land, as it was known until 1853. Discipline was especially harsh here, with the chain gang, the lash, and the noose always present. Some convicts died trying to escape, others became bushrangers, and still others stowed away on American whalers. One notable Irish prisoner escaped and eventually became governor of Montana. But most prisoners served out their sentences and then remained on the island as citizens of the new colony. Today's Tasmanians proudly research their family trees in the hope of discovering a convict.

In a country whose treatment of its original inhabitants, the aboriginals, has long drawn criticism, the Tasmanian experience is a particularly sad one. Aboriginals are presumed to have arrived in Tasmania about 30,000 years ago, across a land bridge that then connected the island to mainland Australia. Within 50 years of white settlement the number of Tasmanian aboriginals had declined from nearly 2,000 to just 200, and by the late 1880s there were no pure-bred Tasmanian aboriginals left at all (though modern-day descendants understandably and emphatically insist that their race never was, nor ever will be, wiped out). The decline in numbers was due to several factors: susceptibility to diseases that accompanied the white settlers; imbalance of the sexes resulting from capture of aboriginal women by the newcomers; and a deliberate policy of extermination. There was even an attempt in 1830 to round up all of the colony's aboriginals and place them in separate areas away from white settlement. Though they would eventually lose the war, the aborigi-

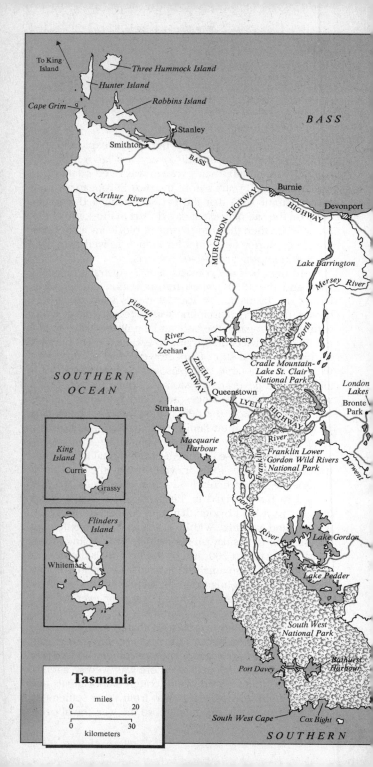

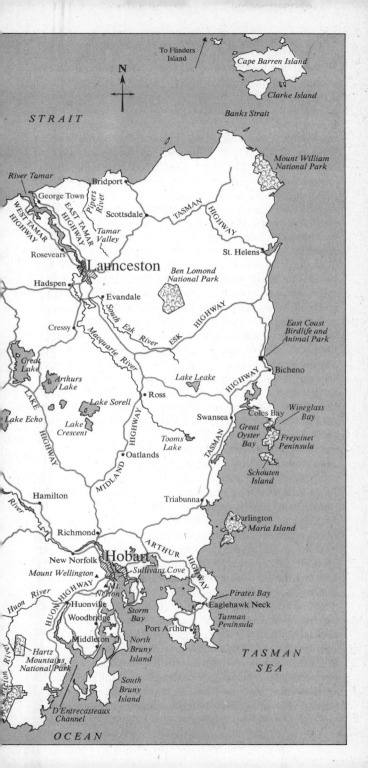

nals did win that battle—six whites were killed, but only two aboriginals were captured.

Lying some 200 miles south of the Australian mainland, Tasmania lacked the industrial base and transport advantages of Australia's other eastern states and thus developed much more slowly. These seeming disadvantages have produced a lasting benefit, particularly for the visitor, because, unlike the other states, Tasmania retains superb and substantial echoes of its colonial past: the penal settlement at Port Arthur, quaint villages and towns rich in Georgian architecture, elegant colonial mansions, and the colorful Hobart port area, Sullivans Cove.

Tasmania's total population is small—only about 460,000—and so are its major cities (Hobart has about 175,000 inhabitants and Launceston about 65,000). Life here lacks many of the urban pressures experienced on the mainland. Hobart's traffic peak, for example, lasts for only about ten minutes twice a day, and some city workers still go home during their one-hour lunch break.

Tasmania's other major attraction, even more enduring than the relics of its colonial beginnings, is its extraordinary wilderness areas. The state has a strong conservation movement and boasts Australia's oldest conservation authority. In the 1970s Tasmania was the center of Australia's first major conservation struggle—the ultimately unsuccessful fight to save Lake Pedder from flooding for a hydroelectric project. The conservationists lost that round but today Tasmania has more than 20 percent of its land registered as national parks. There are a total of 14 national parks, the largest and most rugged of which is the South West National Park, a World Heritage area. In recent years Tasmania has been the center of fierce controversy over attempts to dam its wild rivers and log some of the world's finest temperate rain forests. Experiencing this wilderness, whether through a one-day flight from Hobart, a 14-day rafting trip along the Franklin River, or a seven-day bushwalk through South West National Park, is one of the very best reasons for visiting the state.

Late summer and autumn (roughly December to May) are the best times to visit Tasmania, especially from mid-February, when schools reopen and accommodation problems disappear. The temperature varies around the island: The east coast is generally the warmest and driest, and the west coast and central highlands are often the coldest and certainly the wettest. Many North Americans who have visited Tasmania compare the climate in Hobart and

Launceston with that of Seattle in the United States and Vancouver in British Columbia, Canada.

Summer temperatures can climb to the high 70s or low 80s F, and the usually dry autumns peak at about 65 degrees. Temperatures in winter can drop to below freezing at night, especially in the highlands, but during the day they range from about 53 to 60 degrees. Nights are cool year-round, however, and it is advisable to have a light jacket or sweater handy. In the wilderness areas, be prepared for sudden changes in the weather.

The area codes for Tasmania are 002 through 004; when dialing from outside the country drop the first zero.

The Food and Wine of Tasmania

Tasmania offers chefs an abundance of excellent raw materials. Its seafood—especially crustaceans and mollusks, including crayfish (which in Australia are called lobsters), abalone, oysters, mussels, and scallops—is exported around the world and is of a very high standard. Inland waters contain fine trout, both brown and rainbow. One of the state's newest and most promising industries is the farming of Atlantic salmon and the fabled sea-run trout. Other tasty fish well worth trying include trevalla (a large deep-sea fish caught off the edge of the continental shelf), trevally (a smaller coastal and estuary fish), stripey trumpeter, and orange roughy.

The cool Tasmanian climate is ideal for growing a wide range of fruits and vegetables; visitors should especially look for berry fruits, such as strawberries, raspberries, and blueberries. The state is also renowned for its dairy foods, the finest coming from the northwest. One of the largest producers, Lactos, has won many awards for its cheeses, including its new, creamy blue cheese called True Blue. King Island, off the far northwestern tip of Tasmania proper, is renowned for its cream, butter, cheddar, and Brie, and also for excellent specialty foods such as salami and smoked beef.

Tasmania's lamb, too, is of a high standard, and there is an increasing demand for local game meats such as venison, hare, quail, duck, spatchcock, and even wallaby. Increasing local awareness of the fine quality of produce, dairy goods, and meat products has resulted in far better access to them. Most delicatessens and even some supermarkets and suburban shops now carry Tasmanian specialty foods.

The Tasmanian wine industry is still quite a new one, but production has expanded substantially over the past couple of years and the wines are much more readily available. Tasmania has a cooler climate than most grape-growing districts on the mainland, and the resultant wines are elegant and delicately flavored. Many of the best wines still come from the "big three"—Pipers Brook, Heemskerk, and Moorilla Estate—but smaller producers are also hitting the market with good wines. Other names to look for include Freycinet Vineyard, Spring Vale, St. Matthias Vineyard, Elsewhere Vineyard (so named because the owners noted that weather reports invariably seem to conclude with "and fine elsewhere," and that's where they wanted to put their vineyard), Panorama Vineyard, Meadowbank, Nottley Gorge, Rochecombe, Bream Creek, Wellington, Wattley Creek, and Tasman Wines. Tasmania has great potential for producing premium-quality sparkling wines, and two of the great Champagne houses of France, Roederer and Moët & Chandon, have developed associations with Tasmanian vineyards. The first product of the association between Roederer and Heemskerk was released in late 1991—it's called "Jansz" after Gerrit Jansz, the captain of Abel Tasman's second ship, the *Zeehan* (Heemskerk itself takes its name from Tasman's main ship). Jansz and subsequent releases have drawn lavish praise from wine writers around Australia.

With the increased supply of local wines has come an increased emphasis on offering cellar-door tastings and sales. Wineries that do so include **St. Matthias Vineyard** and **Marion's Vineyard** (in the Tamar Valley, north of Launceston), **Rochecombe** (which has a good restaurant), **Pipers Brook**, and **Delamere** (in the Pipers River district, northeast of Launceston), **Freycinet Vineyard** (on the east coast, 18 km/11 miles south of Bicheno), **Meadowbank** (at Glenora, about 60 km/37 miles northwest of Hobart on the Derwent River), **D'Entrecasteaux Vineyard** (midway between Woodbridge and Cygnet, about 40 km/25 miles south of Hobart), and **Moorilla Estate** (in Berriedale, a northern suburb of Hobart). Moorilla has established an impressive vineyard restaurant that specializes in local produce and should be on every wine-and-food-lover's itinerary.

Availability of Tasmanian wines through bottle shops has also increased. Among the best are Aberfeldy Cellars, Tasmanian Wine Cellars, Vaughn's Wine Cellars, and the Brooker Inn in Hobart; the Royal Oak Hotel and

Vaughan's Wine Cellars in Launceston; the Gateway Inn in Devonport; and the Regent Hotel in Burnie. David Johnstone & Associates, in Montpelier Retreat, in the Hobart suburb of Battery Point, is the leading wholesaler of Tasmanian wines and also sells directly to the public.

HOBART
Sullivans Cove

The water dominates Hobart, as it does any great maritime city, and a tour of Hobart should begin at the docks around Sullivans Cove. Three 19th-century docks—Victoria Dock, Constitution Dock, and Watermen's Dock—still line the waterfront, which in the era of whalers and tall-masted trading vessels earned a reputation as one of the busiest and wildest ports in the Pacific. Things are quieter now, but the port is still alive with fishing vessels, yachts, ships that service Australia's Antarctic bases, and the occasional cruise ship. In late December and early January the port welcomes the fleet at the end of the Sydney–Hobart yacht race, one of the world's great ocean classics. Increasingly, the end of the race is being used to promote ancillary activities such as the Taste of Tasmania festival, which gives visitors and locals alike a great opportunity to sample the state's fine foods and wines.

The warehouses that line **Salamanca Place** south of the harbor and **Victoria Dock** have been renovated and given new life as restaurants, art galleries, and shops for the many skilled craftspeople who have gravitated to Tasmania. There's a street market in Salamanca Place on Saturday mornings, but the best woodwork, jewelry, pottery, and weaving are in the little shops, where visitors can often watch local artists at work. To gain an idea of the range and quality of their wares, visit the **Handmark Gallery** (77 Salamanca Place, Tel: 002/23-7895) or the workshop of internationally renowned jeweler **Phill Mason** (Galleria Building, Salamanca Place, Tel: 002/23-3412). The **Wilderness Shop** (Galleria Building, Salamanca Place, Tel: 002/34-9370) is brimming with information about the state's wilderness areas and has an excellent range of locally produced souvenirs. A particularly interesting **art gallery** is in the University of Tasmania's Arts School in the renovated IXL jam factory across the road from Victoria Dock.

Hobart

miles

kilometers

RIVER DERWENT

SULLIVANS COVE

N

Macquarie Wharf

EVANS STREET

HUNTER STREET

Victoria Dock

Constitution Dock

Elizabeth Street Pier

Ferry Terminal

Watermen's Dock

Franklin Wharf

Princes Wharf

Theatre Royal

CAMPBELL STREET

DUNN PLACE

MARKET STREET

Tasmanian Museum and Art Gallery

Town Hall

Customs House

Parliament House

CASTRAY ESPLANADE

SALAMANCA PLACE

Arthurs Circus

Van Diemens Land Museum

HAMPDEN ROAD

To St. Georges Church

SECHERON STREET

Maritime Museum

BATTERY POINT

MONTPELIER RETREAT

ARGYLE STREET

St. Davids Cathedral

St. Davids Park

ELIZABETH STREET

MURRAY STREET

HARRINGTON STREET

BATHURST STREET

BARRACK STREET

MOLLE STREET

COLLINS STREET

LIVERPOOL STREET

MACQUARIE STREET

DAVEY STREET

Anglesea Barracks

SANDY BAY ROAD

To Sandy Bay and Mount Nelson

FORREST ROAD

PATRICK STREET

The City Center

Hobart's two main thoroughfares, Davey Street and Macquarie Street, have more than 30 buildings apiece that are classified by the National Trust. Particularly worth visiting is the **Anglesea Barracks**, the oldest military establishment in Australia. It is still used by the army, and there are tours every Tuesday morning at 11:00. Other fine examples of colonial architecture are the **Customs House**, **St. David's Cathedral**, and the **Town Hall**.

The **Tasmanian Museum and Art Gallery**, on the corner of Argyle and Macquarie streets, houses some outstanding examples of colonial art and furniture and has interesting displays on Antarctic exploration, Tasmanian aboriginals, and the state's maritime history. The **Theatre Royal** (1837), on Campbell Street, was described by Sir Laurence Olivier as the "greatest little theatre in the world" and is Australia's oldest theater. It was gutted by fire in 1984 but has been totally restored. Visitors are welcome to inspect the theater from 10:00 A.M. to 5:30 P.M. Monday through Friday, except when rehearsals are in progress; Tel: (002) 34-6266.

Battery Point

Overlooking Sullivans Cove from the south, Battery Point was so named because of the gun emplacements that protected the infant colony in the 19th century. Like the cove, it was a hive of maritime activity, filled with shipbuilding yards, chandlers's shops, pubs, and seedy residential areas. Much of it still stands—now forming the heart of a trendy area of restored dwellings, craft shops, restaurants, and historic pubs. This hodgepodge of winding streets is far more easily explored on foot than by car. Take a guided walking tour, or pick up a free brochure and find your own way about. (The Tasmanian Travel Centre in the city center at 80 Elizabeth Street can give advice on both.) The area is very compact, and, as with most of Hobart, the streets are safe, even in the evening. Allow two or three hours for a leisurely stroll, and browse the antiques shops en route for colonial bric-a-brac. Battery Point has its own village green—the tiny Arthurs Circus—and the magnificent St. George's Church, as well as a number of excellent museums.

The **Van Diemen's Land Memorial Folk Museum** is housed in Narryna, a fine colonial mansion built in 1834 on Hampden Road. Many of the rooms have been furnished and decorated to reflect the life of the first settlers, and the outbuildings contain period vehicles and tools. Nearby Secheron House, with its wide verandahs and classic design, is regarded by many as the best example of Georgian architecture in Hobart. These days it houses the **Maritime Museum**, a vast collection of maritime memorabilia and models covering everything nautical from the whaling days right up to the present.

Dining in Hobart

For many years Tasmania was considered a backwater when it came to good restaurants, but now an increasing number of chefs have come to realize what an asset they have in the high quality of the fresh ingredients available here. The standard of service has improved markedly, although opening hours can still leave something to be desired.

For seafood the most famous name in Tasmania is Mures. George and Jill Mure established their reputation with Mures Fish House in Battery Point, but that has now been closed and they are concentrating their activities in the **Mures Fish Centre**, at Victoria Dock, right in the heart of Sullivans Cove. In addition to the top-class **Upper Deck** (Tel: 002/31-1999), the center contains a sushi bar, a bistro, a bakery, an ice-cream bar, a travel agency, a convention bureau, and a fish-processing facility where the public can purchase fresh seafood.

Other restaurants worth trying in the city center area include **Sisco's**, at 121 Macquarie Street (Tel: 002/23-2059), a popular venue for businesspeople and politicians, and one of Australia's few, perhaps only, Catalan-style Spanish restaurants; the **Aegean**, 121 Collins Street (Tel: 002/31-1000), a bright, classy Greek restaurant with rollicking evening entertainment; and **Dear Friends**, 8 Brook Street (Tel: 002/23-2646), an upscale, silver-service restaurant specializing in dishes made from local produce.

Elizabeth Street in North Hobart is emerging as a cosmopolitan restaurant area with many cheap, good-quality B.Y.O. restaurants such as **Ali Akbar**, for Lebanese food, with lots of choice for vegetarians (Tel: 002/31-1770), and **Marti Zucco's**, for pasta, pizza, and natter about the horseraces (Tel: 002/34-9611).

Just on the edge of the city are two excellent B.Y.O.'s with a French provincial flavor: **The Paris**, at 356 Macquarie Street, South Hobart (Tel: 002/24-2200), and **Mawson's Hut**, 80 Queen Street, Sandy Bay (Tel: 002/23-

3969). The latter has been decorated to evoke the atmosphere of the Antarctic hut used by a great early 20th-century Australian polar explorer, Sir Douglas Mawson.

Prosser's on the Beach, located south of Hobart on Beach Road in the trendy riverside suburb of Sandy Bay, is doing great things with seafood; the chef, Stuart Prosser, is renowned for his innovative menus. Try his famous strawberry-chile prawns and his Louisiana-style blackened fish. The atmosphere here is relaxed elegance, and the view over the water makes the restaurant especially appealing at lunchtime. It is advisable to reserve your table; Tel: (002) 25-2276.

Also in Sandy Bay, in the Mayfair at the Bay shopping center, is the **Bay Hamper** delicatessen, the best place to find many of the state's gourmet delights. The shop also has a small dining room that specializes in showing people how to make good use of items stocked in the deli.

At the more formal end of the scale is the **Revolving Restaurant** at the Wrest Point Hotel Casino (see below). Even if you dine elsewhere it is worth visiting for the views alone, and the weekday business lunches are an especially good value.

Staying in Hobart

The ▶ **Sheraton Hotel Hobart** opened on Davey Street in 1987 and provided Hobart's central business district with its first (and still only) international-standard hotel. Its opening forced other hotels to reconsider their operations, and the overall effect has been an improvement in room standards and service.

About 4 km (2½ miles) down the Derwent River from Hobart in Sandy Bay is the ▶ **Wrest Point Hotel Casino**, which was the first casino in Australia when it was built 20 years ago. It is indicative of Tasmania's north-south rivalry that Australia's second casino—the Federal Country Club—opened a few years later in Launceston in the north. Both casinos offer luxury accommodation and are the centers of nightlife in the two cities—if *anything* in Tasmania can really be called nightlife.

Fine bed-and-breakfast accommodation is available at ▶ **Barton Cottage** in Battery Point. Built in 1850, this delightful colonial building has attic bedrooms. The ▶ **Salamanca Inn**, on Gladstone Street in Battery Point, is Hobart's first apartment-style hotel and features a beef-and-seafood grill and an indoor pool. It's situated just a few paces from Salamanca Place and is within easy walking distance of the city center.

Also noteworthy is ▶ **Hadleys Hotel** on Murray Street in the city center. It was from here in 1911 that Norwegian explorer Roald Amundsen telegraphed the world to proclaim his successful expedition to the South Pole.

An excellent place to taste Tasmanian wines—and enjoy some fine food and hospitality—is the prettily situated ▶ **Woodbridge Hotel**, overlooking the D'Entrecasteaux Channel about 35 km (22 miles) south of Hobart. It offers more than 20 local wines by the glass or bottle. Its popular dining room serves a broad selection of dishes based on fresh local produce. The hotel provides clean, comfortable country-pub-style accommodation (shared bathrooms). The farmhouse breakfasts are delicious—and huge.

Mount Wellington
and Mount Nelson

Mount Wellington (about 4,000 feet), Hobart's most famous landmark, is located about 7 km (4 miles) west of the city center. The locals have great fondness for the mountain, whose moods vary from brooding and menacing to kindly and protective. It's a 30-minute drive from the city to the summit where you'll have panoramic views of Hobart, the Derwent Valley and estuary, the D'Entrecasteaux Channel, and the rugged wilderness to the southwest. Half-day tours are run by a number of companies, including Hobart Coaches; Tel: (002) 34-4077.

Less ambitious, but still enjoyable, is the 15-minute drive south from the city to the top of Mount Nelson. Apart from the view of the city and the Derwent River, there are tearooms, a restaurant, a shop with high-quality, mostly locally produced souvenirs, and relics of the old signal station used in the communications chain linking Hobart and Port Arthur. Mount Nelson is serviced regularly by public transport. Contact the city's transportation authority, the MTT (Tel: 002/71-3232), for bus schedules.

DAY TRIPS FROM HOBART
Port Arthur

The most infamous of the old penal settlements in Tasmania is Port Arthur, established in 1830. If visitors to Tasmania see no other attraction, they should at least experience the eerie serenity and stark beauty of Port Arthur, 110 km (68 miles) southeast of Hobart on the Tasman Peninsula. From the city center take the Tasman Highway across the Tasman Bridge to Sorrell, and then turn right on to the Arthur Highway. Allow 90 minutes for the drive along the winding road.

A few minutes in the solitary-confinement cell of the **Model Prison** is sufficient to imagine what it must have been like to spend half a lifetime or more at His Majesty's pleasure in one of the world's most dehumanizing outposts. It's quite easy to spend a day wandering around the ruins and restored buildings—the asylum, church, penitentiary, commandant's house, hospital, and so forth. There are also boat trips to the **Isle of the Dead**, where nearly 2,000 convicts and free settlers were buried on a remarkably small piece of land.

Also worth seeing in the area is the **Remarkable Cave**. This cave, part of a stunningly rugged coastline on the Tasman Peninsula, faces the Tasman Sea and is reached by a steep flight of steps from the headland above. Even when the sea seems relatively calm elsewhere, it still "boils" into the cave.

On the drive back toward Hobart you'll cross **Eaglehawk Neck**, a narrow stretch of land connecting the Tasman Peninsula to the Tasmanian mainland. Convicts attempting to escape from the penal settlement at Port Arthur had the option of swimming through cold, rough seas over considerable distances or attempting to elude the dogs and guards here at the Neck; none is known to have fled successfully.

The ► **Lufra Hotel**, right on Eaglehawk Neck, offers comfortable accommodation and an excellent dining room overlooking Pirates Bay. (For further accommodations in the Port Arthur area, see Host Farms and Colonial Cottages, below.)

Richmond

Richmond, 27 km (17 miles) northeast of Hobart, was founded in 1824 as a stopping point on the old road from Hobart to Port Arthur, and it quickly became one of the colony's most important rural centers. In a state that has many charming historic villages, Richmond is perhaps the most charming, and certainly the best preserved.

The convict-built **Richmond Bridge** is the oldest in Australia. Local legend has it that the bridge is haunted by

the ghost of a particularly harsh overseer who was mur-
dered there by convicts and thrown into the river.

Sandstone cottages, Georgian mansions, and Gothic
churches abound. Of particular interest is the Richmond
jail, which predates anything at Port Arthur by about five
years. Many of the other old buildings have been restored
as private homes, shops, and art galleries. Richmond is
second only to Hobart's Salamanca Place for those interested in arts and crafts. **Saddlers Court Gallery**, on Bridge
Street, has an excellent selection of paintings by Tasmanian artists, as well as pieces by two of the state's best
potters, Les Blakebrough and Derek Smith.

The **Richmond Wine Centre**, also on Bridge Street,
offers a wide range of Tasmanian wines for tasting and
incorporates a restaurant specializing in local produce.
▶ **Prospect House**, half a mile or so out of town on the
road to Hobart, is one of Tasmania's finest colonial-style
buildings. It offers good accommodations and a fine restaurant.

FROM HOBART TO LAUNCESTON

There are a number of ways to travel between the state's
two major cities, and each has its own attractions: the
Midland Highway, a quick route with a couple of good
stops; the Tasman Highway, which follows the beautiful
east coast; and a strenuous but rewarding trip up the
state's west coast.

The Midland Highway

This is the most direct and by far the quickest route north
to Launceston, making it possible to do the trip in little
more than two hours. It would be a shame, though, to
stay on the fast lane of this modern highway for the entire
journey, because some of the byways are paved with
history. The town of **Oatlands** has Australia's largest collection of Georgian architecture, and gained notoriety last
century as the starting point of the futile aboriginal
roundup instigated by Governor George Arthur (founder
of Port Arthur).

Farther north on the highway is **Ross**, once an important military post and coaching stop. These days it is the
center of a thriving wool industry but is nonetheless a

sleepy town with a convict-built bridge to rival that of Richmond and many other relics of its colonial past. Both Oatlands and Ross are classified by the National Trust. When the Midlands Highway was upgraded it was decided to bypass both towns, leaving each a few minutes away from the main road. Rather than causing them to decline, as some people initially predicted, the move has enhanced the charm of their village atmosphere and firmly established the towns as tourist attractions. Leave five or six hours for this trip if you want to do some sightseeing.

The East Coast

Travelling from Hobart to Launceston via the Tasman Highway on the east coast extends the driving time to about five or six hours, and there's not as much history along this route. The compensation is the beauty of the coastline, particularly in the vicinity of the Freycinet Peninsula and of St. Helens.

MARIA ISLAND

The introduction of fast catamaran service—25 minutes each way—from Triabunna and from the East Coaster resort at Louisville, near Orford, has greatly improved visitor access to Maria Island, which was declared a national park in 1971. A penal settlement was established on Maria Island in 1825—five years before that at Port Arthur—and plenty of evidence of the convict era remains, especially at the settlement of **Darlington**. It also has a fascinating industrial history: Late last century, Diego Bernacchi established vineyards, a silk industry, and cement works on the island. Rugged scenery, including cliffs that drop straight into the ocean, and abundant wildlife add to the appeal of Maria Island, much of which is accessible by foot or bicycle. There are campsites and bunkhouse accommodations at Darlington, but the facilities are primitive to say the least. Unless you're prepared to rough it, stay at the ▶ **East Coaster** resort and take a day trip to the island. The resort has both motel-style and self-contained accommodations, a restaurant, and a pub, plus indoor and outdoor swimming pools, squash courts, tennis courts, and a mini golf course. There are no shops on Maria Island so you must take all your provisions with you.

FREYCINET PENINSULA

If you've got the time, a detour to Coles Bay and the Freycinet Peninsula National Park is well worthwhile. The wallabies will eat out of your hand, and there are many hiking trails of varying duration and difficulty. Especially appealing is the walk to **Wine Glass Bay**—about an hour each way from the Coles Bay parking lot.

EAST COAST BIRDLIFE AND ANIMAL PARK

Nearby **Bicheno**, which began its existence in 1803 as a port for sealers and whalers, is another attractive seaside town, with fine beaches and comfortable motels such as the ▶ **Silver Sands Resort**. Special craybakes are held at the Silver Sands every Saturday during the crayfishing season (usually November to the end of April). Just outside of town is the East Coast Birdlife and Animal Park, which is set in natural coastal bushland. There are wallabies and kangaroos to hand-feed, emus, native birds, and, of course, Tasmanian devils. Tasmanian devils are small marsupials, and though their menacing growl and bared teeth are mainly bluster, it is best to treat them with care. If provoked they can bite, and because they feed almost exclusively on carrion, their bites can cause infections. Fairy penguins nest along the town's beaches, and schools of dolphins and the occasional seal can be seen.

If you want to do any serious walking or sightseeing on the east coast, the trip to Launceston will take more than a day. Accommodation is available in a number of the coastal towns near the park. There are a number of reasonable motels offering private bathrooms, telephones, television/radio, refrigerators, room-service breakfast, coffee- and tea-making equipment, and sometimes stocked bars.

The best of the conventional accommodations in Tasmania are offered by the ▶ **Innkeepers/Tas Villas Group**, ▶ **Flag International**, and ▶ **Best Western Australia**, all of which list moderate to first-class properties throughout the state. Around **Swansea** are some excellent colonial-cottage accommodations, such as ▶ **Wagners Cottage**.

The West Coast

It is also possible to travel between Hobart and Launceston via **Queenstown** on Tasmania's wild west coast and Burnie on the northwest coast. The west coast is a rugged, mountainous area with high rainfall, raging rivers, and dense forests. Harsh conditions and isolation have made its inhabitants—many of them miners—a tough, independent breed, often initially suspicious of strangers but also capable of extending warm hospitality. Places worth visiting include the **West Coast Pioneers' Memorial Museum** in Zeehan, the **Mt. Lyell Mine** (tours available) at Queenstown, and, near Strahan, windswept **Ocean Beach**, whose rolling breakers haven't seen land since departing South America, half a world away.

The trip up the west coast is certainly much longer than a day trip, and the weather can be far from hospitable and the driving conditions hazardous. If you do go this way, stay overnight at Queenstown or nearby **Strahan** and take the river cruise along the Gordon River and Macquarie Harbour (see The Wilderness section below). It's one of the best ways of experiencing just what the conservation battles are all about.

The ▶ **Strahan Inn** in Strahan and the ▶ **Silver Hills Motel** in Queenstown offer comfortable mid-range accommodations. The Strahan Inn is especially convenient to the take-off point for the Gordon River cruises and has an attractive outlook over the town and Macquarie Harbour. The recently restored ▶ **Franklin Manor** at Strahan offers a high standard of colonial-style accommodation and has brought to the west coast a touch of elegance previously unheard of in this remote part of Tasmania. The development of the historic fishing port of Strahan as a major wilderness gateway has also seen the addition of ▶ **Strahan Village**, a collection of harborside cottages—some equipped with spas—and a major upgrade of the nearby pub, ▶ **Hamer's Hotel**. Much of the crayfishing fleet ties up at the wharf across the road from the pub, and its catch features on the menu.

Near Queenstown is the southern end of Cradle Mountain–Lake St. Clair National Park (see The Wilderness section below).

LAUNCESTON AND THE NORTH

Launceston, founded in 1805, is Tasmania's second-largest and second-oldest city. It rapidly developed into a river port of considerable importance and became the commercial center of a rich agricultural district.

The town has magnificent public and private gardens, including the 30-acre **City Park**, with its enormous oaks and elms dating back to the 1820s. There are also many buildings to delight those interested in history and grand architecture. The **Queen Victoria Museum and Art Gallery**, opened in 1891, was built to celebrate the queen's jubilee. It houses outstanding exhibitions of Tasmanian flora and fauna, aboriginal and convict relics, and both early and contemporary art. There is also a Chinese joss house (shrine) that was built during the mining boom last century and was donated to the museum by the Chinese families of northeastern Tasmania.

The **Customs House** is considered by many to be the city's most attractive building, and though it isn't open to the public, its magnificence is a reminder of the days when Launceston was a prosperous port. The **Old Umbrella Shop**, the last genuine period shop in Tasmania, was built entirely from Tasmanian blackwood in the 1860s. In addition to housing a fine permanent collection of these wet-weather mainstays, the shop sells new umbrellas and other knickknacks and serves as an information center for the National Trust.

Launceston's **Penny Royal World** complex is one of Tasmania's most imaginative tourism creations. A working corn mill that was originally located near Cressy, south of Launceston, was moved stone by stone and reconstructed at Launceston. The complex has a 19th-century gunpowder mill, a cannon foundry, a restored tramway, a replica paddle steamer, a museum, and a lake complete with old ships. There are accommodations on the grounds.

STAYING AND DINING IN LAUNCESTON

There are international-standard accommodations at the ► **Federal Country Club Hotel** (Launceston's casino, which also has a golf course, squash courts, tennis courts, and an indoor swimming pool) and the ► **Launceston Novotel**.

The reputation of Launceston's restaurants has slipped a bit in recent years, particularly in comparison with those in Hobart, but there is still some very good food to be had here. The best seafood is at **Shrimps** (Tel: 003/34-0584) on George Street. Both **The Folly** (Tel: 003/31-7900), in the Old Bakery tourist complex, and **Fee and Me** (Tel: 003/31-3195), on the corner of Frederick and Charles streets, offer exciting, innovative menus, good food made from local ingredients, attentive service, and an elegant but relaxed atmosphere. **Posh Nosh**, at 127 St.

John Street, sells Tasmanian-produced gourmet foods and has a small dining room where you can sample its wares.

Around Launceston

Launceston makes a good base for visiting the many historic villages in the north of the island. **Evandale**, 18 km (11 miles) south of Launceston, and **Hadspen**, 11 km (7 miles) west of Launceston, are both small settlements that retain much of their 19th-century charm. Browse for antiques, and enjoy the leisurely pace of life.

Clarendon, 8 km (5 miles) south of Evandale, is one of Australia's most magnificent Georgian mansions. Built in 1838 as a residence for the wealthy merchant James Cox, it is now owned by the National Trust, which is gradually restoring the house and its surroundings to their full 19th-century grandeur. It is open to the public daily except during July.

Entally House, at Hadspen, is a delightful whitewashed country house set among beautiful gardens and interesting outbuildings, including a bluestone church and a two-story coach house. Entally was built in 1820 by Thomas Reibey, whose mother arrived in Sydney as a 13-year-old convict and became a highly successful businesswoman. Reibey's son, also named Thomas, was premier of Tasmania, a fact that clearly demonstrates how quickly descendants of convicts could gain high standing in colonies, which lacked the rigid social structure of their English homeland.

THE NORTHWEST COAST

Tasmania's northwest coast is a rich agricultural area that produces fine fruits and vegetables and top-class dairy foods. The scenery can be spectacular, especially in the vicinity of **Table Cape**, near Wynyard. Here, the patchwork of lush pasture and rich brown earth extends right up to the edge of cliffs that plunge into Bass Strait. The fertile coastal strip is a narrow one, and cleared, gently rolling hills quickly give way to forested mountains. Of particular interest is **Stanley**, the oldest settlement in the northwest, founded in 1826 as the headquarters for the Van Diemen's Land Company, a mighty London-based outfit set up to breed fine-wool sheep in the colony. The town is dominated by the Nut, a huge volcanic outcrop that these days can be reached by cable car. In town are many fine examples of colonial architecture as well as some excellent craft shops. **Hursey Seafoods**, on the waterfront in Stanley, has one of the best selections of freshly caught fish and shellfish in Australia—when you buy fish and chips you'll have to choose from some 15 different types. Fish is available fresh or cooked.

Cape Grim, on the northwestern extremity of Tasmania, is reputed to have the cleanest air in the world, and is used by scientists as a monitoring station to provide baseline data for experiments on atmospheric pollution worldwide.

THE WILDERNESS

You don't have to be an experienced backpacker or mountain climber to experience and enjoy Tasmania's wilderness areas. Access can be as quick and comfortable as a one-day aerial outing, or an overnight stay in a wilderness lodge. There are three major "gateways" to the most spectacular of the areas—Cradle Mountain, in the northwest; the small fishing port of Strahan, on the west coast; and Hobart.

▶ **Cradle Mountain Lodge**, at the northern end of the vast **Cradle Mountain–Lake St. Clair National Park**, offers comfortable log-cabin-style accommodations on the edge of the wilderness. Bushwalks begin from the grounds of the property. In addition to bushwalking and organized activities such as canoeing and fly-fishing, the lodge offers hearty, fireside meals in the main dining room and plentiful access to wildlife. In the evening, native animals such as wallabies, opossums, native spotted cats, and Tasmanian devils gather outside the main lodge building to be fed.

Strahan, on Macquarie Harbour, is the departure point for cruises across the harbor and up the **Gordon River**. These cruises are among the easiest and most comfortable means of experiencing the Tasmanian wilderness. Macquarie Harbour is a large, deep, usually placid body of water surrounded by mountains and dense forests. The cruises also take in the lower reaches of the Gordon River which enters the southern end of the harbor. The water here is a deep tea color due to staining by button grass. At Heritage Landing there is the opportunity to wander through myrtle rain forest along well-constructed walkways. Most of the cruises also stop at **Sarah Island**, Tasmania's first and most brutal penal settlement. Half-day and full-day cruises are available, and meals are usually included. Operators include World Heritage Cruises (Tel: 004/71-7174) and Gordon River Cruises (Tel: 004/71-7187). Bookings are essential.

Also worth experiencing are rain-forest tours and a seaplane flight over the World Heritage **South West National Park**. The South West National Park is a 40-minute flight west of Hobart by light plane. Two airlines, Par-Avion and Tasair, operate a variety of trips from Cambridge Aerodrome, which is just across the road from Hobart's main airport. Tasair has a flight along the rugged southern coast, including a coffee break on a remote beach, before flying over Bathurst Harbour, Lake Pedder, and Federation Peak on the return flight. The cost is A$135 per person. Par-Avion follows a similar route but includes a landing at Melaleuca, on the shores of Bathurst Harbour. Cost is A$125 per person.

Another option from Par-Avion is a day in the wilderness. After the plane lands at Melaleuca passengers take a land-and-water trip to a bush camp. After lunch there's time to explore the forest or to climb a nearby peak before returning to Hobart. Hotel pickup and return is included in the price of A$265 per person. The adventurous can also opt for an overnight stay in the bush camp (A$380). For details, contact Par-Avion, Cambridge Aerodrome, Hobart 7170 (Tel: 002/48-5390; Fax: 002/48-5117); Tasair, Cambridge Aerodrome, Hobart 7170 (Tel: 002/48-5088, Fax: 002/48-5528).

The ultimate wilderness experiences—rafting down the wild **Franklin River**, or trekking into the national park—are only for those with five to 14 days to spare. Peregrine Adventures, a Hobart company, offers a five-day rafting trip that includes transport from Hobart to the Franklin River by four-wheel drive. The return to Hobart is by seaplane from the Gordon River on the west coast; the cost is A$880. Peregrine also has a series of shorter adventures involving rafting, sailing, cycling, walking, or spelunking. A one-day rafting trip to the **Picton River**, near Hobart, including all transport and lunch, is A$95 per person. A three-day rafting-walking-spelunking-sailing option from Hobart costs A$350 per person. It features rafting on the Picton River, a walk in the **Hartz Mountains National Park** south of Hobart, a journey through limestone caves, and a return to Hobart under sail. All camping equipment, meals, and transport and the services of a professional guide are included. The tours operate from December 1 until the end of April. For details, contact Peregrine Adventures, 164 Liverpool Street, Hobart 7000; Tel: (002) 31-0977.

Tasmania's rivers and lakes, many within two hours' drive of Hobart and Launceston, provide good **trout fishing**. The majority of the highland lakes have shallow edges and fish can be seen feeding in water only a few inches deep. **London Lakes** in the center of the state are Australia's largest privately owned trout-fishing waters, and the well-stocked lakes are a delight for fly fishing. ▶ **London Lakes Fly Fishing Lodge** provides first-class accommodation for ten guests at an all-inclusive rate of A$495 per person per day. Limousine transfers are available, at extra cost, from Devonport, Launceston, and Hobart airports.

Host Farms and Colonial Cottages

One way to enhance your Tasmanian experience is to spend a night or two at a private home or host farm. Many suburban and country homes are listed with ▶ **Homehost & Heritage Tasmania** (P.O. Box 780, Sandy Bay, Tasmania, 7005; Tel: 002/24-1612; Fax 002/24-0472). They provide lodging and a cooked breakfast, with prices starting at $53 single and $76 double. Many of the host farms are listed under Tasmanian Country Retreats, which operates a central reservations office; Tel: (003) 30-1744; Fax: (003) 30-2035. Tasmanian Travel Centres, in Hobart, can also make bookings for these and other properties; Tel: (002) 30-0250. Host farm rates range from A$55 to A$85 per couple, including breakfast. Most of the farms are small—50 to 200 acres—and operate a mix of crops, dairying, and livestock for meat production. Some, like ▶ **Holly Tree Farm** at Middleton, 40 minutes south of Hobart, also produce fruit and flowers on a small scale. A herd of tame donkeys, two pet sheep, chickens, ducks, and rabbits in the bottom paddock here are a bonus for visitors. Holly Tree Farm has two guest rooms, both with private bathrooms.

In keeping with its reputation as Australia's most history-conscious state, Tasmania has develped a fine network of self-contained accommodations based in colonial cottages—some of which date back to the 1850s. First settled in 1803, Tasmania is Australia's second-oldest state, and the colonial heritage is better preserved here than anywhere else in the country. Most cottages boast modern bathrooms and kitchens. A typical colonial cottage is ▶ **Ivy Cottage**, in the center of Launceston. It has two bedrooms, a living room, a fully equipped kitchen, and a bathroom. The shelves are lined with 19th-century books and bric-a-brac, and guests are encouraged to make use of the lovely vegetable garden in the back.

Other cottages of merit include ▶ **Molecombe Cottage** in Launceston, ▶ **Wagners Cottage** near Swansea on the east coast, ▶ **Emma's Cottage** at Hamilton, the ▶ **Waverley Cottage** collection at Oatlands, and ▶ **Cascades Colonial Accommodation** at Koonya, not far from Port Arthur. The last utilizes an old convict outstation and hospital. There are many other cottages located elsewhere throughout the state. They may not have all the facilities of international-standard hotels, and the floors may sometimes creak, but if you want to stay somewhere with a bit of atmosphere and a lived-in feeling, colonial cottages are hard to beat. Many of these properties are represented by the Tasmanian Colonial Accommodation Association; Tel: (003) 31-7900. Tasmanian Travel Centres also carry full listings: in Hobart, at 80 Elizabeth Street, Tel: (002) 30-0250; in Launceston, at the corner of Saint John and Paterson streets, Tel: (003) 37-3111; in Burnie, at 48 Cattley Street, Tel: (004) 31-8111; and in Devonport, at 18 Rooke Street, Tel: (004) 24-1526.

GETTING AROUND

Tasmania is one hour by air from Melbourne; direct flights from Sydney take 90 minutes. The island has two major jet airports—at Hobart and Launceston—as well as smaller airports at Burnie and Devonport on the northwest coast. Ansett Australia and Qantas operate daily from Melbourne and Sydney to Launceston and Hobart. Air New Zealand and Qantas operate flights between Christchurch, New Zealand and Hobart every Saturday.

Access to the state is also provided by the *Spirit of Tasmania,* an overnight vehicular ferry service that links Melbourne to Devonport on the north coast. Most accommodation is in cabins, with some dormitory accommodation for backpackers. There are a number of restaurant and entertainment areas on board. The overnight crossing takes about 13 hours; for schedule information call the Tasmanian Travel Centre, Tel: (008) 030-131.

A new sea link for both passengers and vehicles has been established between George Town (north of Launceston) and Port Welshpool (on the southeastern coast of Victoria). This is via the *Seacat Tasmania,* a locally built, high-speed, wave-piercing catamaran that completes the crossing in about four and a half hours. It is similar in design to the *Hoverspeed Great Britain,* which earned the Hales Trophy for the fastest passenger-ship crossing of the Atlantic Ocean. The service operates from early December through April.

The roads in Tasmania are good but, taxis apart, the public transport system is poor, so plan on renting a car. On an island just 200 miles from north to south, and just a little bit wider, driving is fun.

Gasoline prices in Tasmania are about A\$.70 a liter, but the compactness of the island lessens the impact on the wallet. Launceston is only a two-hour drive from Hobart. Hobart to Strahan is about four and a half hours, Hobart to Port Arthur on the Tasman Peninsula is about 90 minutes, and Hobart to the historic village of Richmond is a mere 25 minutes.

ACCOMMODATIONS REFERENCE

The rates given here are projections *for 1994. Where a range of rates is given, the lower figure is the low-season rate, the higher figure the high-season rate. Unless otherwise indicated, rates are for double room, double occupancy. As prices are subject to change, always double-check before booking.*

▶ **Barton Cottage.** 72 Hampden Road, Battery Point, **Hobart,** Tasmania 7004. Tel: (002) 24-1606; Fax: (002) 24-1724. A\$90 including cooked breakfast.

▶ **Best Western Australia.** 81a George Street, **Launceston,** Tasmania 7250. Tel: (003) 31-9366; toll-free within Australia (008) 222-422; Fax: (003) 31-3048. Properties throughout Tasmania. A\$60–A\$90 depending on property and season.

▶ **Cascades Colonial Accommodation.** Nubeena Road, **Koonya,** Tasmania 7817. Tel: (002) 50-3121; Fax: (002) 50-3121. A\$75 for self-contained accommodation including ingredients for continental breakfast.

▶ **Cradle Mountain Lodge. Cradle Mountain,** Tasmania 7306. Tel: (004) 92-1303; Fax: (004) 92-1309. Lodge (shared bathrooms) A\$80; self-contained cabins A\$135; special winter rates available.

▶ **East Coaster Resort.** Louisville Road, **Louisville,** Tasmania 7190. Tel: (002) 57-1172; Fax: (002) 57-1564. Motel-style accommodation, A\$70, self-contained cabins, A\$90.

▶ **Emma's Cottage.** "Uralla," Main Road, **Hamilton,** Tasmania 7140. Tel: (002) 86-3270; Fax: (002) 86-3270. A$80–A$85 including provisions for breakfast.

▶ **Federal Country Club Hotel.** Country Club Avenue, Prospect Vale, **Launceston,** Tasmania 7250. Tel: (003) 35-5777; Fax: (003) 35-5788. A$205; special off-season (winter) rates are available.

▶ **Flag International.** Shop 3, CML Building, corner of George and Brisbane streets, **Launceston,** Tasmania 7250. Tel: (003) 31-1222; Fax: (003) 34-4772; in U.S. and Canada, (800) 624-FLAG. Properties throughout Tasmania. A$44–A$125, depending on property and season.

▶ **Franklin Manor.** The Esplanade, **Strahan,** Tasmania 7468. Tel: (004) 71-7311; Fax: (004) 71-7267. A$112 including breakfast; winter specials available for two-night stays.

▶ **Hadleys Hotel.** 34 Murray Street, **Hobart,** Tasmania 7000. Tel: (002) 23-4355; Fax: (002) 24-0303. A$85.

▶ **Hamer's Hotel.** The Esplanade, **Strahan,** Tasmania 7468. Tel: (004) 71-7191; Fax: (004) 71-7389. A$50–A$75.

▶ **Holly Tree Farm.** Channel Highway, **Middleton,** Tasmania 7163. Tel: (002) 92-1680. A$64 including cooked breakfast. Smoking not permitted inside the house.

▶ **Innkeepers.** Central reservations: 31 Elizabeth Street, **Launceston,** Tasmania 7250. Tel: (003) 31-8899; Fax: (003) 31-2168. Properties throughout Tasmania. A$80–A$120, depending on property and season.

▶ **Ivy Cottage.** 17 York Street, **Launceston,** Tasmania 7250. Tel: (003) 34-2231. Self-contained cottage, A$115 including provisions for cooked breakfast. Self-contained cottage sleeps up to four (third and fourth persons A$25 each).

▶ **Launceston Novotel.** 29 Cameron Street, **Launceston,** Tasmania 7250. Tel: (003) 34-3434; toll-free within Australia (008) 030-123; Fax: (003) 31-7347. A$160; special low-season (winter) rates available.

▶ **London Lakes Fly Fishing Lodge.** Post Office, **Bronte Park,** Tasmania 7140. Tel: (002) 89-1159. A$440–A$1,100 all inclusive.

▶ **Lufra Hotel.** Main Road, **Eaglehawk Neck,** Tasmania 7179. Tel: (002) 50-3262; Fax: (002) 50-3460. A$55.

▶ **Molecombe Cottage.** 23 Kenyon Street, **Newstead** (Launceston), Tasmania 7250. Tel: (003) 31-1355; Fax: (003) 34-3645. A$80 including provisions for light breakfast.

▶ **Prospect House.** **Richmond,** Tasmania 7025. Tel: (002) 62-2207; Fax: (002) 62-2551. A$96.

► **Salamanca Inn**. 10 Gladstone Street, **Battery Point** (Hobart), Tasmania 7004. Tel: (002) 23-3300; Fax: (002) 23-7167. A$154.

► **Sheraton Hotel Hobart**. 1 Davey Street, **Hobart**, Tasmania 7000. Tel: (002) 35-4535; Fax: (002) 23-8175; in U.S., (800) 325-3535. A$200–A$230; special low-season (winter) rates available.

► **Silver Hills Motel**. Penghana Road, **Queenstown**, Tasmania 7467. Tel: (004) 71-1755; Fax: (004) 71-1452. A$67.

► **Silver Sands Resort Hotel/Motel**. Peggy's Point, **Bicheno**, Tasmania 7215. Tel: (003) 75-1266; Fax: (003) 75-1168. A$50.

► **Strahan Inn**. Jolly Street, **Strahan**, Tasmania 7468. Tel: (004) 71-7160; Fax: (004) 71-7372. A$99; special low-season (winter) rates available.

► **Strahan Village**. The Esplanade, **Strahan**, Tasmania 7468. Tel: (004) 71-7191; Fax: (004) 71-7389. A$75–A$115 including breakfast; top rate includes spa-equipped room.

► **Wagners Cottage**. Tasman Highway, **Swansea**, Tasmania 7190. Tel: (002) 57-8494. A$95 including provisions for breakfast.

► **Waverley Cottage and associated cottages**. **Oatlands**, Tasmania 7120. Tel: (002) 54-1264; Fax: (002) 54-1527. A$90 including provisions for breakfast.

► **Woodbridge Hotel**. Channel Highway, **Woodbridge**, Tasmania 7162. Tel: (002) 67-4604; Fax: (002) 67-4828. A$85 including cooked farmhouse breakfast. Shared bathrooms.

► **Wrest Point Hotel Casino**. 410 Sandy Bay Road, **Sandy Bay** (Hobart), Tasmania 7005. Tel: (002) 25-0112; Fax: (002) 25-3909; in U.S., (800) 44-UTELL; in Canada, (800) 387-8842. Tower rooms, A$198–A$220; motor inn, A$89–A$99; special low-season (winter) rates available.

MELBOURNE AND VICTORIA

By Ian Marshman

Ian Marshman, a lifelong resident of Melbourne, is senior writer for Traveltrade, *the country's leading travel-industry publication, and hosts a travel-oriented radio talk show. He is the author of a major study of tourism in Australia.*

Marvelous Melbourne, Australia's industrial, financial, and commercial heart, is also one of the world's best preserved Victorian cities. Dubbed "marvelous" by newspapers in Europe and North America in the 1880s, Melbourne at that time had the most rapid growth of any city in the Western world.

From a few ragged tents and small sheep runs in the 1840s, Melbourne expanded to stage the Great Exhibition of 1888, which celebrated the first century of Australia's European settlement. The catalyst for this growth was the discovery of gold in 1854 at Ballarat and Bendigo in Victoria, the biggest gold rush the world had then experienced. As the mines and creeks of California became less and less lucrative, the richest alluvial and surface gold-mining regions ever discovered lured miners to Victoria from North America, Europe, and China.

Melbourne's boom lasted until the great crash of the 1890s, whose severity far exceeded the later financial crises of 1929 and 1987. The boom over, Melbourne never rivaled New York or London as a world capital but evolved instead into a 20th-century metropolis that retains much of the charm of the previous century in an architectural and overall visual style that reflects gold-generated wealth and the boom. Gothic cathedrals reminiscent of Paris or Vienna, steel and glass skyscrapers, and rivers that recall European canals create a stylish and beautiful city.

The "most European" of Australia's cities, Melbourne is home to nearly three million people who have moved here from throughout the world to enjoy its temperate climate and, some say, in contrast to its slightly larger rival, Sydney, a quiet, undemanding lifestyle. Melbourne is also the gateway to Phillip Island, with its highly entertaining "penguin parade," the spectacular Great Ocean Road, and the Murray River, the "highway" to the Outback. The city's proximity to the great Australian wilderness allows easy access to snow-covered mountains in winter and rolling surf in summer. It's also the east coast city closest to the Outback.

MAJOR INTEREST

Melbourne
Victorian-era terrace houses with iron-lacework
    verandahs
Quiet, small-town ambience
Cosmopolitan ethnic makeup
Pubs and dining
The arts
Sports

Victoria outside Melbourne
Phillip Island: the penguin parade, wildlife,
    beaches
Great Ocean Road's scenery and nature
Gold country, including the cities of Ballarat and
    Bendigo
Murray River region

MELBOURNE

Nearly every writer who has attempted to capture on paper the spirit of Melbourne has devoted pages to space: space to move and breathe clean fresh air and enjoy a personal freedom not common in most of the modern world. Despite its size and key role as a business and industrial center, the city has retained the feel of an outsized country town. It's easy to feel at home in Melbourne. The people are friendly, the pace is slow, the restaurants are good, the weather is temperate. Life seems easy.

Melbourne is Australia's Detroit, with three vehicle manufacturers; it's the center of the oil and gas industry, with refineries and shipping; it's the country's biggest shipping terminal; and it's the retail heart of the nation. It was the first Australian landfall for the millions who came from Europe via South Africa's Cape of Good Hope, and the destination for nearly one million postwar immigrants fleeing a war-devastated Europe; more recently, thousands have made new homes in its suburbs as an alternative to the rice fields and sprawling cities of Southeast Asia. There are nearly a hundred languages in daily use here, but every person you meet will say "G'day," and all will extol the virtues of their city.

Melbourne was Australia's capital from 1901 to 1927 and over the years has been host to hundreds of thousands of American troops—and to General Douglas MacArthur, who initially established his headquarters here for the fight to regain the Philippines and Singapore during World War II.

Today Melbourne is a hub of the Australian film industry (albeit with rivals in Sydney and Adelaide), the center of Australian fashion and art, and the only city in the world to grant its citizens a public holiday to attend a horse race. The **Melbourne Cup**, staged since 1867, carries more than A\$1 million in prize money and is the major attraction of a racing carnival the first week of each November, with the big race at Flemington on Tuesday. It's "anything goes" on racing day, and people dress to the nines in everything from top hats to beachwear and guzzle Champagne at lavish parking-lot parties. Not even the U.S. presidential elections, usually held on the same day, divert attention from the big race.

The first Melburnian was John Batman (the Australian-born son of a transported English convict), who purchased much of the region from local aboriginal tribes for a handful of beads and trinkets. It was never a destination for convicts or administered by the British military but rather was settled by people who chose it as a home in the wake of the gold rush and 19th-century land booms. This boom mentality is still in evidence, with most residents choosing to buy and sell their own homes at auctions, a system of land transfer uncommon outside Australia. Sociologists say the auction system reflects Melburnians' propensity to take a gamble, to let it ride—even

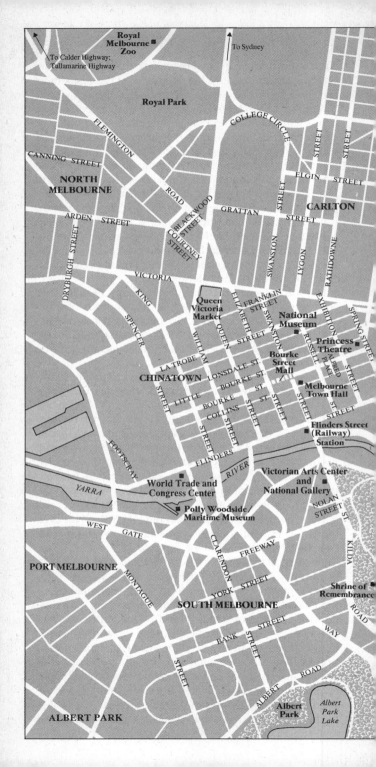

with their homes. It's easy to see an auction in progress; just look for the flags flying outside a house on any Saturday. A sign placed by the real-estate agent handling the sale will advise the time. Crowds of more than 100 are not unusual, and bids may run up by A$10,000 at a time. It often seems that little has changed since the city's residents abandoned everything to search for gold.

Melbourne is sometimes described as the most Australian of cities, being the home of both Foster's beer (brewed at the Carlton Brewery, on Bouverie Street at the top end of Swanston) and Australian Rules football.

"Aussie Rules footy" is a rugged game that is sometimes said to have evolved from Gaelic football, which was brought to Australia by Irish immigrants in pursuit of gold. It is played from February to September each year. Try to catch a game at the MCG (Melbourne Cricket Ground), an immense stadium near the central business district that can handle 120,000-plus crowds. Games are played Friday nights and Saturday and Sunday afternoons from March to September; call the Australian Football League for information, Tel: (03) 654-1244. (The MCG was also the site of the opening and closing ceremonies of the 1956 Olympic Games.) The **Australian Gallery of Sports and Olympic Museum**, also at the MCG, reflects Melbourne's claim to be Australia's sports capital, housing fascinating collections of items relating to cricket, Australian Rules football, cycling, tennis, boxing, lawn bowls, rowing, hockey, lacrosse, yachting, and other sports.

Like all cities, this one has its famous sons and daughters. In Melbourne's case they include opera star Dame Nellie Melba (1861–1931); rock stars Olivia Newton-John, Men at Work, and Little River Band; actors Mel Gibson and Sigrid Thornton; business tycoon Rupert Murdoch; and Wimbledon winner Pat Cash. Melbourne has also been home to some famous temporary residents, including Lyndon B. Johnson, who was here as a young naval officer, and Prince Charles, who went to school here.

Melbourne's trams, reminiscent of San Francisco's cable cars, travel a huge network and have been an integral part of the city's public transport system for more than a century. It's easy to catch a tram: Signal the driver at a designated stop, but be careful of cars when you step off the curbside and even more so when you leave the tram. Tram stops are easily identified by safety zones in the center of the street designed to isolate people from cars. If there is not a safety zone, look for a sign that identifies the stop number, wait on the curb until a tram approaches, and then signal the driver that you wish to board. An excellent book, *See Melbourne by Tram,* by Lacy Lowe, is available at most bookstores in the city, and certainly in the book department of Myers department store, on the ground floor near the Lonsdale Street entrance. It details all the major routes with a stop-by-stop guide to sights of interest.

Aside from Melbourne's sights and festivals, it is Melbourne's style and ambience that most visitors remember, from its elegant, lovingly restored pubs to its superb restaurants (there may be more restaurants per person in Melbourne than in any other city in the world, except perhaps Paris), and its gracious manners. It has to be said, too, that the other side of Melbourne's Old World and unhurried style is that it does not have the street life or nightlife of a Paris or New York; you have to make your own fun here.

The two peak holiday seasons correspond with major festivals in March and November. Melbourne enjoys sunny autumn weather in March for the **Moomba Festival** (*moomba* is aboriginal for "Let's get together and have fun"). The festival includes one of the world's outstanding water-skiing events (on the Yarra River), dozens of concerts of all types, and a huge carnival in the Alexandra Gardens. The **Melbourne Comedy Festival** in late March each year attracts new- and old-wave comedians from around the world. Dozens of venues stage comic revues, plays, stand-up routines, and satire. In November, the Spring Racing Carnival includes the **Melbourne Cup** on the first Tuesday of the month.

Around in Melbourne

Melbourne is a fully planned city built on a grid system, with the commercial section measuring exactly one square mile—although a major redevelopment of the nearby docklands is expected to enlarge the city considerably by early next century. The central city, too, is based on a grid, with Swanston Street on the north–south axis and **Bourke Street** on the east–west axis. Bourke is the major retail street, but the better shops and arcades front **Collins Street** one block to the south. **Chinatown**, with dozens of restaurants, is only a block north of Bourke on Little Bourke Street. In the heart of this precinct the **Museum of Chinese History** captures the impact that Chinese immigrants have had on Australia, from the earliest arrivals during the gold rush to the merchants who make up Chinatown today.

The city's major boulevard, St. Kilda Road, begins just south of the Swanston Street Walk on the south side of the Yarra River. **St. Kilda Beach** is 6 km (3½ miles) south of Flinders Street Station, the sandstone edifice that dominates the southern gateway to the commercial district. The trip to the beach takes about 20 minutes on a number 15 or 16 tram (see Getting Around, below). From its position as the city's premier suburb a century ago, **St. Kilda** degenerated to become Melbourne's red-light area in the 1970s, with a high incidence of drug-related street crime. However, in more recent times St. Kilda has been gentrified, and the district now offers a cosmopolitan mix of the bohemian and the trendy with its ethnic restaurants, 19th-century mansions converted into chic apartments, and palm-studded beachfront parks that give it an Art Deco atmosphere. St. Kilda's Acland Street is great for a Sunday stroll; it has dozens of Jewish bakeries and academic bookshops. Craftsmen sell their work each Sunday on the beachfront Esplanade, and it's common to find artists capturing St. Kilda on canvas. Nearby Port Melbourne has recently become the focus of groups that want to preserve the old buildings and bohemian, albeit slightly seedy, atmosphere of the area. They are objecting to a A\$2 billion development plan that would turn it into Melbourne's premier upscale shopping and tourism precinct.

On another excursion from the center of the city, a number 8 tram will take you southeast, along the south bank of the Yarra, first to **South Yarra**'s rows of terrace houses, with their verandahs covered in cast-iron lace, and then to **Toorak**, a neighborhood that is home to some of Australia's wealthiest residents.

Parks

Melbourne's parks constitute one of the biggest urban networks anywhere and range from the open sports fields of Royal Park to the 102.5-acre Royal Botanic Gardens.

A highlight of a visit to the city is the famous **Royal Melbourne Zoo**, which displays animals in their natural habitat. The zoo, housing about 4,000 species, is the third oldest in the world (dating to 1857) and is in Royal Park, only a few minutes north of the city center in the suburb of Parkville. The most popular animal residents are the gorillas born as a result of artificial insemination. There is a bear enclosure and the world's biggest butterfly house, where visitors stroll through a lush tropical jungle as the butterflies fly free around them. The zoo is a great place to see native Australian species: kangaroos, emus, wombats, platypuses, and koalas—animals that won't be found anywhere else in Melbourne. Trams leave for the zoo from Elizabeth Street; check with the driver to be sure you are on the right one.

The **Royal Botanic Gardens**, on the southern banks of the Yarra River, is home to 12,000 plant species and plenty of ducks and other wildlife. Fitzroy and Treasury gardens adjoin each other at the eastern end of Flinders and Collins streets, providing a place of solitude in the heart of the city. Albert Park Lake in South Melbourne is a former swamp turned into a home for ducks, black swans, and small yachts.

One of the newest attractions in town is the **National Tennis Centre** in Flinders Park, just southeast of the city center. Home of the Australian Open, the center is also used to stage rock concerts and other big events and is considered one of the best tennis facilities in existence. It is possible to play tennis here, however not on center court, famous for its unique opening roof. For information, Tel: 655-1234.

The **Shrine of Remembrance** in King's Domain Park dominates the downtown portion of St. Kilda Road. It was built as a memorial to World War I soldiers, ironically by many of those who survived, as a WPA-type project during the depression of the 1930s. The Acropolis-like structure has become a permanent reminder of the horrors of war. Some of the best views of the city can be seen from its balconies (a favorite of photographers); the names of all of Australia's war dead are inscribed on its granite walls.

Museums and Mansions

Historic attractions in Melbourne include the sailing ship *Polly Woodside* and the **Melbourne Maritime Museum**, on the south bank of the river opposite the World Trade and Congress Centre. (Don't be put off because the area looks like a construction zone; by 1996 the Maritime Museum will be part of a museum complex that will also include the **National Museum of Victoria**, currently on the corner of Swanston and La Trobe Streets.) When it opens, the National Museum will house the world's largest collection of aboriginal art. The deep-water, square-rigged *Polly Woodside* is one of the last boats of its type still afloat; only the fifth such vessel to be so recognized, it was recently awarded the World Ship Trust Heritage Medal.

Many historic mansions remain from the time when gold-rich miners and wool-wealthy graziers built houses to rival any in Europe and North America. **Como House**, in South Yarra, was the home of a single family for more than a century and is a fine example of the elegant, iron-lace-fronted edifices that housed the privileged during the last century. Its acres of Victorian gardens and authentic period furnishings, including many of the family's possessions, accurately capture the colonial period. **Ripponlea** in Elsternwick (south of the city via St. Kilda Road) is an even grander house, built in the Romanesque style with a huge fernery set in nearly ten acres of gardens.

The Arts

More contemporary attractions in Melbourne include the **Victorian Arts Centre and National Gallery** complex on the south bank of the Yarra, across from Flinders Street Station. The gallery is located in a striking building designed by the Australian architect Roy Grounds; from St. Kilda Road it looks rather like a jail. The gallery houses Australia's most famous collection, including the best-known works of Australian artists Tom Roberts, Arthur Streeton, William Dobell, Russell Drysdale, Sidney Nolan, and Frederick McCubbin. (Melbourne's inner eastern suburbs—once a bushland area—formed the scenic backdrop that motivated many of these artists to create the so-called Heidelberg-school style last century.) The gallery also houses works by Picasso, Renoir, Turner, Degas, Van Gogh, and Constable in its three main courts. Leonard French's spectacular stained glass roof, the largest in the world, stretches over the Great Hall.

The main theater building is topped by a spire (which critics say makes the whole center look as if it were still under construction), and the **Concert Hall** is housed in the circular (and mostly underground) building closest to the river. The 2,000-seat hall is the home of the Melbourne Symphony Orchestra and is also used for major theater productions and concerts. The entire complex generates considerable comment, with architecture critics sometimes claiming it offers on the inside what the Sydney Opera House does on the outside (what a pity they didn't get together). The center stages a wide range of productions; tickets can be purchased from the ticket office or through the BASS (Best Available Seating Service) booking agency. Half-price theater tickets for same-day performances can often be purchased at the Halftix booth in the Bourke Street Mall off Swanston.

The Arts Centre complex also includes the **Performing Arts Museum**, with more than a quarter of a million items of performing-arts memorabilia on view, as well as an extensive video library. There is the Southbank River Walk (which offers an excellent view of the Melbourne skyline) from the Arts Center to the Sheraton Towers Southgate Hotel, the World Trade and Conference Centre located downstream on the northern bank of the Yarra, and the National Museum of Victoria site.

Melbourne has hundreds of commercial galleries, a comprehensive list of which may be found in the *Art Almanac* (available from most city bookstores). Also, the Friday edition of the newspaper *The Age* lists current exhibitions. There are several galleries specializing in Australian paintings and crafts; **Toorak Road** in South Yarra (tram route 8) is a good place to stroll when looking for some unique Australian art. Particularly interesting is the **Graphic Illusion Gallery** at 68 Davis Avenue (a small street off Toorak Road near tram stop number 15), which specializes in contemporary painting, jewelry, ceramic sculpture, drawings, and prints.

The **Meat Market Craft Centre** at Courtney and Blackwood streets in North Melbourne houses the Victorian State Craft Collection and operates as a resource and information center for artists. Its shop displays contemporary work by 450 local craftspeople in several mediums, including ceramics, pottery, glass, and wood, and there is a range of jewelry. The superbly restored Meat Market itself displays crafts of almost every kind and houses frequently changing exhibitions.

Another good spot to shop for arts and crafts is the **Queen Victoria Antique Arts and Crafts Centre**, a complex of laneways and old warehouses with more than 100 traders, located on the northern edge of the commercial district off Franklin Street near the Queen Victoria Market.

Shopping in Melbourne

Melbourne's chic boutiques and big department stores market home-grown designers such as Prue Acton, Rodney Clarke, Adele Palmer, and Sally Browne, as well as all the big-name Paris, London, Milan, and New York labels. There are several different shopping streets in Melbourne, each with a very definite personality of its own. The bustling **Bourke Street Mall** is big. The stores are big, the selection is big, and the crowds are big. Here you'll find the major department stores of **David Jones** and **Myer**, the latter the largest such retail establishment in the Southern Hemisphere. David Jones, on the south side of the Bourke Street Mall (the side opposite Myer) is worth the visit; it is regarded as one of the world's finest examples of Art Deco architecture and is classified by the National Trust. Across Lonsdale Street at the rear of Myer is the 300-store **Melbourne Central** shopping center, which includes the Japanese store **Daimaru** offering six floors of the best merchandise Asia and the Pacific region have to offer, coupled with traditional service. There is direct access to the complex from the Museum underground station or from Myer via a pedestrian bridge. **Collins Street** is spoiled rotten with exclusive boutiques and stores such as **Georges** and **Henry Buck**, selling nothing but the best. The stores on Collins Street specialize in better clothing, imported designs, and quality goods, especially jewelry and leather. The **Sportsgirl** complex near the Swanston Street Mall is noted for its chic, high-fashion stores and food hall on the upper level.

Two interesting shopping arcades were built here in the last century: the **Block Arcade**, with a high-domed ceiling and mosaic-tiled roof that make you think of Milan, and the **Royal Arcade**, which is home to some of the city's most exclusive retailers. Here you will find Australia's best shoe shops, women's high-fashion boutiques, and specialty accessory stores.

Australia's most up-scale shopping street is 3 km (2 miles) south of downtown on **Toorak Road**; from Punt Road to Orrong Road the price tags are strictly high-altitude. The **Como Center** on Toorak Road offers an up-to-the-minute range of locally produced high fashion, and **The Place** in Toorak Village (last of the stops on the number 8 tram line) houses many specialist designer outlets.

The prices can also induce vertigo on **High Street** in **Armadale** (south of Prahran), which is well known for its antiques shops, furniture stores, and exclusive boutiques. **Splashes** has a huge range of swimwear and rainwear, much of it not available anywhere else. Dozens of shops in this neighborhood offer everything from Australian-built furniture to very old books and advertising posters. Most of the shops are owned by the people who serve you, and they nearly always know their stock well.

Chapel Street in Prahran (number 78 or 79 tram from Toorak Road) is the best street for young and trendy fashion, with a style range from way-out to off-the-planet. **Morrisons** has Akubra (Crocodile Dundee) hats, moleskin trousers, and R. M. Williams boots; it's possible to walk out of here and look as if you're ready to herd mountain cattle.

Melbourne's newest shopping experience is the tourist oriented **Southbank** opposite Flinders Street Station and adjacent to the Victorian Arts Centre and Sheraton Towers Southgate Hotel. Designed to be the city's answer to Sydney's Darling Harbour, it features more than 20 restaurants, most with superb views of the city skyline, and shops specializing in Australian goods ranging from souvenirs to highly crafted pottery, glass, and other works of art. A highlight is the Australia Experience, a 45 minute audio visual presentation which focuses on Southern Australia and is a good place to begin a tour of Melbourne.

Back downtown, the **Opal Mine**, at 125 Bourke Street, stocks thousands of individually designed pieces of jewelry, especially, of course, Australian opals. Prices range from moderate to ultraexpensive. **Altmann and Cherny**, at 120 Exhibition Street, displays the world's largest and most valuable opal (estimated at over A$2.5 million), but it stocks more moderate pieces as well.

The **Queen Victoria Market**, on Victoria Street at the northern edge of the commercial district, is one of the biggest markets in the world, with goods ranging from fresh produce to cheap clothes, antiques, and bric-a-brac, plus prints and crafts. It's open from 6:00 A.M. every day but Monday and Wednesday.

Dining in Melbourne

Melbourne is very big on the good life—its residents keep more than 2,000 restaurants in business. If you decide to eat at a non-hotel restaurant, though, check whether it is licensed to sell liquor (even wine and beer) or if it's a B.Y.O. (bring your own). B.Y.O.s account for about one-third of all the city's restaurants; residents often favor them because it is cheaper to buy wine or other drinks from a licensed liquor retailer than it is to purchase the same bottle in a restaurant. State law permits you to bring in alcohol bought from a liquor store or hotel even if you are dining at a licensed restaurant, but the restaurant is entitled to charge a corkage fee to serve you.

Restaurant prices range from moderate to expensive, and good service is almost guaranteed because of the number of competitors. Among the top-priced eateries, **Fannys** in Lonsdale Street is a very formal French restaurant with food that would pass muster in Paris (Tel: 03/663-3017); **Mietta's,** also in the city center, on Alfred Place, offers formal dining in a historic building that started out as the German Club and was later General MacArthur's headquarters; Tel: (03) 654-2366. **Jean Jacques** on the St. Kilda beachfront has been judged by many to be Australia's top seafood restaurant; it offers superb bay views and an ambience that relies heavily on discreet service and pastel peach decor; Tel: (03) 534-8221. And on Collins Street the Regent Hotel's 35th-floor **Le Restaurant** serves classic French cuisine with the best views of the Melbourne skyline; Tel: (03) 653-0000. Also on Collins Street, **Maxi's** at the Grand Hyatt rivals Jean Jacques for seafood; Tel: (03) 657-1234.

More moderate are **Café Palma** on Little Bourke Street, with dining in a garden beneath a sliding-glass roof that allows diners to take advantage of the sun or a warm starlit night; and **Mario's** at 303 Brunswick Street, Fitzroy, where they serve great gnocchi. Those yearning for New York might try **Scheherezade** at 99 Acland Street, St. Kilda, which keeps late hours and serves the best chicken soup in town; Tel: (03) 534-2722.

Treble Clef, part of the Victorian Arts Centre complex, is the ideal place for before- or after-theater dining, with its excellent service, international cuisine, and views of the city across the Yarra; Tel: (03) 684-8264. **The Last Laugh** on Smith Street in Collingwood, a ten-minute cab ride northeast of downtown, features good meals and a comedy show followed by dancing. It is the focal point of Melbourne's Comedy Festival held each March.

The **Colonial Tramcar Restaurant** is a 1927 tram converted into a stylish mobile restaurant that offers good French cuisine. The tram's route passes through the city's best suburbs and the commercial district; it is essential to reserve at least a couple of days in advance; Tel: (03) 696-4000. The tram departs from tram stop number 12 on Southbank Boulevard near the National Gallery. **Vlados Charcoal Grill** at 61 Bridge Road, Richmond, attracts regular visitors from Southeast Asia and Japan, who come to eat the biggest steaks served in Melbourne (although not everyone enjoys the large photographs of beef cattle that pass as decor here). More refined is the city-center **Windsor Grill** at the Hotel Windsor on Spring Street; excellent service and style have been the norm here since the 19th century.

Melbourne boasts more than a thousand ethnic restaurants, including dozens of Chinese, Thai, Malaysian, and Indonesian places on Little Bourke Street, Italian on Lygon Street (just north of the commercial district), Greek on Sydney Road, Jewish on Acland Street (Sydney and Acland are both about 6 km/3½ miles south of the city center), Vietnamese on Victoria Street, and Indian, Middle Eastern, and even Mexican spread throughout the city. **Fortuna Village** at 235 Little Bourke Street is typical of those in Chinatown, with a wide range of dishes from different regions of China. Most people prefer to let the chef here select their dishes. The Chinese community favors the **North Garden** on the corner of Little Bourke and Russell streets. It hosts a unique government-sponsored chef-training program for cooks from major cities in China including Shanghai and Beijing. Cuisine is authentic; reservations are not necessary. A few doors west, the **Shark Fin** is pure Hong Kong.

Lygon Street's Italian restaurants offer the city's best dining value, and the quality is not matched elsewhere in Australia. It is easy to believe you are in Rome here—old men talk politics over big plates of pasta, and more often than not the decor relies on clippings of newspaper reviews. It's best just to catch a cab to Lygon Street and peruse the menu displayed outside each establishment; most places here do not accept reservations. An exception is **Florentino's**, at 80 Bourke Street, long regarded as the city's premier Italian restaurant, with wood-paneled walls and homemade pasta; Tel: (03) 662-1811. Any Melbourne bookstore or newsstand will have copies of *The Age Good Food Guide*—an excellent listing of the city's best eateries in every price range.

Nightlife in Melbourne

PUBS

One of the best ways to experience Melbourne and mix in with the locals is at a pub. All Australian cities have pubs, heaven knows, but in Melbourne they are different. The city has never permitted bars that don't offer food and accommodation, and it is only in recent years that the sale of liquor has even been permitted in most restaurants. So the pubs—almost all are called "hotels"—have emerged as the focus of entertainment in the city.

Pubs range from those that have barely changed since the days when they hosted huge crowds prior to closing the doors at 6:00 P.M. each afternoon, to those that specialize in high-class food service and chic decor. In between are the suburban watering holes, sometimes described as beer factories surrounded by parking lots, and the **Melbourne pub circuit**, a series of pubs that provide various kinds of musical entertainment. The pub circuit, the birthplace of several bands and artists who have gone on to be worldwide stars—including AC/DC, the Bee Gees, and Olivia Newton-John—is an informal grouping, with establishments entering and dropping out on a regular basis. At any time there are about 50 pubs within three miles of the commercial district. They feature a wide range of music, including jazz, folk, country and western (in Melbourne it's mostly American-style country and western), and even classical. The daily papers, particularly Friday's edition of *The Age,* offer the best guide to what is happening in the pubs. Ask around Melbourne to find out which pubs are "in." Be aware that the list changes frequently; the regular patrons on the circuit change their focus quickly.

The most interesting pubs are found in the suburbs of Carlton, Fitzroy, Albert Park, South Melbourne, Richmond, and Prahran. It's here that Melbourne people gather to discuss the events that really matter in this city: politics and football (cricket in summer). The best way to get to one of the pubs is by cab, as walking in most of the areas is not recommended after dark. Besides, temperatures here often fall below freezing from March through October.

The **Lemon Tree**, north of the city center at 10 Grattan Street in Carlton, specializes in wine, seafood, and vocal patrons. It is a favorite of the literary set and a good spot to talk left-wing politics. The **Royal Oak Hotel** at 527 Bridge Road, Richmond, has a huge atrium, a small beer garden, and a wide selection of wines; there's often a classical trio or a pianist playing here. The **Red Eagle Hotel**, at 111 Victoria Avenue in Albert Park, is the type of place where owning a Porsche helps conversation. The Art Deco–style **Botanical Hotel** at 169 Domain Road bordering the botanical gardens offers Melbourne's most comprehensive wine list. The **Fawkner Club** at 52 Toorak Road is the best spot in the city to sit outside, enjoy a cool drink, and eat a big steak. The place to find Melbourne really at play is the **Loaded Dog Pub and Brewery** at 324 St. Georges Road, a North Fitzroy landmark known to every cab driver in the city. Its claims to fame are its more than 200 brands of beer and a live-music policy that ranges from new wave to 1950s-style rock 'n' roll. It's always crowded, loud, and fun. Similar in style and usually even louder are the **Star** on Clarendon Street in South Melbourne and the **Roxy**, just around the corner at 172 York Street.

In the city center the bar in Collins Chase, at the corner of Collins and Russell streets in the Grand Hyatt, is a favorite of the smart set; the entrance is through the Hyatt from either street. The **Sportsgirl Bar** on the upper level of the Sportsgirl shopping complex in Collins Street near the Swanston Street Mall is another favorite of the fashion conscious. The **News Bar** in Collins Place on Flinders Lane near Exhibition Street is a haunt of journalists.

THEATER AND CLUBS

Although Melbourne's after-dark life tends to be firmly centered on restaurants and pubs, there is a handful of theaters on Russell and Exhibition streets that stage well-known productions such as *Phantom of the Opera, Buddy,* and *Miss Saigon.* (Daily papers carry full details of theater productions and the more than 30 cinemas located within walking distance of the major hotels.) The recently restored **Princess Theatre** on Spring Street is one of Melbourne's classic Victorian buildings and forms an architectural triangle with the Windsor Hotel and Parliament House. More than 20 other theaters in the inner suburbs stage everything from former Broadway or West End shows to avant-garde productions. The **Universal Theatre** in Fitzroy is the most active of the theaters that stage original works. The Halftix booth in the Bourke Street Mall sells same-night tickets for most productions.

It is late at night when the dance clubs kick up their heels—patrons tend to be under 25 and definitely under 30. The most popular is the **Metro**, at the top end of Bourke Street. On a Thursday, Friday, or Saturday night upwards of 3,000 people crowd in to dance or hear top-line bands. Other favored clubs include **Inflation**, the **Underground**, and **York Butter Factory**, all on King Street in the western part of the city. The chicest club is **Monsoons**, at the Grand Hyatt. The **Ivy Club**, at the corner of Flinders Lane and Russell Street next to the Hyatt, is one of the "in" places in Melbourne. It offers dancing and bars on three levels, has an excellent restaurant with an international menu, and is frequented by actors and rock stars; look your most chic at the door to be admitted.

Nearly all the clubs feature a combination of live and

recorded music. There are more than 20 of them listed in the newspapers' entertainment sections, and they cater to a wide range of tastes, from jazz to new-wave rock. **The Troubador** at 388 Brunswick Street in Fitzroy features live original folk music and music with a mild country feel, and also serves a set menu at a good price. One of the top jazz clubs is the **Station Tavern and Brewery** on Greville Street in Prahran, about 4 km (2½ miles) south of the commercial district.

Expect to pay up to A$40 for a theater ticket, about A$15 for entry to a club plus about A$4 per drink, and about A$20 for entry to a live-music venue.

Staying in Melbourne

Melbourne hotels offer a high standard of accommodation, which, like those in all of Australia's major cities, owes much to the standards set by Asian competitors: Business and pleasure travellers have become used to the excellent amenities they receive in Hong Kong, Singapore, and Bangkok, so Australia's big-city hoteliers have to offer room quality and services matched only by the very best hotels in other Western countries. The luxurious ▶ **Grand Hyatt** at the corner of Collins and Exhibition streets, as an example, is considered by the Chicago-based chain to be its international flagship hotel; it boasts a marble foyer and an arcade of shops with a busy bar sunk in its center, and rooms with views across the Yarra River to the parks on its southern bank. The Hyatt's restaurant and shopping complex, called Collins Chase, is popular with Melburnians and visitors alike. The Art Deco–style decor of the Hyatt is designed to reflect the character of the eastern precinct of the city's commercial center.

▶ **Sheraton Towers Southgate** is said by Boston-based ITT Sheraton to be its global flagship. The hotel offers a style reminiscent of one of Melbourne's boom-time mansions with features such as butler service on every floor. The hotel is located across the river from Flinders Street Station and has its own footbridge access to the city center. Its north-facing rooms enjoy superb views of the city skyline and river, and south-facing rooms have views to St. Kilda and Port Phillip Bay.

The most unusual hotel in the city is ▶ **The Regent of Melbourne** on Collins Street, which has its lobby at ground-floor level, function rooms on the first floor, bars and restaurants on the 35th floor, and guest rooms extending from the 36th to the 50th floor (there are offices on the interim floors). Every room has a spectacular view, but ask for one facing the southeast toward the Dandenongs and the Alexandra Gardens.

Melbourne makes good use of its wonderful Victorian architecture in some accommodations. A good example in the city center is ▶ **Gordon Place**, a complex of competitively priced suites with their own kitchens, open fires, and antique furniture. The hotel started as a refuge for homeless men last century, but is known now for its well-appointed rooms, its courtyard housing a tropical garden, and its superb restaurant—not to mention its New Orleans–like feel.

The ▶ **Parkroyal Melbourne** on the corner of Little Collins Street and Alfred Place is one of Melbourne's newest hotels, but it has the ambience of a traditional establishment that you would expect to find in London or San Francisco. Its large rooms have full kitchen facilities and a well-stocked bar. The ▶ **Radisson President** at 65 Queens Road offers unbeatable views of Albert Park and the St. Kilda Beach area (ask for a west-facing room). The hotel honors several U.S. presidents from George Washington to George Bush with bars and restaurants named after them.

It is surprising that more accommodation in Melbourne isn't built to capitalize on the city's fabulous bay views, but there is one hotel that makes up for the shortage of options: The ▶ **Parkroyal on St. Kilda Road** is the premier hotel on the city's southern side, offering unmatched views from its southern-exposure rooms across Albert Park Lake and the bay.

The ▶ **Windsor Hotel** on Spring Street is a century-old colonial-era hotel in the style of the Oriental in Bangkok and Raffle's in Singapore. Promoted as Australia's only Grand Hotel, it is operated by the Indian Oberoi chain, and its rooms are furnished with genuine antiques; its reasonable rates make it an excellent alternative to the better-known chain hotels, although its accommodations fall short of the opulence suggested by its public areas.

▶ **Rockman's Regency Hotel** on Exhibition Street is a favorite of visiting celebrities because of its location in the theater district, larger-than-average rooms (all with VCRs), and midrange rates. ▶ **Country Comfort Old Melbourne**, north of the city on Flemington Road (the route from the airport), is built around a cobblestone courtyard; its rooms are designed to re-create the era of the gold rush. (The walk from downtown takes about 15 minutes, and the number 55 tram to Elizabeth Street stops right outside.) The ▶ **Hilton on the Park** offers superb views, particularly from its southern side, and is an easy walk across the Treasury Gardens from the major shopping and theater district.

Other good hotels include the ▶ **Le Meridien Melbourne**, a delight for architecture enthusiasts, as it occupies two 19th-century wool stores; the laneway between serves as its lobby. The ▶ **Victoria Hotel** on Little Collins Street is more than 50 years old, but it continues to offer quality accommodation and service at rates that will let you leave with your credit rating intact.

▶ **Flag International** operates an Australia-wide chain of motor inns, with about 20 in Melbourne that offer good rooms with private bathrooms, free parking, and restaurants at the lowest rates available. Similarly, the ▶ **Best Western** chain can be relied upon for reasonably priced accommodation in Melbourne.

Close to the Toorak Road shopping precinct, the ▶ **Hotel Como** offers Melbourne's best suites, with separate dining rooms and kitchens and high-quality furnishings. It is not unusual to find visiting rock bands staying here. Some rooms offer accommodations on two levels, and most enjoy views of the Yarra River and city skyline.

Golf in Melbourne

Melbourne claims more golf courses than any other city in the world; they range from public courses that charge a nominal fee to exclusive, expensive clubs.

One of the most popular tours with international visitors offers the opportunity to play some of the city's golf courses. An early-morning round of golf at **Albert Park Lake**, followed by breakfast at the Radisson President (opposite the course, overlooking the lake), shopping at Myer's and in the city's labyrinth of arcades, lunch in the Dandenongs (see Day Trips, below), and dinner in Lygon Street (Little Italy) comes close to making up the perfect day in Melbourne.

The **National Golf Club** is two hours south of Melbourne at Cape Schanck. Its course, with views of the rugged southern coast, is acclaimed as one of the best in the world, and it is rarely crowded. Tel: (059) 88-6666.

Golf enthusiasts should visit Melbourne in November for the Australian Open at Metropolitan Golf Club. Tel: (03) 579-3122.

DAY TRIPS FROM MELBOURNE
Port Phillip Bay

Melbourne is built on the shores of Port Phillip Bay, a huge expanse of shallow water, and is about 112 km (70 miles) from the open ocean. One of the most interesting tours here runs along the east side of the bay via the **Nepean Highway**. Hundreds of the city's finest houses are built here facing the bay (a cool million or so will buy a two-story Edwardian home with a view). From the main street in Mornington (south of the city along the east shore of the bay), farther along to Mount Martha and Rosebud, the coastal road winds around the bay shore, with spectacular holiday homes and safe swimming beaches contributing to an atmosphere of peaceful seclusion.

The beaches are open to everyone, and most have changing and toilet facilities. Nude bathing is restricted to the designated areas (which are much farther from the city), but topless bathing and very revealing swimsuits are common everywhere. The bay provides safe swimming, but take notice if a light aircraft sounds a siren; it's telling you there is a shark in the vicinity. (It happens only a couple of times a season.) Information is available from the Flinders Tourist Information Centre on the Nepean Highway at Dromana.

It's best to drive along the Beach Road and stop at the beach that strikes your fancy. The most interesting of the beaches close to Melbourne is at **Brighton**, where bathing boxes look more like something at a resort on the English coast than the South Pacific.

Farther south, **Rosebud** offers exceptional white sand and perfect swimming conditions. There is a good three-mile walk along the bayshore from St. Kilda to Station Pier at Port Melbourne, where you can catch a tram to the city center. (Port Melbourne is also the terminus for the overnight ferry service to Tasmania.)

Arthur's Seat, along the bay just before Rosebud, offers superb views of the Mornington Peninsula, and is on the road to Red Hill, an old farming community that is rapidly evolving into a hobby-farm area for people who want to live within commuting distance of Melbourne. It's inhabited by television personalities and former hippies turned yuppies—chopping down a tree is a crime ranked with multiple murder and drug running in these parts.

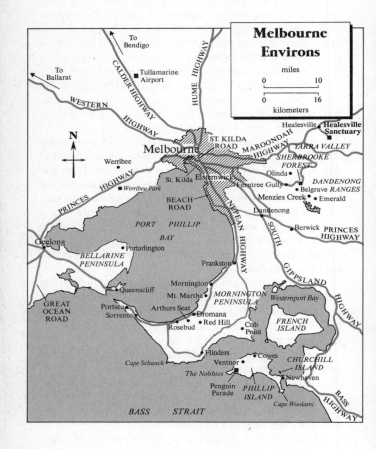

The Dandenong Ranges

Every visit to Melbourne should include at least one day in the Dandenong Ranges, about an hour's drive east of the city. Hundreds of varieties of Northern Hemisphere trees provide a spectacular show when their leaves change color throughout the ranges between March and June. (Australian trees do not lose their leaves in winter, although eucalyptus trees shed their bark—but that's in summer.)

Sherbrooke Forest, a rain forest deep in the mountains, is home to the rare lyrebird (so named because the courting male's tail feathers are shaped like the ancient Greek instrument; the lyrebird is pictured on the Australian 10-cent coin). It's sometimes possible to catch a glimpse of the shy and beautiful lyrebird from the secluded bush tracks that wander through the forest—but be very quiet and wear soft-soled shoes. The lyrebird is an excellent mimic, so if you hear something that sounds out of place among the trees, such as a chain saw or doorbell, there may be a lyrebird nearby.

The gardens in this region have won for Victoria the moniker "The Garden State"; take a short trip to the **National Rhododendron Garden** at Olinda to see why. North of Olinda on Mount Dandenong Tourist Road is the **William Ricketts Sanctuary**, one of the most unusual potteries anywhere. Set on a fern-covered slope beneath towering mountain ash trees, it features hundreds of aboriginal clay figures portraying the mythology and symbolism of Australia's oldest culture. Sculptor William Ricketts painstakingly created the figures between 1932 and 1961; open daily from 10:00 A.M. to 4:30 P.M.

Train buffs will be impressed with **Puffing Billy** near Belgrave, a 19th-century narrow-gauge steam train that has been restored to make a walking-pace journey from Belgrave to Emerald. It's one of the best ways to see the forest, and there are great views all the way to the so-called Australian Alps.

The **Healesville Sanctuary** to the northeast is one of the best places in Australia to see this continent's unique wildlife, with koalas, lyrebirds, cockatoos (including the showy pink galah), and kangaroos living in an environment much like their natural habitat; open daily from 9:00 A.M. to 5:00 P.M. A few miles past the sanctuary, the Maroondah Highway crosses the **Black Spur**, a rain forest with tall trees and deep fern glades.

STAYING AND DINING IN THE DANDENONGS

Bavarian- and Swiss-style restaurants are a feature of every village in this area; English-style Devonshire tea establishments serve scones with jam and tea. **Clover Cottage Restaurant and Strawberry Terrace**, on Manuka Road in Berwick, about 35 km (22 miles) east of the city on Highway 1, serves a wide range of French-style dishes in the dining room of a Georgian-era country mansion. It is classically tasteful, with excellent service; Tel: (03) 707-1066. The **Cotswold House Country Restaurant**, in the heart of the mountains on Blackhill Road in Menzies Creek, offers nouvelle cuisine in an Australian homestead. It specializes in local wine, and you can enjoy views across the valley as you dine; Tel: (03) 754-7884. The **Micawber Park Tavern**, on the corner of Monbulk and Gully Crescent roads in Belgrave, is set among three acres of magnificent fern glades and towering gum trees adjacent to Sherbrooke Forest. It's also a good spot to stop for Devonshire tea in the afternoon; Tel: (03) 754-2014. It is important to reserve at any restaurant in the Dandenongs on weekends and public holidays, whether for lunch or dinner.

The region has many accommodation options, but the pick of the bunch is the ▶ **Burnham Beeches Country House**, built for the Nicholas family in the 1930s. Close to Olinda, it is regarded as Australia's finest example of Art Deco architecture. The house now offers 36 very expensive suites and hosts many of the famous personalities who pass through Melbourne each year. Its pricey restaurant ranks as one of the country's finest dining rooms, the atmosphere enhanced by superb views of the forest and flocks of brilliantly colored parrots. The house offers excellent health and fitness facilities, including a swimming pool, tennis courts, and jogging tracks through the bush. ▶ **The Loft in the Mill** offers bed-and-breakfast accommodation in a bushland setting close to the top of Mount Dandenong.

The Yarra Valley

The Dandenongs can be combined with a trip through the Yarra Valley wine region northeast of Melbourne near Healesville, where there are seven vineyards open to the public for tastings and sales. The Yarra Valley is renowned for its full-bodied reds, fruity whites such as Chardonnay and Rhine Riesling, and fortified wines, including some of Australia's best Port-type wines. Wineries are well sign-posted from the Maroondah Highway, which travels the full length of the valley. Most offer tastings and sales and will be happy to ship a dozen bottles to your home (but keep in mind customs regulations, which might mean you will have to pay import duty before the wine can be delivered).

PHILLIP ISLAND
The Fairy Penguins

It is hard to imagine a visitor to Melbourne not making the journey to Phillip Island, 72 km (45 miles) southeast of Melbourne on the other side of the Mornington penin-sula, to experience one of nature's great wonders, the nightly parade of the fairy penguins as they return to their cliff-top homes at Summerland Beach after a day's fishing at sea.

Phillip Island is one of only a handful of places in the world where it's possible to see these remarkable birds at all, and among those Phillip Island is certainly the easiest to get to. The fairy penguin is the smallest penguin, about a foot tall, and lives in several remote spots along the south-ern Victoria coast and on islands of the Bass Strait. These birds spend days at sea catching fish, which they then regurgitate after returning to their nests in the evening, to feed their young, who remain on Phillip Island.

The parade of birds as they flop out of the surf and waddle up the steep surrounding hills provides visitors with one of the most entertaining experiences in Victoria.

The first stop on a trip to Phillip Island should be the tourist information center at Newhaven; Tel: (059) 56-7447. The center has a comprehensive range of informa-tion, including maps and suggested cliff walks.

Don't forget to take warm clothing, even on the hottest summer day. On a spring or autumn night, the tempera-ture can drop below freezing if a gale-force wind is blowing off the Antarctic icecap.

It's a good idea to arrive early during peak holiday periods, because a maximum of 3,500 people are permit-ted to view the birds on any one night. The Newhaven information center can advise you what time dusk occurs so you won't miss the parade.

TOURS TO PHILLIP ISLAND

There are several tour options, with more than a dozen bus operators offering half-day and full-day itineraries that include the island's scenic attractions and, of course, the penguin parade at dusk. Departure from Melbourne is usually at midmorning (some tours leave earlier), and arrival back in Melbourne will be some two or three hours after twilight. Australian Pacific Tours has departures for the penguin parade every day; Tel: (03) 598-5355 or, toll-free within Australia, (008) 33-5003. The penguins return from their fishing expeditions in the cold sub-Antarctic waters at dusk; powerful lights—which don't seem to bother the creatures—make viewing easy. The little birds do not like flashbulbs, however, and photographers are asked to use long exposures or purchase preprinted shots rather than use a flash.

A good way to experience the wonder of the fairy penguins without spending a full day in the area is to fly with Penguin Express; Tel: (03) 379-2122. The trip from Melbourne's Essendon Airport begins with a glass of Champagne in the terminal and a 30-minute flight over the city's southern suburbs and beaches and along the rugged southern coast. The tour starts at A$217 and includes a chance to see koalas in the wild as well as the penguins, and the return journey provides spectacular views of Melbourne at night.

OTHER PHILLIP ISLAND ATTRACTIONS

Phillip Island is about a two-hour drive south-southeast from Melbourne and is connected to the mainland by a bridge that permits easy access to its 58-mile-long coastline (see Getting Around, below). The terrain varies from rocky outcrops and steep cliffs to superb surfing beaches and safe swimming areas. The surf is biggest at **Cape Woolami**, but for swimming the north coast offers dozens of equally good choices. Just drive along the shore and stop where you want. The inland is studded with some of Victoria's prettiest farms and several old chicory kilns (the plant, an alternative to coffee, was once widely grown on the island).

The real reason to visit Phillip Island—aside from viewing the penguin parade—is to experience the region's wildlife and scenery. Its fauna is amazing: more than 200 species of birds in addition to penguins, seals, and koalas. It is one of the few places in Australia where koalas can easily be seen in the wild. Visitors and Melburnians alike are enthralled by the koalas, but the park rangers charged with their protection do ask that the animals be left alone. Simply enjoy these symbols of Australia as they lazily munch on eucalyptus leaves and look down at you, almost mocking the busy life of a traveller. If you drive to Phillip Island, it is also important to watch for signs that warn where koalas cross the road; you must drive very slowly at those points.

Sea gulls by the millions, black swans, pelicans, and ibis call this beautiful island home. Coastal scenery that's a photographer's dream, secluded pockets of bushland inhabited by koalas and wallabies (small kangaroos), and huge sand dunes all combine to create a remarkable place. Beachwalking from Cowes to the Forest Caves or the Colonnades affords fantastic views of the ocean.

The island was among the first spots to be permanently settled on Australia's rugged southern coast, and it has been a popular resort area for more than a century. Just 13 miles long, it is a permanent home to only about 4,000 inhabitants (most of whom live in the town of Cowes), but the population in peak holiday seasons and on sunny weekends expands into the hundreds of thousands. It is a good idea to avoid the island on long weekends, particularly around Christmas and New Year. While the fairy penguins are the highlight of any visit, there are several other attractions that make an excursion to the island memorable, including the **Island Nature Park**, home of wombats and cockatoos.

A ferry from Cowes sails out to **Seal Rock**, a remote rock formation at the entrance to Westernport Bay that is home to a colony of some 5,000 fur seals. The experience of being so close to seals in the wild is exhilarating, if a bit noisy.

The Nobbies, the southwesternmost part of the island, are huge cliffs that block the enormous swells of the Indian Ocean after they've built up over thousands of miles of open sea. The result is breathtaking, as the water crashes into a huge underground cavern known as the Blow Hole, creating a waterspout that towers hundreds of feet into the air when the Roaring Forties are blowing their hardest. Don't be put off if the weather is cold; just bundle up and enjoy nature at its most furious.

Churchill Island is a small landfill connected by a footbridge to Phillip Island—simply follow the signs. Its historic homestead is now operated by the National Trust and is typical of country properties throughout Australia, with a rambling verandah, 15-foot-high ceilings, and more than 20 rooms furnished in colonial-era antiques. The entire island has remained as it was a century ago, and farming here goes on much as it always has.

Phillip Island is famous for being the original home of the Australian Grand Prix, the car-racing circuit immortalized in Neville Shute's *On the Beach,* the novel that portrays Melbourne as the last surviving city on earth after a nuclear holocaust. The movie version, made in 1959, includes a famous scene with Fred Astaire, Gregory Peck, and Ava Gardner at the world's last-ever motor event. Today the circuit at Ventnor in the center of the island is the site of the **Motor Sport Hall of Fame** that displays hundreds of vintage and classic cars and memorabilia from the racing days. The automobile Grand Prix is long gone (to Adelaide), but the track still seems to echo with the roar of the open wheelers. The old racetrack is also the home of hundreds of exotic and colorful parrots, many of them tame enough to eat from your hand. For a while Phillip Island was the site of the Australian Motor Cycle Grand Prix, but the island lost it to Sydney because the Victorian government bans cigarette advertising at sports events.

STAYING AND DINING ON PHILLIP ISLAND

Accommodation on Phillip Island is mostly limited to motels and recreational-vehicle parks. The ▶ **Cowes Colonial Motor Inn** offers high-quality accommodations, lonely walks along the beach, and romantic open-hearth fires at night. ▶ **Trenavin Park**, one of the oldest houses on the island, is now a bed-and-breakfast with two- and three-bedroom guest wings. Accommodation can be booked on a fully inclusive basis, and Trenavin Park's restaurant is famous for its afternoon Devonshire tea. ▶ **Narrabeen Cottage** is a beautifully restored old house with a superb garden and friendly service.

Australian cooking at its best can be sampled at the **Woolshed Restaurant**, which serves huge slabs of beef and lamb and stages a one-hour sheep-shearing, cow-milking, and boomerang-throwing show. **The Jetty** in Cowes serves seafood and beef (the island's two major products) in an indoor garden with a huge open fire and views of Westernport Bay. The century-old **Isle of Wight Hotel** has a good, reasonably priced family restaurant. You can observe nesting mutton birds as you dine at the spectacular cliff-top **Sheerwater Restaurant Observatory**. It's moderately priced and easy to find (as is everything else on Phillip Island) on the tourist road. Sheerwater is closed on Mondays during the winter.

An independent traveller could easily combine Phillip Island with the Mornington Peninsula, the city's major beach and resort region—and even with the Great Ocean Road—by using the 30-minute car-ferry service that operates between Sorrento, near Portsea at the tip of the Mornington Peninsula, and Queenscliff, at the western mouth of Port Phillip Bay on the Bellarine Peninsula near Geelong (A$35 per vehicle and up to four passengers). You can't book passage on the ferry ahead of time, but boats leave every hour.

THE GREAT OCEAN ROAD

There can be few more stimulating experiences for late 20th-century pleasure seekers than to be seated at the wheel of a good car anticipating a 180-mile run along a spectacular cliff-top road with breathtaking views of the Southern Ocean.

Victoria's Great Ocean Road comes close to most drivers' idea of paradise as it snakes westward from Melbourne and Port Phillip Bay, past Geelong along the southern coast from Torquay to Anglesea, through Lorne and Apollo Bay, and on to Port Campbell National Park, Warrnambool, and Portland in the direction of Adelaide and South Australia. The road provides some of the best coastal scenery to be viewed anywhere, with a backdrop of rain-forested mountains. Drivers would be well advised to keep their eyes on the road; for passengers, however, there are unmatched vistas of mountains and the Southern Ocean (known to the rest of the world as the Indian Ocean). The coastal villages en route are Victoria's holiday playground, and the surf is recognized as among the most challenging in the world, equaling that of Hawaii and southern California.

The Great Ocean Road was built by World War I veterans as a government project designed to provide these men with employment when they returned home from the European battlefields. It was always intended to be a tourist road; the original plans claimed it would rival the famous California coastal route. It does.

The Great Ocean Road is a high-quality blacktop. From it, photographers can set up some great shots, ranging from board riders hanging ten at Bells Beach, near

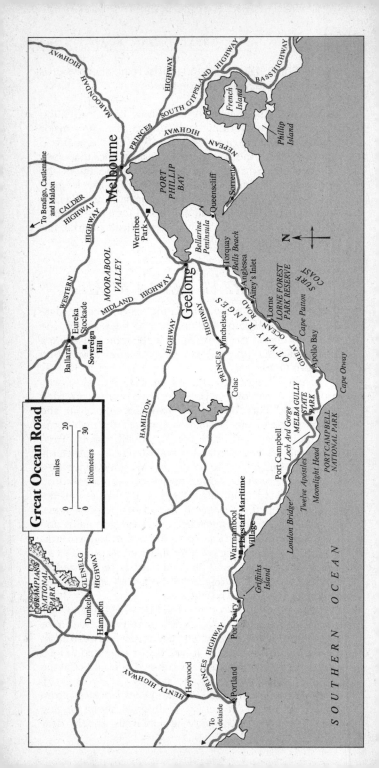

Torquay, to coastal cliffs with sheer drops hundreds of feet into roiling sea. A two- or three-day trip from Melbourne will take in the historic port of Geelong; the wineries and pubs of the Bellarine Peninsula (facing the Mornington Peninsula at the head of Port Phillip Bay); the big surf at Bells Beach and Lorne; the ancient rain forest of Cape Otway; the spectacular southern cliffs and rock formations created by the ocean as it pounds the Australian continent; coves and bays where 19th-century mariners and passengers scrambled ashore from the more than 500 tall ships wrecked in the area; and historic fishing villages, once among the world's busiest ports and the landing points for thousands of miners bound for Victoria's goldfields.

Most Melbourne-based car-rental companies have vehicles that are certain to make the Great Ocean Road a memorable trip. Hertz offers the biggest sports-car fleet, including Ford Capri convertibles (known as Mercury Capri in the U.S.). They start at around A$100 a day on an unlimited-mileage basis, although a more sedate car will cost you less.

Bus tours of the region are conducted by Australian Pacific and Trans Otway Tours, both located in the Melbourne central business district.

It is possible to undertake only part of this trip and make it a one-day outing from the city if time is limited. The first hour or so on Highway 1 (Princes Highway), through the city's western suburbs, across the giant Westgate Bridge over the docklands, and then by freeway to Geelong, is fairly dull. The only worthwhile detour is to **Werribee Park**, whose main attraction is a magnificent 60-room Italianate mansion built in the 1870s. The stately home is located in a huge formal garden that reflects the flamboyant emergence of the "squattocracy" in Victoria, the pioneer families who rode to prominence on the sheep's back. (The early pioneers were known as squatters because they simply moved in and claimed land as their own.)

Homesteads of equal grandeur extend through western Victoria and into South Australia. They were once the centers of station properties that sprawled for hundreds of square miles. Most are retained by the descendants of the original builders; many have been refurbished in recent years as wool has reemerged as Australia's biggest agricultural export. The trip to Geelong, on the western shore of Port Phillip Bay, is through country once largely controlled from Werribee Park.

Geelong

Victoria's second-largest city, Geelong is home to a number of major industrial complexes. It began its life as a seaport, a place where clipper ships picked up wool for the mills of Europe and North America. The waterfront is still dominated by huge 19th-century wool warehouses bearing the names of companies (such as Dalgety and Elders) that have survived to be numbered among Australia's biggest corporations. One of the former wool houses has been turned into Geelong's biggest shopping center. Another has been renovated and is now the **National Wool Museum**, with exhibits that detail the history of the industry that opened up Australia's interior more than a century ago.

The National Trust operates several historic properties close to the city, notably **The Heights** and **Barwon Grange**, both excellent examples of privileged life in the last century. Both are well signposted from Highway 1.

Little evidence is left of the region's original inhabitants, the Wathaurung aboriginal tribe, who lived throughout the south coast area for more than 4,000 years until the 1840s. Like the aboriginal population in most of Australia, the Wathaurung did not survive long when Europeans arrived. They had no immunity to European diseases, particularly measles (which was nearly always fatal to them), and were pushed off their traditional hunting grounds by the encroaching settlers. Fewer than 20,000 aboriginal people live in Victoria today, mostly in suburban Melbourne, and most are descendants of people from Queensland and the Northern Territory.

The probable source of one of Australia's great colloquialisms involves a white man named William Buckley, a convict who escaped to live with the Wathaurung. It was thought that he had no chance of survival; hence, Australians will give a person or project that seems to have no chance of success a "Buckley's chance." Buckley *did* survive, and lived in the Geelong area as an aboriginal for 32 years, coming out of the bush only when the white settlers arrived around 1835.

Four of the area's several cool-climate wineries are open for public tastings and cellar-door sales; one of them is the **Tarcoola Estate**, about 32 km (20 miles) northwest of the city in the Moorabool Valley. It is also the home of several hundred koalas. They range freely around the property but are usually easy to find.

Wines from around Geelong are noted for their full, fruity flavor, particularly the reds made from Shiraz and Cabernet Sauvignon grapes. The tourist information office on Ryrie Street in central Geelong has comprehensive guidebooks to the city and its varied attractions, including Tarcoola Estate and National Trust houses.

Queenscliff

Geelong is the gateway to the Bellarine Peninsula, a region best known for its safe swimming beaches and the historic settlement of **Queenscliff**.

Several pubs remain from the time when the town, at the western head of the entrance to Port Phillip Bay, was the preferred holiday resort of Melbourne's landed gentry. ▶ **Mietta's Queenscliff Hotel**, the ▶ **Ozone Hotel**, and the ▶ **Vue Grand Private Hotel** all offer fine, colonial-style accommodation and dining rooms that have changed little since the days when tall ships stopped here en route to Melbourne. **Mietta's Restaurant** at the Queenscliff Hotel is recognized as among the best in the state serving traditional French fare.

Fort Queenscliff, Australia's largest and best-preserved military fortress, was, like many other coastal fortifications around the country, built in the last century to ward off an anticipated Russian attack.

The Road Begins

The Great Ocean Road has three parts, each with a distinct character: The first, from Torquay to Apollo Bay, is a Riviera-like playground with wide sandy beaches, such as Bells Beach near Torquay, that spread out from the feet of the high, tree-clad slopes of the Otway Ranges. As you travel south along the second section of the road, the trees become bigger and the mountains taller until the landscape is dominated by rain forest and wet, dark fern glades. In the third part of the drive the forest gives way to the spectacular cliffs and coastal scenery of the **Port Campbell National Park**, where the Indian Ocean swell crashes into the Australian continent. The memory of the many ships that sailed the waves right into the cliffs is strong here. There are numerous beaches, as well as surf that attracts many of the best board riders in the world—the region has hosted world surfing championships several times. It's easy to rent a board and try the big waves, but you're advised to stick to beaches with a lifeguard patrol unless you have already found the breakers on Honolulu's North Shore to be "no worries, mate."

Surfing was introduced to Australia by Hawaii's Duke Kahanamoku in 1915; since then it has become part of the national culture, with south coast beaches and the associated hedonistic lifestyle the best-known images of the area. Old Holdens (the Australian version of Chevrolets) and Fords with boards on their roofs are permanent fixtures; the beaches of Winki Pop, Jan Juc, Point Impossible, and Spout Creek are among surfers' favorites.

The **Angahook Forest Park**, near Anglesea at the start of the drive, is home to a wide range of native and European birds, including spectacularly bright parrots that will eat out of your hand. The park has several superb, well-marked trails, and is a good place to see hundreds of different wildflowers and wattle (native acacia trees whose spikes were used by early settlers to make fences), particularly in the spring, i.e., from September to November.

The bushland setting of the **Anglesea Golf Course** down the highway from Torquay provides the unique experience of teeing off among the local kangaroos, which live on the grounds and often refuse to move—making for another hazard on a course that isn't easy in the first place. Anglesea is a public course and reservations are usually not necessary, unless you plan on going there on a sunny weekend or major holiday; Tel: (052) 63-1582.

Between Torquay and Anglesea is the **Southern Rose**, a lavish restaurant with views over an eight-acre rose garden. It's possible to stop just for a drink, for morning or afternoon tea, or for a full meal in the late evening. Reservations are not necessary to enjoy its excellent Australian food and warm, cozy atmosphere.

The headlands that frame the surf beaches offer some of Australia's best surf fishing for whiting, snapper, gummy (a small shark), and salmon. Fishing gear and bait can be rented at most gas stations; it's best to adhere to local advice to find out where the fish are biting. Many people fish the rock pools, which act as natural fish traps at low tide—but be careful of the incoming tide.

As the Great Ocean Road winds into Airey's Inlet, the bush takes on a ghostly gray hue, with thousands of tall gum trees standing dead and gaunt over a lush undergrowth. This area was hit in 1983 by a bush wildfire that wiped out some 2,000 homes and destroyed thousands of square miles of forest.

Victoria and South Australia are the most bushfireprone regions in the world, and the fire known as Ash Wednesday was the worst in 40 years. It is a natural function of the Australian eucalyptus bush to burn— indeed, several varieties of trees need the heat of fire to germinate seed—but the 1983 fire was much hotter than normal and many of the trees never recovered. It's easy to catch a glimpse of the harshness of the Australian conti- nent here by witnessing the birth of a new generation of forest. Farther west along the road it's easy to see how the rain forest looked before the fire. It will take at least 50 years for the bush to recover fully from the devastation— and then the law of the Australian bush dictates it will happen again.

Lorne, about 30 km (19 miles) out of Torquay, is the largest of the coastal towns. With an almost Mediterra- nean atmosphere in the summer, in midwinter it be- comes a lonely and isolated outpost bearing the brunt of the worst the Indian Ocean can provide. Its most famous attraction is the beach, but behind the town the rain forest creates a dense canopy of foliage; bush tracks here lead to high waterfalls and lookouts. **Lorne Forest Park Reserve** is lush in the extreme, with walks that make it easy to experience what much of southern Australia was like prior to white settlement. The easiest is the five- minute signposted walk from the parking lot to Erskine Falls. Comprehensive maps of the forest area and the various bushwalks are available at the BP gas station and supermarket as you enter the town from Melbourne.

STAYING IN AND AROUND LORNE

Accommodations on the Great Ocean Road are mostly limited to chain motels, residential resorts, and guest- houses. Victour in Melbourne and the tourist office in Geelong can assist with reservations. Flag International has several motels in the region and offers the only interna- tional reservations service (see Accommodations Refer- ence). Reservations are definitely needed during school holidays (April, June, and September), long weekends, and from mid-December to mid-February. The ► **Light- keeper's Inn** at Airey's Inlet offers high-standard accommo- dation at reasonable rates and is one of the handful of motels situated on the Great Ocean Road. In Lorne, the ► **Cumberland Lorne Resort** offers condominium-style accommodation with views of the rugged southwest coast. ► **Cape Otway Cottage** is a rural retreat on a farm se- cluded in a hidden valley close to Lorne. Trail riding by horse in the area is easily arranged at ► **Seamist**, a mountain facility that also has nice log-cabin accommodations in Winchelsea, about 16 km (10 miles) north of Lorne.

The Shipwreck Coast

The road continues to track around the cliff tops by way of the extraordinarily rugged Cape Patton to the pretty town of **Apollo Bay**. The last of the surf beaches is not far outside town. The scenery then changes to dramatic and dark rain forest. Tall trees and ferns lap the road as it traverses the massive bulk of **Cape Otway**, the southernmost point along the Great Ocean Road. **Melba Gully State Park**, on the far side of the cape, is particularly beautiful, its valley of ferns and glowworms covered by trees, some nearly as tall as California's giant redwoods.

An unpaved side road leads to the lighthouse at Cape Otway, which has protected ships rounding one of the continent's southernmost points for more than a century. The 14-km (8½-mile) road leads to cliffs towering some 300 feet up from the ocean, cliffs that mark the start of the shipwreck coast, the graveyard of more than 500 clippers, brigantines, and barquentines from the last century. Relics of the disasters still litter some of the region's wild, isolated beaches, and tales of heroic rescues are entwined in the folk history of the fishing hamlets that dot the coast. The anchors of the *Fiji,* wrecked in 1891, and the *Marie Gabrielle* (in 1869) can be seen half-buried in sand at Moonlight Head.

The fern glens and waterfalls of the rain forest give way here to the almost unbelievably rugged west coast, and to **Port Campbell National Park**. The rock formations created by the relentless ocean as it slams into Australia after an uninterrupted stretch extending from South America 15,000 miles away carry names such as the Twelve Apostles and London Bridge that evoke more civilized images. There is a penguin parade near the Twelve Apostles every evening that surpasses the much better known event at Phillip Island. Here it's quite isolated, and often you will be alone to witness the hundreds of penguins struggling ashore at dusk. But the site is hard to find, so it's best to seek local information when you are in the area. The park extends for 21 miles and offers unmatched scenery, but it is only easily accessed in two places, at Loch Ard Gorge and at another signposted entry about 3 km (2 miles) farther along the road.

Loch Ard Gorge is the best spot to imagine what it must have been like to be aboard a fragile 19th-century sailing ship on a bitterly cold night as the Roaring Forties whipped up 50-foot waves. The clipper *Loch Ard* sank in this place on just such a night; the few survivors washed up here on a beach that can now be reached by a wooden stairway. A memorial to those who were lost and a graveyard that contains the few bodies recovered lie at the top of the gorge.

The best place to learn more about the coast and its link with the days of sail is the **Flagstaff Hill Maritime Village** in Warrnambool, farther down the highway. The museum complex has its own clipper and is itself a re-creation of a 19th-century port on the city's foreshore.

The **Tower Hill State Game Reserve** near Warrnambool features an extinct volcano that, like many others in the area, has sunk into the plain and become a lake.

Close to the coast is **Griffiths Island**, home each summer to thousands of mutton birds. These remarkable birds leave the area every year on or about April 26 to spend the northern summer in Siberia and then return around September 22.

STAYING IN WARRNAMBOOL AND PORT FAIRY

Warrnambool, the major city in the area, offers a wide range of accommodations. The ▶ **Mid City Motor Inn** and the ▶ **Olde Maritime Motor Inn** are good choices offering high-standard motel accommodations with room service, swimming pools, and licensed restaurants.

The Great Ocean Road continues on to the pretty fishing village of Port Fairy, which has excellent colonial accommodation at the ▶ **Dublin House Inn**, an 1855 pub whose facilities rival the standards of big-city hotels. The inn has at various times been a general store, a bakery, and a liquor store.

There are several places along the Great Ocean Road where it's possible to return to Melbourne on the more direct Highway 1 (Princes Highway). All are well sign-posted, and the highway will return you to Geelong, then to Melbourne via the Westgate Freeway.

The Western District

Your trip along the Great Ocean Road could be extended easily to include Victoria's oldest town, the coastal city of **Portland**, which includes several historic buildings, and then branch off through the Western District to **Gariwerd**

National Park, formerly known as the Grampian Ranges. These undulating hills from the coast to the mountains comprise part of the world's biggest volcanic plain, with extinct craters dotting the landscape. Take the Henty Highway north to Hamilton and turn right onto the Glenelg Highway in the direction of Ballarat and Melbourne. A left turn onto Route 111 in the town of Dunkeld will take you north through the mountains to Halls Gap and ultimately to Highway 8 (Western Highway), the major Adelaide–Melbourne route. It would be best to allow at least two days for this trip and stop overnight in Hamilton, Stawell (on Highway 8), or Ballarat. Accommodations in this area remain limited to motels (contact Flag or Best Western) and friendly pubs without reservations facilities.

Gariwerd is the traditional aboriginal name for the Grampians, which were named after similar rugged ranges in Scotland. The area offers a rich variety of native flora, brilliant in spring. The easiest spot in Victoria to pet a kangaroo is here at **Zumsteins**, a small town about a half-hour drive across the Sierra Range from the main center of Halls Gap. It is easy to find; only two roads traverse the Grampians and the area is well signposted. There are several significant aboriginal sites in the ranges; stop at the ranger station at Halls Gap for information. ▶ **Glenisla Homestead**, between Hamilton and Horsham just west of the Gariwerd boundary, is renowned as one of Australia's best country houses, and it offers a high standard of accommodation on a working sheep property.

If you turn left and stay on Highway 1 at the town of Heywood on the way north from Portland to Hamilton, you will continue west along the coast through the town of Mount Gambier in the state of South Australia and on up to Adelaide.

Ballarat and Back to Melbourne

The return journey to Melbourne is via Ballarat, once the site of the richest gold mines in the world. A pitched battle was fought here at the Eureka Stockade in 1854 between British forces and miners seeking political representation (and the repeal of mining licenses)—the nearest thing Australia ever had to a revolution. Ballarat is the site of Sovereign Hill, a re-creation of life in a gold township in the 1850s, and the **Gold Museum**. At the latter, there are displays of huge nuggets, which attracted miners from around the world, as well as exhibits of 19th-century mining equipment and original miners' licenses.

The story of Eureka and the events that led to Victoria's independence from England is told with original documents and photographs. Particularly interesting is the story of the California Militia, a group of miners who organized under the U.S. flag in 1854.

A visit to **Sovereign Hill** can easily take most of the day. It has a main street complete with boardwalks, the New York Bakery, the United States Hotel (now a restaurant), a working mine (a gold-train ride down the shaft is great fun), and the museum, which details the huge Ballarat and Bendigo strikes.

Superb, reasonably priced accommodation in a colonial-style structure is available at the ► **Miners Retreat**, a Victorian-era home with iron-lacework verandahs and suites furnished with antiques. The return journey to Melbourne from Ballarat is via the Western Highway and takes about two hours.

BENDIGO, THE GOLDFIELDS, AND THE MURRAY

Two hours northwest of Melbourne on the Calder Highway you could be forgiven for thinking you've entered some kind of time warp. The goldfields city of **Bendigo** here is a living example of life 130 years ago—but not as it was lived in Australia. When the gold miners arrived from San Francisco's Barbary Coast, Dublin, and Shanghai in search of instant wealth, their intention was not to build a city. But as the gold ran out they turned to farming, and the former shantytown became a commercial center for the surrounding countryside. From a tent city, Bendigo evolved into a place that is part California, part Ireland, and part China, but its wide streets are unable to mask a strong feel of the Australian bush even in the city center. A statue of Queen Victoria marks the entrance to the city, whose affluence is evidenced by superb Victorian-era public buildings that are among the finest in Australia. The Court House and Post Office in Pall Mall evoke a confidence and optimism few modern governments could hope to emulate. The Joss House has remained in continuous use as a Chinese temple since the 1860s. Gold mining was obviously a thirsty business, as it left to Bendigo a legacy of more than 50 pubs.

The road from Melbourne passes the **Central Deborah Gold Mine**, which provides visitors an opportunity to go underground and experience something of the life of a gold miner. The best way to see Bendigo is to take the tram that runs from the Central Deborah mine to the Joss House and provides an audio commentary.

DINING AND STAYING IN BENDIGO

The **Copper Pot** at 8 Howard Place in Bendigo has been recognized as one of Victoria's best restaurants for more than 20 years. It offers an unusual combination of international, Asian, and Middle Eastern cuisine. The **Bar Blacksheep** at 58 Bull Street is a former garage that serves great burgers, satay, and onion rings. Little has changed at the **Rifle Brigade** since it served thirsty goldminers in the 1850s, although the diverse menu, which includes trout and steak, is a big improvement on the "bully beef" of the time. They brew their own beer here, and it is worth a try (but don't drink too much if you're driving—the Victoria Police strictly enforce a .05 percent blood alcohol limit, the equivalent of three beers in one hour).

There is a wide range of accommodation in Bendigo; the ▶ **Shamrock Hotel**, built in 1897, is the most notable. In the 1970s the state government spent more than A$2 million to restore the hotel to its original condition. The Shamrock is a magnificent example of Victorian-era architecture, a four-story visual delight of towers, balconies, and iron lacework that also offers good accommodations and an excellent restaurant. Located on Pall Mall, the hotel forms part of a precinct of Victorian buildings that also includes the Post Office and Courthouse, all of which are protected by the National Trust. ▶ **Australian Designer Travel** (Tel: 054/41-5133) can arrange private accommodations in historic houses in Bendigo.

Castlemaine

About 32 km (20 miles) south of Bendigo is Castlemaine, another former gold town turned service center for the surrounding country communities. Its **Castlemaine Market**, built in the style of a Roman basilica, was once the region's center of commercial life, where miners came to sell their gold and buy their provisions. A National Trust monument, today it houses a heritage exhibition and arts and crafts displays. Castlemaine was the original home of Castlemaine XXXX beer, better known as the national drink of Queensland. When the brewery faced financial ruin early in the century, it was sold and moved to Brisbane. The ▶ **Midland Hotel** at 2 Templeton Street dates from 1879 and offers unusual accommodations (lots of dark Edwardian-era furniture) and a sitting room with a huge open-hearth fireplace.

Maldon

Twenty kilometers (12 miles) northwest of Castlemaine is Maldon, a true step back in time. Known as Australia's first "notable town," Maldon has not seen a single new building constructed in nearly a century. As a result, the town has been the location for many of Australia's films, particularly in the 1970s, when Australian filmmaking was dominated by historical dramas such as *My Brilliant Career* and more offbeat works such as *Picnic at Hanging Rock*. Timber buildings with shady verandahs and old-fashioned, handmade-brick and stone cottages line the town's wide streets, which were planted with Dutch elms in 1875. The Beehive Chimney smokestack, built in 1862, is a landmark. Gracious public buildings, churches, and old hotels add charm to the township. There are many small accommodation options in Maldon. Typical is the ► **Scotch-Pie House Stables** with one double and one twin room located, as the name implies, in former horse stables. ► **School Cottage**, which also provides good accommodations, was built in the 1860s and now offers two double rooms and one twin room. Its former role as a school gives it a unique ambience.

The Murray

The Murray River originates in the Snowy Mountains in Eastern Victoria and twists and turns for nearly 2,000 miles west to the coast near Adelaide. But it is at its most accessible (and some say its most attractive) about two hours north of Bendigo, particularly around the old river port of Echuca, once the busiest in Australia. In the days before rail and highway transport, the Murray was the only way to move produce from the Outback and to take provisions inland to the pioneer settlers. A rather thin band of water, the river follows a tortuous path through one of the world's harshest environments. It remains today the lifeblood of towns such as Echuca and Swan Hill.

Echuca, whose name is the Koorie aboriginal word for "meeting of the waters," lies at the junction of the Murray and Campaspie rivers. A section of the magnificent red-gum wharf still stands, a reminder of the thriving paddle steamer industry. Echuca's past was immortalized in the television series "All the Rivers Run," which featured a boat named the *Philadelphia*, one of several paddle steamers that remain on the river. Day trips can be booked at the Port of Echuca, a National Trust area. A unique feature of the town is an old building close to the wharf, the only former brothel in Australia preserved by the National Trust.

Farther downriver is **Swan Hill**, another former port. The Murray Valley Highway roughly parallels the river, and the journey by road between the towns will take about four hours. Although not as well preserved as Echuca, Swan Hill is home to the **Pioneer Museum**, which features a large riverside exhibition of 19th-century life in the region.

It is easy to see why Australia's early explorers were so confused when they first began to chart the Murray. Between Echuca and Swan Hill (and for another 300 miles beyond that), it flows northwest toward the continent's barren interior, and until the 1840s it was assumed that the river must flow into an inland sea. Eventually it was discovered that the Darling River (which originates in Queensland) joins the Murray, soon after which it abruptly turns south and ultimately flows into the Indian Ocean. There was no inland sea—just the Outback.

Accommodation in the area is plentiful, but mostly of the motel type, with ▶ **Flag International** or ▶ **Best Western** offering the most options. There is also a good range of farm accommodations, which can be arranged by ▶ **Australian Homestays and Farm Holidays** or the ▶ **Host Farms Association**. ▶ **Inhouse Bed and Breakfast Australia** also has a range of accommodation options throughout the area. (See the Accommodations Reference list at the end of this chapter.)

GETTING AROUND

Melbourne is the gateway to southern Australia, with good domestic air connections to Sydney and other cities and direct international service from North America (via Qantas, United, Continental, and Air New Zealand), Asia, and Europe (British Airways, Qantas, Cathay Pacific, and Singapore Airlines) to Tullamarine Airport. The airport is about 20 km (12 miles) from the central business district and the major hotels; cab fares average A$22.

It is easy to find your way around Melbourne, but if you

rent a car and drive, beware of trams (you'll know this already if you've seen the charming 1986 Australian film *Malcolm*). Trams travel on fixed rails. They will not swerve in front of your vehicle, but they will continue exactly where they intended to go—regardless of where you are at the time. Cars must stop when trams stop, to permit disembarking passengers to use the road with safety. You may only pass a tram on the left. You can ride the tram all day for A$8.20; purchase passes at railway stations or onboard trams.

The commercial district has several unusual intersections where right-hand turns are made from the left-hand lane in order for drivers to avoid the unpleasant experience of being sandwiched between two trams.

There are hundreds of tour options in Melbourne, including helicopter tours, chauffeured limousine tours (Budget operates chauffeured cars and has an extensive tour program; Tel: 03/429-4900), vintage-car tours, and even tours by horse-drawn coach. The RACV (Royal Automobile Club of Victoria) Travel office on Collins Street near the Melbourne Town Hall has information and brochures on touring, and can provide detailed maps.

Travelling out of the city is easy; major freeways and highways are clearly marked. To get onto the freeway to Geelong via the Westgate Bridge, simply proceed to the southern end of the city and cross the river at Spencer, William, Queen, or Swanston Street; signs will clearly direct you from there. There are two routes to the Dandenongs: Drive east on either the Eastern Freeway or South Eastern Arterial, and to the Mornington Peninsula travel straight down St. Kilda Road to the Nepean Highway. If you are heading to Phillip Island, follow signs to the South Eastern Arterial. It is a 28-km (17-mile) trip to the South Gippsland Highway. Be careful of this road—it looks like a freeway, but there are four major intersections along it. Get an early start, because traffic on the arterial after 3:00 P.M. can be so bad that you might miss the Penguin Parade.

ACCOMMODATIONS REFERENCE

The rates given here are projections for 1994. Where a range of rates is given, the lower figure is the low-season rate, the higher figure the high-season rate. Unless otherwise indicated, rates are for double room, double occupancy. As prices are subject to change, always double-check before booking.

▶ **Australian Designer Travel.** 112 Queen Street, **Bendigo**, Vic. 3550. Tel: (054) 41-5133; Fax: (054) 41-1694. A$80–A$120.

▶ **Australian Homestays and Farm Holidays.** First floor, Albert Park Hotel, 83 Dundas Place, **Albert Park**, Vic. 3206. Tel: (03) 696-0433; Fax: (03) 696-0329. A$50–A$90.

▶ **Best Western.** 27 Raglan Street, **South Melbourne**, Vic. 3000. Tel: (03) 690-4722; toll-free in Australia, (008) 222-2166. A$60–A$150.

▶ **Burnham Beeches Country House.** Sherbrooke Road, **Sherbrooke**, Vic. 3789. Tel: (03) 755-1903. A$225–A$285.

▶ **Cape Otway Cottage.** Hordernvale Road, **Hordernvale**, Vic. 3238. Tel: (052) 37-9256. A$140.

▶ **Country Comfort Old Melbourne.** 5-17 Flemington Road, **North Melbourne**, Vic. 3051. Tel: (03) 329-9344; Fax: (03) 328-4870; in U.S., (800) 44-UTELL; in Canada, (800) 387-8842. A$140.

▶ **Cowes Colonial Motor Inn.** 192 Thompson Avenue, **Cowes**, Vic. 3922. Tel: (059) 52-2486. A$65–A$85.

▶ **Cumberland Lorne Resort.** 150 Mountjoy Parade, **Lorne**, Vic. 3232. Tel: (052) 892-400; Fax: (052) 892-256; toll-free in Australia, (008) 037-010; in U.S., (800) 44-UTELL; in Canada, (800) 387-8842. A$165–A$210.

▶ **Dublin House Inn.** 57 Bank Street, **Port Fairy**, Vic. 3284. Tel: (055) 681-822. A$64.

▶ **Flag International.** 132 Bank Street, **South Melbourne**, Vic. 3205. Tel: (03) 132-400; toll-free in Australia, (008) 028-889; in U.S. and Canada, (800) 624-FLAG; in Los Angeles, (213) 277-9037. A$60–A$200.

▶ **Glenisla Homestead.** Hamilton Highway, **Cavendish**, Vic. 3408. Tel: (053) 80-1532. A$195.

▶ **Gordon Place.** 24-32 Little Bourke Street, **Melbourne**, Vic. 3000. Tel: (03) 663-2888; Fax: (03) 639-1537; in U.S., (800) 44-UTELL; in Canada, (800) 387-8842. A$156.

▶ **Grand Hyatt.** 123 Collins Street, **Melbourne**, Vic. 3000. Tel: (03) 657-1234; Fax: (03) 650-3491; in U.S., (800) 228-9000; in Alaska and Hawaii, (800) 228-9005. A$185–A$265.

▶ **Hilton on the Park.** 192 Wellington Parade, **East Melbourne**, Vic. 3002. Tel: (03) 419-3311; Fax: (03) 419-5630; in U.S., (800) 445-8667. A$150–A$280.

▶ **Host Farms Association.** 322 Banyule Road, **View Bank**, Vic. 3084. Tel: (03) 457-5413; Fax: (03) 457-6725. A$50–A$100.

▶ **Hotel Como.** 630 Chapel Street, **South Yarra**, Vic. 3141. Tel: (03) 824-0400; Fax: (03) 824-1263. A$235.

▶ **Inhouse Bed and Breakfast Australia.** P.O. Box 907, **Bendigo**, Vic. 3550. Tel: (057) 26-9291. A$50–A$100.

▶ **Lightkeeper's Inn.** 64 Great Ocean Road, **Airey's Inlet**, Vic. 3221. Tel: (052) 89-6666; Fax: (052) 89-6806. A$55–A$128.

▶ **Loft in the Mill.** 3 Harold Street, **Olinda**, Vic. 3788. Tel: (03) 751-1700; Fax: (03) 751-2030. A$90.

▶ **Le Meridien Melbourne.** 495 Collins Street, **Melbourne**, Vic. 3000. Tel: (03) 620-9111; Fax: (03) 614-1219; in U.S., (800) 44-UTELL; in Canada, (800) 387-8842. A$225.

▶ **Mid City Motor Inn.** 525 Raglan Parade, **Warrnambool**, Vic. 3280. Tel: (055) 62-3866; Fax: (055) 62-0923. A$76–A$99.

▶ **Midland Hotel.** 2 Templeton Street, **Castlemaine**, Vic. 3450. Tel: (054) 72-1085. A$80.

▶ **Mietta's Queenscliff Hotel.** 16 Gellibrand Street, **Queenscliff**, Vic. 3225. Tel: (052) 52-1066; Fax: (052) 52-1899. A$235–A$270.

▶ **Miners Retreat.** 602 Eureka Street, **Ballarat**, Vic. 3350. Tel: (053) 31-6900. A$46–A$49.

▶ **Narrabeen Cottage.** 16 Steele Street, **Cowes, Phillip Island**, Vic. 3922. Tel: (059) 522-062. A$134–A$220.

▶ **Olde Maritime Motor Inn.** Corner of Banyan and Merri streets, **Warrnambool**, Vic. 3280. Tel: (055) 61-1415; Fax: (055) 62-0767. A$70–A$110.

▶ **Ozone Hotel.** 42 Gellibrand Street, **Queenscliff**, Vic. 3225. Tel: (052) 521-011; Fax: (052) 52-3712. A$95–A$120.

▶ **Parkroyal Melbourne.** 111 Little Collins Street, **Melbourne**, Vic. 3000. Tel: (03) 659-1000; Fax: (03) 659-0999. A$250.

▶ **Parkroyal on St. Kilda Road.** 562 St. Kilda Road, **Melbourne**, Vic. 3004. Tel: (03) 529-8888; Fax: (03) 525-1242. A$215.

▶ **Radisson President.** 65 Queens Road, **South Melbourne**, Vic. 3004. Tel: (03) 529-4300; Fax: (03) 521-3111. A$175.

▶ **The Regent of Melbourne.** 25 Collins Street, **Melbourne**, Vic. 3000. Tel: (03) 653-0000; Fax: (03) 650-4261; in U.S., (800) 545-4000; in Canada, (800) 626-8222. A$260.

▶ **Rockman's Regency Hotel.** Corner Exhibition and Lonsdale streets, **Melbourne**, Vic. 3000. Tel: (03) 662-3900; Fax: (03) 663-4297; in U.S., (800) 223-6800; in Canada, (800) 341-8585. A$295.

▶ **School Cottage.** 115 High Street, **Maldon**, Vic. 3463. Tel: (054) 75-2658. A$60.

▶ **Scotch-Pie House Stables.** 63 Main Street, **Maldon**, Vic. 3463. Tel: (054) 75-2654. A$70.

▶ **Seamist.** Corner of Wensleydale Station and Gum Flat roads, **Winchelsea**, Vic. 3241. Tel: (052) 88-7255 or 88-7365; Fax: (052) 88-7457. A$75–A$80.

▶ **Shamrock Hotel.** Corner of Pall Mall and Williamson Street, **Bendigo**, Vic. 3550. Tel: (054) 43-0333; Fax: (054) 42-4494. A$60–A$170.

▶ **Sheraton Towers Southgate.** Suite 18, 51-55 City Road, **South Melbourne**, Vic. 3205. Tel: (03) 696-3100; Fax: (03) 686-1381. A$280.

▶ **Trenavin Park.** Ventnor Road, **Phillip Island**, Vic. 3922. Tel: (059) 56-8230. A$100.

▶ **Victoria Hotel.** 215 Little Collins Street, **Melbourne**, Vic. 3000. Tel: (03) 653-0441; Fax: (03) 650-9678. A$80–A$99.

▶ **Vue Grand Private Hotel.** 46 Hesse Street, **Queens-cliff**, Vic. 3225. Tel: (052) 52-1544; Fax: (052) 52-3471. A$280.

▶ **Windsor Hotel.** 103-115 Spring Street, **Melbourne**, Vic. 3000. Tel: (03) 653-0653; Fax: (03) 654-5183. A$199–A$260.

ADELAIDE AND SOUTH AUSTRALIA

By Kerry Kenihan

Kerry Kenihan is a journalist, travel writer, and author of six books. She is also an author and coauthor of a series of international travel guides and a member of the Australian Society of Travel Writers. She lives in the Adelaide Hills.

After Edinburgh, there's Adelaide. The Adelaide Festival of the Arts, Australia's best-known biennial arts festival (even-numbered years), evokes cosmopolitan vitality. In odd-numbered years, the internationally acclaimed youth festival Come Out takes place, also in March. And year-round, city, metropolitan, and country festivals abound— enough to earn South Australia its nickname: the Festival State. Visitors also come in ever-increasing numbers for November's Formula One Grand Prix; Adelaide is acclaimed by international drivers for having the world's most outstanding street circuit. And nowhere else in Australia can visitors gamble in such elegant surroundings as those of the Adelaide Casino.

Surrounded by acres of parkland, the state capital, backed by a crescent of hills, is a city of pubs and churches. Its gracious Victorian and Edwardian buildings do not reflect a history of English convict labor; South Australia was the nation's only completely non-convict state. (Ironically, the concept of colonizing the state with free men was planned by Edward Gibbon Wakefield while he served three years (1830–1832) in England's Newgate Gaol for marital indiscretions.)

With only one million people, Adelaide has a small-town, almost folksy atmosphere. You can walk or cycle the parklands and play golf and tennis within a mile of downtown. In the city and close suburbs, more than 600 restaurants and pubs offer international cuisine and fine wines. West of Adelaide, safe swimming beaches extend southward for 18 miles.

Adelaide is also the gateway for numerous attractions in South Australia, including wine country, Kangaroo Island nature preserve, the Riverland, the colorful Flinders Ranges, and the unusual opal-mining town of Coober Pedy in the Outback. The southern wine coast or the Barossa Valley and Clare Valley vineyards can be seen on a day trip from the city, as can Kangaroo Island. A tranquil experience fishing, canoeing, and bird-watching from a Murray River houseboat can be enjoyed in a one-night trip from Adelaide, but for a cruise out of the Riverland's Renmark Harbour on the Southern Hemisphere's biggest paddle wheeler, allocate at least three days and three nights. You should plan at least a one-night stay in the Flinders Ranges or the town of Coober Pedy if you want to have time to appreciate fully the scenic splendor and wildlife of the ancient ranges or the Outback eccentricity of the opal-mining town.

Adelaide's climate is Mediterranean. Summers can include heat waves; winter is cool, and June is the wettest month. September to May is best for a visit. Bring casual dress, of course, but also semiformal wear (coat and tie for men) for the casino and the top restaurants.

MAJOR INTEREST

Adelaide
Parks and gardens
Museums
Pubs and restaurants
Festivals
The Hills

South Australia outside Adelaide
The wine country, especially the Barossa Valley
Kangaroo Island
Coober Pedy: opal mining, underground living

ADELAIDE

Colonel William Light, son of Captain Francis Light, who was the founder of Penang in Malaysia, designed his utopian walking city (named after Queen Adelaide, consort of England's King William IV) like a chessboard, interspersed with and encompassed by parks and gardens. Light had been appointed South Australia's surveyor-general, with executive power over even the governor, to locate and plan the city. The downtown area is one mile square and bordered on all sides by the wide, tree-lined East, South, West, and North terraces; parklands extend back from each of these boulevards.

Adelaide is an easy city to get around on foot; it's flat and compact, and the central parks of Whitmore, Hurtle, Victoria, Hindmarsh, and Light squares offer shady places to relax. East Terrace features some grand old homes (old for South Australia), and edges the Victoria Park Racecourse and Rymill Park, both of which are part of the Grand Prix circuit each November. North Terrace is dotted with outdoor cafés and has many of the city's most gracious buildings—Ayers House, an elegant, bluestone English Regency-style mansion; Parliament House, which is made of marble and granite in the classical revival style; and the Gothic Bonython Hall, which is part of Adelaide University. Bluestone and local sandstone buildings of the past contrast gracefully with the cement and glass of modern structures in Adelaide.

The city's northern parklands, originally laid out by Light, are formal gardens, and include the Botanic Gardens, the Zoological Gardens, the gardens of Government House, and Adelaide Oval and Elder Park. The Torrens River and the man-made Torrens Lake run through these parklands, and beyond the river is the suburb of North Adelaide. North Adelaide's design, unlike Light's grid layout for downtown, was dictated by the relatively hilly topography here. Today it is a cosmopolitan center in its own right: the original settlers' colonial cottages rub shoulders with historic pubs and the mansions in which the 17th-century nouveaux riches lived.

Exploring the City

If your accommodation is centrally located, take to the wide streets on foot. **Victoria Square**, the geographical

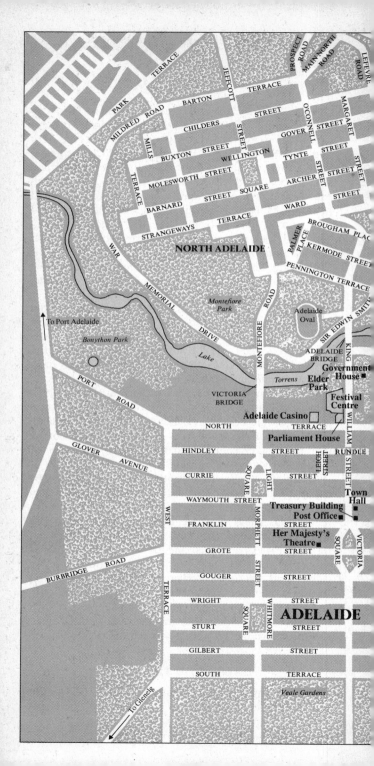

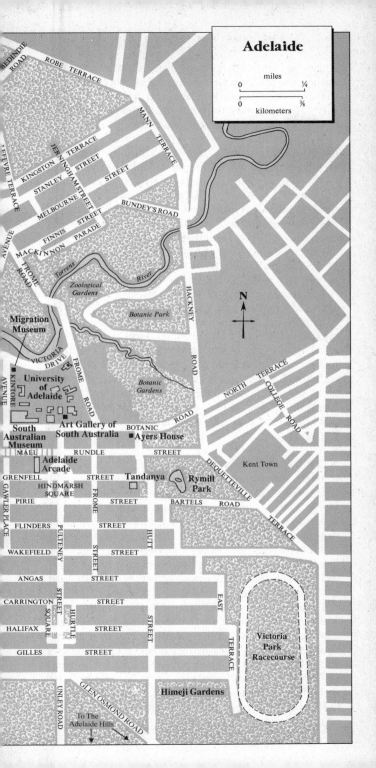

center of Light's city plan, is a good place to start. Just around the corner is **Grote Street**'s colorful market (great for economy al fresco lunches), and opposite is **Her Majesty's Theatre**, which has been refurbished to become one of the city's best and most intimate stage venues.

Walking north along King William Street, you will pass the Post Office (1867), Treasury buildings (dating from 1839), and the Town Hall (1863). Three blocks north of Victoria Square, turn east onto Grenfell Street and at number 252 you will find **Tandanya**, an aboriginal cultural center that reflects the heritage, tradition, language, mythology, crafts, and visual and performing arts of 50 aboriginal groups in South Australia.

One block north of Grenfell Street is **Rundle Mall**, a pedestrian mall that houses Adelaide's best shops—from department stores to boutiques—and street performers.

At the eastern end of Rundle Street just before East Terrace is the **East End Market**. It was originally the city's wholesale produce market, and is now a restored complex of stalls with fresh produce, local handicrafts and jewelry, and second-hand and antiquarian books. At the western end of Rundle Mall, boisterous **Hindley Street** (or Little Europe) boasts clubs and outdoor cafés that are good for people-watching and reflect the city's mix of nationalities. **Marcellina's** at 273 Hindley Street is a café that becomes a club and restaurant after dark (open until 5:00 A.M.).

NORTH TERRACE

Just one street north of Hindley is tree-lined North Terrace, where you'll find the Convention Centre and the Monte Carlo–style **Adelaide Casino**, which has a 1930s atmosphere, created by internal Corinthian columns and magnificent crystal chandeliers above the gaming tables. Its **Pullman** restaurant offers a very good smorgasbord for lunch, dinner, and Sunday brunch in an airy setting, and its cozy **Wine Bar** offers a wide selection of South Australian wines. The casino is open until 4:00 A.M.

To the east of King William Street on North Terrace is the **South Australian Museum**, which houses Australian bird, mammal, fish, and reptile exhibits. The **Art Gallery of South Australia** at North Terrace hosts visiting exhibitions and sells prints from its Australia collection. The nearby University of Adelaide features many fine old buildings, including castlelike Bonython Hall, where concerts are held. Also at the university, the rustic atmosphere, Torrens River view, and fresh seafood, steak, and pasta of the

University Union Bistro draw a cultured and business crowd for lunch and dinner. Call to reserve; Tel: (08) 223-5432. The sidewalk cafés of North Terrace are filled with students in summer.

Ayers House, on the opposite side of North Terrace, is the restored Regency manor of former state premier Henry Ayers (after whom the famous Ayers Rock was named). The house is now the headquarters of the National Trust of South Australia. Open for public inspection (except Mondays), the manor includes the **Henry Ayers Room,** one of Adelaide's most prestigious restaurants, where you dine on local seafood and fresh produce served at well-spaced tables. Surrounded by antiques and art, you will feel transported into the past—almost as if you were a personal guest of Henry Ayers himself. Reservations are a must; Tel: (08) 224-0666. The leafy **Paxton's Conservatory** here is a less formal choice for lunch or dinner.

TO NORTH ADELAIDE

North of North Terrace and close to King William Street is Kintore Avenue, where Australia's only **Migration Museum** stands on the site of the former Destitute Asylum of the 1870s (in which children were imprisoned). The museum traces the history of foreign settlement in Australia and also has changing exhibitions on the impact of various groups in transforming the nation into a multicultural society. On the museum grounds, **Mrs. Gifford's Café** is an old-fashioned, inexpensive, and casual luncheon stop. Its light fare attracts both businesspeople and visitors. Tel: (08) 223-1935.

Just down from the angular Festival Centre on King William Road (King William Street becomes King William Road above North Terrace) you can take a motor-launch cruise of the Torrens River or hire a paddleboat at Captain Jolley's, next to the bridge. Above is the seemingly uninviting **Jolley's Boathouse Bistro,** but inside and on the balcony overlooking the river you'll lunch with local executives on artistically presented and moderately priced cuisine. The decor is simple—potted plants and director's chairs in a casual atmosphere—but chic.

Walk or take the bus along King William Road to North Adelaide, past parks with floral displays and tennis and golf facilities; King William Road becomes O'Connell Street after you reach Brougham Place.

North Adelaide is the city's oldest urban area, with restored bluestone cottages, mansions, terraced houses featuring intricate iron lacework, and many restaurants, pubs, and small contemporary art galleries. You'll find the galleries along **O'Connell Street** and the streets nearby: the **BMG Fine Art Gallery**, for example, at 83 Tynte Street, and **Gallery Bonython-Meadmore** at 88 Jerningham Street.

PORT ADELAIDE

Buses depart from Grenfell Street, the eastern continuation of Currie Street across King William Street, for the 15-km (9-mile) ride north to Port Adelaide, where South Australia's maritime heart is exposed in impressive, restored 19th-century buildings. This is a compact area, so walk and discover the **Maritime Museum**'s seven separate locations around the port, beginning at 119 Lipson Street. There's a lighthouse dating from 1869, and a sound and light show at the Bond Store, built in 1854. Here, in this award-winning museum, you can capture the environment—sights, sounds, and even smells—that immigrants experienced as they sailed into the fledgling colony.

For an intimate guided walk around the port, contact **Tourabout Adelaide**; Tel: (08) 362-9614. Reservations are essential.

End a leisurely stroll around the port at a restored boutique-brewery-brasserie—the **Port Dock Hotel** on Todd Street. The look of this public bar has changed little since its days as a meeting place for former seafarers and clients of its brothel. A lofty covered extension is the place to taste Old Preacher Ale, mischievously named after a temperance preacher who forced the pub's closure for 77 years. In the summer a Sunday lunch here—with seafood and pasta on the menu and live entertainment—is relaxed and inexpensive. The port has a colorful market on Sunday as well.

City Tours

If you don't want to walk, there are other, interesting ways to orient yourself in the city. Between October and April (Adelaide's sunniest months), **pedicab** tours (for two adults, A$20) leave from 400 William Street; Tel: (08) 83-2203 if you don't see a pedicab parked there. You may want to bargain for a point-to-point fee. An elegant, year-round alternative is an hour-long tour of the city or parks tour by horse-drawn **Hansom Cab**. Hansom cabs are also available for romantic day and night tours and for city and garden tours that include a picnic lunch and Champagne.

Adelaide, with its surrounding parks, historic homes, and city night lights, is an enchanting place for a carriage ride. One-hour tours start at A$40; Tel: (08) 212-3355.

Another option is to take an **Explorer Tram** tour from Tourism South Australia's Travel Centre, 1 King William Street at the corner of North Terrace. The tram, actually a bus, departs at 9:20 A.M., 12:05 P.M., and 2:25 P.M. daily, and costs A$16 (A$10 for children). A guide supplies commentary during the trip, and you can alight from the tram at any stop along the way and reboard 90 minutes later. The tram takes in the Adelaide Casino and the **Old Parliament House** on North Terrace. The latter is Australia's only museum dedicated to the nation's political history. It holds changing exhibitions, and shows a video, *The South Australian Story,* that provides visitors with excellent background information. The museum's restaurant, on the rear terrace, is a casual place to lunch and serves good fish and other seafood as well as pasta.

The tram continues on to the **Festival Centre**, which includes a concert hall, the Lyric experimental theater, an amphitheater, and the Playhouse Gallery, which offers changing exhibitions. **Lyrics Restaurant** and the less formal **Playhouse Bistro** overlook Torrens Lake, and are open for lunch, supper, and dinner. The center is home to the internationally renowned biennial **Adelaide Festival of the Arts**, and also of the Fringe. **The Fringe** is a separate experimental arts festival that precedes and follows the Adelaide Festival; it is designed for young people and families on lower budgets and includes all aspects of the arts. Many visitors schedule their Adelaide Festival stays to include Fringe entertainment—the festivals are held during February and March in even-numbered years.

After the Festival Centre, the tram passes the **Botanic Gardens** with its **Botanic Gardens Restaurant**, open daily for lunch only (reservations advisable Fridays, Sundays, and Mondays; Tel: 08/223-3526). The gardens include a space-age conservatory of tropical plants (the largest in the Southern Hemisphere). The tram's next stop is the 112-year-old **Adelaide Zoological Gardens**. This attractive zoo by the Torrens River is small but is an international leader in the preservation of endangered species.

Finally, the Explorer Tram takes you to the seaside suburb of **Glenelg**, which has a marina, a safe beach, and a replica of HMS *Buffalo,* the ship that brought the first governor to South Australia in 1836. The **HMS Buffalo** is both a maritime museum and a fine seafood restaurant; Tel: (08) 294-7000. Glenelg has a variety of other seafood restaurants, and several reflect the ethnic backgrounds of the area's European and Asian settlers. On Glenelg's foreshore, the ▶ **Ramada Grand Hotel**, a restored former pub built at the turn of the century, has accommodations with Victorian elegance as well as a health club and conference facilities. You can reach Glenelg independently by taking Adelaide's only real tram from King William Street at the southern end of Victoria Square in the city center—the ride to Glenelg takes 20 minutes.

If your interest runs to stately mansions, antiques, and English country-style gardens, visit **Carrick Hill**, a Tudor-style manor at 590 Fullarton Road in suburban Springfield, 6½ km (4 miles) from the city. It's open Wednesday to Saturday from 10:00 A.M. to 5:00 P.M.; closed in July.

Staying in Adelaide

Adelaide has three five-star hotels. The central ▶ **Hilton International**, in Victoria Square, has 380 rooms, making it one of the smallest in the Hilton chain. The marbled lobby is a favorite meeting place for locals, who often breakfast in the Hilton's busy coffee shop, the **Marketplace Café**. **The Grange** restaurant has an international menu. The hotel's Margaux nightclub is currently regarded as the best in town.

Only two minutes' walk from the Festival Centre on King William Road and connected by a walkway to the Adelaide Casino, the ▶ **Hyatt Regency Adelaide**, fronting North Terrace, is in the high-price range. Its presidential suite comes equipped with telescope for 360-degree views. The hotel's decor features works by painters, ceramists, potters, and glassblowers commissioned to reflect the past and present of South Australia, and its Japanese **Shiki** restaurant has won awards for its cuisine. The flagship restaurant is **Blake's**; the **Riverside Restaurant** is open from 7:00 A.M. until very late.

Almost directly opposite the Hyatt is the ▶ **Terrace Intercontinental**, which has an intimate atmosphere rare in a five-star hotel. The hotel has 335 rooms, including executive and presidential suites. The gracious **Crystal Room**, serving innovative international cuisine, offers a bird's-eye view of North Terrace and Parliament House. A more earthy view is commanded at **Spices**, where Indian (including Tandoori), Indonesian, Thai, Malaysian, and Hong Kong–style Chinese food is served in the only upscale (but reasonably priced) restaurant of its kind in South Australia.

The ▶ **Country Comfort Inn** (formerly the Parkroyal Motel) at 226 South Terrace is a classy motel with good views of the southern parklands; the ▶ **Hindley Parkroyal**, at 65 Hindley Street, has 39 suites with kitchens (for self-caterers) in addition to its 177 rooms. The rooms are set back from bustling Hindley Street. Old-fashioned service is paramount here. At the quieter end of Hindley Street is the new ▶ **West End All Suite Hotel**, which has roomy self-catering suites and studios. There's also a spa and restaurant here. ▶ **Apartments on the Park**, at 274 South Terrace (between Pulteney and Hutt streets), is another central-Adelaide accommodation appealing to those who want to cook for themselves. Though there isn't a restaurant in this medium-price-range facility, there are plenty close by.

For parkland at your feet and the finest view of the city, day or night, book a south-facing room on an upper floor of the ▶ **Quality Hotel Adelaide** at 62 Brougham Place, which is off O'Connell Street in North Adelaide. (O'Connell Street is a continuation of King William Road.) This hotel was Adelaide's first of international standard. Its **Brougham Restaurant** has a great night view and good food.

For a taste of what life for the landed gentry must have been like in colonial Australia, there's the ▶ **North Adelaide Heritage Apartments** and **Adelaide Heritage Cottages**. Comprised of eight different accommodations ranging in size from one to three bedrooms, the properties are all State Heritage–listed buildings. Decorated with antiques and set within North Adelaide's parklands, the addresses remain private until booking, affording guests the utmost privacy.

▶ **Adelaide's Bed and Breakfast**, an economical boutique hotel, occupies an 1870 sandstone house in the heart of town. It's not ritzy (only one room has a private bath), but fairly oozes historic charm. Adelaide also has several home-style bed-and-breakfast accommodations. Select from 15 city or near-city establishments in the *Bed and Breakfast Town and Country* brochure available at the Travel Centre at 1 King William Street. The brochure also offers 22 alternatives in the Adelaide Hills, between 20 and 40 minutes' drive from the city.

Shopping in Adelaide

Many shops in central **Rundle Mall** and its bordering streets, particularly the northern end of King William

Street, have interesting Australiana items, including books, cuddly stuffed animals, tee-shirts, crafts, original paintings by local artists, pottery, and kangaroo and sheepskin products. If you need a break from browsing, enter a haven reminiscent of Hong Kong—the **Choy Sin** (meaning "drunken saint") at St. James Place off the mall. This plush downstairs restaurant offers all major Chinese cuisines, complemented by excellent S.A. wines; Tel: (08) 346-7343.

For antiques, browse the shops on Unley Road, which leads to the Adelaide Hills (see below). If you are not planning to visit Coober Pedy, visit **Olympic Opal Jewellers**, 5 Rundle Mall, which has a simulated opal mine and offers discounts to overseas visitors. South of Rundle Mall is Gawler Place, where the **Opal Mine**, at number 30, also offers discounts. King William Street has several other opal outlets as well.

Dining in Adelaide

Competition among the large number of restaurants in Adelaide has resulted in high standards and relatively low prices.

King George whiting, a fish specialty of South Australia, is featured on many restaurant menus. Prawns, lobster, and fresh fish (caught locally) are excellent, and Coffin Bay oysters rival the Sydney Rock variety. Stroll Gouger Street, where fish cafés such as **Pauls**, **Stanley's**, **The Gouger**, and **The Rock Lobster** (which may be serving the rare razor fish while you're there) are no-fuss establishments offering good South Australian fish. South Australian restaurants also offer kangaroo meat, which is gamey and tender after hanging, marinating, and roasting or broiling. It is featured at **Chloe's**, a popular restaurant housed in an elegant mansion at 36 College Road, Kent Town, five minutes by cab northeast of the city center. The menu at Chloe's includes smoked fish gâteau, red snapper, and saddle of kangaroo. Chloe's smokes its own fish and boasts more than 20,000 bottles of Australian and imported wines in the cellar. Call for reservations; Tel: (08) 362-2574. For real Aussie "tucker" visit **Kents** in Kent Town at 69 Fullarton Road, where char-grilled witchetty grubs, air-dried emu, and gum-smoked kangaroo are served with flair; Tel: (08) 364-2955.

At 73 Angas Street, an unprepossessing central business location just a short walk east of the Hilton, you will find authentic spicy northern Chinese and top-quality

Szechuan cuisine at the **Beijing**. It's quietly informal and inexpensive, the food is excellent and nicely presented, and the Peking duck doesn't require 24 hours' notice. The silver-threaded bun is a special accompaniment; Tel: (08) 232-1388.

For excellent Italian food, try the rustic yet upscale **Rigoni's Bistro** at 27 Leigh Street, just west of King William Street. It's crowded with businesspeople at lunch, and out-of-town celebrities are likely to be seen choosing from a great salad bar with huge antipasto selections or contemplating the blackboard menu that changes daily. Tel: (08) 231-5160.

Kaiseki-ryori, a refined, delicate form of Japanese cuisine, isn't on the menu at the **Matsuri Restaurant** at 167 Gouger Street, a stroll west from the Hilton, but devotees of this hard-to-find and artistically presented style of food can order it in advance (Tel: 08/231-3494). Decor is authentic, floor-level tables are available, traditional dishes and sushi are on the menu, and the good wine list includes Japanese imports.

Adelaide's only Russian restaurant, the **Volga**, centrally located upstairs at 116 Flinders Street, has established a fine reputation in recent years for authentic cuisine served in a spacious setting that nonetheless has a cozy atmosphere. In summer there's dining outside on the balcony. Fridays and Saturdays, gypsy violins turn the Volga into a dinner-dance night spot where the vodka flows, accompanying caviar. The steak tartare, prepared at table to individual taste, is a dream. Lunch is served from noon Tuesday to Friday, dinner from 6:00 P.M. Monday to Saturday; Tel: (08) 232-0441.

A short walk east from Brougham Place off O'Connell is Melbourne Street, which has a few restored pubs and Adelaide's best Mexican restaurant, **Zapata's**, at number 42. Open for lunch on Fridays and for dinner Tuesday through Saturday, it has a white stucco interior complemented by dark wood furniture, lamps, and Mexican rugs. The food is neither heavy nor expensive; unusual liqueur coffees are featured. Reservations are recommended; Tel: (08) 267-4653.

Pubs and Nightlife in Adelaide

You'd never know South Australia was once a temperance state, as pubs proliferate here. Many of Adelaide's splendid old colonial hotels (pubs) that had fallen into disrepair have been restored. The counter lunch or counter tea is inexpensive, hearty, but fairly unimaginative in pubs that *haven't* been restored; however, those places have an authentic charm of their own.

At the **Earl of Aberdeen** pub, on the corner of Carrington and Pulteney streets not far east of Victoria Square, you can mix with locals as well as other visitors—and also enjoy excellent food. The pub was one of the first to be completely restored, and became a leader in innovative pub food of top quality. The pub's **Gazebo Restaurant**—exposed brick, glass roof, and lush greenery—specializes in aged steaks. You will find a variety of characters in the bar, especially on Saturday nights.

The **Colonel Light** in Light Square (west of King William Street at Currie Street) has also been restored to recapture the old colonial pub atmosphere; it has a balcony bistro.

The **Old Botanic Hotel**, at the corner of North and East terraces, is a good watering hole for a convivial pint or two. You might also get a bite to eat here after wandering the city's museum and art gallery on North Terrace.

At the west end of North Terrace is the Strathmore Hotel, which houses the **Balcony** restaurant, looking down on the bustling, historic street and offering a Sunday brunch and cosmopolitan lunch. The meals are heavy on seafood; also available are charcoal-grilled veal and pork. (The Strathmore has comfortable accommodations as well; see Staying in Adelaide, above.)

On Melbourne Street, North Adelaide, enjoy an ale at the **Old Lion**, whose brasserie includes a 103-year-old grapevine.

There are several discos and night spots in central Hindley Street (west off King William Street, opposite Rundle Mall). Action starts around 9:30 P.M., mostly with deejay music. For a clientele over 25 try **The Cargo Club**, 213 Hindley Street. **Margaux's on the Square** at the Hilton, with brass decor, provides an intimate setting Fridays (when there's an excellent combo) and Saturdays (late-night dancing and drinking). You'll meet out-of-towners here. **Le Rox** is a popular disco at 9 Light Square; it's open Wednesday, Friday, Saturday, and Sunday from 9:00 P.M.

Mystics, in the Terrace Hotel on North Terrace, has live entertainment and caters to an older crowd. It's open until 1:00 A.M. Wednesdays and Thursdays and until 3:00 A.M. Fridays and Saturdays. The Hyatt hotel's **Waves** (on North Terrace, just west of King William Street) claims to feature the world's most advanced computerized video and light technology. The crowd is mixed, from international visitors to young locals. To get into Waves, however, you must be a hotel guest or become a club member for A$10.

There's also the **Adelaide Casino**, next door to the Hyatt; see Exploring the City, above. The **Fezbah** at the Festival Centre swings with slick jazz after theater performances and from 11 P.M. Saturdays.

Don't leave town before experiencing Adelaide's pie floater (meaty pie in thick pea soup), sold evenings until late from curbside carts on North Terrace near the casino and outside the General Post Office in Victoria Square. It's a wake-up or a settler after a night on the town.

The Adelaide Hills

The Mount Lofty Ranges, more commonly known as the Adelaide Hills, embrace the city. Green for three-quarters of the year, they brown off in summer. From the lower hills there are lovely views of the Gulf of St. Vincent and the sea beyond. The Hills are astonishing for their resemblance to parts of England, East Prussia, and Bavaria, for early settlers planted their homelands' trees here to mingle with native Australian flora, and they built their homes in Old World styles.

Most tour-bus companies have Hills tours. The route 100 circle-line bus from Currie Street, for example, offers one-and-a-half-hour tours of the city, the southeast suburbs, and the lower hills. **A Little Shopping and Touring** is a tourism-award-winning company that offers personalized half- and full-day experiences to visitors. As its name suggests, the firm (run by former flight attendants Colleen and Helen) caters to people who like to shop for the unusual. The company also offers unusual tours, such as hot-air ballooning in the Barossa Valley combined with a four-wheel-drive Outback-style adventure on a working sheep ranch and a houseboat cruise on the Murray River—in the same day. Other tours focus on wildlife, wineries, orchards, crafts, museums, and Kangaroo Island (discussed below); Tel: (08) 274-1101. It's best, however, to rent a car, especially in spring. For a particularly scenic view from the Hills follow Unley Road, an extension of Pulteney Street that becomes Belair Road, south for 11 km (7 miles) to **Windy Point**.

Windy Point has an excellent formal—and expensive— à la carte restaurant called the **Starlight Room**, serving international food, and a more casual Italian bistro, **Peppi's**. At either place the city and suburbs are at your feet, with magnificent sunsets over the ocean in winter.

Reservations at both restaurants on Windy Point are essential; Tel: (08) 278-8255.

At 46 Unley Road, just out of the city, is the award-winning Indian restaurant the **Snake Charmer**. In its several rooms (behind a somewhat plain storefront) you will find all styles of Indian cuisine represented, with a wide selection of South Australian wines to accompany them. This is one of Adelaide's most popular eateries, particularly for theatergoers, who can take advantage of a special menu and discount if they dine between 5:30 and 7:00 P.M. The atmosphere here is casual, and the fare authentic, imaginative, and varied. Unley Road is lined with boutiques, restaurants where you can sample most of the world's cuisines, and antiques shops, many of which are worth stopping at to explore.

Southeast of the city, **Mount Lofty** is the highest point in the ranges—drive there for spectacular city views from the summit. Close by on Summit Road is **Cleland Conservation and Wildlife Park**, where you can cuddle a koala. Nighttime walks make it possible for visitors to observe nocturnal animals feeding. It is essential to book one week in advance; Tel: (08) 339-2444.

In addition to koalas, you can meet Australian species you never knew existed—pademelons, bettongs, and potoroos, marsupials all—on weekend dawn, day, and sunset walks (or by arrangement) at **Warrawong Sanctuary**, Stock Road, Mylor, not far off the South Eastern Freeway's Stirling exit. Reservations are necessary to visit Warrawong—Tel: (08) 388-5380—where creatures wander in their natural environment. You can breakfast with native birds in the sanctuary at the **Bird Garden Tearoom**.

The Hills' hub is **Hahndorf**, about 40 minutes from Adelaide on the South Eastern Freeway. The town, which resembles a German village, has a clock museum, galleries, and crafts shops selling calico, lace, copper, and woollen goods along one main street. Each January it hosts Schutzenfest; the name means "shooting festival," but the event really serves as an excuse to get into German costume, sing, dance, parade, and eat and drink German-style.

Hahndorf was home to the great landscapist Sir Hans Heysen. Heysen immigrated to Adelaide from Germany in 1883 and became Hahndorf's and Australia's most important artist. The Academy here has some of his works, which frequently depict the Adelaide Hills that he so loved. (Ask locally about hiking the so-called Heysen Trail.)

Towns in the Adelaide Hills are not far apart, being separated only by valleys, orchards, and groves that are most beautiful in spring and fall. Several towns spin off the freeway, though it's nicest to drive through the back roads to, for example, **Aldgate**, with its award-winning **Aldgate Crafts** shop featuring local woollen goods, pottery, art, and leatherware, or **Bridgewater**, an old flour-mill town, where the restored mill is now the winery of one of South Australia's most renowned small wine-makers, **Petaluma**. The vineyards spread over low, rolling hills.

Get a map from the Tourist Information Centre on Hahndorf's Main Street and wend your way on back roads to the city. You can also pick up an excellent map at any post office or gas station in Adelaide and the Hills. Another good resource is the *Adelaide Hills Weekender,* a free monthly newspaper listing regional happenings.

DINING AND STAYING IN THE ADELAIDE HILLS

For fresh, originally prepared produce and cozy atmos-phere in the Hills, try the **Petaluma Mill** or the ▶ **Uraidla Aristologist** (meaning "student of dining"), past Somer-ton at Uraidla on Greenhill Road, 30 minutes from the city. The Uraidla Aristologist also offers comfortably reno-vated stone cottages. The restaurant is open on weekends only, but during the rest of the week guests are welcome to cook for themselves in the kitchen.

A tranquil place to spend the night in the Hills is ▶ **Apple Tree Cottage**, an English-style country cottage with two period-furnished bedrooms and a fireplace. The cottage sits beside a lake and an apple orchard. ▶ **Gum Tree Cottage**, an affiliated establishment, lets you experience an Australian pioneer cottage in typical setting—with all modern conveniences. Both places supply breakfast, and are located in Oakbank, not far from the freeway.

More homey accommodations that will enable you to mix with locals in the city, Hills, Barossa Valley, and farther afield are listed in the *Bed and Breakfast Town and Country Guide*. Some luxury accommodations are listed here as well. The South Australia Host Farms' Asso-ciation also has an excellent guide—*Farm Holidays South Australia Guide*—that lists 51 accommodation op-tions on farms and vineyards in all areas of the state. Visitors can participate in farm life at many of these. Another brochure worth getting is *South Australian Shorts,* which details more than 150 short (two- to seven-day) and unusual holiday packages available statewide. They include canoeing, whale-watching, ballooning, horseback riding, and simply being pampered in luxury accommodations. *South Australia's Out of the Ordinary Holiday Book* contains scores more unusual vacation options. All of these brochures are available free of charge from the South Australian Travel Centre at 1 King William Street in Adelaide.

SOUTH AUSTRALIA'S WINE COUNTRY

South Australia's five major wine regions—the Riverland, Southern Vales, Coonawarra, Clare Valley, and Barossa Valley—encourage wonderful self-indulgence. More than 50 percent of Australia's wine is produced in South Australia and much of it never leaves the state.

RIVERLAND

The red-soiled Riverland region starts one hour's drive northeast of Adelaide on the **Murray River**, where you can rent a **houseboat**. (Book at Tourism South Australia, 1 King William Street, Adelaide 5000; Tel: 08/212-1505.) Self-contained vessels that you skipper yourself are based at many locations on the Murray, including the towns of Renmark, Paringa, Berri, Loxton, and Waikerie.

To reach these river towns, drive the South Eastern Freeway out of Adelaide to Tailem Bend, leave the freeway, then follow the clearly signposted road along the river. A houseboat stay will reveal the native birdlife of the Murray, spectacular red cliffs, ancient gum trees, and historic towns. There is good fishing and also water sports on most reaches of the river. The citrus fruit here is Australia's best.

A relaxed, pampered way to experience the river is on the intimate, 40-passenger luxury paddle steamer **Proud Mary**, which plies out of Murray Bridge for a variety of overnight (or longer) cruises that can be combined with a trip to the Barossa Valley. Activities can include exploring hidden lagoons to see prolific birdlife and sunken petrified forests, canoeing, and tracing the historic riverboat days through shore excursions; Tel: (08) 231-9472; or write to Proud Australia Cruises; 33 Pirie Street, Suite 12C, Adelaide, S.A. 5000.

The Riverland is one of Australia's biggest wine producing areas, and most of the 44 grape varieties cultivated in South Australia's wine-growing regions are represented here. The main varieties of white grapes produced are Chardonnay, Chenin Blanc, Frontignac, Rhine Riesling, Sauvignon Blanc, Sémillon, and Traminer. The Riverland's red grapes are Cabernet Sauvignon, Malbec, Pinot Noir, and Shiraz. Fine Sherry-style wines are also produced.

SOUTHERN VALES

The Southern Vales region, edged along the Fleurieu Peninsula facing Gulf St. Vincent, includes Australia's densest concentration of wineries (more than 40), just 40 km (25 miles) south of Adelaide. You can sun on one of several wide, sandy beaches (there's nude bathing at Maslin's Beach) before tasting crisp whites and full-flavored reds and perhaps lunching at a winery. Several, including **Middlebrook** on Sand Road, with a barbecue grill and an à la carte menu, have excellent tables. An unusual complex is ▶ **McLarens on the Lake** in McLaren Vale; set lakeside, it includes country-style cottage units, a silver-service restaurant, a more casual courtyard bar and grill, and the Andrew Garrett Winery on its grounds. Be sure to taste Andrew's Fumé Blanc and Cabernet Merlot. You can buy opals here, too. Directions to the wineries are well signposted as you drive above and along the coast on South Road out of Adelaide.

COONAWARRA

Coonawarra, about 400 km (250 miles) southeast of Adelaide near the Victorian state border, is a small town in a region of the same name—a cigar-shaped plain of red volcanic soil about eight miles long—that, since the beginning of the century, has produced some of Australia's finest reds. Particularly noteworthy are its Cabernet Sauvignons. The region also produces Rhine Rieslings, which are emerging as whites of great quality. Labels to look for include Penfolds/Wynns, Mildara, Hungerford Hill, and Petaluma. (The grapes for Petaluma are also grown in the Adelaide Hills.)

You might approach the Coonawarra region from the state of Victoria along the Great Ocean Road (see the Melbourne and Victoria chapter above), one of the nation's most spectacular drives, with breathtaking views of the ocean from high cliffs. **Mount Gambier**, just over the border in South Australia, overlooks the mysterious Blue Lake, which changes from gray to brilliant blue from November to March. The puzzle of the color change was solved in 1979, when Australian scientists discovered that the lake's deep bottom was composed of pure calcium carbonate and that tiny suspended crystals of this material refracted mainly the blue line of the light spectrum.

After visiting the Coonawarra area north of Mount Gambier you can explore several spectacular caves with marine fossils north of the town of **Naracoorte** before returning to Adelaide via the town of Keith. If you return to the coast instead, you'll cross the **Coorong**, a narrow, unspoiled, virtually uninhabited region of dunes, ocean, and inland waters abounding with birdlife.

CLARE VALLEY

The Clare Valley, 135 km (84 miles) north of Adelaide, has 22 wineries that stem from 1851 plantings by Jesuit priests needing sacramental wine. The Clare Riesling is a unique variety introduced by the priests. The vines are a variety of *cruchen,* widely grown in Europe. Other white grapes grown are Rhine Riesling, white Hermitage, and white Pinot, and also some Verdelho, used mainly in blending. Red varieties, as in most of the other South Australian wine districts, are principally Shiraz, Cabernet Sauvignon, and Pinot Noir.

The Barossa Valley

The most popular wine district in the state is the Barossa Valley, an hour northeast of Adelaide. Australia's best-known grapes grow here among pastures, gum trees, and almond and olive groves.

The Barossa, named (but misspelled) by Adelaide's founder, Colonel Light, after Spain's Barrosa (Hill of Roses) Sherry region, is a small area, 5 by 19 miles. The Barossa's small towns, churches, quaint buildings, cuisine, and festivals reflect the traditions of the Lutheran settlers who came here in the 1800s, fleeing persecution in Silesia and Prussia. Each town has its share of trees, vines, old buildings, Lutheran churches, and charm.

It is possible, but not recommended, to tour the Barossa Valley in one day by rented car or chauffeured limousine, helicopter, or cab from Adelaide with the option of getting around locally by limo, car, cab, or moped (these can be hired at Tanunda). Try to allocate three days if you are doing it on your own. Tight schedules are likely to come unstuck despite the short hops between towns. If you're driving up, head for Nuriootpa, a logical beginning for your visit. (Stop at old Gawler to

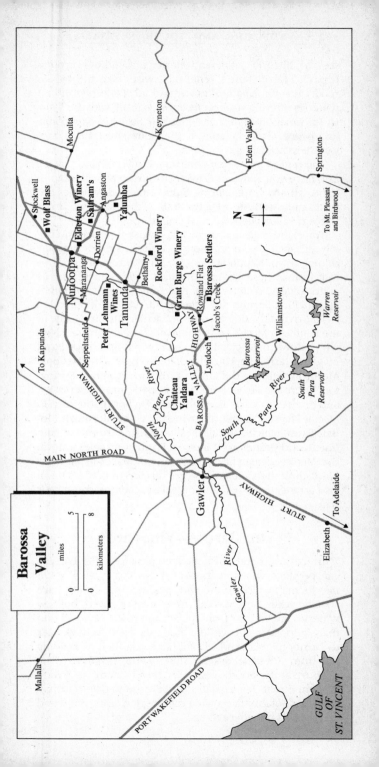

see its historic pubs and heritage buildings around Church Hill if there's time; otherwise, take the bypass road.) For information, maps, and advice, especially on wineries offering your preferences, consult with the Tourist Information Centre at 66 Murray Street in Nuriootpa. (Maps are also available at the South Australia Travel Centre in Adelaide.)

The region may seem confusing but you'll find that it's not, once you arrive in Gawler or Nuriootpa with map in hand. All accommodations, attractions, and wineries are well signposted. Sturt Highway skirts the valley, while the Barossa Valley Highway runs right through.

Travel the area in a roughly clockwise direction, gradually zigzagging your way south. Australia's oldest copper-mining town, **Kapunda**, is located in the region's north; a folk festival here in April features Celtic music. For its crafts gallery, country pub, and hollow tree, you might also include **Springton**, to the south, on your itinerary.

Return to Adelaide via the spectacular **Torrens Gorge** in the southern Mount Lofty Range above the Torrens River, which flows to the city. The route is winding and bordered by glens, farms, and bushland. It also passes the **National Motor Museum** at the Mill in Birdwood, south of Springton. There are a trout farm, wildlife park, and conservation and recreation areas along the way. On Springton Road in Mount Pleasant, south of Springton, is the **Merindah Mohair Farm**, which sells clothes hand made from goat hair. **Cafe C and Craneford Winery** in Springton serves innovative Mediterranean fare with Asian influences in a former blacksmith shop and grain store; Tel (085) 68-2633. They'll also arrange local bed-and-breakfast accommodations for you.

The Barossa Vineyards

With its varied soils and climate conditions, the Barossa can produce wines in most of the world's styles. You'll need a map to locate the wineries, as some do not have specific addresses. Several roads are not paved, but few wineries are very far from the arterial roads. You will find that signposting is excellent along the road from Gawler to Nuriootpa via Lyndoch and Tanunda. Before heading out from Adelaide, ask for the *Touring Guide to Wine Country* at the South Australian Travel Centre, at 1 King William Street. It's free and contains up-to-date information on all of the state's wine regions, including maps and suggestions on where to eat.

About 45 Barossa Valley wineries offer free tastings, and wines are for sale at outlets known as "cellar doors"—sometimes for quaffing with a picnic on winery grounds, or at other picnic spots throughout the valley. To enjoy picnicking on vineyard grounds, come to the Barossa Valley in spring blossom time, summer, or fall; dress casually. If you visit any of the family wineries, you may well have the special treat of meeting the winemakers.

If you enter via **Gawler**, the usual gateway to the valley, the Baroque-style **Château Yaldara**, just before the town of Lyndoch, offers an imposing welcome to the Barossa. Fine antiques are displayed in the château's ballroom, and its buildings are set in lovely gardens.

Barossa Settlers, in Trial Hill Road in Lyndoch, is a small premium winery set in an 1860s stone stable, where you can sample its distinctive late-harvest Rhine Riesling.

Following the road from Lyndoch you'll reach **Tanunda**, where you will find outstanding wines at **Peter Lehmann Wines**. Peter is a winemaker's winemaker; any of his professional peers would be thrilled if he made wine for them. His brilliant Sémillon Sauternes stand out, as does his Cabernet Sauvignon. This riverside winery has picnic facilities.

A number of wineries lie along a roughly clockwise route northeast out of Tanunda. At the entrance to **Nuriootpa** is the **Elderton Winery**, which produces, among other wines, a delightful red Beaujolais-style wine. There is a riverside picnic area here, and bicycles can be hired to tour the vineyard or small cars to tour the winery.

Wolf Blass, on the Sturt Highway in Nuriootpa, is Australia's most successful red-wine exhibitor. His black-label reds, Cabernet Sauvignon or Shiraz, are great wines, particularly when they've been put down for at least ten years. Blass's large vine-draped tasting area is German in style, and the winery includes a museum tracing the history of wine making.

Saltram's, on the main Nuriootpa-Angaston road just before the town of Angaston, is famed for its Mr. Pickwick Port, and its selection of nonfortified wines—both reds and whites—is commendable, too. There is a picnic area. **Yalumba**, just out of Angaston as you head north, is a big old bluestone winery set in lovely gardens. Its Heggies' Rhine Riesling is most appealing.

Circling back to Tanunda, you'll find **Rockford Winery** on Krondorf Road. Try the big, bold reds in the old Australian tradition. Also near Tanunda is **Grant Burge**,

which is rapidly becoming one of the region's most notable labels. Vineyard operations are located in a beautifully restored old building off Barossa Valley Highway at
Jacob's Creek.

Barossa Valley Festivals

On the Sunday of Australia Day weekend (a three-day
weekend falling on or just after the official date of January
26), the Oom Pah Fest brass-band festival, with frolic and
food, takes place in Tanunda. Essenfest, the German food
festival, is celebrated here on the first Sunday in March.
Biennial Easter Monday (1993, 1995, and so on) is the
best time to visit for the week-long **Barossa Valley Vintage
Festival**, the world's biggest wine fest. Book accommodations well in advance, as beds are hard to find in the
valley at any festival time. Every October the Barossa
Valley hosts an **International Music Festival**, with concerts in wineries, churches, and villages. Ask at the Travel
Centre in Adelaide for details and dates of this year's
music fest, the only one of its kind in Australia. Adelaide
Cup weekend (including the third Monday in May) brings
a hot-air balloon regatta to Tanunda.

The winemakers of the valley welcome visitors to the
August **Barossa Valley Classic Gourmet Weekend**. Partici-
pating wineries team up with South Australia's best chefs
to serve the finest food and wine in friendly settings, with
live music appropriate to each winery's atmosphere. The
host wineries vary from year to year, as does the date,
which always falls on a mid-August weekend. Inquire at
Tourism South Australia, 1 King William Street, Adelaide,
for the specific dates and wineries. You'll have to drive
from winery to winery in the Barossa, but distances are
short, and the food, wine, and entertainment—from jazz
bands to string quartets—are memorable.

Staying in the Barossa Valley

Motels and pubs in the area have adequate, moderately
priced bed-and-breakfast accommodations, but the most
interesting places to stay are restored homesteads or
cottages such as those listed in the *Bed and Breakfast
Town and Country Guide* or *Farm Holidays South Australia Guide*.

The homestead of the pioneer wine-making Seppelt
family, ▶ **The Lodge**, a licensed country guesthouse with
four rooms opposite Seppeltsfield, is not cheap but offers
a most gracious environment. At Marananga, a village on

the way to Seppeltsfield, there are lovely views and cozy accommodations at ▶ **The Hermitage**. The date-palm avenue planted by the Seppelt family's employees during the Depression begins at Marananga.

▶ **Stonewell Cottages**, between Tanunda and Seppeltsfield, has lake views in two units, and room for a maximum of eight guests. The peaceful four-room ▶ **Lawley Farm Cottage and Barn** (1850) in Tanunda has been restored as a bed-and-breakfast accommodation, while the ▶ **Collingrove Homestead** in Angaston has been classified by the National Trust. Accommodation is in nicely refurbished maids' quarters, and formal dining is available by request. The ▶ **Landhaus**, a restored shepherd's cottage at Bethany, is a romantic bed and breakfast with a spa. Up to 12 can dine by reservation here at one of the valley's most elegant tables. Halfway between Tanunda and Nuriootpa is the ▶ **Barossa Junction Resort**, a novel motel-restaurant incorporating vintage railway carriages.

Dining in the Barossa Valley

The valley was settled in the mid-1800s by Prussians and Silesians fleeing religious persecution in their homelands—now regions in Poland and Germany. They were joined by migrating British, and the cultural traditions have been maintained. Informal cafés and coffee shops in the area reflect German/Northern European traditions, while old pubs, many restored, provide reasonably priced, no-nonsense, and sometimes quite good fare—and opportunities to meet the locals. For a palate-cleansing ale, pause at the beer garden at the 1846 **Tanunda Hotel** on Tanunda's Main Street. **Bergman's** on Murray Street in Tanunda, retains its old country-store atmosphere; snack here or dine at leisure in the *weingarten*. The **Lyndoch Hotel** in Lyndoch has good steaks. **Barossa Bakery** on Nuriootpa's Murray Street offers traditional German lunches, and the coffee's fine at **Linke's Family Bakery**, also in Nuriootpa.

Several restaurants and some wineries (lunch only) have interesting menus, but two, in addition to the Landhaus in Bethany, stand out. Well-presented, stylish dining—with an emphasis on fresh local produce—in an informal, vine-shaded atmosphere can be had at **The Vintners**, on Nuriootpa Road in Angaston. It's open for dinner Friday and Saturday nights and for lunch every day except Monday; Tel: (085) 64-2488. Game is the specialty of the award-winning **Pheasant Farm**, an operating pheasant farm with a lake, off Samuels Road near Marananga (closed February); Tel: (085) 62-1286.

Local fruits dried by Angaston's **Angas Park Fruit Company** make a good accompaniment to picnic fare, which can be bought from the valley's butcher shops, bakeries, and delicatessens.

Prepacked picnic hampers, from a ploughman's lunch to a gourmet's picnic (24 hours notice for the latter), are available from **Gnadenfrei Estate Winery** in Marananga, which also has restaurant facilities; Tel: (085) 62-2522.

Several of the valley's wineries have pleasant picnic spots, but you might also picnic at Bethany Reserve, a tranquil spot in the village with a trickling creek and gum trees. Kaiser Stuhl Conservation Park, near Mengler's Hill, affords panoramic views of the valley. Both the reserve and the park lie on a scenic route east from Tanunda to Angaston, via Bethany.

KANGAROO ISLAND

Kangaroo Island, Australia's third-largest island, is a place of spectacular natural contrasts, a mix of farmland and wildlife areas. Although day-trippers come just to mingle with the seals at Seal Bay, 60 km (36 miles) south of the main town of Kingscote, five days is a more adequate stay. Permission from park rangers is required to enter some areas, but rangers are helpful and can conduct independent travellers to otherwise inaccessible places.

The island was first circumnavigated in 1802 by Frenchman Nicolas Baudin (many signposts on the island mark this event). In 1803 unofficial settlers—brutal sealers and renegades—arrived at Kangaroo Island. Tales of their exploits can be heard at the coastal town of American River (so named because many of the sealers were American), where they lived a primitive existence. South Australia's first official English settlement was established near **Kingscote** in 1836.

It's quite an experience to stroll among rare sea lions at **Seal Bay**, one of the world's largest accessible colonies. Visitors can also camel-trek in southwest **Flinders Chase**, the largest of 15 national and conservation parks on the island. You can swim with the seals or scuba dive around shipwrecks circling the rugged 281-mile-long coastline, and there's whale-watching in August.

Other possible activities include angling for game fish or joining National Parks and Wildlife Service rangers to descend escarpments for swimming in secluded bays and exploring the Kelly Hill Caves. Visitors can stay—comfortably, albeit with minimal amenities—at light-houses; contact the National Parks Authority (Tel: 0848/22-381).

The less intrepid can sunbathe on the superb beaches on the island's northern side or bird-watch either by the sea or the lagoons: The hundreds of birds include alba-tross and fairy penguins. Visitors can also see protected kangaroos (first observed by Captain Matthew Flinders, who named the island while passing it in 1802), wallabies, koalas, possums, bandicoots, New Zealand fur seals, goannas (a kind of monitor lizard), and platypuses in their natural habitat, or photograph some 50 kinds of orchids and hundreds of other wildflower species from August to November.

Ocean currents make Kangaroo Island's winters cold, but the Southern Ocean (next stop, Antarctica) crashing against high southern cliffs is a not-to-be-missed spectacle. Swim in summer, beachcomb the rest of the year, when the landscape is greenest.

Most people come in December, January, and February; the last weekend in February is Kangaroo Island's racing carnival.

Dress informally on the island, and in summer take warm tops for sudden changes in the weather. Watch for snakes, particularly beneath and around the Yakka bushes (or grass trees, a unique Australian palm). They resemble huge pineapple tops. Walking shoes and a hat are musts.

National Parks and Wildlife Service officers at the office on Dauncey Street in Kingscote (Tel: 0848/22-381), as well as staff at the Travel Centre in Adelaide, the tour operators mentioned in the next section on touring, and airline and ferry service personnel listed under Getting Around can all give details on how to participate in Kangaroo Island's varied activities.

Touring Kangaroo Island

Kangaroo Island, 91 miles long, has 1,000 miles of roads, but the only paved ones run between the three main towns at the east—Kingscote (population 1,700), American River, and Penneshaw—with a bit more running to central Parndana and beyond. There is no public transportation. Rental-car charges include expensive insurance, because the unpaved roads mean accident risks. If you are wary of driving, consider taking a tour.

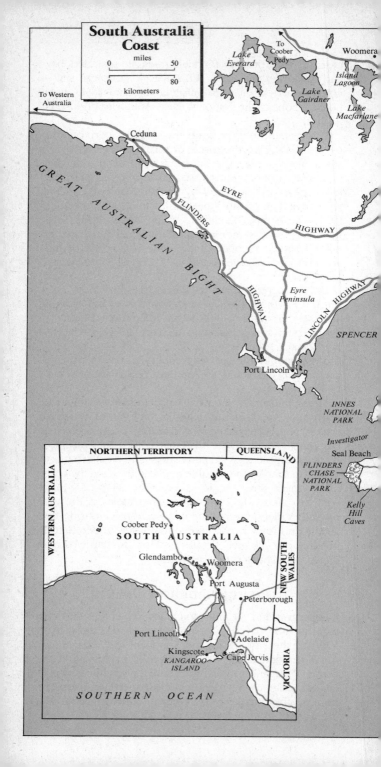

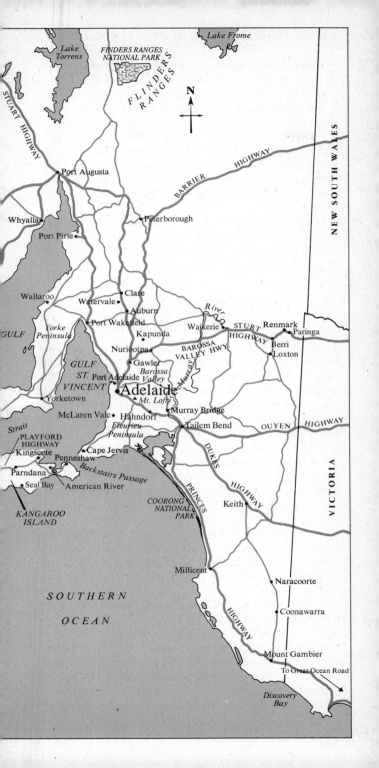

Kingscote's Kangaroo Island Explorer Tours (Tel: 0848/ 22-640) offers trips to major scenic and historic areas as well as four-wheel-drive excursions to more isolated spots. **Australian Odysseys'** Anna Howard offers day and night wildlife excursions in the bush. Anna also organizes special no-frills stays with environmental scientists involved in the tracking of echidnas (spiny hedgehogs), the banding of native birds, and many other studies. Tourists live and work with these American researchers. She also tailors special tours for the visually impaired; Tel: (0848) 31-294.

Linnett's Island Club in American River, the Sorrento Resort in Penneshaw, and the Ozone Seafront Hotel in Kingscote organize tours as well. You can also book tours in Adelaide or at any Qantas office.

Staying and Dining
on Kangaroo Island

Kingscote's main accommodations are right in town. ▶ **Wisteria Lodge and Motel**'s modern second-story suites have sea views. The ▶ **Ozone Seafront Hotel**, facing the sunset's reflections on Nepean Bay, is a stylish old place with a pool. Its fine dining room features local seafood and top South Australian wines. Kangaroo Island's local lobster is good eating; do ask for it, particularly at the Ozone.

▶ **Linnett's Island Club**, overlooking American River and the coast, has comfortable full-service and self-contained units and excellent facilities, including a pool, spa, sauna, and tennis courts. The hotel's dining room specializes in seafood. American River is on Eastern Cove, a great fishing spot. Pelican Lagoon, at the southern end of Eastern Cove, is part of a conservation park. Although there is no fishing allowed here, canoeing, bird-watching and walking the lagoon's edge are tranquil alternative pastimes.

In Penneshaw, a small fishing village, you can stay at the ▶ **Sorrento Resort Motel**, an attractive modern facility— and the only hotel in town—but the real local surprise is **Muggleton's General Store**, a licensed restaurant that also allows you to bring your own drinks. The atmosphere is Old World; good Mediterranean-influenced lunches are prepared here by Rowan Muggleton-Mole, a former Melbourne Cup caterer who now presents gourmet fare at the

Kangaroo Island Cup. Reservations are suggested; Tel: (0848) 31-151.

As for nightlife on the island, entertainment takes an animal rather than a human form: Fairy penguins parade at Penneshaw and on the Kingscote foreshores.

The eucalyptus oil that is processed locally is marvelous for rubbing into aching muscles or congested chests and will clear nasal passages instantly. Ceramic witchetty grubs, modeled on the fat, wormlike creatures that are considered a delicacy by aboriginals, are sold at **Kingscote's Gallery** in Murray Street, as are other ceramic items, paintings, hand-spun and -woven goods, prints, wildflowers in glass, pressed wildflowers, and macramé pieces, all made on the island.

SOUTH AUSTRALIAN OUTBACK

Travelling north through the Barossa and Clare valleys you come to the edge of the dramatically colorful **Flinders Ranges**, a series of ancient rugged mountains that are now designated national parks. Here you can bushwalk, rock climb, discover old aboriginal cave paintings, and ride horseback in a region immortalized by the artist Sir Hans Heysen.

Port Augusta, 130 km (80 miles) north of Adelaide at the top of Spencer Gulf, is the jumping-off point for people travelling to the Northern Flinders Ranges, the Outback, and Eyre Peninsula. Known as the crossroads of Australia, Port Augusta is a railhead and historic port, with well-preserved colonial buildings. Stop at the Flying Doctor Base and the School of the Air, which educates isolated Outback kids by radio. You might also visit the **Wadlata Outback Centre**, which interprets the aboriginal Dreamtime and charts the opening up of the region by explorers, pioneer pastoralists, and railway men. Reasonably priced, standard motels and restaurants are available in Port Augusta, and seafood is a specialty.

To make a detour along the Eyre Peninsula's coast on your way to Western Australia, take the Lincoln Highway at Port Augusta and drive 140 km (87 miles) southwest through the steel-manufacturing town of Whyalla to **Port Lincoln**. South Australia's tuna capital, Port Lincoln offers thrilling yacht charters on Boston Bay, which is five times larger than Sydney Harbour. You can visit deserted islands, fish, watch frolicking dolphins, or simply marvel at being in the closest charter area to Antarctica and yet in a warm, Mediterranean climate. Lincoln Cove Yacht Charter (Tel: 086/82-1124 in Port Lincoln or 08/271-9492 in Adelaide) has a fleet of luxury Benetaus (or you can go bareboating) for trips in the bay and beyond in Spencer Gulf around uninhabited islands rich in birdlife. Try swimming with sea lions in the gulf; they love company.

From Port Lincoln, travel northwest along the Flinders Highway above spectacular cliffs and deserted beaches to link up with the Eyre Highway at Ceduna before continuing to Western Australia. For those short on time, Kendell Airlines serves Whyalla and Port Lincoln and also offers special packages from Adelaide to sail with Lincoln Cove Yacht charters.

Tours of the Flinders Ranges can be booked at Adelaide's South Australia Travel Centre or in Port Augusta. Port Augusta–based Augusta Airways offers one-day tours out of Adelaide that give a glimpse of the Outback; reservations can be made in Port Augusta or in Adelaide through Ansett Australia.

COOBER PEDY

Looking like a moonscape of craters and hills from the air, at ground level much of Coober Pedy resembles a wrecker's junkyard.

Coober Pedy (from the aboriginal *kupa piti*—"white fellow's burrow"—and pronounced "Coober PEE-dee"), 863 km (535 miles) north of Adelaide on the Stuart Highway—and the Outback's last frontier—hides its wealth beneath its pockmarked surface: It produces 80 percent of the world's opals.

This is a place of polarized fortunes, where dynamite is discounted at the supermarket. The 4,000 inhabitants—give or take a thousand who avoid the census or drifters seeking the big strike—comprise about 45 nationalities.

Roughly 80 percent of the town's residents live underground, following the example of the miners who arrived after the discovery of opals here in 1915. The miners escaped the desert's searing daytime heat and frigid night-time cold by digging homes into bare hillsides.

Today visitors come for the underground museum here (see below) and art galleries, to buy pottery and fiery opals more cheaply than in the cities, and to noodle or fossick (rummage) for them across the lunarlike landscape. Heed local boasts that the town is so progressive that everyone moves forward; walking backwards you run the risk of falling down one of the thousands of deep mineshafts no one has bothered to fill in. If you are serious about mining, get a permit from the South Australia Department of Mines and Energy on Hutchison Street.

It's best to visit Coober Pedy between April and October, when it's pleasantly warm. Summer temperatures can reach 129 degrees F, although buses and many aboveground buildings are air-conditioned. Underground temperatures remain at 77 degrees F. Wear light, casual clothes, with a warm jacket or wrap for cool nights. Hats, sunglasses, and walking shoes are essential.

Coober Pedy comes alive during the second weekend in October, the date of the annual horse- and camel-race meet, and at Easter's Opal Festival, which features aboriginal arts and crafts and multicultural events including dancing and feasting. July's Greek Glendi Festival of music, dance, feasting, and celebrating Hellenic traditions is also fun.

Around in Coober Pedy

At the very least, walk down Hutchison Street, Coober Pedy's main street. Hotel staff can arrange sightseeing flights or rental cars, but if you're driving beyond town, be careful: While signposted, many of the narrow, unpaved roads through rubbled hills have few landmarks. You can easily lose your sense of direction. As an alternative, there are taxis and comprehensive, locally operated tours.

Hutchison Street yields the ▶ **Umoona Opal Mine Museum and Motel**, which has seven motel-style units, communal facilities, and above- and below-ground camping. Umoona also features local aboriginal heritage exhibits, art, a mine, and a display home. Also on Hutchison Street are the **Underground Gallery and Bookshop** and various shops (some underground) selling opals, local art, and souvenirs.

Like early Christians in Roman catacombs, it is possible to worship underground in the Roman Catholic St. Peter and Paul's Church on Hutchison Street, and the Anglican Catacomb Church east of Hutchison Street on Catacomb Road.

The **Big Winch** retail complex atop a hill (the highest point in town, with spectacular views) off Umoona Road, offers paintings and opals (set or unset) for sale, and gives cutting demonstrations. There are tables outside for picnicking in the cooler months. The giant winch and bucket symbolize the determination of the miners. Down the road, noodling (searching for gems with your bare hands) is permitted in an area known as the Jeweller's Shop.

Visible to the east from the Big Winch is the **Old Timer's Mine**, an original mine that has been restored to show visitors how it was worked (the mine closed in 1918). While refurbishing, the owners found opals just inches from where the old-timers had stopped chipping away.

The **Breakaways**, 28 km (17 miles) north of town, is an exposed sandstone range. The plain beneath it, known as the **Painted Desert**, was the movie setting for *Mad Max: Beyond Thunderdome;* the reserve is so named because the sun's position constantly alters the vibrant colors of the landscape. A round trip of 40 miles by four-wheel drive north from Coober Pedy returns visitors along part of the 5,937-mile-long Dog Fence, erected to protect grazing sheep from dingoes. This barrier stretches from Surfers Paradise on the coast of Queensland to the Great Australian Bight, the wild, open stretch of water that pounds the state's south coast. The fence is regularly checked by boundary riders in three states. Fossilized shells 100 million years old can be found along the fence and on the desolate Moon Plain to the east, about 20 km (12 miles) from Coober Pedy.

Staying in Coober Pedy

You can sample a bit of Coober Pedy's unique lifestyle by staying in an underground motel—just don't expect views! The award-winning ▶ **Desert Cave Hotel** on Hutchison Street claims to be the only international-standard underground motel in the world, and it offers a novel experience in complete comfort. The motel also has a lively bar (underground), an international menu at its **Umberto's Restaurant**, and an underground gallery tracing the history of opals. The less luxurious ▶ **Underground Motel** is a little away from the main action of Hutchison Street, on Catacomb Road. The underground accommodations here, gouged out of the sides of bare hills, have walls of sealed, colorful textured sandstone. Rooms at both motels have doors to the outside, and the claustrophobic can request an above-ground suite at the Desert Cave. The ▶ **Opal Inn Hotel-Motel**, built on the surface, is at the epicenter of Coober Pedy's miners' nightlife; order a schooner of beer and chat with the locals in the hotel's public bar. ▶ **Radekas**

Motel and Backpacker's Inn has self-contained underground units alongside youth accommodations.

Dining and Nightlife
in Coober Pedy

The town's nightlife focuses on a few spots: the Desert
Cave's bar and restaurant ('roo is on the menu, in addition
to well-presented international dishes); the Opal Inn,
which frequently features visiting entertainers; the Greek,
Italian, and Yugoslav clubs, which welcome visitors; and
the casual restaurants lining Hutchison Street. These last
include the upstairs **Traces** and, opposite, **Tom and Mary's
Taverna**, good Greek establishments with grills and, surprisingly, seafood, at very reasonable prices.

Sergio's Restaurant is small but offers huge servings of
imaginatively cooked Italian food. The **Old Miner's Dugout Café** is underground and goes for the country-
cuisine-and-casserole (European-influenced) approach at
reasonable prices. The American proprietress serves old-
fashioned apple pie—U.S. style. All these are licensed
and have fair selections of South Australian wines.

You can eat and drink at almost any time of day or night
in Coober Pedy, but, with the exception of Umberto's at the
Desert Cave Hotel, don't expect silver service. It's all
hearty, informal Outback fun, and the interaction of residents and visitors means that many places kick on till about
4:00 A.M.

GETTING AROUND

Adelaide
From the United States Qantas flies weekly from San
Francisco to Sydney with domestic connections to
Adelaide. Air New Zealand flies weekly from Los Angeles
via Auckland to Melbourne. Continental and United
flights terminate in either Sydney or Melbourne, necessi-
tating a one- or two-hour domestic flight to Adelaide via
Qantas or Ansett Australia. A connecting flight is also
necessary for passengers from Toronto or Vancouver fly-
ing Qantas into Sydney or Melbourne. British Airways and
Qantas have direct flights from London to Adelaide; Singapore Airlines has flights from most European capitals via
Singapore and Malaysia Airlines offers connections out of
London and Kuala Lumpur.

Transit airport buses and cabs meet international and

domestic flights at opposite terminals. It's 15 minutes by bus or cab to central Adelaide. Interstate trains disembark passengers for Adelaide at inner-suburban Keswick Station; from there it is an easy, ten-minute cab ride to the city that costs about A$12.

Kangaroo Island

Air Kangaroo has a separate terminal signposted on the right just before Adelaide's small domestic airport building, from which through-passengers can fly to Kangaroo Island via Air Kangaroo or Kendell Airlines. The flight takes 25 minutes, and it's ten minutes by bus from the island's airport to Kingscote. Albatross Airlines and Air Emu operate smaller planes to the island from Adelaide airport.

The trip from Port Adelaide to Kingscote via the car-ferry *Island Seaway* takes six hours. For reservations, Tel: (08) 47-5577. Alternatively, drive or take the bus for two hours through scenic mainland Fleurieu Peninsula to Cape Jervis, then make the hour-long crossing of Backstairs Passage on Kangaroo Island Sealink ferries from Cape Jervis to tiny Penneshaw on the island. To reserve, call toll-free, Tel: (008) 088-836. Buses leave the Adelaide bus terminal at 101 Franklin Street (Tel: 08/384-6860) to connect with the ferries at Cape Jervis.

Kingscote Yacht Club welcomes charter yachtsmen from the mainland.

Coober Pedy

From Adelaide Kendell Airlines has five flights weekly. Make independent ground arrangements or take a three-day air package combining Coober Pedy with Ayers Rock, the Olgas, and Alice Springs. (See the Northern Territory chapter.) Call Kendell through Ansett Australia at (08) 13-1300 in Adelaide.

Bus Australia's six-night Outback tour includes Coober Pedy along with Ayers Rock, the Olgas, and Alice Springs; Tel: (008) 132-323 toll-free from anywhere in Australia. In cooperation with Stateliner-Greyhound and Ansett Pioneer, through-coach services extend to Ayers Rock and Alice Springs. Additional stopovers can be arranged. Make arrangements in Adelaide or with Qantas abroad.

It is also possible to rent a car or camper in Adelaide, but the ten-plus hours' drive from Adelaide to Coober Pedy becomes tedious after the Stuart Highway leaves coastal Port Augusta. Brief or overnight stops can be scheduled at ▶ **Woomera ELDO Hotel** (South Australia's third-biggest hotel) in Woomera, a former British rocket range, and/or the ▶ **Glendambo Tourist Centre** in Glendambo. The ELDO Hotel is a stoic cement building with comfortable rooms refurbished from a 1950s British Royal Air Force Officers' mess. The award-winning Glendambo Tourist Centre is a spacious motel in the middle of no-man's-land.

Carry drinking water. Glendambo's roadhouse sign says: "No fresh rain water. Don't ask." When driving at night, be on the lookout for emus and kangaroos; a collision with one of these creatures may damage your vehicle more than the vehicle will damage the animal.

ACCOMMODATIONS REFERENCE

The rates given here are projections *for 1994. Unless otherwise indicated, rates are for double room, double occupancy. As prices are subject to change, always double-check before booking.*

▶ **Adelaide's Bed and Breakfast.** 239 Franklin Street, **Adelaide**, S.A. 5000. Tel: (08) 231-3124; Fax: (08) 212-7974. A$75–A$85.

▶ **Apartments on the Park.** 274 South Terrace, **Adelaide**, S.A. 5000. Tel: (08) 232-0555; Fax: (08) 223-3457. From A$110.

▶ **Apple Tree Cottage** and **Gum Tree Cottage.** P. O. Box 100, **Oakbank**, S.A. 5243. Tel: (08) 388-4193. From A$100. Continental breakfast.

▶ **Barossa Junction Resort.** Barossa Valley Highway, **Tanunda**, S.A. 5353. Tel: (085) 63-3400; Fax: (085) 63-3660. From A$81. Continental breakfast.

▶ **Collingrove Homestead.** Eden Valley Road, **Angaston**, S.A. 5353. Tel: (085) 64-2061; Fax: (085) 64-2061. A$100. Cooked breakfast.

▶ **Country Comfort Inn.** 226 South Terrace, **Adelaide**, S.A. 5000. Tel: (08) 223-4355; Fax: (08) 232-5997. From A$85–A$108.

▶ **Desert Cave Hotel.** Hutchison Street, **Coober Pedy**, S.A. 5723. Tel: (086) 72-5688; Fax: (086) 72-5198. A$112.

▶ **Glendambo Tourist Centre.** Stuart Highway, **Glendambo**, S.A. 5710. Tel: (086) 72-1030; Fax: (086) 72-1039. A$65–A$73. Continental breakfast.

▶ **The Hermitage of Marananga.** Seppeltsfield Road, **Marananga**, S.A. 5360. Tel: (085) 62-2722; Fax: (085) 62-3133. A$160. Cooked breakfast.

▶ **Hilton International.** 233 Victoria Square, **Adelaide**,

S.A. 5000. Tel: (08) 217-0711; Fax: (08) 231-0158, in U.S. and Canada, (800) 445-8667. From A$130–A$180.

► **Hindley Parkroyal.** 65 Hindley Street, **Adelaide,** S.A. 5000. Tel: (08) 231-5552; Fax: (08) 237-3800. From A$120–A$190.

► **Hyatt Regency Adelaide.** North Terrace, **Adelaide,** S.A. 5000. Tel: (08) 231-1234; Fax: (08) 238-2392; in U.S. and Canada, (800) 223-1234; in Alaska and Hawaii, (800) 228-9005. A$145–A$260.

► **Landhaus.** Bethany Road, **Bethany,** S.A. 5352. Tel: (085) 63-2191. A$145. Cooked breakfast.

► **Lawley Farm Cottage and Barn.** Krondorf Road, **Tanunda,** S.A. 5352. Tel and Fax: (085) 63-2141. A$102–A$120. Cooked breakfast.

► **Linnett's Island Club.** Government Road, **American River,** S.A. 5221. Tel: (0848) 33-053; Fax: (0848) 33-030. A$50–A$92.

► **The Lodge.** Seppeltsfield Road, **Seppeltsfield,** S.A. 5360. Tel: (085) 62-8277; Fax: (085) 62-8344. A$210. Cooked breakfast.

► **McLarens on the Lake.** Kangarilla Road, **McLaren Vale,** S.A. 5143. Tel: (08) 323-8911; Fax: (08) 323-9010. A$85.

► **North Adelaide Heritage Apartments** and **Adelaide Heritage Cottages.** 109 Glen Osmond Road, **Eastwood,** S.A. 5063. Tel: (08) 272-1355; Fax: (08) 272-1355. A$70–A$95.

► **Opal Inn Hotel-Motel.** Hutchison Street, **Coober Pedy,** S.A. 5723. Tel: (086) 72-5054; Fax: (086) 72-5501. From A$70.

► **Ozone Seafront Hotel.** Commercial Street, **Kingscote,** S.A. 5223. Tel: (0848) 22-011; Fax: (0848) 22-249. From A$80.

► **Quality Hotel Adelaide.** 62 Brougham Place, **North Adelaide,** S.A. 5006. Tel: (08) 267-3444; Fax: (08) 239-0189; in U.S., (800) 624-FLAG. A$85–A$120.

► **Radekas Motel and Backpacker's Inn.** Coober Pedy, S.A. 5723. Tel: (086) 72-5223; Fax: (086) 72-5821. From A$70.

► **Ramada Grand Hotel.** 2 Jetty Road, **Glenelg,** S.A. 5045. Tel: (08) 376-1222; toll-free in Australia, (008) 88-2777; Fax: (08) 376-1111; in U.S., (800) 228-2828. A$155–A$440.

► **Sorrento Resort Motel.** North Terrace, **Penneshaw,** S.A. 5222. Tel: (0848) 31-028; Fax: (0848) 31-204. A$75–A$88.

► **Stonewell Cottages.** Stonewell Road, between **Ta-**

nunda and **Seppeltsfield**, S.A. 5352. Tel: (085) 63-2019. A$78–A$98.

▶ **Terrace Intercontinental.** 147-150 North Terrace, **Adelaide**, S.A. 5000. Tel: (08) 217-7552; Fax: (08) 231-7572. A$120–A$250.

▶ **Umoona Opal Mine Museum and Motel.** Hutchison Street, **Coober Pedy**, S.A. 5723. Tel: (086) 72-5288; Fax: (086) 72-5731. A$25.

▶ **Underground Motel.** Catacomb Road, **Coober Pedy**, S.A. 5723. Tel: (086) 72-5324; Fax: (086) 72-5911. From A$70. Continental breakfast.

▶ **Uraidla Aristologist.** Greenhill and Basket Range roads, **Uraidla**, S.A. 5000. Tel: (08) 390-1995. From A$90. Continental breakfast.

▶ **West End All Suite Hotel.** 255 Hindley Street, **Adelaide**, S.A. 5000. Tel: (08) 231-8333; Fax: (08) 231-4741. A$96.

▶ **Wisteria Lodge and Motel.** 7 Cygnet Road, **Kingscote**, S.A. 5223. Tel: (0848) 22-707; Fax: (0848) 22-200. A$100–A$110.

▶ **Woomera ELDO Hotel.** Town Center, Kotara Crescent, **Woomera**, S.A. 5720. Tel: (086) 73-7867; Fax: (086) 73-7226. A$60.

PERTH AND WESTERN AUSTRALIA

By Janis Hadley

Janis Hadley was the first woman editor in the Hong Kong business press, for Asian Business *magazine. Born in the United Kingdom, she has lived in Western Australia for more than ten years, working as a freelance travel writer for publications in Australia and overseas.*

Western Australia, like most other parts of the country, is immense. Most travellers—even those who have lived in the state all their lives—find it hard to come to grips with the distances in this, Australia's largest state. Western Australia covers a staggering 975,920 square miles: 1,550 miles north to south and 1,055 miles west to east. Driving from the capital, Perth, to the beautiful northern tropical town of Broome would take the average motorist 20 hours; it is roughly the equivalent of driving from New York City to Miami, Florida.

Along with these immense distances comes isolation; Perth is credited with being the most isolated provincial capital in the world. It takes half an hour longer to fly from Melbourne to Perth than from Perth to the Indonesian island of Bali. Singapore and Jakarta are as close to Perth as Sydney.

But this relative isolation brings out in Western Australians the fierce determination to succeed against the odds, and a strong loyalty to the state.

As well as being isolated, Western Australia is the most

sparsely populated state of Australia. More than two-thirds of the population of 1.5 million live in Perth, with the remainder living in small mining and agricultural towns hundreds or thousands of miles from one another.

For the traveller, this means that planning a trip here takes a little bit more thought than usual. If your stay is only a short one, then concentrating on the lifestyle and sights of Perth and Fremantle will make a lot more sense than spending days—and lots of money—making epic journeys to the far corners of the state.

If you do have the time and the extra cash to cover the distances, you will be treated to some of the most rugged and seldom-visited scenic grandeur on earth, and a friendly, country way of life that is worlds away from Perth and the usual travel destinations.

MAJOR INTEREST

Perth
Historic buildings
Shopping, especially for diamonds, pearls, and
    aboriginal art
Western Australian Museum and Art Gallery of
    Western Australia
Natural bushland and wildflowers of King's Park
The Swan River for cruises and water sports
Indian Ocean beaches

Fremantle
Round House (historic jail)
Fremantle Gaol
Fremantle Museum and Arts Centre
Maritime Museum
Fremantle Markets
Fishermen's Harbour and South Terrace for
    open-air cafés and restaurants
Offshore island of Rottnest

Around Perth
Indian Ocean beaches
Yanchep National Park
Historic town of York

Elsewhere in Western Australia
Margaret River wine country
Southwest beaches and forests
Gold Country's boom town of Kalgoorlie
Abrolhos coral islands
Kalbarri coastal retreat

The rugged Pilbara
The Kimberley wilderness area
Pearl shopping in Broome
Wildflowers

Separating Western Australia into regions is difficult; even within regions there are immense contrasts. Nonetheless, touristically speaking, it can be divided into six areas:

- *The Southwest* (which includes Perth), the state's most populated area; boutique wineries, wildflowers, and giant trees are among its varied attractions.
- *The Gold Country,* east of Perth and centered around Kalgoorlie, the site of what was once the richest square mile of gold-bearing earth in the world.
- *The Nullarbor Plain,* a huge treeless plain near the South Australia border.
- *The Central Coast,* an area of wildflowers, beaches, coral reefs, and dolphins about five hours' drive north of Perth.
- *The Pilbara,* the mining heart of Western Australia, inland north of Perth up to the Kimberley, with some of the state's most impressive gorges.
- *The Kimberley,* at the northern end of the state, with an unspoiled tropical coastline, vast rivers and gorges, and some of the biggest cattle ranches in the world.

PERTH

Perth is a city of suburban centers spread around the picturesque banks of the Swan River and along 30 miles of Indian Ocean white-sand surf beaches. The actual downtown is in a small, high-rise strip on the northern banks of the Swan. From here the river meanders westward through affluent suburbs to the port of Fremantle at its mouth; to the east of Perth is the Darling Range—a group of low-lying hills that fringe the metropolitan area.

Perth's big attraction is its pressure-free lifestyle. Living tends to focus on the outdoors: On summer Sundays the Swan is awash with colorful yachts and private pleasure cruisers (Perthites really are boat-mad). Getting together for sports, on the beach, or around the family barbecue is a way of life here.

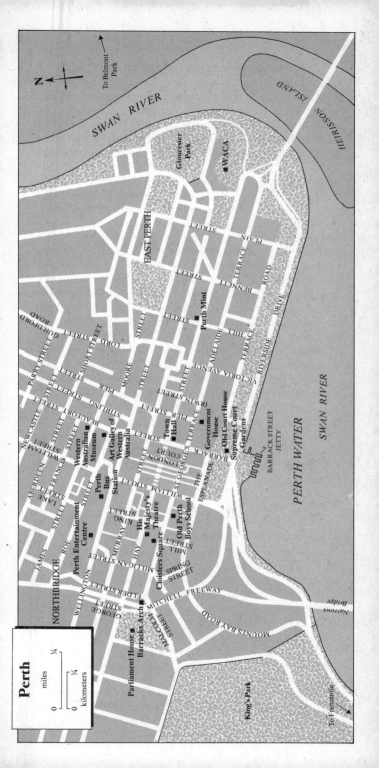

Many visitors' general impression of Perth is one of wealthy people, yachting, and beautiful parks—and they're not far wrong. No matter where you come from you're likely to be impressed by Perth's neat and clean environment. Parks abound; the only concentration of high-rise buildings is in the very center of town, and there is but a single industrial smokestack in the entire urban area.

The city center consists of four main streets running east–west: St. George's Terrace, closest to the river; Hay Street, the main shopping drag to its north; Murray Street; and Wellington Street, nearest to the railway on the northern side. The best place to start a visit to Perth is in **King's Park**, the huge elevated tract of natural Australian bushland at the western end of St. George's Terrace. Take a free Clipper Bus ride (ask at your hotel for a Clipper map) or rent a bicycle on Riverside Drive at the corner of Plain Street. On your bike you may explore King's Park and take in some great views of the city, its suburbs, and the Swan River. You'll see the sparkle of the river, softened by the gray-green bush trees on the Darling Range, which fringes Perth's flat river plain. The suburbs sprawl out to the Darling foothills, and the Swan meanders along the main street in the heart of the business district.

In spring (September to November) King's Park is a good place to view Western Australia's wildflowers growing in their natural habitat. At the end of September each year the park hosts a special display of some 4,000 wildflower species. (For more about wildflowers, see below.)

Historic Perth

Dutch mariners first sighted Western Australia as early as 1616, some 154 years before Captain James Cook sailed into Sydney Harbour. But the British decision to colonize the continent's western reaches and to establish Perth came much later, in 1829, and was actually a move to thwart French interests in the western part of "New Holland." Perth's site was chosen for its access to the plentiful drinking water of the Swan River.

A few buildings dating back to early colonial days have been preserved among the high-rise cityscape, most within easy walking distance of the city center. Some of the buildings are not open to the public but are worth viewing from the outside for their fine colonial architecture. Set aside three hours for a gentle stroll down St. George's

Terrace, or join a historical walking tour with a knowledgeable guide; Tel: (09) 322-6751 for tour information.

At the western end of St. George's Terrace, close to the entrance to King's Park, is **Barracks Arch**. Only the central arch remains of large barracks built in 1863 to house troops used to guard convicts. The rest of the structure was demolished in 1966 to make way for the Mitchell Freeway.

A few minutes' walk south, between Mill and Spring streets, is the Georgian-style **Bishop's House** completed in 1859 for Perth's first Anglican bishop. A short walk east along Mounts Bay Road and north up Mill Street is the **Cloisters**, built in 1859 as an Anglican boys' school and featuring extensive decorative brickwork. Farther east, on the south side of St. George's Terrace, is the **Old Perth Boys' School**, built of local sandstone in the Gothic Revival style by convict labor. Today it houses the Perth headquarters of the National Trust and is open during business hours. Opposite, on King Street, is **His Majesty's Theatre**, built in 1904 in an opulent Edwardian style and recently refurbished to house local opera, music, and ballet companies; Tel: (09) 322-2929 for access details. **King Street**, traditionally the center of Perth's clothing-manufacturing industry, boasts a number of National Trust–preserved turn-of-the-century buildings and is a miniature art- and café-society enclave among the high-rise buildings.

To the east, at the corner of Hay and Barrack streets, is the **Town Hall**, built in an English Jacobean style, also by convict labor. Around the corner on Barrack Street a sidewalk plaque commemorates Perth's founding on August 12, 1829. Opposite the plaque, on the south side of St. George's Terrace, the **Supreme Court Gardens** were set aside in 1829 for botanical gardens and opened in 1899. Set in the colorful gardens are Government House and the Old Court House. **Government House** was completed in 1864 and has been used as the state governor's home ever since. The **Old Court House** dates to 1837 and is one of the oldest surviving buildings in Perth. Today it houses the Law Centre and a law museum; Tel: (09) 325-4787.

The **Perth Mint** at the eastern end of Hay Street, close to the corner of Hill Street, was opened in 1899 as a branch of London's Royal Mint and was Australia's biggest gold refinery for 91 years until the equipment was moved to a more modern refinery near Perth's international airport. Today the Mint houses a display of gold, silver, and platinum worth more than A$1 million and sells legal coins, gold nuggets, and precious-metal bars. The Perth Mint is open from 9:00 A.M. to 4:00 P.M. weekdays and 10:00 A.M. to 1:00 P.M. Saturdays.

Shopping in Perth

For shopping in Perth there is the traffic-free **Hay Street Mall**, right in the center of the city and joined to Murray Street by shopping arcades, and the new **Forrest Chase** complex, straddling Wellington and Murray streets opposite the City Railway Station. Look for the "Olde English" façade of **London Court** in the Hay Street Mall, a good place to find inexpensive souvenirs, including dried Western Australian wildflowers (which can be attractively boxed and mailed home for you), crafts turned from local woods, and attractive silk-screened tee-shirts. In the more upscale Forrest Chase there are numerous specialty shops and a branch of Myer, a national department-store chain. A wide variety of quality European- and Asian-made garments, leathers, and porcelain is sold here, so you won't find too much Australiana—but it's an elegant complex and worth a browse.

If you have a little more money to spend you shouldn't pass up Broome pearls and Argyle diamonds. The Argyle diamond mine in Western Australia's Kimberley has the world's largest output, based on the total number of carats produced. Most prized are the rare pink diamonds—price tags to match—but you'll find white sparklers in every price range.

Broome's pearls, known as South Sea pearls, are cultured on underwater farms. Large in comparison to Japanese pearls, they start at 10 millimeters in diameter; however, the pick of a crop may be twice this size. Avoid the huge markups these goods attract when sold overseas by buying them here in the state where they are produced. **Linneys** in Rokeby Road, Subiaco, specializes in stunningly designed jewelry featuring both pearls and diamonds. (Subiaco is a district west of the city center across King's Park.) Reputable sources of pearls include **House of Pearls** in London Court and **Currie & Smith** in Forrest Chase. More moderately priced jewelry and crafts feature the state's unique wildflowers. A range of sterling-silver jewelry, teaspoons, and letter knives, each individually handcrafted to depict the more unusual flora, is available at **Harris & Son** in the Wesley Centre Arcade in Perth (enter from Hay Street). At the **Flora**

Metallica workshop you can watch as real wildflowers from the bush are encased in gold, silver, or copper to make very moderately priced gifts; the jewelry is sold on the premises (in Glyde Street, Mosman Park, west of the city center off Stirling Highway).

Purely Australian in the Hay Street Mall, next to London Court, and **Creative Native** on King Street (between Hay and Murray streets) are the best places in Perth to buy aboriginal art and crafts. Here you'll find large emu eggs meticulously decorated with stylized animals; carved wooden birds with colorfully painted plumage; and bark paintings depicting kangaroo hunts and other bush scenes. The most dramatic items are huge canvases stippled with thousands of multicolored dots of paint, which are rudimentary maps designed to pass on the stories of the age-old aboriginal culture. This "Western Desert" style of dot painting can differ subtly in color and pattern according to aboriginal group (there are dozens of different aboriginal groups in the eastern and northwestern parts of the state).

For maps of a more modern kind—dating back to the first European discovery and settlement of Australia—**Trowbridge Prints** on Old Theatre Lane in Claremont has a fine selection. (Claremont district is southwest of King's Park on a bay off the Swan.)

Just north of Roe Street, and an easy walk after a day's shopping, is the **Northbridge** area, the cultural, nightclub, and café center of Perth. Here, all within the space of three blocks, you will find the excellent **Art Gallery of Western Australia** and the **Western Australian Museum**. The Art Gallery has a good permanent collection of European, Australian, and Asian-Pacific art. The Western Australian Museum includes a gallery of aboriginal art and houses an impressive meteorite collection. There is also a host of small restaurants and exotic food stores in the Northbridge area—see Dining in Perth, below.

Sports and Beaches

Western Australians of all ages are fanatical about sports—both playing and watching them. The city is sprinkled with sports arenas, including the **WACA** (pronounced "Whacker," the acronym stands for the Western Australian Cricket Association), a few minutes east of the city center off Hay Street. In winter the WACA becomes an Australian-rules football venue. Horse racing is held on Saturday afternoons in winter at **Belmont Park**, five minutes northeast of the city, and in summer at **Ascot**, east of the city center via the Great Eastern Highway. **Gloucester Park**, a one-minute walk north of the WACA, is the place to see pacers. National Basketball League games are played (in winter) at **Perth Entertainment Centre** on Wellington Street, close to the corner of Milligan.

With 30 miles of white-sand coastline no more than 20 minutes from downtown, there's always room on Perth's beaches. One of the best is **Cottesloe Beach**, just above North Fremantle on the north side of the Swan's mouth. Nude bathing is not legal in Western Australia, but that hasn't worried the generations of sun lovers swimming *au naturel* at popular **Swanbourne Beach**, just north of Cottesloe. To catch the waves, surfers head early in the morning for Cottesloe or **Leighton Beach**, a few minutes' drive to the south of Cottesloe.

The Swan River

A visit to Perth is incomplete without a river trip. Walk to the Barrack Street Jetty to choose your cruise. You can spend an hour or two gazing at the millionaires' mansions along the river, have dinner aboard a paddle steamer, or sail upriver to the historic Swan Valley vineyards while you enjoy lunch and wine tasting. **Boat Torque Cruises** (Tel: 09/221-5844) offers a variety of day and evening river cruises and daily trips upriver to the vineyards. **Transperth** (Tel: 09/231-1222) also runs cruises to the vineyards and calls at **Tranby House**, built on the Swan's banks in 1839. It is now a museum showing the elegance of colonial home life at the turn of the century.

The more adventurous can rent a **catamaran** in South Perth, at the north end of Coode Street, and sail on the calm Swan waters with the city skyscrapers as backdrop, or ride the breezier waters at Pelican Point, Crawley, a popular place for windsurfing. Pelican Point is southwest of the city center, a few minutes' drive from King's Park.

The Swan River was named in 1697 by Dutch explorers after the many black swans on the waterway. The black swan is unique to Western Australia and is the state symbol as well as a popular promotional motif, most notably on the label of the state's beer, Swan Lager. Today the best place to see black swans is at Lake Monger, just a few minutes' drive north of the city via the Mitchell Freeway.

Wildflowers

Western Australia's floral emblem is the kangaroo paw, an unusual wildflower with a long red, green, or yellow stem and hairy flowers that, as the name suggests, look like marsupial "hands." The kangaroo paw is just one of some 7,000 different wildflower species that are unique to the state. In fact, Western Australia has the richest collection of wildflowers known in the world, a phenomenon that has become a major seasonal attraction for visitors.

In the northwest and central areas of the state, the arid countryside literally blooms with a profuse and colorful carpet of wildflowers that stretches for miles over rolling hills and craggy rocks. Given the harsh conditions and inhospitable temperatures of some of these northern regions, it is surprising that the flowers cling to life at all, let alone exhibit such robust beauty and vivid hues. The southwest corner of the state boasts the greatest variety of wildflower species, the subtler colorings, and the most delicate of blooms. Here in the southern bushlands new wildflower species continue to be discovered. This area is also the home of more than 30 species of orchids.

Northern wildflowers bloom in late winter; in the south some flowers need the early summer warmth to bring them into bloom. Overall, however, the best time to view wildflowers is in the spring—from mid-September to early November. At this time of year many overseas and interstate tourists, visiting botanists, and botanical artists come to Perth. Perth is the base for wildflower bus tours, with botanist guides. Routes—north to the central coast area, south, or southwest—can vary daily depending on bloom reports from the field. There are many tours to choose from, ranging from day trips to three-, four-, seven-, and ten-day excursions that may also take in other attractions such as Monkey Mia's dolphins to the north or Margaret River's vineyards in the southwest (see below for both). **Feature Tours** (Tel: 09/472-4131) offers one- and five-day wildflower tours, and **Australian Pacific Tours** has a range of one-day wildflower excursions (Tel: 09/325-9377). **Pinnacle Tours** has the best range of longer excursions (Tel: 09/325-9455). Independent travellers can opt to drive through the main wildflower regions with the help of the Western Australian Tourism Commission's publication *Wildflower Discovery: A Guide for the Motorist,* available from any tourism office or the Western Australia Tourist Centre, 772 Hay Street, Perth; Tel: (09) 322-2999.

If your time is limited, make a trip to King's Park in Perth and walk or cycle on the park's bushland tracks to see thousands of wildflower species, including seven varieties of kangaroo paw and at least ten species of orchid. If you would like to take home a lasting memento of these wildflowers, consider the watercolors of the internationally renowned botanical artist Philippa Nikulinsky. She has made Perth her home to study and paint the state's flora. Call for an appointment; Tel: (09) 386-6375.

Dining and Entertainment in Perth

Perth has a lot of restaurants with a wide range of ethnic diversity. Many are B.Y.O., so you don't pay the restaurant wine markup. (Inquire to be sure when you make your reservation.) The better restaurants are closed on Monday nights.

North of Perth's railway station, in a block bounded by William, Lake, Roe, and Aberdeen streets, is the **Northbridge** area, where two can eat handsomely for as little as A\$45 at any of nearly a hundred restaurants and cafés representing most of the world's cuisines. You can't go far wrong stepping into any of these establishments, and what they lack in decor they easily make up for with good food and cheerful service. After dinner, regulars move along to one of the numerous sidewalk cafés in the area for dessert and cappuccino.

The pick of Northbridge's Chinese restaurants includes Choi's Inn and Szechuan Place in Roe Street's tiny Chinatown, and Emperor's Court on Lake Street. **Choi's Inn** offers a quiet and reasonably priced dim sum lunch every weekend; here you'll see the Aussie-Asian young professional set. (If you feel that authentic dim sum must necessarily include the yells of the trolley girls and clash of dishes, try the **Ocean Palace** on nearby Francis Street.) **Szechuan Place** is small and rather starkly decorated, but you'll find an eclectic mix of diners enjoying the excellent spicy cuisine. **Emperor's Court** is a favorite of the upwardly mobile. The decor is tasteful and you'll pay a bit more than A\$55 for two, especially if you pick the house specialties from the "live" tank.

A vast range of Western Australian and Australian seafoods is available at **Simon's Seafood Restaurant** on Francis Street. Do not expect elegant surroundings or service, just fresh produce at moderate prices. There are a lot of Italian restaurants in Northbridge, but the best Italian fare is to be found in Fremantle (see the Fremantle section, below).

On a different level, the **Matilda Bay Restaurant** in Crawley, right next to the Royal Perth Yacht Club south of King's Park, is moderately priced and specializes in seafood. It combines elegant dining with one of the best views of the Swan River; Tel: (09) 386-8014.

Lunching in the garden of the pricey **Mediterranean**, on Rokeby Road in Subiaco, is the way to see Perth's socialites, and to dine on expertly prepared international-style food served with excellent local and other Australian wines; Tel: (09) 381-2188.

Windows, in the Burswood Island Resort Hotel, ranks as Perth's premier restaurant. Time your arrival to see the sun set over the city and the Swan River from the restaurant's windows, then prepare to be pampered. The decor is sumptuous, the service is efficient and discreet, the menu features the finest of Australian produce, and the wine list is simply the best in town. Fellow diners are likely to be Japanese hotel guests and those on large expense accounts, as Windows is expensive even by local standards. However, if you intend to dip into your wallet for one memorable meal, Windows is the place; Tel: (09) 362-7777.

Haskins on Outram Street (West Perth, just minutes from the city center) has an old-fashioned atmosphere. The restaurant, located in a renovated terrace house, is small, so reservations are essential; Tel: (09) 481-6619. The cuisine is nouvelle (with a little more substance than usual) and Haskins remains popular despite having been in operation for a number of years. Moderate prices here, with the B.Y.O. advantage.

For sushi at bargain prices it's worth seeking out **Jun and Tommy's Sushi Bar** at 113 Murray Street in the city. Little more than a hole in the wall, it is popular with city workers at lunchtime and with evening theatergoers.

Early morning sees many Perthites heading for the ocean for a swim, jog, or game of beach volleyball; afterward many of them breakfast at the **Blue Duck Restaurant** on Marine Parade near Eric Street, in the Cottesloe area to the west of the city center. Here you'll see socialites showing off their tans and enjoying hearty fare or lighter specials. The café is located right on Cottesloe Beach and is also open for snacks, lunch, and dinner. Seafood is a specialty and prices are moderate.

Enter most Perth nightclubs feeling sprightly and you'll come out feeling like Methuselah—they are the province of the affluent under-25s. **Geramiah's** in the Orchard Hotel on Wellington Street and **Margaux's** in the Parmelia Hilton, close to King's Park on Mill Street, just off St. George's Terrace, however, cater to a somewhat more mature clientele.

Popular Australian and international entertainers regularly play the theater restaurants of the **Civic** on Beaufort Street, just north of the central city block, and at the Burswood Resort in the Victoria Park area. The **Oz Outback Theatre Restaurant** on James Street provides an Aussie dinner and national comedy acts, and most hotels provide live entertainment by local musicians from rock to jazz and bush bands. Colonial and Irish folk songs and a raucous atmosphere prevail at **Clancy's Tavern** in Fremantle, and jazz can be heard at the **Railway Hotel** in East Fremantle each weekend. (For more on Fremantle, see below.)

Popular cultural events include the **Festival of Perth** in February, and year-round ballet, music, and drama at several venues. Check the daily *West Australian,* particularly the paper's Thursday entertainment section, for details of what's on while you're in town.

Staying in Perth

Nowhere is far from anywhere else in Perth or Fremantle, so you don't need to stay in a centrally located hotel. You can choose from international-standard resort complexes in the city or at the beach, from more moderately priced, old-fashioned pubs in the inner city, or from the good value of the YMCA.

▶ **Burswood Resort and Casino**, located on the main highway running from the airport to the city center, is one of Perth's newest hotels, expensive by West Australian standards but well worth it. Every room in this ten-story hotel affords splendid views over the Swan River. The complex includes Australia's largest one-level casino and the vast Superdome entertainment center, as well as a golf course and a wide range of other entertainment facilities. The only trouble with staying here is dragging yourself away to see the sights.

Located just across the Swan River at Adelaide Terrace

is the ▶ **Hyatt Regency Hotel**. This upscale establishment, popular with businesspeople, has a soaring lobby, great views over the river, and a good shopping arcade and restaurant complex.

For a more moderately priced accommodation in the heart of Perth's shopping center on Murray Street try the ▶ **Wentworth Plaza**. This pleasant, older-style hotel has recently been refurbished. It's a short stroll from here to the best shops, theaters, and restaurants.

The ▶ **Hotel Regatta,** in the heart of downtown on the corner of Hay and Pier streets, offers budget-style accommodation that is not too bare or basic. The hotel was one of Perth's first, built in 1850, and it was the first public building in the city to be electrified. From here it is a short walk to all the Perth action. The Regatta is a lively hotel with friendly, helpful staff. The two bars are popular with the locals, however, so noise can be a disadvantage. Room rates include a cooked breakfast.

▶ **Jewell House**, a YMCA hotel, is less noisy, even more moderately priced than the Regatta, and centrally located on Goderich Street, a few minutes' walk east of the main city block. The hotel is tidy, represents good value for the money, and has to be the most cheerful of the city's cheap accommodations for the traveller on a limited budget.

The place to stay if you want good beachside accommodation is the ▶ **Observation City Resort Hotel**. Prices are on the high side but you are paying for a great Indian Ocean location. Built to capture views of the 1987 America's Cup yacht racing, it's situated on **Scarborough Beach**, just 20 minutes northwest of Perth. Unlike those in other hotels, the shops in Observation City stay open seven days a week. The **Spice Market** restaurant in this shopping arcade specializes in Mongolian barbecue, where your selection of wafer-thin meats, vegetables, and exotic sauces is cooked by the chef on a hot plate at your table. This fun way to dine is popular with hotel guests and adventurous locals.

FREMANTLE

Although only 20 minutes by taxi from Perth's central business district, historic Freo (as it's affectionately known) was originally a separate port city servicing Perth and is completely different from its skyscrapered neighbor. While Fremantle is almost engulfed by subur-

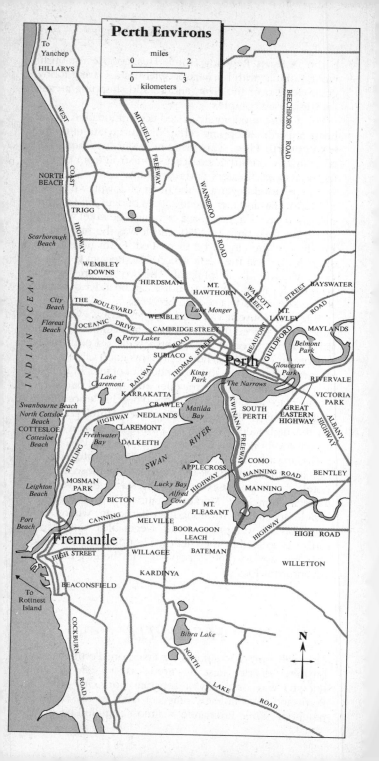

bia, fortunately this has not destroyed its historical charm, for the city has been described as having the best intact collection of 19th-century British Colonial architecture in the world. These buildings owe their elegance and abundance to the arrival of convicts in 1850, who provided the labor for construction; to the discovery of gold in Kalgoorlie in the 1890s, which created a boom economy, an influx of prospectors, and a perceived need for public buildings in the port town; and to the foresight of engineer C.Y. O'Connor, who dredged the harbor to make Fremantle a viable port.

The **Round House**, at the waterfront end of High Street, is the oldest public building in Western Australia, completed in 1831 as the colony's first jail for local felons. The small, rudimentary cells were crowded from 1850 on, when convicts began arriving from Britain. A tunnel underneath the Round House was where whales were dragged from shore to be stripped of blubber.

Fremantle Gaol was built of local stone by convict labor from 1851 to 1859. It was occupied as a prison from 1855 until just three years ago, when the inmates were moved to a new facility. The complex is now open to the public every day. The gaol museum has an extensive photographic history from the early convict days to the present. The gaol is east of the city center at 1 The Terrace, best reached via Fothergill Street.

The **Fremantle Museum and Arts Centre** on Finnerty Street was built from 1860 to 1864 as an insane asylum and is considered one of the finest examples of convict-built Colonial Gothic architecture in Australia. It is worth spending time here to understand the hardships of the early days, Fremantle's convict history, and the port's role in providing Britain and other Commonwealth countries with wheat, meat, and wool. (Open Monday to Thursday from 10:30 A.M. to 5:00 P.M.; Friday to Sunday, afternoons only.)

Old sea stories abound in Fremantle. The **Maritime Museum** on Cliff Street illustrates how Dutch mariners bound for the Spice Islands (Indonesia) were blown east by the Roaring Forties to hit the treacherous Western Australian coastline. The main feature is a reconstruction of part of the hull of the *Batavia,* which sank off the Abrolhos Islands in 1629. The mutiny of the ship's crew and the murder of many of the passengers aboard make a harrowing tale. Visitors can see work in progress on the fragile, waterlogged timbers. Relics on display from other early Dutch wrecks include cannonballs, elephant tusks, navigational instruments, and armor. The oldest section of the museum building dates back to 1852, when it was used as the Commissariat for the Convict Establishment; by 1878 it was a customshouse and bonded warehouse. (Open Monday to Thursday from 10:30 A.M. to 5:00 P.M.; Friday to Sunday, afternoons only.)

Also on Cliff Street is the home of Lionel and Fanny Samson, one of Fremantle's founding families. Lionel bought the land in 1829—the year he was granted a merchant's spirit license. (His descendants still run a liquor importing business.) His first house burned down, and the existing building was erected in 1898. Lionel's house is not open to the public, but on Ellen Street, a short walk from the city center, the home built for his son Michael is open Thursdays and Sundays from 1:00 P.M. to 4:30 P.M. This house, completed between 1888 and 1900, gives an idea of how affluent Fremantle families lived at the turn of the century.

Fremantle now boasts more than 160 buildings from the 19th century on Australia's National Heritage list. Fremantle's tourist information center, located in the town hall on St. Johns Square in the center of the city, offers a number of brochures that give details of historical walks to see the best of the colonial architecture. Fremantle's "tram" (in fact a motorized vehicle) also takes visitors on a historical tour every day. Details of the tram's schedule are available at the town hall.

The **Endeavour replica** on Mews Road is an ambitious project to build in local jarrah timber a copy of the vessel James Cook sailed to reach and explore Australia. When completed in 1994 the ship will sail to Sydney. It is worth setting aside an hour to see the construction area, adjacent sail loft, and informative video about the project.

On South Terrace are the bustling **Fremantle Markets** (open from Friday to Sunday), originally built in 1897, where locals shop for food, cheap and cheerful clothing, and even antiques. Good buys for visitors are the Aussie handicrafts, including jewelry, toys, and leatherwork. For more gifts and souvenirs try the **Bannister Street Craftworks** on nearby Bannister Street.

Around the corner on High Street is the **Birrukmarri Gallery**, which sells an impressive collection of aboriginal wooden handicrafts and art; on the pedestrian mall section of High Street at **Desert Designs and Friends**, vibrant aboriginal-design fabrics are made up into a range of casual clothes for men and women.

Staying and Dining in Fremantle

Thanks to the impetus provided by modern-day sailing and especially by Fremantle's role as host for the 1987 America's Cup yacht race, the city received a major shot in the arm to renovate some of the seedier pubs and restaurants and build new facilities for the influx of yachtsmen and spectators. This spate of restoration and new construction intensified Fremantle's resortlike character. Cup-inspired meeting places include **Lombardo's Restaurant and Bar** complex, built over Fishing Boat Harbour; the courtyard restaurant of the refurbished **Esplanade Fremantle Hotel** on Marine Terrace; and **Old Papa's and Gino's**, the best known of the open-air cafés on South Terrace.

The Cup transformed many of the old run-down sailors' hotels, and making a pub crawl in Fremantle today is a delight. Typical is the **Sail and Anchor** on South Terrace, which makes its own "real ale." The **Norfolk** is across the street, and a two-minute walk north brings you to the **Newport**—both pubs with a laid-back Fremantle atmosphere.

Western Australia's lobster, known as crayfish, is a specialty at the **Oyster Beds Restaurant**, set on the Swan River at the north end of town. It is easy to spend a leisurely afternoon here watching the yachts while dining alfresco on superb seafood at very reasonable prices.

Two good places for Italian food are Apicius and Café Amadeus. **Apicius**, on Wray Avenue (a ten-minute walk southeast from Fremantle Markets), serves Tuscan-style cuisine with the emphasis on innovative sauces and simply perfect pasta. Apicius is open for dinner from Wednesday to Sunday, and for lunch on Fridays and Sundays. It is a B.Y.O. restaurant, and prices are moderate. **Café Amadeus**, located in a turn-of-the-century house on George Street complete with roaring log fires in winter, serves excellent pasta as well as other Italian and European dishes.

Sails, on Mews Road overlooking Bather's Beach, is the place to watch the sun set over the Indian Ocean. Here you can have a romantic meal and dine on seafood without breaking the bank. The terrace catches the winter sun, making Sails a comfortable outdoor spot in cooler weather. Opposite Sails is the **Chunagon Japanese Restaurant**, where you'll be treated to a total Japanese dining experience. Daily specials can make dining here quite inexpensive.

The ▶ **Esplanade Fremantle Hotel** on Marine Terrace is the place to stay if you want to make Fremantle your base. Popular with those who love Fremantle's relaxed atmosphere, this 19th-century hotel had a splendid refitting for the America's Cup and offers the best of the old and the new at a moderate price.

The ▶ **Trade Winds Hotel** on Canning Highway is a little far from town but remains a popular spot with families and businesspeople for its reasonable rates and special accommodation packages. With an old-style façade and modern interior, it maintains a hint of the Freo atmosphere. **Trader Morgan's Bar** in the hotel is a gathering place for locals.

ROTTNEST ISLAND

Perth's island playground, just 11 miles offshore from Fremantle, was given its name from the first Dutch mariners, who called it "Rat's Nest," believing that the small animals they found on the island were vermin. Actually they are quokkas: small, friendly marsupials that delight in being fed from your hand. By day they stay under shady trees; at night, when they get more adventurous, they are everywhere.

In 1831, just two years after the founding of the Swan River Settlement (in Perth), the Thomson family moved to Rottnest and scratched out a living collecting salt and curing fish until the government reclaimed the land for an aboriginal prison. The jail (now part of the Rottnest Lodge Resort), warders' cottages, and church were all built by prison labor. In 1903 the prison was closed and by 1917 locals were vacationing on the island.

During World War II Rottnest's strategic location was important in the planned defense of Perth, and today the gun emplacements, ammunition tunnels, and engine rooms on Oliver's Hill have been restored. Check at the museum at Thomson Bay for the schedule of the guided tour of the facility.

Rottnest is a special place. Only the locals have cars and there are few phones. The island has gently rolling hills, shaded wooded valleys where you're sure to find quokkas, salt lakes teeming with birdlife, secluded coves, clean white beaches, and safe anchorages. Visiting here is what vacations must have been like before resorts were invented.

You can't take a motor vehicle to Rottnest, so island transport is by bicycle or on foot. This is no hardship, however, as the island is roughly seven miles long and a round-island trip on the coast-hugging road is about 17 miles—a two-hour cycle at the most. (You can rent an inexpensive bicycle at Thomson Bay from the shop behind the pub.)

If pedal power isn't your style, you'll find that most interesting spots are within easy walking distance. There's also a bus at the ferry berth to take you around the island to get your bearings and see the sights.

The settlement in **Thomson Bay** is the center of activity. In January the bay is covered with yachts and power boats, and the settlement hums day and night. Of the island's two hotels, young people gather at the ▶ **Rottnest Hotel**, originally the summer home for West Australian governors. This moderately priced establishment is nicknamed the Quokka Arms by locals, and its beer garden is the scene of much raucous activity during summer weekends. It has a great location right on Thomson Bay beach, but can be noisy during school vacations and public holidays. As elsewhere, rates are lower in the off season (May through November). The more upscale (though likewise moderately priced) ▶ **All Seasons Rottnest Lodge Resort** is popular with an older, more sedate clientele. The resort is peaceful even though it's only a couple of minutes' walk from the main action at Thomson Bay.

▶ **Rottnest Island Self Catering Cottages** are budget-priced family accommodations in well-equipped cottages dotted around Thomson, Longreach, and Geordie bays, which, except for school holidays, can be booked at relatively short notice. A villa in Thompson Bay overlooking the ocean sleeps four and rents by the week; rates are lower from May to September, higher during peak season, with an additional fee for sheets, towels, and cutlery.

Sampling the local seafood is imperative on the island. Both hotels offer inexpensive buffet lunches featuring a "bottomless" platter of prawns. The Lodge Resort throws shrimp on the barbie for lunch at least once a week and has a moderately priced à la carte menu in the evening. But the dining spot that offers the most fun is the **Rottnest Restaurant** in the heart of Thomson Bay. It features a view of the passing parade on foot, bicycle, and afloat, and a huge seafood menu—with portion sizes to match—at low prices. The atmosphere is unpretentious and tables are squashed together, so in no time you may find yourself sharing a bottle of wine with neighboring diners.

Rottnest's many protected bays, with white-sand beaches and fringing coral reefs, are ideal boat havens. The beaches at Thomson Bay, and Longreach and Geordie bays (just a 20-minute stroll north from Thomson), are best for safe swimming. Fishermen may prefer the wilder waters at Rocky Bay or West Point at the western end of the island. Divers can visit the museum at Thomson Bay for the **Rottnest Wreck Trail** brochure, which shows locations of 11 wrecks accessible to scuba divers or snorkelers. You can rent gear at Thomson Bay, or contact Diving Ventures in Fremantle (Tel: 09/336-1664) to arrange an all-inclusive scuba package for a day's diving in the waters around the island. Rottnest is a reserve, so no spear guns are allowed. If you're not quite so adventurous, take in the best of the coral and shipwrecks on the mini-submarine at Thomson Bay.

Getting to Rottnest is easy. If you want to combine a sea trip with a river trip you can take a ferry from the Barrack Street Jetty in Perth; otherwise, catch ferries directly either from Fremantle or from the boat harbor at Hillarys, in Perth's northern beach area (see below). The trip downriver from Perth takes about 40 minutes, and it is half an hour over the sea from both coastal exit points.

Alternatively, you can fly to Rottnest in just 12 minutes at low cost from both Perth and Jandakot airports (the latter is a 30-minute drive south of the city, off the Roe Highway).

ATTRACTIONS NEAR PERTH

Drive north on the West Coast Highway to Perth's new beachside suburbs and you probably won't be able to resist a cooling dip in the Indian Ocean. At **Mettam's** and **Hamersley Pools**—between Trigg and North Beach—natural rock formations have formed shallow, safe swimming areas that are pleasantly warm year round.

Farther along the highway—some 30 minutes from the city—is **Hillarys Boat Harbour**, which serves as a private marina, the public ferry berth for excursions to Rottnest Island, and a tourist center with shops, outdoor restaurants, and children's activities. At **Underwater World** in this complex visitors walk through underwater tunnels and view sharks, turtles, rays, and all kinds of local fish.

Thirty minutes farther north, **Yanchep National Park** has a colony of koalas, typical bush birdlife, and limestone caves.

Just over an hour's drive east of Perth through the Avon Valley is the old town of **York**, with its fine historic buildings. **Faversham House**, completed in the 1850s, was built with the profits of an early sandalwood-cutting industry. It is a fine example of a country colonial mansion and is open to the public. Car enthusiasts should not miss the collection of antique and vintage cars, motorcycles, and horse-drawn vehicles at the **York Motor Museum** on the main street, and the **Residency Museum** has a display of artifacts that catalogue daily village life in the 1890s. Accommodation options in York include the four-poster beds of the gracious ▶ **Settlers' House** on the main street. It's rather expensive, but well worth it for the experience.

At **Armadale**, 30 km (19 miles) southeast of Perth, artists and craftspeople at **Pioneer World**, a re-creation of a colonial village, make and sell pottery, ornaments turned from local jarrah and blackboy woods, ironwork, wooden toys, and woollen clothing. There is more craft than culture, but it is fun all the same. You'll find street theater, turn-of-the-century costumes, and the opportunity to buy copies of the necessities of a bygone age such as flour-sack shirts and those fly-deflecting hats with corks dangling around the brim.

THE SOUTHWEST

A couple of hours' drive south from Perth leads to **Bunbury**, a cooler, mixed-farming area that produces wheat, wool, and beef. There are two routes from Perth, either via the South Western Highway from Armadale through the vegetable- and fruit-growing districts of Harvey or via the Coast Road through the beachside resort of Mandurah and windswept sand-dune country. Bunbury is Western Australia's commercial and shipping center and, with a population of 40,000, is the second-largest city in the state, after greater Perth. At **Koombana Bay**, just minutes from the city center, dolphins play close to shore and allow swimmers to approach them.

THE MARGARET RIVER REGION
Drive for less than an hour southwest of Bunbury on the Bussell Highway via the coastal holiday resort of

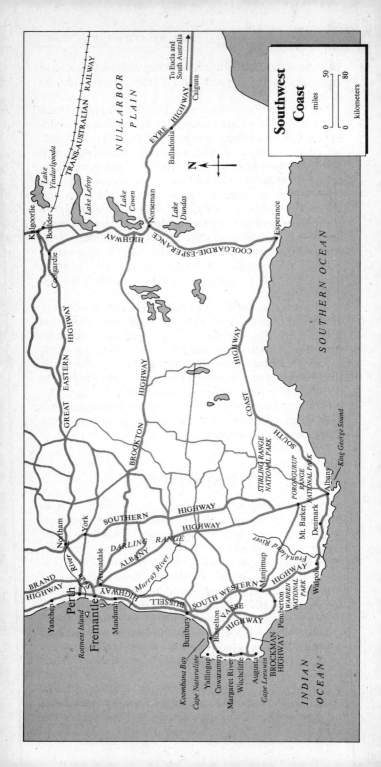

Busselton and you're in one of the finest wine-growing areas in Australia. On the well-signposted 25-km (40-mile) drive south to the town of **Margaret River**, more than 30 wineries welcome visitors to taste and buy from their cellars. Many have restaurants serving simple or more elaborate fare.

Perhaps the best known of the wineries is **Leeuwin Estate** (designed with the help of Robert Mondavi of California's Napa Valley), ten minutes south of Margaret River. Leeuwin's Chardonnay is internationally acclaimed, and the winery produces a wide range of wine styles, all of which are Australian medal winners. The winery has a fine restaurant featuring local produce—beef, freshwater crustaceans called marrons, and local Brie-type cheese. Each February Leeuwin hosts an open-air concert as part of the Festival of Perth. Artists who have performed here include Dionne Warwick, Ray Charles, and the London Philharmonic Orchestra with Dame Kiri Te Kanawa. Other wineries in the area with a top range of wines and attractive restaurants include **Amberley Estate** at **Yallingup** (15 miles west of Busselton) and **Brookland Valley Vineyard** on the banks of the Willyabrup Brook, 10 miles north of Margaret River, near Cowaramup.

Other attractions in the region from Busselton to Augusta include limestone caves at Yallingup near Witchcliffe (10 miles south of Margaret River), and at Augusta (25 miles south of Margaret River). They are all open to the public every day. The coast due west of Margaret River has wide beaches and is a venue for international **surfing** events; the rugged coastline tracks here are at their best in spring, when wildflowers are in bloom. The town of Margaret River itself is an artists' enclave, and there are numerous art galleries and crafts shops in the district.

MARGARET RIVER TO PEMBERTON

Pemberton is 90 minutes' drive from Margaret River. The route runs east on the Brockman Highway on the fringe of the southwestern wilderness area, where there are few tracks, and where botanists are still finding wildflower species unknown elsewhere in the world, then south on the Vasse Highway through the tall-timber country. **Pemberton** is a tiny sawmill town (population 1,000) in the heart of forest country dominated by giant karri trees. The tallest known karri is 288 feet, towering over the other hardwoods—marri, tingle, and jarrah—that make up the region's temperate rain forest. A karri's circumference measured in millimeters is roughly equal to its age in years, so be sure to pack a tape measure.

There are many signposted driving trails through the forests. The tallest accessible karri—236 feet high—is in the **Warren National Park**, just minutes from Pemberton; at the eastern end of the township is the **Gloucester Tree** fire lookout, where the fit and fearless can climb the huge karri's 153 rungs to reach a viewing platform 200 feet high. The Pemberton tram runs on old bush rail tracks through magnificent forest country; in spring this is a perfect way to view wildflowers.

The place to stay is in the heart of the forest at ▶ **Quality Karri Valley Resort** on the Vasse Highway just east of Pemberton. You can stay in a motel-style accommodation, where you can fish from your bedroom window for trout in the large lake, or you might opt for a self-contained chalet.

Other attractions in the region include a trout hatchery, the **Fine Woodcraft Gallery** in Pemberton, which shows superb crafted work in local woods, and historical and modern sawmills. At **Manjimup**, a 30-minute drive north on the South Western Highway, the **Timber Park and Museum** illustrates the logging history of the area from the first sawpits in 1830; exhibits include a mill steam engine and a karri log "time clock" with 350 years of historic events displayed on its growth rings.

PEMBERTON TO ALBANY

Albany, about 210 km (130 miles) southeast of Pemberton, is a good base from which to explore the diverse scenery of the southern tip of the state: To the east are calm inlets fringed by giant karri trees; the port of Albany is dominated by huge granite rock formations; and, to the north near Mount Barker, the Stirling Range and Porongurup national parks have popular walking trails amid stark rock peaks that rise to heights of more than 3,000 feet. The best route to Albany from Pemberton is via the tiny town of Walpole, an hour's drive south on the South West Highway. This is big-timber country, with plenty of well-signposted lookouts and scenic drives through the forests. The coast from Walpole 66 km (41 miles) east to **Denmark** has a number of broad inlets with fine white sands ideal for water sports, boating, and fishing. At Denmark, Goundrey and Tinglewood wineries offer tastings, and there are a number of art and craft shops featuring locally made ceramics, turned-wood artifacts, and woollen items.

Albany, 48 km (30 miles) further east, has an impressive setting on wild cliffs and majestic rock formations. The port was settled in 1826, 30 months before Perth was founded. Within walking distance of the main street is the **Old Gaol,** which now houses a museum detailing the settlement of the town and a replica of the ship *Amity,* which brought the first settlers to Albany. To the east is Strawberry Hill Farm, built in 1836 as the home of Albany's resident (or governor).

A ten-minute drive around the southern side of the King George Sound Inlet brings you to the rocky outcrop that bears the full force of the Southern Ocean. The granite "Bridge" and the infamous "Gap" (where unwary fishermen and star-crossed lovers have fallen 75 feet to their death) are at their most spectacular when the sea is running high. A few minutes' drive away is **Whaleworld,** set in the town's former whaling station. Whaling was Albany's largest industry from early colonial days until as recently as 1978, and Whaleworld's museum tells the bloody story through photographs and artifacts.

ALONG THE ALBANY HIGHWAY

The five-hour drive from Albany back to Perth via the Albany Highway passes through the state's major sheep-herding and wheat-growing region of **Mount Barker** (now also becoming known for its wines). Thirty-three kilometers (20 miles) east of Mount Barker is **Porongurup National Park,** offering accessible and popular walking tracks through the steep granite outcrops. There are many well-signposted trails to choose from, depending on how much time you have and your level of fitness. Two trails recommended for the spectacular views of seas of wheat and wildflowers are the ones to Castle Rock (more than 1,700 feet high), which takes 90 minutes including return, and to Devil's Slide (more than 2,000 feet high), which will take about two hours. Committed hiking enthusiasts should head to the **Stirling Range National Park,** 56 km (35 miles) to the north, where the peaks rise to more than 3,000 feet and the rigorous climbs can take up to five hours.

THE GOLD COUNTRY

It was the discovery of gold in **Kalgoorlie** by Paddy Hannan in 1893 that made the powers in the east of Australia sit up and take notice of Western Australia, for the resulting gold rush doubled the state's population in three years and provided an economic boost for development statewide.

Kalgoorlie and its sister town, **Boulder**, are located about six hours' drive east of Perth via the Great Eastern Highway (or overnight by train). Between the twin towns is the so-called **Golden Mile**, site of one of the world's richest gold seams. Under present-day suburban streets lies a rabbit warren of mine tunnels, many of which were in use up until five years ago, when a consortium of gold-mining companies began the "Super Pit." This vast, open-cut mine is three miles long by one mile wide and 300 feet deep.

At the **Hainault Tourist Mine**, visitors can go 200 feet underground in an abandoned mine with ex-miner guides. On the surface you'll see demonstrations of molten gold being poured into molds, as well as a display of old mining tools and relics. The Loop Line railway, which leaves daily from Boulder City station, circuits the Golden Mile via Golden Gate (once the busiest station in the state), the old headframes, and the vast mine waste dumps. There's more history of the magical metal at the new **Museum of the Goldfields**. Here visitors take an elevator up the headframe of the defunct Ivanhoe mine for panoramic views of the Golden Mile and down into the vaults to see gold ingots, jewelry, and a fascinating collection of photographs that catalogues every facet of life during the gold-rush years.

Kalgoorlie has legal brothels, many hard-drinking bars, and no shortage of players for Two-Up, a traditional Australian gambling game played by tossing two coins. Most hotels and bars here are basic but full of atmosphere. The most comfortable place to stay is the ▶ **Quality Plaza Hotel** on Egan Street, just off Hannan, the town's main street. It is modern and reasonably priced, but has none of the hard-drinking, hard-talking action for which Kalgoorlie is renowned. For atmosphere and a bargain price, try the ▶ **Palace Hotel**. This gracious old inn on the corner of Maritana and Hannan has seen better days but is brimming with atmosphere. Its bars are the haunts of many a local character with a tall tale to tell. And do visit the other hotels—there are plenty to choose from.

At **Coolgardie**, 40 km (25 miles) west of Kalgoorlie, the Goldfields Exhibition shows what life was like for prospectors in 1898, when the town supported two stock exchanges and 23 hotels and had a population of 15,000 (today it is 1,500).

THE NULLARBOR PLAIN

This vast, virtually treeless and waterless plain in the central south of Australia is crossed by the Eyre Highway, which runs inland east from Norseman (south of Kalgoorlie) along the southern coast of Australia to Adelaide. This is a memorable drive for the achievement you feel in completing it, for the wildlife, and for the acute sense you gain of nature's harshness.

The west–east Eyre Highway is named after Edward Eyre, who in 1841 was the first European explorer to trek some 1,000 miles west around the coast of the Great Australian Bight—a formidable accomplishment. To drive across the Nullarbor today requires stamina and two to three days. The softer option is to take one of the world's most exciting train journeys, either on the Indian Pacific (Perth to Sydney) or the Trans Australian (Perth to Port Pirie, just outside Adelaide) route. From Norseman, at the start of the Eyre Highway (and 725 km/450 miles southeast of Perth), to the Western Australian–South Australian border is 725 km (450 miles); from here it is another 1,275 km (790 miles) to Adelaide.

Along the route are roadhouses with basic accommodations, restaurants, and gas and water. Whatever you do, fill up, for there is virtually nothing in between stops. The tourism department in **Norseman** will book accommodation ahead and advise you on driving conditions. Travellers share the road with all manner of vehicles, from family sedans to buses and four-wheel-drive trucks, and share the adjoining country with kangaroos, emus, camels, dingoes, and birdlife, including wedge-tailed eagles.

Tackling the Eyre Highway is no mean feat, and winter is the only time recommended for visitors to attempt the drive; in summer temperatures can soar as high as 122 degrees F. There are plenty of points of interest along the way, none more than a mile or two from the highway. What appears to be a "tabletop" mountain at Norseman is, in fact, a four-million-ton tailings dump of crushed gold-bearing quartz. **Balladonia** is where the Skylab satellite fell to earth, and from here to the next settlement, Caiguna, is, at 145 km (90 miles), the longest straight stretch of road in the world. At **Eucla**, close to the border, are the ruins of a turn-of-the-century telegraph station that once linked the eastern and western parts of the continent. Just over the border on the South Australian side, the road nears limestone cliffs that drop hundreds of feet down to the foaming ocean.

THE CENTRAL COAST

The major port town of **Geraldton**, five hours north of Perth, is the center of an area that offers many sightseeing opportunities. Perhaps the best of these are the protected, unspoiled coral islands of the Abrolhos group, which can be visited by charter boat, and the now-famous wild **dolphins** that come into the shallows to be fed and patted at Monkey Mia 300 km (186 miles) farther up the coast.

You can take a weekend cruise to the **Abrolhos Islands** from Geraldton aboard a 75-foot schooner equipped with diving and fishing gear; check Geraldton's tourism office on Chapman Road for details. The Abrolhos Islands, a chain of dozens of small, low-lying rocky outcrops, are a base for the local lobster-fishing fleet and a haven for seabirds. The islands are not particularly attractive; what draws visitors here is the excellent fishing in the surrounding waters, the tropical corals and fish visible through the pristinely clear water, and the opportunity to dive into historic wrecks (including the *Batavia,* marked by an underwater plaque, a reconstruction of whose hull is featured in Fremantle's Maritime Museum). The islands are a six-hour motor-sail from the port, so this is a trip in itself.

A visit to **Monkey Mia** is best combined with a general Central Coast trip taking in Geraldton, the seaside retreat of Kalbarri and nearby gorges to its north, and the eerie **Pinnacles** limestone formations near Cervantes, halfway between Perth and Geraldton.

Kalbarri is the ideal base from which to see the region; here you can choose between river and sea for your recreation activities. The tiny town is at the mouth of the Murchison River, which has scoured the landscape to form 50 miles of spectacular gorges. The **Murchison Gorges** feature dramatic, massive cliffs that drop sheer to the river below and have been eroded over the centuries to reveal red, white, cream, and orange bands of sandstone. The Loop and Z Bend gorges are just 64 km (40 miles) east from Kalbarri and easily accessible by car. Hawks Head Lookout, a 40-km (25-mile) drive northeast of the town, is a popular picnic spot overlooking the gorges. Four-wheel-drive gorge tours are available for visitors who want to

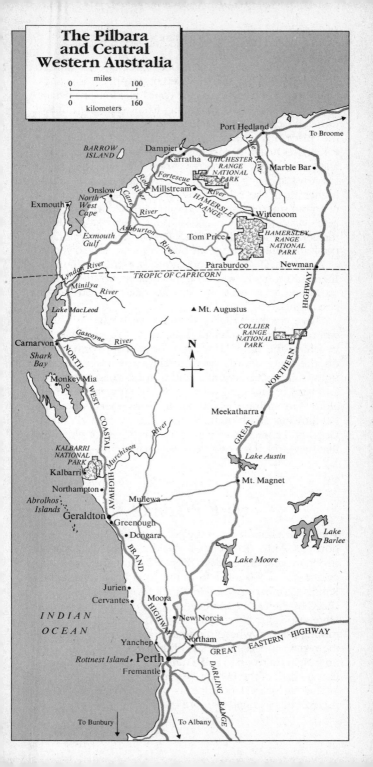

reach some of the less easily accessible places, and there are air charters that take in views of the Abrolhos Islands, **Shark Bay**, and the gorges. See your hotel for tour details.

There is also excellent fishing from white-sand Indian Ocean beaches in the Kalbarri region. The river estuary is the place for safe swimming and water skiing. The ▶ **Kalbarri Beach Resort** has a prime position for estuary and ocean views, a good restaurant, a popular bar, and a range of sporting facilities. The room rates are a little higher than the other family-style accommodations in town but still represent good value. For a more moderate price visitors can choose a self-catering two-story villa in the centrally located ▶ **Reef Villas** complex, which has a pool and offers free use of bikes, canoes, and rowboats.

The Central Coast is not noted for its fine cuisine. Increased tourism will no doubt change this, but in the meantime it is best to ask the locals for advice on restaurants.

There are three flights a week from Perth to Kalbarri, where you can rent a car at the airport for side trips. If you have the time, however, a drive from Perth to the Central Coast affords views of craggy, windswept coastlines, rolling farm country, and historic stone flour mills and farm cottages at Dongara and Greenough, near Geraldton. In spring (September to November), when the wildflowers are blooming, the country from Perth to Geraldton comes alive with colorful carpets of blossoms that may stretch for two to three square miles.

THE PILBARA

The Pilbara region spans the center of the state 600 miles north of Perth. To the west are the coastal fishing and diving meccas of Coral Bay, Exmouth, and Onslow. In the center, some 300 miles from the coast in the **Hamersley Range National Park**, ancient rock formations have been sliced by the Fortescue River to form magnificent gorges. Here also is the heart of the state's billion-dollar iron-ore mining district, where mountains are literally moved as the red, iron-bearing rock is blasted, crushed, and carted on freight trains up to half a mile long up to Port Hedland in the north of the Pilbara, where the ore is exported.

The Pilbara's landscape is characterized by large, jagged ranges tinged iron-ore red; sparse, low-lying bush;

and arid, inhospitable terrain. There are no facilities between settlements. Winter is the best time to visit, for in the summer heavy rain can make roads impassable and temperatures are almost unbearable. It is such a vast area that most visitors choose to fly into the gorge country, then drive north via the tropical oasis of Millstream to Karratha and fly farther afield from there. (See Getting Around, below, for more information on driving in the Pilbara.)

Wittenoom is the base from which to see the gorges of the Hammersley Range, but it is not possible to fly there directly. There are daily flights from Perth to the mining town of **Tom Price**, where, at the airport, you can rent a car to drive the 70 km (43 miles) northeast to Wittenoom. A visit to the mine at Tom Price is interesting because it gives an idea of the enormous scale of the operation.

The only hotel in Wittenoom is the ▶ **Hotel Fortescue** on Gregory Street. Fewer than 100 people live in town, so visitors are always given a friendly welcome and plenty of tourist information. In the 1960s the town was the biggest in the state's northwest because of blue asbestos deposits that were used in home construction and fencing. When it was discovered that asbestos fibers may cause lung cancer the mine was closed. Even today visitors are advised to close car windows in windy or dusty conditions and to avoid getting too near asbestos-tailings deposits.

The gorges are south and southeast of Wittenoom. The best route is to begin with a drive through **Yampire Gorge**, just 24 km (15 miles) southeast of the town, where multicolored banded rock towers in sheer cliffs high above. Sixteen kilometers (10 miles) farther south, **Circular Pool** and **Fortesque Falls** feature waterfalls and deep pools fringed by lush palms and ferns. At **Kalamina Gorge** easy walking trails wind through tropical vegetation, and at **Joffre** and **Red Gorges** the cliffs are so steep that sunlight rarely penetrates to the pools below, and their water's temperature is near freezing.

From Wittenoom it is a four-hour drive on unpaved roads to **Karratha**. The drive passes through cattle country; this is where some of Western Australia's biggest cattle ranches are. **Millstream**, in the Chichester National Park, is at the halfway point and is a well-signposted 10-km (6-mile) detour off the main road. Here there are cool pools surrounded by lush ferns, date palms (complete with a colony of fruit bats), and tropical river gums. You can camp at Millstream, but there are no facilities.

THE KIMBERLEY

The Kimberley Plateau region in the northwest is Western Australia's last frontier, poised to become one of the country's major tourism drawing cards. It's an awesome area. In the remote hinterland you can gaze over craggy, million-year-old landscapes, dramatic gorges, and thousands of square miles of rugged bushland on which no one has ever stood. To the west is the historic pearling port of Broome, magnificent beaches, and a rugged coast deserted except for isolated aboriginal missions. In the northeast, close to the Northern Territory border, are tropical Kununurra and Lake Argyle—the largest man-made lake in Australia.

The best time to visit the Kimberley is in the dry season from April to September, when the (albeit tropical) climate is warm to hot. At other times the weather is unbearably hot and humid, and there is the likelihood of a journey's being cut off by flash flooding.

It is impossible to see everything in the vast Kimberley region, so first-time visitors might make their base in the Kununurra region, a four-hour flight from Perth, then take a four-wheel-drive tour with experienced bush guides to the remote wilderness of the Bungle Bungle mountain region to the south of Kununurra, and finish with some R&R in Broome, just a two-hour flight west of Kununurra on the Indian Ocean. Seven days is the minimum for such a Kimberley experience.

The Kununurra Region

Flights leave Perth daily for Kununurra. Be sure to ask for a window seat on the plane so you can marvel at the thousands of miles of rugged coast and the remote, red interior you'll see en route.

Kununurra is a modern town, built in the 1960s to service the huge **Ord River** dam and irrigation scheme. The innovative plan was to turn desert into a major fruit- and sugar-producing area—and the land is certainly green—but falling sugar prices and the site's remoteness from main markets have impeded the project's success.

The region has a major attraction for visitors, though: When the Ord was dammed, **Lake Argyle** was formed, and it is now the biggest man-made lake in the Southern Hemisphere. Here you can take your pick from a wide

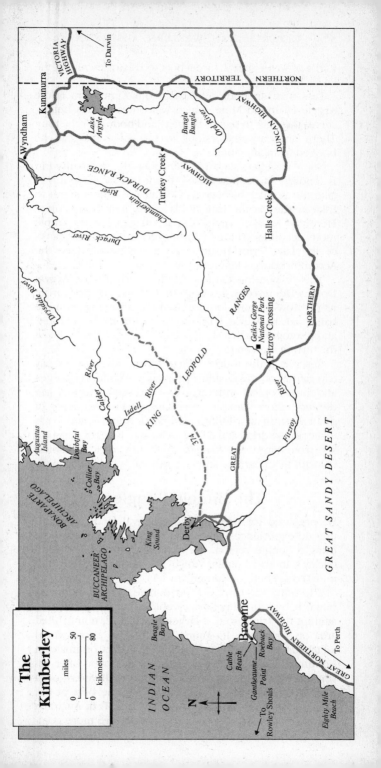

range of water sports, hire a boat to fish, or picnic on the lake's lush banks.

Less than an hour by coach from Kununurra is the **Argyle Diamond Mine**, which welcomes visitors but reserves the right to search baggage and body after the tour. There are daily excursions to the mine that can be booked from any hotel.

Some travellers stay in Kununurra—the ► **Quality Inn** is modern and comfortable—but it is a lot more fun to take the regular bus service 75 km (46 miles) south to Lake Argyle via the fruit fields of the irrigation project. Here the ► **Lake Argyle Tourist Village** provides simple motel accommodation in a removed setting on the banks of the lake. Prior reservations are advisable (see the Accommodations Reference list below).

The pioneering Durack family's early home, **Argyle Downs Homestead**, has been moved brick by brick from its previous remote location to the tourist village on the banks of Lake Argyle. It is now a museum and has exhibits and photographs that show the hardships of station life at the turn of the century.

Reserve at the tourist village for an adventurous day trip **rafting** on the Ord River through magnificent gorges and thick tropical undergrowth—and seeing, from a safe distance, those famous crocodiles. You'll see plenty of other Australian wildlife in the area. Animals and birds that come to drink at the lake include all types of marsupials, from large red kangaroos to tiny rock wallabies, colorful bush parrots, storks, cormorants, and pelicans.

The Bungle Bungles

Be prepared for breathtaking primeval landscapes and unique experiences when you venture into the remote Bungle Bungle region, the most dramatic of The Kimberley's interior sights, which lies about 200 km (122 miles) due south of Kununurra.

The only way to reach the Bungle Bungle mountain range is by four-wheel-drive vehicle, but it is unwise to attempt the trip into this largely uncharted, uninhabited area on your own. It's much safer to take a four-wheel safari run by skilled bushmen. Safari tours originate in Kununurra, and there are many operators who offer adventure trips of up to ten days' duration. If you're on a limited timetable, it is possible to see the best of the sights on a three- or four-day trek. (**SafariTrek Australia** includes many extras to make the adventure more comfortable. It operates a variety of tours from May to August and can be contacted at its Perth office; Tel: 09/322-2188.) Prices are moderate and all-inclusive. If time is really short you can take an air charter from Kununurra for a bird's-eye view of the Bungle Bungle and surrounding district.

When you join a four-wheel-drive adventure trek there's a 150-km (90-mile) drive south from Kununurra on paved roads through cattle country, then it's unpaved roads through the bush some 50 km (30 miles) to the Bungle Bungles.

Declared a national park in 1987, the Bungle Bungle range covers 270 square miles and is at least 350 million years old. It is characterized by beehive-shaped formations banded by lichens that live on water droplets trapped in the rock. (Because these formations are so fragile, you are not allowed to climb them.) You'll need to hang on to your hat—and your stomach—as your vehicle grinds up huge rock inclines and down precipitous slopes, but any discomfort is offset by the overwhelming beauty of the terrain. This is a magnificent world of cavernous gorges, sheer massifs, fragile sandstone pinnacles, and eerie landscapes that resemble the moon's surface more than they do anything on earth.

Peer down the deep gorges and you'll see thick, lush plant life. These palms and creepers are remnants of primitive tropical vegetation. Yet far above on the craggy slopes the searing heat makes even the desert lizards shudder.

There are plenty of stops on the way: to clamber up a rock slope, to picnic overlooking awesome, age-old ridges, to listen to the silence. Each night of the safari is spent under canvas on the banks of one of the many tributaries of the Ord River. The sunsets are breathtaking in this dramatic setting. After a bush barbecue, watch the Southern Cross constellation rise in the night sky and listen to the yarns of your bush guides around the campfire. The Bungle Bungle National Park is visited by a relative handful of travellers—little more than a thousand each year—so this is a very special wilderness experience.

Broome

Broome, on the coast on the southwest tip of The Kimberley, is a perfect spot for some relaxation after a rigorous Kimberley safari. There are daily flights from Perth (five hours) or from Kununurra (two hours). The main attractions here are the 18-mile Cable Beach on the town's western edge and the opportunity to buy pearls directly from pearl farmers.

Broome has a leisurely, tropical atmosphere—warm in winter, the best time to visit, and hot and humid in summer. The town is green and lush year round, with colorful tropical vegetation, including palms and the unusual baobab trees that look as though they're growing upside down.

Broome is built on a small inlet, so there's an interesting mix of landscapes. On the coast, the broad white sands of **Cable Beach** stretch for miles and miles. It's never crowded and nobody minds if you bare it all. To the east of the town are the mangrove flats, which experience 30-foot tides, and on the ocean side of town at the south end of Cable Beach are the rugged cliffs of Gantheaume Point, where at low tide you can see fossilized dinosaur tracks embedded in the sandstone rocks. In 1989 local dinosaur enthusiast Paul Foulkes discovered some 4,000 footprints belonging to 15 dinosaur species. He organizes supervised tours of some of the prints, tides permitting, every day. Your hotel can arrange tour bookings, or you can contact him directly; Tel: (091) 92-1371.

Broome was founded in the 1880s when pearls were discovered in the Indian Ocean. The find sparked a huge export trade to Europe, where the mother-of-pearl was made into buttons and the pearls adorned the necks of European wives and mistresses. When plastics came along Broome's pearl-shell trade died, but pearling has more recently been rekindled on cultured-pearl farms.

The **Broome Historical Society Museum** on Saville Street tells the story of pearling and how many Asians, particularly Japanese, came to Broome at the turn of the century to dive for pearls. At first they free-dived, then they wore rudimentary suits with oxygen pipes in order to pluck the oysters off the sea bottom. Many didn't live long to spend their riches. As you'll see by the numerous rough-hewn rock gravestones at the large Japanese cemetery on Port Drive, many died from the bends or simply by drowning.

The Asian influence is evident in Broome's **Chinatown** area between Dampier Terrace and Carnarvon Street. This is the place to buy pearls, less expensive mother-of-pearl jewelry, and aboriginal carvings of native animals. **Linneys** on Dampier Terrace supplies pearls to the finest jewelers on London's Bond Street and New York's Fifth Avenue, but here you can buy direct, and the prices reflect the absence of middlemen. Nearby, **Buccaneer Pearls** offers regular factory tours to see the jewelers at their work.

At **Willie Creek Pearl Farm**, 30 km (19 miles) north of Broome, visitors can watch the pearl cultivation process. Here you'll see the "seeding" of the oyster with a tiny bead to prompt the growth of a pearl, how the oysters mature on underwater racks, and the harvesting of the precious crop.

The **Shinju Matsuri Pearl Festival**, in early August, is a week-long salute to the pearl industry and features a national pearl-jewelry design competition, street theater, performances from the region's top country-music artists, a street parade, and—it must be admitted—a fair amount of drinking. If you are not faint-hearted and want to experience the festival's fun, you'll want to make flight and accommodation bookings well in advance.

Modern-day Broome has had a major tourist boost from an unlikely source. Lord Alistair McAlpine of England has adopted Broome as his home away from home and injected capital into the town to restore turn-of-the-century buildings and establish tourist attractions. Beneficiaries have included the Cable Beach Club hotel, the Pearl Coast Zoological Gardens, the adjacent Crocodile Park, and a Hovercraft service that tours the mangrove swamps. You can arrange transport to the zoological gardens and Hovercraft bookings through your hotel.

The **Pearl Coast Zoological Gardens** has the most comprehensive collection of birds in Australia and a good range of native fauna. Visitors view the collection from elevated walkways stretching for almost a mile.

It's a good idea to rent a car—all hotels can arrange this for you—to get around the town and to and from the beach. Volkswagen-type convertibles are the popular vehicles. You can't drive far out of town before the paved roads turn into unsignposted bush tracks suitable only for four-wheel-drive vehicles, so it's safer to take a day tour with a local guide or to get a group together to see the dramatic bush landscape by air. Check with your hotel for details on the various excursions.

STAYING AND DINING IN BROOME

The ▶ **Roebuck Bay Resort Hotel**, at the southern end of Broome overlooking the small town beach, offers motel and studio-unit accommodation and stunning modern interior design in the main bar. Each studio has a spacious lounge area. The recently completed ▶ **Cable**

Beach Club overlooks the beach and is a popular spot to sip a drink and watch the sun set over the Indian Ocean. Its facilities include 12 tennis courts and two pools, and its bungalows, though costlier than the other styles of accommodation offered here, have a luxurious colonial charm. You'll pay a little more at both these resort hotels than at other accommodations in Broome, but if you've come all this way it's worth it.

The two resort hotels are the best places to eat in town. The Cable Beach Club's **Club Restaurant** takes you back to old Singapore days with a Raffle's Hotel–style decor (the original Sidney Nolan paintings looking incongruous among the antique bird cages and old-style furniture). Locals have been known to travel hundreds of miles for the Kimberley beef rib, which is so large it may daunt those who haven't been "mustering" (herding) cattle all day. Other specialties on the vast menu include lobster served with tropical fruit, and pork Wellington. Diners usually include casually dressed locals, a cattle baron or two, and hotel guests. Prices are moderate.

Roebuck Bay's **Cherabin Restaurant** sits beneath a high conical roof of jarrah wood beams and thatching, a spectacular setting for enjoying a vast array of seafood. There's live entertainment on the weekends, when an extensive seafood buffet is served and the locals come for the best-value meal in Broome. The Cherabin is open for dinner only and the prices are low.

Divers will doubtless appreciate the pristine coral of the **Rowley Shoals**, 120-odd miles off Broome's coast. This remote spot in the Indian Ocean is considered to have the finest unspoiled atolls left in the world. This is a divers' paradise; the action is under the water and the atolls themselves only appear as rocky crags at high tide. In this untroubled underwater world you can feed rock cod by hand and dive in incredibly secluded waters. Boats leave Broome for the Rowley Shoals in the winter months for a 12-day charter. For details check with the Holiday Western Australia Centre in Perth; Tel: (09) 322-2999.

GETTING AROUND

Perth is the main entry point to Western Australia by air, train, bus, and car. The international airport is modern and efficient. The only delay is customs processing, which usually takes about an hour. The domestic terminal is straight across the runways from international arrivals, but it's 10 km (6 miles) between the two by taxi or bus.

Allow 15 minutes for the trip if you have to make a connection.

From either terminal there are no tricks to getting to the city, not more than 20 minutes away, or to your hotel. Many hotels have courtesy minibuses. All entry points have bus services, and Perth taxis in particular set very high standards. Taxi drivers are friendly, and many are well-educated and multilingual. Cab fare from the international airport into the city is A$20; from the domestic airport, the fare is A$17.

Getting around in Perth and Fremantle is exceptionally easy by bus, train, or rental car. Perth even has free Clipper buses that circle the city center. Fremantle has a distinctive tram circling the main attractions. There's also a good train that runs between Perth and Fremantle. The Perth rail and bus stations are located on Wellington Street. Bus tours are available from the major hotels to sights both in the city and nearby. Or you may prefer the independence of a rental car. Apart from short peak-hour bursts of traffic, you can go anywhere quite quickly in Perth.

There are daily flights from Perth Airport to all major towns in Western Australia, and this is the way to go if you don't want to spend hours on long, straight roads. However, direct flights between some major towns are not as frequent and sometimes involve returning to Perth before flying on. A trip from Kalgoorlie to Geraldton, for example, requires a plane change in Perth.

If you rent a car, note that gas stations are generally open from 7:00 A.M. to 6:00 P.M. After 6:00 P.M. there is a gas station open in each Perth suburb or in major towns. Renting a car in the larger provincial towns can be considerably more expensive than in Perth, mainly because provincial operators have awakened to some of the inhospitable places people take rental cars in the countryside.

Travelling to the southwest of the state is easy by car (and fairly expensive by air). Distances are quite manageable in a day—Albany is about 400 km (250 miles) from Perth via Albany Highway and through the wheat belt of the state, or a little longer through Bunbury on the coast and via forested Manjimup in the tall-timber country. Many communities in this area use the money from speeding fines to repair their roads and for other worthy causes, so watch out for the speed signs. There is train service from Perth to Bunbury. There are daily flights and a train service from Perth to Kalgoorlie, and a taxi service in the town, but you'll need a car to venture farther afield. The roads are good but facilities are few.

Driving Precautions

If you're venturing across the Nullarbor or driving in the Pilbara, Kimberley, or goldfields areas, you're in remote country with few facilities, low rainfall for most of the year, and flash floods in the summer months, so a few driving precautions are advisable.

The vehicle should be fully serviced; see that tires are in good condition—including the spare—and tire pressures are correct. Make sure the vehicle has a full tool kit; and for the Nullarbor and more remote areas of the Kimberley, take a range of spare parts. It is advisable to carry ample water—for drinking *and* for the car's radiator.

It is not a good idea to drive at dusk, because kangaroos, emus, and stray cattle choose this time to go foraging for food and can wander across the road and cause major accidents.

Most inland roads in the Pilbara are unpaved, but you can tackle the main highways easily in an ordinary car. Move off the major tracks, though, and you'll need a four-wheel-drive vehicle. Check with the tourism departments or gas stations in each town about the state of the roads, especially if you are travelling during the wet season.

Distances are so vast in the Kimberley that most visitors fly between the main towns of Broome and Kununurra. However, if you have the time and the stamina, the drive is 1,200 km (745 miles) on the Great Northern Highway, which loops around the lower edge of The Kimberley, adjacent to the Great Sandy Desert. The interior is four-wheel-drive country and it is unwise to tackle it without proper preparation. This is remote, uninhabited wilderness with no facilities, so everything must be taken with you. Even in the Bungle Bungle area there are few signposts, and it is easy to get stranded with vehicle problems or no water.

When to Go

Perth's hot summers and mild winters attract visitors year round, but September to December is ideal sightseeing weather. For those who don't mind the heat, January to March is consistently 90 degrees F or warmer, but the humidity is low. The occasional bursts of 100-degree heat in late January and February do not suit everybody.

When the mercury rises in Perth you can always head south, where it is cooler; high summer is a very pleasant time in the southwestern corner. Not so the northwest and Kimberley regions, which get very hot and rainy from November to March, much like the climate during the Wet in Asia. In the northwest 100-degree days are the norm rather than the exception. Traditionally, the best time to visit up north is April to September, when days are clear and warm.

What to Wear

In Perth people dress up to go to work, but apart from that, Western Australia is delightfully informal, opting for color and comfort in fashion, day and night. Exceptions are a few places (such as the International Room at the Burswood Casino) that require a jacket at all times. Some visitors might be surprised to find notices outside bars and restaurants along the coast insisting on minimum dress standards—usually no bare feet or bare chests.

The health and safety slogan "Slip, slop, slap" is aimed at educating everyone about the dangers of skin cancer. The strong Australian sun can cause damage to the skin in summer or winter, so heed the slogan, which means it's advisable to *slip* on a shirt, *slop* on some sunscreen, and *slap* on a hat during the dangerous hours of 11:00 A.M. to 3:00 P.M. If you venture from Perth north into the Pilbara or the Kimberley, do pack a hat, sunblock, and a large container of fly and mosquito repellent—you'll need them.

ACCOMMODATIONS REFERENCE

The rates given here are projections *for 1994. Where a range of rates is given, the lower figure is the low-season rate, the higher figure the high-season rate. Unless otherwise indicated, rates are for double room, double occupancy.*

▶ **All Seasons Rottnest Lodge Resort.** Rottnest Island, W.A. 6161. Tel: (09) 292-5161; Fax: (09) 292-5158. A$135–A$175.

▶ **Burswood Resort and Casino.** Great Eastern Highway, **Victoria Park**, W.A. 6100. Tel: (09) 362-7777; toll-free within Australia (008) 999-667; Telex: AA 197224; Fax: (09) 470-2553. A$250.

▶ **Cable Beach Club.** Cable Beach Road, **Broome**, W.A. 6725. Tel: (091) 92-2505; toll-free within Australia (008) 095-508; Fax: (091) 92-2249; in U.S. and Canada, (800) 624-3524. A$179–A$219.

▶ **Esplanade Fremantle Hotel.** Corner Marine Terrace

and Collie Street, **Fremantle**, W.A. 6160. Tel: (09) 430-4000; toll-free within Australia (008) 998-201; Fax: (09) 430-4539. From A$150.

▶ **Hotel Fortescue**. Gregory Street, **Wittenoom**, W.A. 6752. Tel: (091) 89-7055; Fax: (091) 89-7012. Motel-style unit A$90.

▶ **Hotel Regatta**. 560 Hay Street, **Perth**, W.A. 6000. Tel: (09) 325-5155; Fax: (09) 325-4176. A$60; includes breakfast.

▶ **Hyatt Regency Hotel**. 99 Adelaide Terrace, **Perth**, W.A. 6000. Tel: (09) 225-1234; Telex: AA 95823; Fax: (09) 325-8899; in U.S. and Canada, (800) A$230–233-1234. A$260.

▶ **Jewell House** (YMCA). 180 Goderich Street, **Perth**, W.A. 6000. Tel: (09) 325-8488; toll-free within Australia (008) 998-212; Fax: (09) 221-4694. A$37.

▶ **Kalbarri Beach Resort**. Grey and Clotworthy streets, **Kalbarri**, W.A. 6536. Tel: (099) 37-1061; toll-free within Australia (008) 096-002; Fax: (099) 37-1323. A$72–A$99.

▶ **Lake Argyle Tourist Village**. P.O. Box 111, **Kununurra**, W.A. 6743. Tel: (091) 68-7360; toll-free within Australia (008) 090-600; Fax: (091) 68-7355. A$65–A$75.

▶ **Observation City Resort Hotel**. The Esplanade, West Coast Highway, **Scarborough**, W.A. 6019. Tel: (09) 245-1000; toll-free within Australia (008) 999-494; Fax: (09) 245-1345; in U.S., (800) 44-UTELL; in Canada, (800) 387-1338. A$155–A$245.

▶ **Palace Hotel**. Maritana Street, **Kalgoorlie**, W.A. 6430. Tel: (090) 21-2788; Fax: (090) 21-1813. A$60.

▶ **Quality Inn**. Duncan Highway, **Kununurra**, W.A. 6743. Tel: (091) 68-1455; toll-free within Australia (008) 090-600; Fax: (091) 68-2622. A$110.

▶ **Quality Karri Valley Resort**. Vasse Highway, **Pemberton**, W.A. 6260. Tel: (097) 76-2020; toll-free within Australia (008) 090-600; Fax: (097) 76-2012. Motel rooms A$105; 2-bedroom chalets A$150.

▶ **Quality Plaza Hotel**. Egan Street, **Kalgoorlie**, W.A. 6430. Tel: (090) 21-4544; toll-free within Australia (008) 090-600; Fax: (090) 91-2195. A$120.

▶ **Reef Villas**. Cole Street, **Kalbarri**, W.A. 6536. Tel: (099) 37-1165; Fax: (099) 37-1465. A$60 low season; A$85 high season (stays of two or more days only).

▶ **Roebuck Bay Resort Hotel**. Hopton Street, **Broome**, W.A. 6725. Tel: (091) 92-1898; toll-free within Australia (008) 09-4848; Fax: (091) 92-2424. A$80–A$165.

▶ **Rottnest Hotel**. Rottnest Island, W.A. 6161. Tel: (09) 292-5011; Fax: (09) 292-5188. A$75–A$160.

► **Rottnest Island Self Catering Cottages**. Rottnest Island Board, **Rottnest Island**, W.A. 6161. Tel: (09) 372-9729; Fax: (09) 372-9715. Per week, A$315 low season; A$395 high season; A$15 per person for linens and cutlery.

► **Settlers' House**. 125 Avon Terrace, **York**, W.A. 6302. Tel: (096) 41-1096; Fax: (096) 411-733. A$80–A$99.

► **Trade Winds Hotel**. 59 Canning Highway, **Fremantle**, W.A. 6160. Tel: (09) 339-8188, toll-free within Australia (008) 999-274; Fax: (09) 339-2266. A$107.

► **Wentworth Plaza**. 300 Murray Street, **Perth**, W.A. 6000. Tel: (09) 481-1000; Fax: (09) 321-2443. A$77.

CHRONOLOGY
OF THE HISTORY
OF AUSTRALIA

- **circa 50,000 B.C.**: The first Australians arrive, crossing the land bridge from New Guinea. Some disputed theories and findings push their arrival back even further.
- **c. 20,000 B.C.**: Nomadic first Australians arrive on the shores of a bay that will someday be called Sydney Harbour.
- **c. 15,000–7,000 B.C.**: Rising seas cover the land between the mainland and Tasmania and the other islands, finally cutting the New Guinea land bridge.
- **A.D.1567**: Alvaro Mendana sails from Peru hunting the fabled *Terra Australis Incognita*.
- **1606**: Dutchman Willem Jansz discovers Cape York Peninsula, but doesn't realize it's part of a continent.
- **1606–1700**: *Terra Australis Incognita* becomes *Hollandia Nova* on Dutch East India Company maps.
- **1642**: Dutch explorer Abel Tasman discovers Tasmania, but the discovery is ignored.
- **1688**: The English buccaneer William Dampier lands on a bleak stretch of the northwest coast.
- **1770**: The *Endeavour* reaches the southeastern corner of Australia, and Captain James Cook then sails north, charting 2,500 miles of coast. He names the land New South Wales and claims it for England.
- **1773**: The first picture of a kangaroo circulates in England.
- **1788 (January 26)**: The First Fleet with its cargo of convicts anchors in Sydney Cove, Port Jackson.

- **1790**: Ships of the Second Fleet arrive.
- **1792**: The young aboriginal Bennelong goes to England.
- **1793**: The first free immigrants arrive.
- **1797**: Merino sheep are imported from Cape of Good Hope.
- **1803**: Publication of the first newspaper, *Sydney Gazette and New South Wales Advertiser.*
- **1804**: Hobart is settled.
- **1811**: Reverend Samuel Marsden ships the first commercial cargo of wool to England.
- **1824**: Wine grape cuttings arrive with James Busby; he plants some at his Hunter River estate.
- **1829**: Settlers land at Fremantle on August 10; Perth is founded two days later.
- **1836**: South Australia settlers land on Kangaroo Island.
- **1837**: A year-old settlement on the banks of the Yarra River is named Melbourne.
- **1851**: Nuggets found at Bathurst, Ballarat, and Bendigo start a California-style gold rush. Work begins on the University of Sydney.
- **1853**: The paddle wheeler *Lady Augusta* carries the first cargo of wool from Swan Hill down the Murray River in South Australia.
- **1854**: First steam train runs from Melbourne to its port.
- **1855**: Striking stonemasons win an eight-hour workday. Shakespearean actor G. V. Brooke and Lola Montez Kelly arrive to entertain Melbourne citizens and miners.
- **1859**: European rabbits are introduced near Geelong; by 1868 they've eaten most of Western Victoria.
- **1860**: The Burke-Wills expedition leaves Melbourne for the crossing of the continent to the Gulf of Carpentaria. Burke and Wills die at Cooper's Creek on return.
- **1861 (November 7)**: A crowd of 4,000 watches first Melbourne Cup horse race.
- **1862**: John McDouall Stuart succeeds in his third try to cross the continent south to north.
- **1868**: Arrival of the last transported convicts.
- **1872**: The Overland Telegraph is finished between Port Augusta and Port Darwin.
- **1878**: The Melbourne telephone exchange opens.

- **1880**: Bushranger Ned Kelly is captured after shoot-out at Mrs. Jones's Hotel, Glenrowan. He hangs at Melbourne Gaol in November.
- **1883**: Claims are pegged for silver lode, leading to the founding of Broken Hill.
- **1886**: Wolseley's powered shearers are introduced to wool sheds.
- **1891**: Delegates from the six colonies gather at Sydney to draft a national constitution.
- **1893**: Patrick Hannan's gold strike sparks the Golden Mile rush in Kalgoorlie, Western Australia.
- **1895**: Andrew Barton "Banjo" Patterson composes "Waltzing Matilda," now the unofficial national anthem.
- **1896**: Runner Edwin Flack represents Australia at the first modern Olympic games.
- **1901 (January 1)**: Birth of the Commonwealth of Australia.
- **1901 (May 9)**: The Commonwealth Parliament convenes in Melbourne.
- **1902**: The "Australian Nightingale," Nellie Melba, comes home for a concert tour after 16 years abroad.
- **1909**: The first Australian flight of a Wright bi-plane, in Sydney. The craft stays aloft for 90 yards.
- **1912**: Swimmers Fanny Durack and Mina Wylie, the first Australian women in the Olympics, place first and second in the 100-meter race.
- **1913**: The new Australian Capital Territory is named Canberra.
- **1914**: Australia joins England in the war against Germany.
- **1915**: Australians land at Gallipoli in present-day Turkey; thousands die in the months-long trench warfare, which ends in defeat for the Allies.
- **1923**: Vegemite is concocted by chemist Cyril Percy Callister. The brown paste is now the national elixir.
- **1927**: Parliament House is opened at Canberra.
- **1928**: Charles Kingsford Smith makes first trans-Pacific crossing from the United States to Brisbane; Royal Flying Doctor Service is founded at Alice Springs.
- **1932**: Sydney Harbour Bridge opens. The same month, Phar Lap wins the Agua Caliente Handicap.
- **1939 (September 3)**: Australia joins England in the war against Germany.

- **1942 (February 19)**: The Japanese bomb Darwin.
- **1942 (May)**: The Battle of the Coral Sea ends the fear of a Japanese invasion.
- **1946**: The start of postwar immigration: a flood of 2.5 million British, Greeks, Italians, Dutch, Germans, Poles, and other New Australians.
- **1951**: The first School of the Air is broadcast in Alice Springs.
- **1951 (January 1)**: 8,250,000 citizens celebrate the Commonwealth of Australia's 50th birthday.
- **1954**: Queen Elizabeth II makes a 58-day state visit.
- **1956**: The XVI Olympic Games take place in Melbourne; the Aussies win 13 gold, 8 silver, and 14 bronze medals.
- **1959**: Construction starts on the Sydney Opera House.
- **1962**: Thirty Australian military advisers go to Vietnam.
- **1963**: Mount Tom Price, Western Australia, is recognized as one of the world's greatest iron-ore deposits.
- **1965**: Robert Helpmann, the Australian Ballet leader, is named the nation's "Man of the Year," and Demetrios Stathopoulos becomes the nation's greatest "gun shearer," with a record clip of 370 sheep in a seven-hour, 48-minute day.
- **1973**: Sydney Opera House opens after 13 years and a cost of $100 million—all lottery money.
- **1974**: On Christmas Eve, the 174-mph winds of Cyclone Tracy flatten 90 percent of Darwin.
- **1975**: Peter Weir's film *Picnic at Hanging Rock* wins international acclaim as the first export in a new wave of Australian arts.
- **1976**: Aboriginal Land Rights (Northern Territory) enacted.
- **1978**: Gagudju aboriginals lease lands known as Kakadu to the Australian National Parks and Wildlife Service to be managed as a national park.
- **1983 (November)**: The yacht *Australia II,* owned by Perth millionaire Alan Bond, wins the America's Cup.
- **1985**: Ayers Rock, the Olgas, and 520 square miles of surrounding desert are returned to traditional aboriginal owners; they then lease the land to the Australian National Parks and Wildlife Service to be managed as a national park.

- **1986**: The Outback Myth is one of Australia's largest exports as Paul Hogan's *Crocodile Dundee* grosses $116 million for the year in the United States.
- **1987**: The tally of Australia's millionaires exceeds 30; off the coast at Fremantle, millionaire Kevin Parry's yacht *Kookaburra* loses the America's Cup to a California challenger.
- **1988**: More than two million people travel Down Under to help Australia celebrate its Bicentennial; Queen Elizabeth II dedicates the new Parliament House in Canberra.
- **1989 (August)**: Australia's tradition of labor-management strife reaches new heights when pilots of major domestic airlines resign en masse, creating national transportation chaos. It takes until March 1990 to get things back to normal.
- **1990**: The airline industry is deregulated, and the first new airline in 40 years takes off.

—Shirley Maas Fockler

INDEX

Aboriginal Arts Australia, 195
Aboriginal Tribal Art Centre, 57, 83
Abrolhos Islands, 368
Adelaide, 12, 301, 304 (map)
Adelaide Casino, 306, 315
Adelaide Festival of the Arts, 309
Adelaide Heritage Cottages, 311, 338
Adelaide Hills, 315
Adelaide's Bed and Breakfast, 311, 337
Adelaide Zoological Gardens, 309
Admiral's, 147
Admiralty House: Darwin, 210; Sydney, 38
Aegean, 238
Agincourt Reef, 171
Airlie Beach, 152, 154
A. J. Hackett Bungy Jump Centre, 170
Albany, 364
Albert Park Lake, 274
Aldgate, 317
Aldgate Crafts, 317
Ali Akbar, 238
Alice Junction Tavern, 196
Alice Springs, 11, 190
Allegro, 114
All Seasons Greenmount Beach Resort, 125, 181
All Seasons Harbour Rocks Hotel, 67
All Seasons Park Regis, 69
All Seasons Rottnest Lodge Resort, 359, 381
Altmann and Cherny, 267
Amberley Estate, 363
ANA Hotel: Surfers Paradise, 121, 181; Sydney, 66
Anchorage Village Beach Resort, 118, 181
Ancient Mariners, 147
Andiamo, 77

Angahook Forest Park, 288
Angas Park Fruit Company, 326
Anglesea Barracks, 237
Anglesea Golf Course, 288
Anne Schofield Antiques, 85
Anne Sullivan, 64
Apartments on the Park, 311, 337
Apicius, 357
Apollo Bay, 290
Apollyon, 95
Apple Tree Cottage, 317, 337
Appley Hoare Antiques, 85
Aquatic Air, 96
Arcadia Resort Hotel, 148, 184
Argyle Arts Centre, 44
Argyle Diamond Mine, 374
Argyle Downs Homestead, 374
Argyle Place, 44
Arltunga, 198
Arltunga Hotel, 199
Armadale: Victoria, 266; Western Australia, 361
Arnhem Land, 219
Arnold's, 98
Art Gallery of New South Wales, 56
Art Gallery of South Australia, 306
Art Gallery of Western Australia, 347
Arthur's Seat, 275
Ascot, 348
The Asian Connection, 166
Atherton Tableland, 170
Atrium Hotel, 213
Aussie World, 130
Australian Aspect, 165
Australian Bush Trading Co., 165
Australian Butterfly Sanctuary, 169
Australian Craftworks: Cairns, 165; Sydney, 42, 83
Australian Designer Travel, 294, 298
Australian Explorer Tours, 159
Australian Gallery of Sports and Olympic Museum, 260

Australian Geographic, 83
Australian Homestays and Farm
    Holidays, 296, 298
Australian Kakadu Tours, 216
Australian Museum (Sydney), 55
Australian National Gallery
    (Canberra), 101
Australian Pacific Tours: Cairns,
    177; Sydney, 64
Australian War Memorial, 101
Australian Woolshed, 118
Ayers House, 307
Ayers Rock, 11, 202
Ayers Rock Resort, 200

Bacchus, 141
The Balcony, 314
Balkan Restaurant, 76
Balkan Seafood, 76
Ballarat, 292
Bally Hooley Express, 171
Balmain, 54
Balmoral Beach, 60
Balmoral House, 92, 105
Bamaga, 178
Banana's Rock Café, 147
Bank Discotheque, 148
Bannister Street Craftworks, 356
Bar Blacksheep, 294
Bar Coluzzi, 77
Bargara Beach, 141
Barnacle Bill's, 164
Barossa Bakery, 325
Barossa Junction Resort, 325, 337
Barossa Settlers, 323
Barossa Valley, 12, 320, 321 (map)
Barracks Arch, 345
Barracks Café, 74
Barra's, 164
Barton Cottage, 239, 252
Barwon Grange, 286
The Basement, 80
The Bathers Pavillion, 60
Bathurst Island, 215
Battery Point, 237
Bay Hamper, 239
Bayswater Brasserie, 77
Beach Road Restaurant, 96
Beaufort Darwin, 212, 226
Bedarra Bay, 157, 184
Bedarra Hideaway, 157, 184
Bedarra Island, 157
Beijing, 313
Belmont Park, 348
Belvoir Street Theatre, 79
Bendigo, 293
Bennelong Restaurant, 45

Beppi's, 75
Bergman's, 325
Berowra Waters Inn, 78
Berserker Range, 142
Best Western (Victoria), 274, 296,
    298
Best Western Australia
    (Tasmania), 244, 252
Best Western Florida Motor Inn,
    71
Bibliophile, 85
Bicheno, 244
Big Winch, 333
Billabong Sanctuary, 146
Bill and Toni's, 75
Bilson's, 75
Binna Burra Mountain Lodge, 125,
    181
Bird Garden Tearoom, 316
Birrukmarri Gallery, 356
Bishop's House, 345
Bistro Moncur, 76
Blackall Ranges, 131
Black Spur, 277
Blake's, 310
Blaxland Galleries, 57
Blaxland Restaurant, 98
Block Arcade, 266
Bloomfield Wilderness Lodge,
    175, 185
Blue Duck Restaurant, 351
Blue Mountains, 90
Blundell's Cottage, 101
BMG Fine Art Gallery, 308
B'nai B'rith Center, 76
Bondi Beach, 58
Botanical Hotel, 270
Botanic Gardens: Adelaide, 309;
    Brisbane, 113; Cooktown, 173;
    Rockhampton, 142
Botanic Gardens Restaurant, 309
Bottom of the Harbour, 60
Boulder, 366
Bounty Cruises, 64
Bourke Street, 261
Bourke Street Mall, 266
Brampton Island, 156
Brampton Island Resort, 156, 184
The Breakaways, 334
Breakfast Creek Boardwalk Tour-
    ist Complex, 117
Breakfast Creek Hotel, 117
Breakfast Creek Wharf Seafood
    Restaurant, 117
Bribie Island, 118
Bridgewater, 317
Brighton Beach, 275

Brisbane, 110, 112 (map), 134
Brisbane Forest Park, 117
Broadbeach, 124
Broken Bay, 89
Broken Hill, 87, 93
Brookland Valley Vineyard, 363
Broome, 375
Broome Historical Society Museum, 376
Brougham Restaurant, 311
Browns Mart, 210
Buccaneer Pearls, 377
Buderim, 130
Buderim Festival Centre, 130
Bunbury, 361
Bundaberg, 140
Bungle Bungles, 374
Burdekin Hotel Dining Room, 81
Burleigh Heads, 124
Burnetts on Buderim, 130
Burnham Beeches Country House, 278, 298
Burswood Resort and Casino, 352, 381
La Bussola, 77
Byron Bay, 89

CAAMA Shop, 195
Cable Beach, 376
Cable Beach Club, 377, 381
Cadman's Cottage, 43
Café Amadeus, 357
Café C and Craneford Winery, 322
Café Mozart, 45
Café Palma, 268
Café Paradiso, 77
Cairns, 134, 161, 162 (map)
Cairns Colonial Club, 166, 185
Cairns International Hotel, 164, 185
Cairns Museum, 165
Caloundra, 129
Cambridge Inn, 68
Camel Cup, 191
Camp Cove, 60
Camphor Cottage, 131
Camp Oven Kitchen, 196
Canberra, 99, 100 (map)
Cannonvale, 154
Canoe Club, 165
Cape Grim, 248
Cape Otway, 290
Cape Otway Cottage, 289, 298
Cape Tribulation, 170
Cape Woolami, 280
Cape York, 175, 176 (map)
Capital Parkroyal, 102, 105

Capitan Torres, 74
Capricorn Coast, 143
Capricorn International Resort, 143, 183
Captain Cook Cruises, 64
Cardwell, 160
Careel Bay Café, 96
The Cargo Club, 314
Carnarvon Gorge, 142
Carriages Guest House, 98, 105
Carrick Hill, 310
Cascades Colonial Accommodation, 251, 252
The Casino, 213
Cassis, 147
Castle Hill, 146
Castlemaine, 294
Castlemaine Market, 294
Casuarina Beach, 214
Casuarina Country Inn, 98, 105
Casuarina Free Beach, 214
Cat and Fiddle, 80
Cat's Tango, 114
The Cauldron, 81
Cav's Steak House, 123
Centenary Lakes, 166
Centennial Park, 52
Centennial Park Café, 52
Central Deborah Gold Mine, 293
Central Great Barrier Reef, 144, 149, 150 (map)
Cessnock, 97
Challenger Charters, 151
Chambers Pillar, 198
Chapel Street, 267
Charcoal Restaurant, 102
Charlies on the Esplanade (Cairns), 165
Charlie's Restaurant (Darwin), 212
Charters Towers, 159
Château Hornsby, 197
Château Yaldara, 323
Cherabin Restaurant, 378
Chill Bar, 115
Chinatown: Broome, 376; Melbourne, 261; Sydney, 49
Chloe's, 312
Choi's Inn, 350
Choy Sin, 312
Christ Church Cathedral, 210
Christo's On The Wharf, 212
Chunagon Japanese Restaurant, 357
Churchill Island, 281
City Hall (Brisbane), 113
City Hall Art Gallery and Museum, 113

City Place, 163
City Place Art Markets, 166
Civic, 352
Clairmont Inn, 70
Clancy's Tavern, 352
Clarendon Mansion, 247
Clarendon Restaurant, 92
Clare Valley, 320
Claude's, 76
Claudine's on Macquarie, 73
Clays, 53
Cleland Conservation and Wildlife Park, 316
Cleopatra Country Guesthouse, 92, 105
The Cleveland, 77
Cloisters, 345
Cloudys, 199
Clover Cottage Restaurant and Strawberry Terrace, 278
Club Crocodile Resort, 154, 184
Club Restaurant, 378
Club Tropical, 171, 185
Cockle Bay Bar, 80
Coconut Beach Rainforest Resort, 172, 185
Coen, 178
Coffs Harbour, 89
Collingrove Homestead, 325, 337
Collins Street, 261, 266
Colonel Light, 314
Colonial Tramcar Restaurant, 268
La Colonna, 75
Comedy Store, 79
Como Center, 266
Como House, 264
Conrad International Hotel and Jupiters Casino, 124, 181
The Convent at Pepper Tree, 98, 105
Conway Range National Park, 154
Coober Pedy, 332
Cooktown, 173
Coolangatta, 124
Coolgardie, 366
Coolum Beach, 130
Coonawarra, 319
Coorong, 320
Copper Pot, 294
Coral Sea Resort, 154, 184
Cordelia Street Antique and Art Centre, 116
Cotswold House Country Restaurant, 278
Cotters Market, 147
Cottesloe Beach, 348

Country Comfort Inn: Adelaide, 311, 337; Rockhampton, 142, 183
Country Comfort Old Melbourne, 273, 298
Country Plaza International, 141, 183
Coventry Gallery, 57
Cowes Colonial Motor Inn, 282, 298
Cradle Mountain–Lake St. Clair National Park, 248
Cradle Mountain Lodge, 248, 252
Crazies Comedy Restaurant, 114
Creative Native, 347
Creme de la Creme, 165
Criterion Hotel, 142, 183
Crocadilliacs, 165
The Crocodile Farm, 214
Crocodylus Village, 172, 185
Crystal Creek/Mount Spec National Park, 160
Crystal Lodge, 93, 105
Crystal Room, 310
Cumberland Lorne Resort, 289, 298
Currie & Smith, 346
Currumbin Sanctuary, 124

Daimaru, 266
Daintree National Park, 172
Dalrymple Hotel, 148
Dandenong Ranges, 277
Daniel's, 121
Danny's: Port Douglas, 171; Surfers Paradise, 121
Darcy's, 76
Darley's, 92
Darley Street Thai, 81
Darling Harbour, 48
Darlinghurst, 50
Darlington, 243
Darwin, 11, 206
Darwin Frontier Hotel, 211, 226
Darwin Travelodge, 213
David Jones': Melbourne, 266; Syndey, 84
Daydream Island, 153
Daydream Island Travelodge Resort, 153, 184
The Deanery, 113
Dear Friends, 238
Deep Sea Divers Den, 175
Delamere Winery, 234
Delprat's, 94
Denisons, 114

Denmark, 364
D'Entrecasteaux Vineyard, 234
Desert Cave Hotel, 334, 337
Desert Designs and Friends, 356
Desert Gardens Hotel, 201, 226
Destination Darwin, 219
Diamond Beach Hotel Casino, 212, 226
Dimensions, 196
Diorama Village, 195
Dixon Street, 49
D.J.'s, 171
Doctor's Gully, 210
Dolphin Arcade, 121
Don Pancho Beach Resort, 141, 183
Double Bay, 53
Dov, 76
Down Under Dive, 174
Doyles On The Beach, 78
Dreamtime Cultural Centre, 142
Dreamworld, 123
Dubbo, 87
Dublin House Inn, 291, 298
Dugout Bar, 81
Dundee's, 165
Dunk Island, 158
Dunk Island Resort, 158, 184
Duthies Leichhardt Hotel, 142, 183
Dynasty Restaurant, 148

Eaglehawk Neck, 241
Earl of Aberdeen, 314
Early Street Historic Village, 118
Earth Exchange, 56
East Coast Birdlife and Animal Park, 244
East Coaster Resort, 243, 252
East End Market, 306
East Point Military Precinct, 211
Echo Point, 90
Echuca, 295
Editions Gallery, 166
Edmund Kennedy National Park, 160
18 Govett's Leap Road, 92
Eight Plates, 114
Elderton Winery, 323
Elizabeth Bay, 53
Elizabeth Bay House, 53
Elizas, 148
Emerald, 142
Emma's Cottage, 251, 253
Emperor's Court, 350
Emperor's Palace, 116

Endeavour replica, 356
Ensemble Theatre, 79
Entally House, 247
Ernest Giles Tavern, 200
L'Escargoterie, 148
The Esplanade, 163
Esplanade Fremantle Hotel, 357, 358, 381
The Ettamogah Pub, 130
Eumundi, 132
Eumundi Antiques, 132
Eumundi Gallery, 132
Eurong Beach Tourist Resort, 129, 181
Evandale, 247

Faces, 114
Fairmont Resort, 92, 105
Fannie Bay Beach, 214
Fannie Bay Gaol, 211
Fannies Nightclub, 213
Fannys, 268
Faversham House, 361
Fawkner Club, 270
Federal Country Club Hotel, 246, 253
Fee and Me, 246
Festival Centre, 309
Festival of Perth, 352
Fezbah, 315
Fine Woodcraft Gallery, 364
Finke Gorge National Park, 198
Fitzroy Island, 168
Fitzroy Island Resort, 169, 185
Flag International: Launceston, 244, 253; Melbourne, 274, 296, 298
Flagstaff Hill Maritime Village, 291
Flaxton, 131
Flaxton Barn, 131
Flaxton Gardens, 131
Flaxton Inn, 131
Flecker Botanical Gardens, 166
Flinders Chase, 326
Flinders Mall, 146
Flinders Ranges, 331
Flinders Street East, 146
Flora Metallica, 346
Florentino's, 269
Flutes, 147
Flynns on the Mall, 196
Folkways, 81, 84
The Folly, 246
Footbridge Theatre, 79
Forecourt, 45, 79
Formula 1, 77

Forrest Beach, 160
Forrest Chase, 346
Fort Dennison, 38
Fortitude Valley, 116
Fortuna Village, 269
Fortune of War, 82
The Forum, 121
Fountain Room, 116
Franklin Manor, 245, 253
Franklin River, 249
Fraser Island, 129
Fremantle, 353
Fremantle Gaol, 355
Fremantle Markets, 356
Fremantle Museum and Arts
    Centre, 355
Freycinet Peninsula, 244
Freycinet Vineyard, 234
Fridays (Brisbane), 115
Fridays on the Wharf (Maroochy),
    130
Fringe Arts Festival, 309
Fringe Benefits Brasserie, 102
Fronds, 130
Frontier Camel Tours, 199
Frontier Kakadu Village, 219, 226
Frontier Oasis Resort, 197, 226
Fun in the Sun Festival, 163

Gabby's Bar and Bistro, 213
Gagudju Crocodile Hotel, 219,
    226
Gagudju Lodge Cooinda, 219, 226
Galaxy, 130
The Galleria, 121
Galleries Primitif, 57
Gallery Bonython-Meadmore, 308
Gallery Primitive, 166
Garden Café, 213
The Gardens Restaurant, 47
Gariwerd National Park, 291
Gawler, 323
Gay and Lesbian Mardi Gras, 51
Gazebo Restaurant, 314
Geelong, 286
Gekko, 68
Gelato Bar, 58
Georges Boutique, 266
George Street, 41
Geraldton, 368
Geramiah's, 352
The Ghan, 191
Ghengis Khan Restaurant, 213
Gladstone, 140
The Glasshouse Café, 73
Glendambo Tourist Centre, 337
Glenelg, 309

Glen Helen Gorge Nature Park,
    199
Glen Helen Lodge, 199, 227
Glenisla Homestead, 292, 298
Gloucester Park, 348
Gloucester Tree, 364
Gnadenfrei Estate Winery, 326
Gold Coast, 10, 110, 119, 120
    (map)
Gold Coast International, 122, 181
Gold Coast Sheraton Mirage Ho-
    tel, 122, 181
Golden Mile, 366
Golden Palace, 116
Gold Museum, 292
Gordon Place, 273, 298
Gordon River, 248
The Gouger, 312
Gove Resort Motel, 221, 227
Government House: Darwin, 210;
    Perth, 345; Sydney, 47
Grand Hyatt (Melbourne), 272,
    298
Grand Staircase, 91
The Grange, 310
Grant Burge, 323
Graphic Illusion Gallery, 265
Graphix Brasserie, 103
Great Barrier Reef, 10, 107, 132;
    maps, 138 (Southern Reef), 168
    (Northern Reef)
Great Barrier Reef Wonderland,
    146
Great Keppel Island, 140
Great Keppel Island Resort, 140,
    183
Great Ocean Road, 10, 283, 284
    (map)
Great Palm Island, 157
The Great Wall, 102
Green Island, 168
Green Island Reef Resort, 168,
    186
Griffiths Island, 291
Grote Street Market, 306
Grumpy's Wharf, 123
Gum Tree Cottage, 317

Haba Dive, 174
Hadleys Hotel, 240, 253
Hadspen, 247
Hahndorf, 316
Hainault Tourist Mine, 366
Hamer's Hotel, 245, 253
Hamersley Pools, 360
Hamersley Range National Park,
    370

Hamilton Island, 152
Hamilton Island Resort, 153, 184
Handmark Gallery, 235
Harbour Restaurant, 45
Harbourside Brasserie, 80
Harold Park Hotel, 79
Harris & Son, 346
Hartley's Creek Zoo, 170
Hartz Mountains National Park, 249
Haskins, 351
Hastings Street, 127
Hawkesbury Explorer, 96
Hawkesbury 4WD Bush Treks, 96
Hawkesbury River, 89, 96
Hayman Island, 152
Hayman Resort, 152, 184
Hay Street Mall, 346
Healesville Sanctuary, 277
The Heights, 286
Henry Ayers Room, 307
Henry Buck, 266
Heritage Hotel, 115, 181
Heritage Rainforest Market, 169
Heritage Walk, 194
Her Majesty's Theatre: Adelaide, 306; Sydney, 79
The Hermitage of Marananga, 325, 337
Heron Island, 139
Heron Island Resort, 140, 183
Hero of Waterloo, 43
Hideaway Safari Lodge, 221, 227
High Street, 266
Hillarys Boat Harbour, 360
Hilton International: Adelaide, 310, 337; Brisbane, 115, 181; Cairns, 164, 186; Sydney, 68
Hilton on the Park (East Melbourne), 274, 298
Hinchinbrook Island, 157
Hinchinbrook Island Resort, 157, 184
Hindley Parkroyal, 311, 338
Hindley Street, 306
His Majesty's Theatre (Perth), 345
HMS Buffalo, 309
Hobart, 235, 236 (map)
Hogarth Gallery, 57
Hog's Breath Cafe, 148
Holdsworth Galleries, 57
Holidays Afloat, 96
Holly Tree Farm, 250, 253
Holy Mackerel, 123
Home Hospitality, 72
Homehost & Heritage Tasmania, 250

Hook Island, 149
Hordern House, 85
Host Farms Association, 296, 298
Hotel Como, 274, 298
Hotel Darwin, 212, 213, 227
Hotel Fortescue, 371, 382
Hotel Manly, 82
Hotel Nikko Darling Harbour, 69
Hotel Nikko Sydney, 70
Hotel Regatta, 353, 382
Hot Gossip Entertainment Complex, 213
House of Pearls, 346
Hunter Valley, 96
Hursey Seafoods, 248
Hyatt Canberra, 102, 105
Hyatt Kingsgate, 70
Hyatt Regency Hotel: Adelaide, 310, 338; Coolum, 130, 182; Perth, 353, 382
Hyatt Regency at Sanctuary Cove, 123, 182
Hyde Park, 48
Hyde Park Barracks, 46
Hydro Majestic Hotel, 92, 105

Illusions, 148
Imperial Peking, 77
Imperial Peking Harborside, 75
Indo-Pacific Marine, 211
Inflation, 271
Inhouse Bed and Breakfast Australia, 296, 299
Innkeepers/Tas Villas Group, 244, 253
Inter-Continental (Sydney), 67
Iron Range National Park, 178
Island Nature Park, 281
Isle of Wight Hotel, 282
Ivy Club, 271
Ivy Cottage, 251, 253

Jabiru Township, 219
Jacksons on George, 80
James Cook Historical Museum, 173
Jazz and Blues Bar, 115
Jean Jacques, 268
Jemby-Rinja Lodge, 93, 105
Jenolan, 91
Jenolan Caves House, 91, 105
The Jetty, 282
Jewell House, 353, 382
Jim Jim Falls, 218
Jimmys on the Mall, 114
Jolley's Boathouse Bistro, 307
Jourama Falls National Park, 160

Juniper Hall, 51
Jun and Tommy's Sushi Bar, 351

Kables Restaurant, 65, 73
Kakadu National Park, 11, 217
Kalbarri, 368
Kalbarri Beach Resort, 370, 382
Kalgoorlie, 365
Kalkarri Visitor Centre, 95
Kamogawa, 69, 74
Kangaroo Island, 326
Kapunda, 322
Karratha, 371
Katherine, 222
Katherine Gorge, 223
Katoomba, 90
Katoomba Mountains Lodge, 92, 105
Keisan, 73
Kelso Reef, 149
Ken Done, 83
Kents, 312
Kewarra Beach Resort, 168, 186
Kiama, 87
Kimberley Plateau, 12, 372, 373 (map)
Kinchega National Park, 95
Kingfisher Bay Resort, 129, 182
Kings Canyon, 198
Kings Canyon Frontier Lodge, 198, 227
Kingscote, 326
Kingscote's Gallery, 331
Kings Cross, 52
Kings Cross Walkabout Tours, 64
King's Park (Perth), 344
King Street (Perth), 345
Kohuna Village Resort, 156, 184
Koombana Bay, 361
Kununurra, 372
Kuranda Gallery, 170
Kuranda Railway, 169
Kuranda Rainforest Resort, 170, 186
Kuranda Wildlife Noctarium, 169
Ku-ring-Gai Chase National Park, 95

Lady Bay (Beach), 60
Lady Elliot Island, 139
Lady Elliot Island Resort, 139, 183
Lady Musgrave Island, 139
Lake Argyle, 372
Lake Argyle Tourist Village, 374, 382
Lakefield National Park, 178
Lakeland, 177

Lake's Folly, 98
Lakeside International, 102, 105
Lake Street Gallery, 166
Lamington National Park, 125
Landhaus, 325, 338
Lasseters Hotel Casino, 197, 227
The Last Aussie Fishcaf, 77
The Last Laugh, 268
Latitude 19 Resort, 148, 184
Launceston, 245
Launceston Novotel, 246, 253
Laura, 177
Lawley Farm Cottage and Barn, 325, 338
Leeuwin Estate, 363
Leighton Beach, 348
Lemon Tree, 270
Leura, 91
Leura Hotel, 92
Lightkeeper's Inn, 289, 299
Lilianfels, 92, 105
Lindeman Island Resort, 154, 184
Lindeman's Winery, 98
Linke's Family Bakery, 325
Linnett's Island Club, 330, 338
Linneys, 346, 376
Litchfield Park, 213
Lizard Island, 173
Lizard Island Lodge, 174, 186
Loaded Dog Pub and Brewery, 270
Loch Ard Gorge, 290
The Lodge, 324, 338
The Loft in the Mill, 278, 299
The Loft Restaurant, 121
Lombardo's Restaurant and Bar, 357
London Court, 346
London Lakes, 250
London Lakes Fly Fishing Lodge, 250, 253
London Tavern, 52
Lone Pine Koala Sanctuary, 117
Long Island, 154
Long Island Palm Bay Hideaway, 154, 184
Longreach, 143
The Lord Dudley, 82
The Lord Nelson, 43, 82
Lorne, 289
Lorne Forest Park Reserve, 289
Lorraine Outback Sheep Station, 187
Low Isles, 171
Lucio's, 76
Lufra Hotel, 241, 253
Luvit Pancake Parlor, 147

Lyndoch Hotel, 325
Lyon's Cottage, 207
Lyrebird Restaurant, 116
Lyrics Restaurant, 309

MacDonnel Siding, 191
Machiavelli Ristorante, 73
Mackay, 156
Macleay Street Bistro, 77
Macquarie Galleries, 57
Macquarie Street, 40, 45
Macrossans, 171
Maldon, 295
Maleny, 131
Maleny Lodge Guest House, 131, 182
The Manhattan, 70
Manjimup, 364
Manly Beach, 58
Mapleton, 131
Mapleton Tavern, 131
Marcellina's, 306
Margaret River, 361, 363
Margaux's (Perth), 352
Margaux's on the Square (Adelaide), 314
Margherita, 156
Maria Island, 243
Marian Street Theatre, 79
The Marigold, 74
Marion's Vineyard, 234
Mario's, 268
Maritime Museum: Fremantle, 355; Hobart, 238; Port Adelaide, 308
Marketplace Café, 310
Marlin Coast, 168
Maroochy, 129
Maroubra, 58
Marrakai Luxury Apartments, 212, 227
Marti Zucco's, 238
Maruku Arts and Craft Centre, 204
Mary Cairncross Park, 131
Mataranka Homestead Tourist Resort, 223, 227
Mataranka Thermal Pools, 223
Matilda Bay Restaurant, 351
Matilda Cruises, 64
Matsuri Restaurant, 313
Mawson's Hut, 238
Maxi's, 268
Mayfair Crest International Hotel, 115, 181
McLarens on the Lake, 319, 338
McWhirters Marketplace, 116
McWilliams Mount Pleasant, 98

Meadowbank, 234
Meat Market Craft Centre, 265
The Medina, 71
Mediterranean Restaurant, 351
M. E. Humfress and Co., 114
Melba Guily State Park, 290
Melbourne, 10, 255, 258 (map)
Melbourne Central, 266
Melbourne Comedy Festival, 261
Melbourne Cup, 257, 261
Melbourne Environs, 276 (map)
Melbourne Maritime Museum, 263
Melia Alice Springs Hotel, 197, 227
Melia Darwin Hotel, 212, 227
Melton's, 147
Melville Island, 215
Le Meridien Melbourne, 274, 299
Merindah Mohair Farm, 322
Merrony's, 75
Metro, 271
Metro Apartments Darling Harbour, 71
Metro Eastside, 147
Mettam's, 360
Micawber Park Tavern, 278
Michael's Riverside, 114
Mid City Motor Inn, 291, 299
Middlebrook, 319
Middle Island Underwater Observatory, 143
Midland Highway, 242
Midland Hotel, 294, 299
Mietta's Queenscliff Hotel, 287, 299
Mietta's Restaurant: Melbourne, 268; Queenscliff, 287
Migration Museum, 307
Millstream, 371
Mindil Beach, 214
Miners Heritage Walk-In Mine, 142
Miners Retreat, 293, 299
Mint Museum, 47
Mirrabook, 102
Mission Beach, 160
Mrs. Gifford's Café, 307
Mrs. Macquarie's Chair, 48
Mistys Mountain Restaurant, 131
MLC Centre, 84
Molecombe Cottage, 251, 253
Monkey Mia, 368
Mon Repos Environmental Park, 141
Monsoons, 271
Montville, 131

Moomba Festival, 261
Moorilla Estate, 234
Mootwingee National Park, 95
Moreton Bay Islands, 118
Moreton Island, 118
Morgans, 77
Morrisons, 267
Mossman River Gorge, 172
Mother of Pearl and Sons, 84
Motor Sport Hall of Fame, 282
Mountain Heritage Country
  House Retreat, 92, 105
Mount Barker, 365
Mount Coot-tha, 117
Mount Coot-tha Botanic Gardens,
  117
Mount Gambier, 319
Mount Lofty, 316
Mount Morgan, 142
Mount Nelson, 240
Mount Wellington, 240
Mud Markets, 166
Muggleton's General Store, 330
Murchison Gorges, 368
Mures Fish Centre, 238
Murray Falls, 160
Murray River, 295, 318
Museum of Chinese History, 261
Museum of Contemporary Art
  (Sydney), 56
Museum of the Goldfields, 366
Musgrave Homestead, 178
Myer, 266
Mystics, 314

Nags Head, 81
Nambour, 131
Naracoorte, 320
Nara Resort Hotel, 122, 182
Narrabeen Cottage, 282, 299
National Film and Sound Archive,
  101
National Golf Club, 274
National Library (Canberra), 101
National Maritime Museum (Syd-
  ney), 49, 55
National Motor Museum, 322
National Museum of Victoria, 263
National Rhododendron Garden,
  277
National Science Centre, 101
National Tennis Centre, 263
National Wool Museum, 286
Nautilus Restaurant, 171
Neo Pharaoh, 69, 81
Nepean Highway, 275
Netanya Noosa Resort, 128, 182

New Brighton, 82
New Edition Bookshop, 85
The New Marigold, 74
Newport, 357
News Bar, 271
New South Wales Parliament
  House, 46
Newstead Park, 116
New Theatre, 79
Nhulunbuy, 220
Nightcliff, 214
Night Tokyo, 213
Niugini Gallery, 166
The Nobbies, 281
No Names, 75
Noosa, 127
Noosa Heads, 127
Noosa International Holiday
  Resort, 128, 182
Noosa National Park, 128
Noosa River, 128
Norfolk, 357
Norseman, 367
North Adelaide Heritage Apart-
  ments, 311, 338
Northbridge, 347, 350
Northern Great Barrier Reef, 161,
  167 (map), 174
Northern Territory, 11, 188
Northern Territory Museum of
  Arts and Sciences, 211
North Garden, 269
North Stradbroke Island, 118
North Terrace, 306
Nostalgia Town, 130
Nourlangie Rock, 218
Novotel on Darling Harbour, 69
Novotel Twin Waters Resort, 130,
  182
Nowra, 87
Nullarbor Plain, 367
No. 1 Hastings Street, 128, 182
No. 7 at the Park, 75
Nuriootpa, 323

Oak Room, 102
The Oaks, 82
Oasis Hotel, 129, 182
Oasis Seros, 76
Oasis Shopping Center, 124
Oatlands, 242
Observation City Resort Hotel,
  353, 382
Observatory Hill, 44
Observatory Hotel, 66
The Observer, 82
Ocean Breeze Resort, 128, 182

Ocean Palace, 350
Ocean Seafoods, 60
O'Connell Street, 308
The Old Alice Inn, 196
Old Botanic Hotel, 314
Old Court House, 345
Olde Maritime Motor Inn, 291, 299
Old Gaol, 365
Old Lion, 314
Old Miner's Dugout Café, 335
Old Papa's and Gino's, 357
Old Parliament House, 309
Old Perth Boys' School, 345
Old Post Office, 210
Old Sydney Parkroyal, 66
Old Telegraph Station, 191
Old Timer's Mine, 334
Old Umbrella Shop, 246
Old Willyama Motor Inn, 95, 105
Old Windmill, 113
The Olgas, 201
Olive Pink Flora Reserve, 195
Olympic Opal Jewellers, 312
Omeros Seafood Restaurant, 123
191 Oxford Street, 76
Opal Inn Hotel-Motel, 334, 338
Opal Lovers, 165
Opal Mine: Adelaide, 312; Mel-
    bourne, 267
Opera House Drama Theatre, 79
Orchid Avenue, 121
Ord River, 372
O'Reilly's Rainforest Guest House,
    125, 182
The Orient, 80, 82
Orpheus Island, 157
Orpheus Island Resort, 157, 184
Oskars Seafood Bar and Grill
    (Port Douglas), 171
Oskar's Seafood Restaurant
    (Coolangatta), 125
Outback, 11, 107, 158
Outback Pioneer Hotel, 201, 227
Overlander Steakhouse, 196
Oxford Street, 52
Oyster Beds Restaurant, 357
Ozone Hotel (Queenscliff), 287,
    299
Ozone Seafront Hotel
    (Kingscote), 330, 338
Oz Outback Theatre Restaurant,
    352
Oz Tours Safaris, 177

Pacific Fair Shopping Centre, 124
Pacific International Hotel, 164,
    186

Pacific Sailing School, 39
Paddington, 50
Paddington Market, 85
Painted Desert, 334
Pajinka Wilderness Lodge, 178, 186
Palace Hotel, 366, 382
Palm Beach, 60, 89, 96
Palm Cove, 168
Palm Cove Travelodge Resort,
    168, 186
Palmer's, 147
Palm Valley, 198
Panorama Guth, 195
Pan Pacific Gold Coast Hotel, 124,
    182
Papunya Tula Artists, 195
Paradise Centre, 121
Paradise Palms Golf Course, 170
Paradise Point, 123
Paragon Café, 75
Paragon Hotel, 80, 81
The Paris, 238
Park Hyatt, 66
Park Lane Hotel, 68
Parkroyal at Darling Harbour, 69,
    80
Parkroyal Melbourne, 273, 299
Parkroyal on St. Kilda Road, 273,
    299
Parliament House, 101
Pauls, 312
Pavilion Hotel, 102, 106
Pavilions Restaurant, 127
Paxton's Conservatory, 307
Pearl Coast Zoological Gardens,
    377
Pegum's, 93, 106
Pemberton, 363
Penny Royal World, 246
Peppers Cosmopolitan Double
    Bay (Sydney) 70
Peppers Guest House (Pokolbin),
    98, 106
Peppi's, 315
Perc Tucker Art Gallery, 146
Performing Arts Complex (Bris-
    bane), 116
Performing Arts Museum, 265
Perth, 12, 340, 343 (map)
Perth Entertainment Centre, 348
Perth Environs, 354 (map)
Perth Mint, 345
Petaluma Mill, 317
Peter Lehmann Wines, 323
Peter Tibbs Scuba School, 175
Pheasant Farm, 325
Phillip Island, 11, 279

Phill Mason, 235
Phoenician Club, 81
Phoenix Hotel, 81
Piccolo Bar, 77
Picton River, 249
The Pier, 78
Pier Gallery, 166
Pier Nine Seafood Restaurant, 114
Pilbara, 369 (map), 370
Pilbeam Theatre/Art Gallery, 142
Pinnacles, 368
Pioneer World, 361
Pipers Brook, 234
Pitchi Richi Sanctuary, 195
Pitt Street, 41
Pittwater, 96
Pittwater Yacht Charter, 96
The Place, 266
Planet Downs Resort, 187
Playhouse Bistro, 309
The Point, 70, 77
Pokolbin Cellars, 98
Porongurup National Park, 365
Port Adelaide, 308
Port Arthur, 240
Port Augusta, 331
Port Campbell National Park, 287, 290
Port Dock Hotel, 308
Port Douglas, 170
Portland, 291
Port Lincoln, 331
Port Phillip Bay, 275
Portraits Wine Bar, 148
Posh Nosh, 246
The Potters' Gallery, 116
Pottery Place, 166
Pottinger's Restaurant, 131
Powerhouse Museum, 55
Presenting Australia, 165
Pro Hart, 94
Prospect House, 242, 253
Prosser's on the Beach, 239
Proud Australian, 114
Proud Mary, 318
The Pub, 213
Puffing Billy, 277
Pullman Restaurant, 306
Pumphouse Brewery Tavern, 81, 82
Punsand Bay Private Reserve, 178, 186
Purely Australian, 347
Pyrmont Bridge, 48

Quality Hotel Adelaide, 311, 338
Quality Inn (Kununurra), 374, 382

Quality Karri Valley Resort, 364, 382
Quality Plaza Hotel (Kalgoorlie), 366, 382
The Quarterdeck, 148
Queen Elizabeth Lookout, 90
Queenscliff, 287
Queensland, 107, 108 (map)
Queensland Aboriginal Creations, 114
Queensland Art Gallery, 116
Queensland Cultural Centre, 115
Queensland Museum, 116
Queenstown, 244
Queen Street Mall, 111
Queen Victoria Antique Arts and Crafts Centre, 265
Queen Victoria Building, 83
Queen Victoria Market, 267
Queen Victoria Museum and Art Gallery, 246
Quicksilver Connections Company, 171
Quinkan Reserve, 177

Radekas Motel and Backpacker's Inn, 334, 338
Radisson Long Island Resort, 154, 185
Radisson Plaza Hotel (Cairns), 164, 186
Radisson President (South Melbourne), 273, 299
Radisson Royal Palms Resort, 171, 186
Rafferty's, 212
Railway Hotel, 352
Rainbow Beach, 128
Rainforest Habitat, 172
Ramada Grand Hotel (Glenelg), 310, 338
Ramada Great Barrier Reef Resort, 168, 186
Ramada Hotel (Surfers Paradise), 121, 182
Raphael's, 66
Raptis Plaza, 121
Real Ale Café, 80
Red Centre, 11, 188, 192 (map)
Red Eagle Hotel, 270
Red Hands Cave, 90
Reef Enterprise, 156
Reef House Resort, 168, 186
Reef Villas, 370, 382
Reflections Restaurant, 129
The Regal, 74
Regent of Melbourne, 272, 299

Regent of Sydney, 65
Remarkable Cave, 241
Residence Restaurant, 196
Residency, 194
Residency Museum, 361
Le Restaurant (Melbourne), 268
The Restaurant (Sydney), 74
Retreat Restaurant, 196
Revolving Restaurant, 239
Ribbons, 165
Riberries, 75
Richmond, 241
Richmond Bridge, 241
Richmond Wine Centre, 242
Rifle Brigade, 294
Rigoni's Bistro, 313
Rio Rock, 148
Ripponlea, 264
Riverland, 318
Riverside Restaurant, 310
R. M. Williams Bushman's Outfitters, 82
Robert's, 98
Robin Gibson Galleries, 57
Rochecombe, 234
Rockford Winery, 323
Rockhampton, 141
The Rock Lobster, 312
Rockman's Regency Hotel, 273, 299
Rockpool Restaurant, 42, 74
The Rocks, 41
The Rock Shop, 114
Rocks Visitors Center, 43
Roebuck Bay Resort Hotel, 377, 382
Rogues, 81
Rogue II, 156
Rolling Rock Nightclub, 127
Rollingstone, 160
Roser's, 127
Rose, Shamrock and Thistle, 81
Roseville Restaurant, 117
Rosie's Tavern, 115
Ross, 242
Rosslyn Bay, 143
Rosslyn Bay Inn Resort, 143, 183
Rothbury Estate, 98
Rottnest Hotel, 359, 382
Rottnest Island, 358
Rottnest Island Self Catering Cottages, 359, 383
Rottnest Restaurant, 359
Round House, 355
Round Midnight, 80
Rowley Shoals, 378
Le Rox, 314

Roxy, 271
The Royal, 79
Royal Arcade, 266
Royal Botanic Gardens: Melbourne, 263; Sydney, 47
Royal Flying Doctor Service, 194
Royal Flying Doctor Visitor Centre, 166
Royal Hotel, 51
Royal Melbourne Zoo, 262
Royal Oak Hotel, 270
Ruby, 102
Rum Jungle Motor Inn, 214, 227
Rum Runner, 174
Runaway Bay, 123
Rundle Mall, 306, 311
Rushcutters Bay, 53
Russell Hotel, 67
Rusty's Bazaar, 166

Saddlers Court Gallery, 242
SafariTrek Australia, 374
Sail and Anchor, 357
Sail on the Edge, 64
Sails, 357
Sails in the Desert Hotel, 201, 227
St. Andrew's Anglican Cathedral, 41
St. George's Terrace, 344
St. Helena Island, 118
St. Kilda, 262
St. Kilda Beach, 262
St. Matthias Vineyard, 234
La Sala, 92
Salamanca Inn, 239, 254
Salamanca Place, 235
Saltram's, 323
Sanctuary Cove Resort, 123
San Remo, 77
Sapphire and Opal Center, 165
Sarah Island, 249
Sassi at Island Point, 171
The Savoy, 71
Scandals, 213
Scarborough Beach, 353
Scenic Railway, 91
Scheherezade, 268
School of the Air, 194
School Cottage, 295, 299
Scotch-Pie House Stables, 295, 299
Seahaven Beachfront Resort, 128, 182
Seal Bay, 326
Seal Rock, 281
Seamist, 289, 300
Seaview Hotel, 148

Sea World, 122
Sebel Town House, 70
Sergio's Restaurant, 335
Settlers' House, 361, 383
Seven Spirit Bay, 220, 227
Seymour Centre, 79
Shakespeare Hotel, 80
Shamrock Hotel, 294, 300
Shannon Park, 96
Shark Bay, 370
Shark Fin, 269
Sheerwater Restaurant Observatory, 282
Sheraton Breakwater Casino/Hotel, 147, 185
Sheraton Brisbane Hotel & Towers, 115, 181
Sheraton Hotel Hobart, 239, 254
Sheraton Lobby Lounge (Townsville), 148
Sheraton Mirage Resort, 171, 186
Sheraton Noosa Resort, 128, 182
Sheraton Towers Southgate (Melbourne), 272, 300
Sheraton Wentworth (Sydney), 68
Sherbrooke Forest, 277
S. H. Ervin Gallery, 57
Shiki, 310
Shinju Matsuri Pearl Festival, 377
Shrimps, 246
Shute Harbour, 154
Siggi's: Brisbane, 114; Darwin, 212
Silky Oaks Lodge, 172, 186
Silver Hills Motel, 245, 254
Silver Sands Resort Hotel/Motel, 244, 254
Silverton, 94
Simon's Seafood Restaurant, 351
Sir Thomas Brisbane Planetarium, 117
Sisco's, 238
Sketches Bar and Bistro, 67
Skipper-a-Clipper, 96
Sky Garden, 84
Smith Street Mall, 206
Snake Charmer, 316
Solothurn Rural Resort, 131, 183
Some Place Else, 115
Sorrento Resort Motel, 330, 338
Soup Plus, 80
South Australia, 12, 301; 321 (Barossa Valley map), 328 (South Australia Coast map)
South Australian Museum, 306
Southbank, 267
South Bank Parklands, 116

Southern Great Barrier Reef, 137, 138 (map)
Southern Rose, 288
Southern Vales, 319
South Head, 54
South Molle Island Resort, 153, 185
Southport, 122
South Stradbroke Island, 123
South West National Park, 249
South Yarra, 262
Sovereign Hill, 293
Sovereign Hotel, 173, 187
Spice Market, 353
Spices, 310
Splashes, 266
Sportsgirl Bar, 271
Sportsgirl Mall, 266
Springton, 322
Squires Tavern, 213
Squirrels, 116
The Stables Theatre, 79
Stafford Hotel, 67
Stanley, 247
Stanley's Restaurant, 312
Star, 271
Starlight Room, 315
State Library (Brisbane), 116
State Library of New South Wales (Sydney), 47, 85
State Theatre, 79
Station Tavern and Brewery, 272
Steaks Down Under, 92
Steyne, 82
Stirling Range National Park, 365
Stockman's Hall of Fame, 143
Stonewell Cottages, 325, 338
Strahan, 245
Strahan Inn, 245, 254
Strahan Village, 245, 254
Strand Arcade, 83
Strawberry Hills Hotel, 80
Strehlow Research Centre, 204
Stuart Auto Museum, 197
Studebaker's, 81
Suez Canal, 43
Sugareef, 81
Sullivans Cove, 235
Summit Restaurant, 117
Sunshine Beach, 128
Sunshine Coast, 10, 110, 125, 126 (map)
Sunshine Plantation, 130
Supreme Court Gardens, 345
Surfers Paradise, 119
Surfers Paradise Travelodge, 122, 183

Swaggy's Australian Restaurant, 141
Swanbourne Beach, 348
Swan Hill, 296
Swan River, 348
Swansea, 244
Sydney, 10, 33; maps, 34 (Sydney Center), 59, 88 (Environs)
Sydney Antique Centre, 84
Sydney Aquarium, 48, 55
Sydney Boulevard, 68
Sydney Cricket Ground, 57
Sydney Ferries, 63
Sydney Football Stadium, 57
Sydney Harbour, 37
Sydney International Film Festival, 79
Sydney Maritime Museum, 49
Sydney Marriott, 68
Sydney Opera House, 44
Sydney Renaissance, 66
Sydney Showboat, 64
Szechuan Place, 350

Table Cape, 247
Table Manners, 92
Tamarama Beach, 58
Tamworth, 89
Tandanya, 306
Tangalooma Moreton Island Resort, 118, 181
Tanunda, 323
Tanunda Hotel, 325
Taracumbie Falls, 216
Tarcoola Estate, 286
Taronga Zoo, 38
Tasmania, 11, 228, 230 (map)
Tasmanian Museum and Art Gallery, 237
Tawny's, 164
Taylors Beach, 160
Taylor Square, 50
Taylor Square Restaurant, 76
Teewah Coloured Sands, 128
Terrace Intercontinental, 310, 339
La Terrasse, 130
Theatre Royal, 237
Thomson Bay, 359
Three Sisters, 90
Thursday Island, 178
Timber Park and Museum, 364
Tim McCormick, 85
Tipplers Tourist Resort, 123, 183
Tiwi Tours, 216
Tjapukai Aboriginal Dance Theatre, 170
Tom and Mary's Taverna, 335

Tom Price, 371
Tondoon Botanic Gardens, 141
Toorak Road, 265, 266
Top End, 188, 205, 208 (map)
Torrens Gorge, 322
Touche Noosa, 127
Tower Hill State Game Reserve, 291
Town and County Hosts, 72
Town Gallery, 114
Town Hall: Darwin, 210; Perth, 345; Sydney, 41, 79
Townsville, 134, 144, 145 (map)
Townsville Ambassador, 147, 185
Townsville Environmental Park, 146
Townsville Palmetum, 147
Townsville Reef International, 147, 185
Townsville Travelodge Hotel, 147, 185
Traces, 335
Trader Morgan's Bar, 358
Trade Winds Hotel, 358, 383
Tranby House, 348
Travel Bookshop, 85
The Treasure House, 114
Treasury Room, 67, 73
Treble Clef, 268
Trenavin Park, 282, 300
Tre Scalini, 75
Trianon Challis Avenue, 77
Trinity Wharf, 164
Tropical Wines, 141
Tropicana Gelato, 77
The Troubador, 272
Trowbridge Prints, 347
Tully, 160
Twentyone Espresso, 78
Twin Falls, 218
Tyrrell's Bookstore, 85, 97
Tyrrell's Winery, 97

Ubirr, 218
Uluru National Park, 200
Umberto's Restaurant, 334
Umoona Opal Mine Museum and Motel, 333, 339
Umorrdul, 220
The Underground: Brisbane, 115; Melbourne, 271
Underground Gallery and Bookshop, 333
Underground Motel, 334, 339
Underwater World: Hillarys Boat Harbour, 360; Maroochy, 129
Universal Theatre, 271

University Union Bistro, 307
Upper Deck, 238
Uraidla Aristologist, 317, 339

Van Diemen's Land Memorial
    Folk Museum, 237
Vaucluse, 53
Vaucluse House, 53
Verandahs, 165
Vesteys, 214
Vic Hislop's Shark Show, 170
Victoria, 255
Victoria Dock, 235
Victoria Hotel: Darwin, 213; Mel-
    bourne, 274, 300
Victorian Arts Centre and National
    Gallery, 264
Victoria's, 114
Victoria Square, 303
The Vintners, 325
Vista Alice Springs, 197, 227
Vlados Charcoal Grill, 268
Voices Theatre Co-op, 79
Volga, 313
Vue Grand Private Hotel, 287, 300

WACA Sports Arena, 347
Wagners Cottage, 244, 251, 254
Walkabout Clay Crafts, 195
Wapparaburra Haven, 140, 183
Warana Festival, 115
Warrawong Sanctuary, 316
Warren National Park, 364
Waterfront Restaurant, 43
Watson's Bay, 60
Watters Gallery, 57
Waverley Cottage, 251, 254
Waves, 314
W. B. Movie World, 123
Wentworth Plaza, 353, 383
Werribee Park, 285
West End All Suite Hotel, 311, 339
Western Australia, 12, 340, 369
    (map)
Western Australian Museum, 347
Whaleworld, 365
The Wharf, 129
Wharf Restaurant, 39
Wharf Theatre, 79
Whispers Cocktail and Piano Bar,
    213
White Cliffs, 95

White Lace Motel, 156, 185
Whitfield Range Environmental
    Park, 166
Whitsunday Islands, 10, 152
Whitsunday Terraces Resort, 154,
    185
Whitsunday Wanderers Resort,
    154, 185
Wild Art Gallery, 170
Wilderness Shop, 235
Wild Track Adventure Safaris, 177
Wild World, 170
William Ricketts Sanctuary, 277
Willie Creek Pearl Farm, 377
Wilson Island, 140, 183
Windows, 351
Windsor Grill, 268
Windsor Hotel, 273, 300
Windy Point, 315
Wine Bar, 306
Wine Glass Bay, 244
Winton, 143
Wistari Reef, 140
Wisteria Lodge and Motel, 330,
    339
Wittenoom, 371
Wolf Blass, 323
Wollongong, 87
Woodbridge Hotel, 240, 254
Woollahra, 52
Woollahra Antiques Centre, 85
Woolshed Restaurant, 282
Woomera ELDO Hotel, 336, 339
Wrest Point Hotel Casino, 239,
    254

Yallingup, 363
Yalumba, 323
Yamagen, 165
Yanchep National Park, 361
Yandina, 132
Yarra Valley, 278
Yeppoon, 143
York, 361
The York Apartments, 71
York Butter Factory, 271
York Motor Museum, 361
Yum Cha at the Golden Harbour,
    74

Zapata's, 313
Zumsteins, 292